Scriptures and the Guidance of Language

In this book, Steven G. Smith focuses on the guidance function in language and scripture and evaluates the assumptions and ideals of scriptural religion in global perspective. He brings to language studies a new pragmatic emphasis on the shared modeling of life-in-the-world by communicators constantly depending on each other's guidance. Using concepts of axiality and axialization derived from Jaspers's description of the "Axial Age," he shows the essential role of scripture in the historical progress of communicative action. This volume clarifies the formative power of scriptures in religions of the "world religion" type and brings scripture into philosophy of religion as a major cross-cultural category of study, thereby helping philosophy of religion find a needed cross-cultural footing.

Steven G. Smith is Professor of Philosophy and Religious Studies at Millsaps College and the author of numerous works in philosophy of religion and related fields, including *The Concept of the Spiritual, Gender Thinking, Worth Doing, Appeal and Attitude, Full History,* and *Centering and Extending.*

Scriptures and the Guidance of Language

Evaluating a Religious Authority in Communicative Action

STEVEN G. SMITH

Millsaps College

CAMBRIDGE
UNIVERSITY PRESS

CAMBRIDGE
UNIVERSITY PRESS

University Printing House, Cambridge CB2 8BS, United Kingdom

One Liberty Plaza, 20th Floor, New York, NY 10006, USA

477 Williamstown Road, Port Melbourne, VIC 3207, Australia

314–321, 3rd Floor, Plot 3, Splendor Forum, Jasola District Centre,
New Delhi – 110025, India

79 Anson Road, #06-04/06, Singapore 079906

Cambridge University Press is part of the University of Cambridge.

It furthers the University's mission by disseminating knowledge in the pursuit of
education, learning, and research at the highest international levels of excellence.

www.cambridge.org
Information on this title: www.cambridge.org/9781108473217
DOI: 10.1017/9781108580441

© Cambridge University Press 2018

First published 2018

Printed in the United States of America by Sheridan Books, Inc.

A catalogue record for this publication is available from the British Library.

Library of Congress Cataloging-in-Publication Data
NAMES: Smith, Steven G., author.
TITLE: Scriptures and the guidance of language : evaluating a religious authority
in communicative action / Steven G. Smith.
DESCRIPTION: Cambridge, United Kingdom ; New York, NY :
Cambridge University Press, 2018. | Includes bibliographical references and index.
IDENTIFIERS: LCCN 2018013093 | ISBN 9781108473217 (hardback : alk. paper)
SUBJECTS: LCSH: Language and languages–Religious aspects. | Sacred books.
CLASSIFICATION: LCC BL65.L2 S58 2018 | DDC 208/.2014–dc23
LC record available at https://lccn.loc.gov/2018013093

ISBN 978-1-108-47321-7 Hardback

Contents

Acknowledgments

I would like to acknowledge the stimulation and support of the intrepid Millsaps College students who joined me for the philosophy of scriptures adventure: Derek Anderson, Jason Bronson, Steven Campbell, Brad Corban, Akanksha Gupta, Khyati Gupta, Kelsey Hall, Katherine Henry, Veronica Herrin, Ricky James, Camille Maker, Payal Patel, Ben Ross, Mary Schmidt, and Jake Wilson.

I got helpful readings of Chapter 5 from my Millsaps faculty colleagues James Bowley, Elizabeth Egan, Rahel Fischbach, Anne MacMaster, Shelli Poe, Elise Smith, and Lola Williamson, as well as from Tim Knepper in the context of the Global-Critical Philosophy of Religion Seminar in the American Academy of Religion.

Kevin Vanhoozer and Martin Warner gave me important advice on the whole project as it was shaping up. The final book benefits from suggestions made by two anonymous readers for Cambridge University Press.

I dedicate the book to my esteemed undergraduate teachers at Florida State University who hooked me on this subject matter: Walter Moore, John Priest, Bob Spivey, and Bill Swain.

PART I

PROBLEMATICS OF COMMUNICATIVE ACTION

Introduction

On the Powers and Problematics of Language

In language we exercise immense powers of revelation and coordination. As a revealer, language models all the beings that are, were, or may be; we devise new expressions to discriminate as many different referents as we are capable of noticing, and we class things comparatively from as many points of view as our endlessly juxtaposable expressions suggest. As a coordinator, language directs a nuanced partnership of communicators living in that illuminated world.

These powers are known to be dangerous. Clumsily, carelessly, or all too efficiently, language can disastrously mislead. We learned early in life how seriously the danger is taken. Almost as soon as we were first coaxed to speak, we were warned that lying is intolerable. Then we were warned against exaggeration, unfounded generalization, repetition of the baseless or malicious statements of others, obscenity, cursing, and misplaced intimacy or levity. It became clear that the ethics, etiquette, and sheer technique of speaking and understanding rightly would be an intensely monitored lifetime study.

An utterance can have great consequences in a moment; for example, a passenger looking out for a driver trying to enter a busy highway can instantly cause multiple deaths by saying "You can go now." In comparison with a shove or a tap, the linguistic signal is loaded with understanding and pertinence. Word senses stretch our awareness across space and time: when I summon you with such ready authority by your instituted name or by the pronouns "you" and "we"; when I characterize a particular by implementing a concept ("Remember, we're in a Prius"); when I conditionalize ("A Prius can't accelerate fast enough in this situation"); when I quantify ("None of those drivers can see you"); or when I use

3

tense to project into the past or future ("You won't be able to get on this road till rush hour is over").

One sort of maximum of linguistic power is on view when we use language to characterize everything characterizable ("Everything consists of energy") or to prescribe everything prescribable ("Act always for the greatest utility"). Such claims are contestable, of course, and even when accepted leave plenty of room to settle specific issues in different ways. But our ability to deploy such comprehensive frames for life-in-the-world forces us to consider and discuss how claims on that scale could be valid.

Another linguistic power affects relationships, sometimes creatively and sometimes destructively. The commitment expression "I love you" is notable for making all of the speaker's important evaluations and decisions revolve henceforth around the addressee, who is now irrevocably connected to the loving "I" as its "you." It will be a challenge to *substantiate* this expression – but it *can* be substantiated, and our awareness of this possibility makes the utterance of the words a major event. Much harder to substantiate but breathtaking in its presumption is "God damn you!" which paradoxically negates all communion.

We constantly face problems in determining when linguistic acts are acceptable. There is possible abuse of language in making assertions that are false or not appropriately grounded or connected, or in giving orders that are not helpful or not authorized. And there is a possibility of pushing language too hard, making assertions with sketchy or obnoxious entailments. (Let us confess that we do such things frequently, seeing what we can get away with.) To address the problems in each area methodically, it helps to recognize a whole *problematic* of speaking and understanding rightly in each kind of case.

The problematic of truth, for example, involves an array of situations and a history of cases in which debatable lines have been drawn or still need to be drawn between sense and lack of sense, accuracy and inaccuracy, adequacy and inadequacy of disclosure, or the relevant respect and lack of respect among interlocutors. So long as we are enmeshed in such a problematic, we get a sense of orientation from a regulating ideal such as truthfulness. The ideal is an attractor in our problematized practice: we do not always know what truthfulness will involve, and we will disagree about the specimens and standards, but we have a sense of what we are after – a useful, benign, reliable sharing of information about life-in-the-world among all communicating colleagues. We may take what seems to be a tenable general position with respect to this ideal, like "Assert only what you know by direct observation." In the second-order truth problematic of philosophy, we try out specifications of the ideal to orient the explanation and justification of truth claims generally (*adaequatio intellectus et rei*, warranted assertibility), hoping to ground it in a tenable comprehensive position (realism, pragmatism).

Communicative action might therefore be characterized as our exploration of a field of ideally regulated communicative problematics. We are always grappling with problems when we speak and understand, but we are never clueless about what the relevant problems are or what might be a tolerable approximation of a solution.

A premise of the present study is that there is a significant overlap between the ideals at the heart of two problematics of utterance that may seem remote from each other: the perfectly general problematic of everyday communication, in which all humans are enmeshed just by virtue of living humanly, and the intensely special problematic of taking direction from a text of paramount religious authority – a text that will virtually always be placed in its own exalted category as "scripture," "Veda," or "classic" (*jing*) – which seems to concern only members of voluntary religious communities. ("Scripture" is the most commonly used general term for such texts and will be used in this sense henceforth.)[1] One indication of the connection is the inescapable relevance of the idea of "the guidance" in explaining each problematic: what language use is always supposed to do is provide guidance, more particularly *the* applicable guidance to subject matter and performance at each juncture of communication; what scripture is distinctively supposed to do is provide the supremely relevant guidance (the Guidance) for the ultimate goal of optimizing human life.

The connection involves also a reciprocal dependence. Scriptural guidance is one of the ultimate tests of ordinary guidance insofar as it serves, whether by design or as the result of an evolution of textual guidance, as a distillation and maximally heightened emphasis of the ideals in the general communicative problematic. In Christian scripture, for instance, a "father of lies" character, Satan, intensely emphasizes the negative side of the ideal of truth telling, and the assertion that "God is love" (comparable to dramatizations of infinite compassion in Buddhist scriptures) intensely emphasizes the moral ideal of interpersonal solidarity.[2] If this religious visioning makes sense, the ordinary ideals it assumes make all the more

---

[1] On "scripture" as a cross-cultural category, see Section 5.4.
[2] Satan as "father of lies," John 8:44; "God is love," 1 John 4:8; infinite compassion, e.g., Greater Pure Land Sutra 7 (Dharmakara/Amitabha's vows).

sense; if it does not, the ordinary ideals are weaker. On the other side of the dependence, we can tell that scriptural guidance has gone off the rails when we notice ordinary communicative failures – as in a mystifying esotericism or a bullying fanaticism. We cannot defend positions within scripture's own problematic without relying on procedures we use within the general problematic of linguistic action.

There is an *aleph, bet* argument associated with Hillel and others to the effect that it could not make sense to reject the guidance of a scripture given that all of us have already accepted the direction of an existing language and tradition on which we are fundamentally dependent.[3] While this is obviously no proof of scriptural authority or value, it does serve as a useful reminder that the teleology of scripturalism is entangled with the teleology of linguistic communication more generally wherever we can assume broad literacy.

I propose to make the most of a two-sided continuity thesis relating scriptural guidance to linguistic guidance in general. This thesis disagrees with those who make the strongest devout claims for the incomparable properties of scriptural guidance and also with those who completely deny scripture's ideal relevance. According to the first part of the thesis, the vaulting ambition of scriptural guidance fails if it violates basic norms of regular linguistic guidance; this seems to me a sound, commonsensical approach to determining what reasonable scripturalism does and does not involve. The less commonsensical second part of the thesis affirms a corresponding dependence of the terms of regular guidance on their scriptural amplifications.

The chief evaluative question I wish to raise is this: Under what conditions does the idea of Scripture (supreme Guidance in a paramount Text) make generally appreciable sense?

Religious scripturalists will answer this question variously, according to conceptions of scripture supported by their traditions; they may even disagree with their coreligionists about how to take scripture and whether to adopt a scripturalist style of religiosity. Relatively detached observers of scripture's place in our world will answer variously as well. On a negative view, scriptural guidance may be seen as false in substance (if it is supernaturalistic), epistemically treacherous (if it relies on myth or demands faith), and culturally and ethically pernicious (if it

---

[3] See Section 6.2. On the Hillel story, see Steven D. Fraade, "Concepts of Scripture in Rabbinic Judaism: Oral Torah and Written Torah," in *Jewish Concepts of Scripture* (ed. Benjamin Sommer, NYU Press, 2012), pp. 34–36.

is ethnocentric or sexist). One may judge historically that the most important reason that a scripture exists and the prime determinant of its content and application is the domination project of a social elite. Thus the "insights" and "values" we may continue to glean from scripture are incidental: nothing about the general process of generating or using scriptures warrants trust in scriptural guidance. On a positive view, however, scripture generally is or can be of compelling intellectual and spiritual value to its readers – a classic, in effect, perhaps of a more potent kind than literary classics as such – and of great coordinating help to communities both synchronically and diachronically – a constitution, in effect, perhaps of a more potent kind than a political constitution, given that distinctively advantageous promptings and selections of utterances have occurred in the process of generating and using scriptures. (One can take this positive view without being a devout scripturalist.) Finally, taking all these possibilities into account, a neutral view would allow that scripture can be harmful, harmless, or helpful depending on its particular forms, contexts, and uses.

How one sees the ideal relevance of scripture will probably be tied to one's historical view of scripture's prospects for continuing to exert influence. One may judge that scripture plays an enduring key role in the ecology of human guidance, in principle and perhaps demonstrably in living cultures; or that scripture has effectively been replaced by other kinds of great Text; or that the age of literacy ruled by Texts is giving way to a different communicative regime altogether. Or one may reject the premise that scripture or literacy have in fact been as culturally dominant as they are usually supposed to have been. In any case, it will be hard to separate ideal from historical assessments.

In the spirit of my suggestion that the sense of ordinary communicative guidance can be seen as dependent on scriptural guidance, a turn-the-tables question worth asking is this: How could life in a literate civilization make sufficient sense *without* scripture? If it is granted that we receive crucial guidance from utterances (a point to be developed in Chapter 1); that we rely on specially amplified modes of guiding utterance, including religious discourse (Chapter 2); that with writing we can publish refined packages of guidance for endless application and reconsideration, our greatest texts hitting a maximum of guidance utility (Chapter 3); and that our most ambitious language can have guiding value despite its inadequacy in representing the ultimate reference of guidance (Chapter 4) – granting these features of our communicative scene, can the ideal relevance of the category of scripture and thus potentially of a particular scripture be denied without denying the human project of optimizing guidance?

There are appreciable motives for denying the project of optimizing guidance. One may wish to live more independently. One may fear human overreaching. But these motives become reasons only if one engages in reasoning, which is, among other things, a guidance-optimizing activity. From the perspective of reasoners, one either joins in this activity or stays outside it like a barbarian beyond the gates. If we *are* engaged in reasoning and are reflecting seriously upon it, then it seems we are obliged to consider the maximally ambitious scriptural way of establishing guidance and to try to determine which positions we ought to take in negotiating scripture's internal sense-making problematic, on the one hand, and the external problematic of its proper place in our world, on the other.

*

For religious studies purposes, there are compelling reasons to define scripture generically as Guidance. These will be discussed when we turn our attention to the problematic of scripture in Part II, having worked our way up to that supposed maximum of powerful guidance by examining in Part I the main typical ways in which guidance is achieved in utterance.

On the side of philosophy of language, a focus on guidance in communicative action is advantageous even beyond bringing out relations between ordinary and scriptural language use. There are of course good reasons to focus on the representational or expressive elements of language, or on signification or symbolization, or on information transfer, or even on subjective experience. But asking how language use accomplishes guidance is deeply and extensively revealing. Among the best-known major programs in the philosophy of language, one sees the power of the guidance question best, I think, in Wittgenstein and Habermas – although Wittgenstein's explicit discussions of guidance tend to resolve it into the ultrabasic phenomenon of "agreement,"[4] and Habermas's linguistic pragmatics is geared toward free individuals' pursuit of shared understanding rather than toward an optimal relationship between

---

[4] Ludwig Wittgenstein, *Philosophical Investigations* (trans. G. E. M. Anscombe, Macmillan, 1958), §§138–243, pp. 53–88; see also *Remarks on the Foundations of Mathematics*, rev. ed., ed. G. H. von Wright, R. Rhees, and G. E. M. Anscombe, parts VI and VII, pp. 303–437.

guided and guide.[5] Remarkably, it seems that no one has yet been prompted by the profound communicative interdependence of humans to look carefully at the common human interest in guidance as a determinant of the concept. "Beliefs about what words mean guide how to use those words ... beliefs about the content of thinking guide what inferences to draw ... Thoughts about meaning guide our use of language" (Allan Gibbard).[6] What is this "guiding"? Well – what do we want guiding to be? Let us see how things look when we are guided by that question.

---

[5] Jürgen Habermas, *Theory of Communicative Action*, vol. 1 (trans. Thomas McCarthy, Beacon, 1984), chap. 3, pp. 273–337; see also "What Is Universal Pragmatics?" in *Communication and the Evolution of Society* (trans. Thomas McCarthy, Beacon, 1979), pp. 1–68.
[6] Allan Gibbard, *Meaning and Normativity* (Oxford University Press, 2013), p. 238.

I

The Guidance Problematic

When I say to myself: "But I *am* guided" – I make perhaps a movement with my hand, which expresses guiding. – Ludwig Wittgenstein[1]

1.1 ORIENTED AND GUIDED: THE GIVEN SITUATION

Humans are intensely communicative and interdependent, and language is obviously an indispensable human "guidance system." But what does that claim mean in depth? As guided beings and guidance-scrutinizing beings, what are we doing?

Let us try first to sound out the basic practicality of the guidance situation. We can start with a double question of orientation that applies to anyone simply as a movable being: Of all the beings in the world, which do I address, and which might I address? The word "address" already takes a position in the basic problematic of orientation, implying a possible stability in relations.

We see the rudiments of addressing in how two mountains address each other across a valley. There is even a sense in which mountains can have something at stake in the way they address each other, an interest, if their erosion patterns are affected by their channeling of weather. But we are reluctant to attribute that sort of practicality to nonliving beings. Their nature is just to be the result of whatever happens.

Self-moving beings are another story because they have their own programs of addressing. For example, a sunflower follows the sun across the sky. One might like to interpret the sunflower's movement as a

[1] *Philosophical Investigations* §178.

mechanical process of the same kind as weather passing through a valley, but the self-maintaining structural integrity of the sunflower is such that the "process" of its movement is properly conceived as its *action*, and its evolutionary history is such that its action is properly conceived as purposive. Over time, the sunflower species is enmeshed in a problematic of survivable orientation. Each living sunflower actively assumes the successful position that the species has hit upon within that problematic.

Building up the biology of orientation, we have yet another kind of case when a pollinating bee darts into flowers of a certain shape, color, and scent. Here it is not too great a stretch to say that a being's orientation is established by its elective response to the perceived appeal of another being. The bee notices and becomes interested in the flower. But something more than an instantaneous appeal-orientation has been established. The relation between the bee and the flower develops in a structured way through the bee's actions and the flower's affordances so that it seems appropriate to say that the flower *guides* the bee. The flower's guidance of the bee is the diachronic practicality of its appeal; it is how the flower's promise of shared advantage is implemented productively.

Does the flower really guide the bee, or is there only a vague analogy between the flower-bee interaction and guidance proper as found among rational agents? One might be pulled one way or another on this question depending on one's intuitions about naturalism and reason, but the answer may not matter. Whether we prefer to say that there is a natural phenomenon of guidance exemplified by bees in bee fashion and by people in rational fashion or to say instead that bees exemplify some biological preconditions of guidance, while people alone exemplify guidance proper – either way, there is an important continuity between these cases that will have to be taken into account in ascertaining what the most practically meaningful examples of guidance involve. For it undeniably belongs to our animal condition that we depend on cues from other beings and consistencies in our interactions with them to live successfully. The human experience of "relationship" and practical "knowledge" is based on this relatedness. One could not carry on a human conversation if one did not possess beelike perceptual and motor responsiveness and if one's interlocutor did not provide a flowerlike structuring of the situation. One had best be aware that one's prospects for successful life can be affected favorably or unfavorably by changes in these dimensions of the interactive situation.

The sunflower aims to be powered sufficiently by the sun, implicitly aware of its daily heliotropic exercise; the bee aims to collect sufficient food for its community, aware as a perceiver and flier of each of its trips out to the flowers and back; then, by means of the waggle dance, the bee shares with other bees its awareness of the flowers' location. We humans aim to realize rewarding relationships with each other and to learn as much as possible about the world, conscious that both of these pursuits are lifelong and even multigenerational. The very large spatiotemporal scale on which we live, thanks to our linguistically mediated representation of life-in-the-world, makes our natural model of purposive movement not the sunflower's daily bend or the bee's frequent shuttle to food sources but the *journey*. When the orientation of our journey becomes a question, as at the beginning of Dante's *Comedy*, we naturally imagine ourselves having to cross a wild landscape where the solution we need consists of being on the right path.[2]

Usually we are mostly on track already, proceeding down a multitude of densely intertwined paths that have been well enough defined for us. What to notice and value – the menu of appellant types – has largely been determined by our culture, building on our biological base. The possibilities of communication have largely been determined by our language. But our culture and language have in turn been determined by the exigencies of a journeying, path-seeking mode of existence. That is why the generality of meaning in our thoughts and words reaches so much farther than the generality in the animal recognition of, say, "snake (dangerous)!" For us, a snake can be a path starter or a journey ender, and we put that deeply interesting recognition in play when we say "snake." We do that when we use any noun. Further, we range through the illimitable past and future of journeys in conjugating our verbs, and we activate our freedom in path taking in using our pronouns (don't *you* agree?).

The journey/path scenario shows one layer of the structural relevance of guidance in our lives. Another equally basic layer for us is our profound investment as a species in functional interdependence and cooperative trust. This too is in crucial part a language-based phenomenon. Necessarily, the social insects have their own means of guidance in pheromones or waggle dancing; we, however, are primate individualists whose great experiment in coordination (on a vastly enlarged

---

[2] "Midway in our life's journey, I went astray / From the straight road and woke to find myself / Alone in a dark wood." Dante, *Inferno* I.1–3, in *The Divine Comedy* (trans. John Ciardi, New American Library, 2003), p. 16.

spatiotemporal scale) must be carried out by advising, commanding, imploring, and other chancy illocutionary acts. We could not make a success of depending so heavily on each other for material and intellectual help if we did not have a guidance system that is spiritually powerful (providing for the mutually acceptable regulating of relationships) as well as cognitively incisive. This is one of the chief things to be grasped respecting what language *is*: the instrumentality and practice of coordinating free individuals so that their lives will not be isolated, nasty, and short. The result of language's work is the success of their fellowship.

We may frame this point as Thesis #1 on language: *The ideal relevance of language generally, and of any particular linguistic act basically, is a function of its effectiveness in sustaining cooperation.*

Another factor in the guidance situation that deserves more attention is the motivation we ideally bring to the discernment of paths and the labor of coordination. We do not perceive like a camera or solve problems like a calculator: we *want* to take vital steps forward, our momentum in that direction generating questions that we feel we need to answer and options we want to try out. We have this desire in several main modes, on several prime premises: (1) we are *optimistic* – that is, we expect success and gain encouragement from manifestations of success; (2) we are *responsible* – that is, we are moved to act beneficently by awareness of the dependence of the success and well-being of others on our own actions; and (3) we are *intelligent* – that is, we endeavor to make the best possible use of our perceptual and rational capacities to determine the best ends and best means to those ends.

1.2 OPTIMISM AND FANTASTICALITY

Now, what do you think, Shariputra, for what reason is that world called Sukhavati (the happy)? In that world Sukhavati, O Shariputra, there is neither bodily nor mental pain for living beings. The sources of happiness are innumerable there. – The Shorter Pure Land Sutra §2[3]

Virtually all of our actions are powered by optimism in an animal way – as in the optimism of the bird that boldly launches itself and expects to land on a safe perch (and otherwise would not fly), to find a worm (and otherwise would not hunt), and to connect with a mate (and otherwise

---

[3] Trans. F. Max Müller, in *Buddhist Mahayana Texts* (ed. E. B. Cowell, Dover, 1969), p. 91.

would not sing) – and in a more precarious psychological way, subject to our turbulent moods and conflicting beliefs. We project success in paying attention, in being careful, and in thinking things over, but also in surfing on our emotions. In addition, we are spiritual optimists. With the sad exception of those who are severely emotionally or cognitively impaired, all of us are more or less always willing to move into coordination with each other in a somewhat confident, encourageable manner and to risk personal or communal setbacks for a chance of increased collaborative success. Language is the instrumentality and practice of this optimism.

Thesis #2 on language: *The ideal relevance of language and linguistic acts is a function of their support of communicative optimism.* You may say bitterly negative things about the state of life-in-the-world, but you are to be listened to so long as you seem to be acting to improve our shared awareness of the situation.

While sustaining cooperation, optimism powers competition as well – in our animal expectations of being able to pull off actions we undertake, including communicative actions (as in calling out and interrupting), and in our intellectual and spiritual expectations that the ideal superiority of our proposals will be vindicated over the proposals of others (as in debating and teaching).

Optimism is supported by a basic realism of ongoing life: if our experience of scuffling to meet our needs confirms that we can at least expect to continue in the same mode, that gives us a platform on which other goods may be encountered. This is security optimism. There is also an insurgent prosperity optimism proceeding from the sheer energy and volatility of desire. If one thing is wanted and arrives, the same should come again and more: whenever experience gives openings for more ambitious projections of desire, desire may rise to that occasion. Desire is ready to shift its target from the good (the permissively eligible) to the best. As prosperity optimists we may disagree with each other about what is really possible, but we will not disagree about expecting as much as possibility will allow and expecting the best possibility whenever a best is discernible.

The assumptions and aims of our optimism are frequently affected by encounters with unexpectedly impressive appellants. For example, anyone who has come to know a splendid human being has, as a result, a raised platform of security optimism about human nature and a new inflammation of prosperity optimism with respect to relationships one might have. Eliade's term "hierophany" suits this circumstance when the manifested higher good is a *hieros*, a holy being that seems to belong on a higher plane than ordinary life and yet encourages us in a very deep way by enlarging the possibilities of being.

As a flying bird expects that there will be a branch to land on, the inquiring mind expects that a perception or thought will speak to its question and that a truth or norm will resolve it. The earnest collaborator expects that there will be a path and a choreography suited to successful collaboration despite the fact that these elements are always subject to new future determinations even in the best-settled channels of activity. Because we fulfill these conditions by prompting and informing each other as we go along, our optimism about collaboration is an optimism about guidance. When our optimism increases to religious strength, it includes optimism about religious guidance.

Quite apart from any religious hierophany, optimism about the formation of action motivates the cultivation of planned action in general and of ritual in particular, which in turn expands optimism's horizons. Ritualistic optimism asserts itself in the teeth of a very inconsistently cooperative world. We know from experience that actions with extensive causal linkages are easily interrupted or disfigured. They come off well only with luck. By ritualization, however, it is possible on the one hand to give a desired meaning to actions that are unlikely to fail, such as simple gestures (smiles, handshakes) and most of the ordinary actions of speech, and on the other hand to carry out religiously ambitious, highly articulate, and intricately collaborative actions with an assured idealized upshot. The ritual has an agreed rationale and fully specified plan; the qualifications of the actors and the conditions for performing the action are controlled; if something goes wrong, the problem can be diagnosed, and the actors can try again later to do the ritual properly. Optimism about the possibility of performing a perfect action and optimism about the availability of good ritual guidance are mutually reinforcing.

Our conception of success, optimism's primary term of reference, is optimistically volatile. If a newly offered practice promises me a higher happiness or a long-term securing of happiness in a "heaven," or if a new religious philosophy promises me something higher even than any heaven, I will at least wonder if the promise is credible. As Bishop Butler observed, if I wonder *seriously* about a religious prospect, even without believing in it, my life will be on a different footing.[4] My working

---

[4] Joseph Butler, *The Analogy of Religion* (Ungar, 1961) II.6, p. 196.

parameters of security and prosperity optimism will be shadowed by beckoning alternatives.

If we are religiously optimistic, then in facing the general question of living successfully we are disposed to think that optimal life *would* in principle be and *will* in fact be attainable. In facing the problem of thinking coherently about the prospect of optimal life, we are disposed to think that there would and will be adequate doctrine, theory, and pedagogy, based on the provision of all needed assistance from divine being, with all needed concurrence from our fellow agents in a holy community, and with all needed capacities activated in ourselves. In a literate context, the religious optimist will feel force in the idea that all the information needed for the ultimate optimization of human existence would and will be available in a preeminent text or set of texts, a scripture, because the greatest power and guide that could exist, as we know from a supreme hierophany (or as we seriously suspect about a claimed supremely-great-and-good reality), *would* make and so *must have* made that information generally accessible.[5]

Optimism may be the riskiest thing about us – especially our wildly variable prosperity optimism but also our gullible security optimism. We can lose heart between launch and landing, settling for too little at the point of completing an action, or we can let optimism take us too far. Worries about religion are mostly on the side of excess. A well-known undesirable state that is logically related to optimism is *fantasticality* – that is, unrealistic belief in a realized or realizable good.

Fantasticality is excessive confidence in what is optimistically intended, so that fantasy is treated as reality and reality is occluded. The two main forms of unworldliness in religion, one based on a willful reshaping of the manifest forms of the world and the other based on renouncing the world in principle, are both prone to fantasticality. Fantastical optimists may get ahead of themselves on a massive scale, living their lives as though in an enchanted world, or they may indulge in fantasticality only on particular occasions in particular domains – such as during worship (filtering out the reminders of reality that worship services often include) or while reading a religious text (suppressing its worldly relevance). Their ordinarily important connections of cognitive sharing with real interlocutors get broken off. The worldly practicality of their actions gets impaired. They think their children will be spiritually protected and do not get them vaccinated.

---

[5] Richard Swinburne, *Revelation: From Metaphor to Analogy* (Oxford University Press, 1992), p. 72.

Although we are far from having drawn a complete map of the problematic of optimism, I think I have picked out the parts of that problematic on which issues of religious justification most often turn. The emphasis on ambition in my portrayal of optimism in human nature and religion is meant to offset the common presumption that nonlogical, nonempiricist determinants of thought are typically cheats that make for *easier* beliefs and commitments – a view that ignores the idealizing simplifications on the side of logic and science and the zest for the difficult on the side of passion – and to offset as well the notion that believing what is *hard* to believe has its best rationale in proving one's social commitment to others.[6] In sum, my threefold suggestion at this point is that (1) religion characteristically maximizes an optimism that is integral to our biological, intellectual, and spiritual existence; (2) a pertinent way to criticize religious thought or practice is to enforce reasonable checks on optimism; and (3) a pertinent way to vindicate religious thought or practice is to trumpet its unmatchable optimism while separating it from fantasticality.

To be clear, when we refer to the mental state of optimism, we might be referring to any of several distinct sets of issues (and this will be true, mutatis mutandis, for responsibility and intelligence as well).

Such a state is in the first place a *phenomenon*, a fact of life, something we experience in a variety of forms. Optimism may consist of a momentary inspiration to try something, a moderately confident choice of one well-deliberated plan over another, or a soul-shaking passionate acceptance of what is felt to be compelling guidance. It may also be observed on the communal level as a concerted orientation to a plan of life or a guidance. A society exhibits optimism both in holding to its customs and in indulging the freedoms of its members. The relative importance of any of these manifest forms of optimism will be judged differently by diverse observers, no doubt, but a representation of human life that left out optimism altogether would be grossly inaccurate.

Optimism is also a *rule*, a practical requisite of good faith, something asked for even if not yet seen. Like other practical requisites (consistency, carefulness), optimism may or may not be sufficiently marshaled in a given context. Sullen collaborators can let us down. Thus there must be a standing demand for optimism and a discipline. In practice, religion

---

[6] This notion is now popular in the cognitive science of religion. On difficult beliefs as demonstrations of social commitment, see, e.g., Harvey Whitehouse, *Modes of Religiosity* (AltaMira, 2004).

shares in the social-disciplinary work of maintaining a sufficiency of optimism; it is not just a cheerleader for the lushest version.

Theoretically, optimism can also be an *ideal*, an organizing principle for magic, science, politics, and philosophy as well as for religion. On the level of theory, one is concerned with the conceivability and general applicability of the optimistic presumption and with its grounding. How are goodness and optimality to be defined? By what measure or measures can the attainment of good be verified? Can one know or hold a justifiable belief rather than merely a passionate hope that a desired good will be attained? How could there be an ultimate right guidance and happy outcome that did not merely happen to be successful but had some sort of guarantee?

One sees that optimism is vulnerable in all these frames of reference. It obtains massively but not consistently, and individuals and communities can become so demoralized that they lose some of optimism's most basic benefits. It can reasonably be demanded, but it cannot be counted on. It can be thrillingly adduced in an intellectual system, but any pretense of establishing it in a definitive and useful form is highly questionable. (Leibniz's *Theodicy*, the work that introduced *l'optimisme* as a theoretical position, is now proverbial for its repugnant practical implications – justifying the worst things that happen as integral to the "best of all possible worlds" that a beneficent omnipotence must have chosen to realize – even though the position taken abstractly may well be irrefutable insofar as it converges with the Platonic idea that reality and goodness cannot fail to enter into nature as much as the inherent conflicts of nature permit, even as it may be religiously unavoidable for theists who are bound to place the best possible interpretation upon the divine Creator-Ruler's acts.)[7]

Because of the vulnerability of optimism, our techniques for boosting or restoring confidence are almost as important as the spontaneous upsurge of optimism itself. This is something that language as guidance always *is*, besides the provision of direction: an incitement to collaboration and a reassurance of its feasibility. This is why, if I am lost in the wilderness, it lifts my spirits to come upon any sort of message, even a fragment of a magazine ad. This is why I am moved to seek a sensible interpretation of

---

[7] Leibniz's position can be attacked on theist grounds, however. On Leibniz's theist critics see Hernán D. Caro, *The Best of All Possible Worlds? Leibniz's Optimism and Its Critics 1710 – 1755* (Humboldt University dissertation, 2012).

strange things my fellow humans say. It is also why I have some inclination to think that there *would* exist the greatest possible linguistic guidance.

1.3 RESPONSIBILITY AND FANATICISM

And I heard the voice of the Lord, saying, "Whom shall I send, and who will go for us?" And I said, "Here I am; send me." – Isaiah 6:8

Anyone who is alive is responsive; anyone who is committed to a way of being responsive can be called responsible. As cooperative beings, we are all functionally responsible; as collaborative beings, we must address the ideal of an assumption of responsibility that is fully acceptable to all. Speaking is collaborative, and so part of what it means to speak is to endeavor to satisfy everyone (primarily the parties directly involved in the communicative episode but ultimately all parties to communication) with one's response and style of response.

Thesis #3 on language: *The ideal relevance of language and linguistic acts is a function of their effectiveness in realizing responsibility.* Even if you seem to be speaking recklessly about the state of life-in-the-world, you are to be listened to so long as you are possibly acting in benign cognizance of the dependence of others on your speech actions. Without the centripetal force of this presumption, our practical partnerships would be too insecure. Listening to each other would be more like listening to jesters or lunatics. There are occasions when the presumption is relaxed, but the vacation time for loose talk is enabled by putting in a lot of work time of responsible speech.

Responsibility is assumed in proportion to awareness of the agent's power to affect others and the agent's self-control. Some agents want to keep responsibility to a minimum, while others aspire to greater aware-ness and self-control. Some agents, like Aeneas, have so much responsi-bility thrust upon them that they seem like spiritual superheroes in supporting it. So long as it is not crushing, responsibility is a way of having the strongest possible engagement with the world. Responsible agency is a site of importance, of difference making, offering a privileged (but also biased) appreciation of practicalities. Religious responsibility to and for eternal being is a main path of religious enlargement of life, gladly universal and inescapable though not necessarily easy to interpret and fulfill (as Arjuna discovered, faced with the dilemma of internecine war in the Bhagavad-Gita). With crucial assists from their optimism and their serious commitment to mutual aid, religious agents do not shrink from eternal consequences of their choices – a prospect that seems appalling to the nonreligious, who live within a comparatively limited responsibility horizon (though merely ordinary powers give all of us life-or-death responsibility for others).

Fanaticism is a pathology of responsibility, an overly strong insistence on assumptions about responsible practice fueled by an intoxication of self-importance. The problem may be cognitively centered, in drawing monstrous conclusions in one's righteous passion, or more practical, in a patronizing or bullying of one's fellow agents. There is impatience with whatever keeps a desired presence absent and with whatever distracts from the agent's own importance. Militants who fly airplanes into buildings are a compelling example of fanaticism, but there are also fanatics who would not hurt a fly but believe that nothing true can be said that is not stated literally in their scripture and correctly applied by themselves; at the other ideological extreme, there are fanatics who believe that nothing stated in a religious text could be true in any significant way or could properly matter to anyone, given their own contrary commitment.

Increase in responsibility is rewarded in a healthy way by increased practical understanding and in a more dangerous way by increased self-esteem and deference from others. A collaborative culture that promotes responsibility must demand and reward an offsetting humility along with it. We see this in the normal courtesies of assertion and command: "I suggest," "If you would," and "Thank you for considering." The religious courtesy of deferring to the divine is, in principle, radical ("As God wills"), ideally correcting for the extraordinary ambition of taking responsibility for the greatest accessible share of eternity.

1.4 INTELLIGENCE AND SUPERSTITION

The Master said, Among those that "ruled by inactivity" surely Shun may be counted. For what action did he take? He merely placed himself gravely and reverently with his face due south. – *Lunyu* 15:4[8]

It is not polite to characterize a person as unintelligent, but we constantly express our concern about the relative intelligence of particular thoughts

---

[8] *Lunyu* translations are from *The Analects of Confucius* (trans. Arthur Waley, Vintage, 1938).

and actions, prizing what was smart and ruing what was dumb. The issue is this: Did we see the relevant facts and grasp the relevant principles so that we had an adequate view of the best achievable ends and of the best available means to those ends? And were we able to act consistently with that awareness?

It is usually one of the main points of linguistic communication to maintain or enhance the communicators' awareness of relevant facts and principles for the sake of intelligent action. Thus we can state a fourth thesis on language: *The ideal relevance of language and linguistic acts is a function of their appreciable intelligence.* Even if the intelligence in your speaking is sometimes hard to discern, you have the right to be listened to so long as you are possibly contributing to a shared clarity about effective means to the best ends of life.

Intelligence involves rule following at every turn: identifying particulars correctly by general types, recognizing causal consistencies, and taking positions according to practical principles determined by one's culture and by one's roles. That the most desirable intelligence includes recognition of novelty and creative response hardly needs to be stressed, but nevertheless the main armature of intelligent action is regularity combined with correct expectations – the result of good training rather than of genius.

The principles of intelligent action are distilled from logical and empirical investigation. Intelligence cannot require practical connections beyond what logic and experience will vouch for. And yet one manifests religious intelligence only insofar as one is putting into play a venturesome belief about such connections. The pitfall of superstition looms – overly strong expectation of the results or the necessity of a result from an action or occurrence that follows a seductively simple rule. One superstitiously believes without good experiential or logical justification that saying the magic word will produce a desired fruit or ward off an evil. It seems a smart choice of means to ends, but it lacks the experiential funding and discernment of true intelligence.

Superstition may be prompted by an unwise optimism, but its strongest affinity may actually be with fear. It becomes a self-exacerbating syndrome, as a superstitious person who is at all thoughtful recognizes that in spite of the forced technique of superstition, there are many more ways for one's life to go wrong than right and many more life-affecting powers in the world than one's own. Accordingly, classical observers see superstitious religion as a cause of misery; Lucretius, a critic of religion, and

Paul, an evangelist, both appeal for liberation from superstition.[9] The category of superstition is widely applied by religious teachers to immature or pathological forms of religious thinking.[10]

An educational regime provides inducements, resources, and constraints for intelligent living. The desire for the success enabled by intelligent choice (or to avoid the shame and frustration of dumb choices) is perhaps our most inflexible motivation to be serious about guidance in general. But the intelligence about the divine that religious guidance calls for is a risky and debatable enlargement on commonly shared standards of intelligence in the cultural mainstream. Only if one can show that one's religious reference points are not fantastical and one's religious approach is not irresponsible can one expect an extravagant religious identification of means to the best end to be taken seriously.

1.5 GUIDANCE IDEALS AND THE PROBLEMATIC OF AUTONOMY AND HETERONOMY

The concept of guidance plays a crucial role in the analysis of perception, reasoning, communication, and behavior generally, yet it rarely gets its own scrutiny. We talk of guidance in a wide range of contexts – from the semantic guidances of sense and reference to the biological guidance system of flower scent to pollinating bees to the spiritual guidance of a guru to the physical guidance of a pinball guide rail – which raises the question whether there is a clear general sense of guidance embracing the whole range or perhaps a semantic center of the range, a paradigmatic instance or type from which senses are extended.

It seems to me that it is hard to define a clear general sense but easy to pick out a paradigmatic sense.

---

[9] "When human life lay groveling in all men's sight, crushed to the earth under the dead weight of superstition ... a man of Greece [Epicurus] was first to raise mortal eyes in defiance, first to stand erect and brave the challenge." Lucretius, *On the Nature of the Universe* (trans. Ronald Latham, Penguin, 1951), p. 29. Evangelist: Paul, Acts 17:22. Another representative text for the classical problematic of superstition, emphasizing the poisonous effects of fear (and to that extent in agreement with Lucretius, though the goal is to vindicate wholesome religious belief), is Plutarch's essay "On Superstition" (*deisidaimonia*).

[10] A good modern example of a normative religious critique of superstition is Bonaventura Kloppenburg's article "Superstition" in the Roman Catholic manual *Encyclopedia of Theology: The Concise Sacramentum Mundi* (ed. Karl Rahner, Seabury, 1975), pp. 1652–1654.

The problem in defining a general sense encompassing physical guidance is to distinguish guidance from causation. A distinction must be made, because there is an obvious logical difference between "X guides Y" and "X causes Y." In the guidance case, Y must be an actor and not merely a state of affairs. In the causal case, if Y is an actor, then "X causes Y" requires a completion along the lines of "X causes Y to do or to become Z," whereas the proper completion of "X guides Y" is "toward or with respect to a goal Z." (Compare the strained sense in which "gravity guided her to the river" if it did so by making her tumble down the hill with the more proper sense if she noticed the direction taken by water seeping from the ground and intentionally followed it to reach her destination.) Causation is compulsion, and guidance is assistance. A biological "guidance system" assumes a self-moving recipient of help with its own intentional project.[11] Even the pinball guide rail is thought of (under that description) as helping the freely moving pinball to find a destination rather than making the pinball go there in the way that paddles push it. In reality, the pinball situation is causal; the fact that the pinball comes into contact with a guide rail "on its own" does not reduce the determinacy of the system. But we think of this as a guidance situation by extension from a paradigmatic kind of guidance situation in which free beings are genuinely lured and helped.

I suggest that we have a maximum of interest in a humanlike guide because of our profound practical investment in collaborating interdependently with fellow humans. Here is a case to illuminate that interest. Suppose you have signed up for a guided hike in a national park. You show up at the appointed time. After introductions, your ranger guide straps you into a harness studded with electrodes and tells you that for the

---

[11] Michael L. Anderson and Gregg Rosenberg build this into their biological guidance theory of representations: "A token *provides guidance* to a subject by making its features available to the subject's motor systems and rational control processes for use in making discriminating choices between possible actions or possible ways of executing actions." "Content and Action: The Guidance Theory of Representation," *Journal of Mind and Behavior*, 29 (2008), 68. The *intentional* organism, the true "subject," differs from a mechanism (if contemplated only mechanically) in "making discriminating choices" among "available" (not imposed) "features." The informing of Y's action by X occurs in the context of the biological agent pursuing its own purpose with its own prospect of benefit or harm. This gives a sense to X's form being *helpful* to Y – more precisely, being purposely taken by Y as possibly helpful. (If we credit X with the intention to be helpful, X can qualify more fully as a guide; but Anderson and Rosenberg are primarily interested in how a perceiving subject *takes* guidance from anything at all that makes helpful form available, including all environmental stimuli relevant to survival or reproduction.)

duration of the hike, he will determine the exact timing and placement of each of your steps. You object that this arrangement would consist not of the desired *guidance* by him but of a quite alienating *control*. The ranger replies, not without plausibility, that control is the key to successful guidance. He is offering you the benefit of his advanced "guidance system." Suppose you insist on retaining freedom of movement, and the ranger's response is "Well then, you don't want to be guided, you merely want to be supplied with information to use as you see fit. You'll find literature on the park in the Visitor Center." How would you explain that you do not want merely to be informed any more than you want to be a puppet – you want a *guide*? You might say you are hoping for a collaboration, a shared action, with a guide advantageously taking the lead – doing more than you alone can do to define the activity as you hope to experience it, but not to the exclusion of your contributing to the activity also according to your own capacities. In *following* your guide, you expect to be obedient, but not mechanistically so.

The point of this example is sensitive and central: we generally care very much about the balance of power between collaborators. More important than exactly specifying or executing "the correct action" is avoiding a relationship disaster at either of the two extremes: being left to one's own devices or being dominated. Guidance in the paradigmatic case is a contextually determined Aristotelian mean between disapproved extremes. It is this concern and ideal rather than any particular phenomenon or formal model that centers our guidance thinking. As the Aristotelian problematic of virtue is structured by the need to balance the energies and sensitivities of the individual subject, the problematic of guidance is structured by the need to balance participants' contributions to collaborative relationships.

We might receive proper guidance or be ready to receive it in a variety of modes. One mode of guidance is the promissory *invitation*, like the one I received from the helpful park brochure showing the opportunity to sign up for a guided hike. I was free to make use of that information however I wished, yet I was directed to a particular time, place, and experience. In the context of my arriving at the park looking for hiking opportunities, the direction was palpably relevant, and I was very likely to follow it.

Had I gone on a guided hike, even without an electrified harness, I would have been subject to a guide's peremptory *commands* at virtually any juncture: "We're going this way now" or "Don't step there!" To disregard such commands or to overlook more subtle indications with similar purport would be to place oneself outside of that guidance.

(For a bee, the sight or scent of the right flower must be commanding, not merely inviting.)

I might have felt a need to understand my situation in greater depth, in such a way that *explanation* would have been the substance of relevant guidance – for example, a geological characterization of the treacherously unstable ground on the side of the ridge the hikers are not going to climb or a historical overview of bear encounters in the park. If I pay no attention to such explanations, I might be missing the best part of the guidance. If I am not given as much explanation as I want, the guide may not be letting me take over the content of the guidance as my own.

"I had the most wonderful guide!" We can imagine many of the ideal attractors of good guidance in this case: that the ranger facilitated a new experience that was fulfilling of my hopes; that he validated my own actions under his guidance as correct conduct in the wilderness; that he made this notable difference to my life congenially, without violating my functional autonomy or disrespecting my values; that he was knowledge-able and a generous sharer of information and perspective, successfully relaying in guidance form an awareness that he had acquired by any number of means; that he lent himself to a sparkling personal relationship without failing to serve the wilderness-revealing purpose of the hike; that he set great examples for hiking and for social intercourse generally; and that he inspired loyalty so that I might call myself (in this case, jokingly) his disciple. This is how a guide can convincingly justify having been trusted with the leading role in defining a shared action. A richly justified guide seems an imperative choice: "If you go on that hike, you must try to get that ranger!" It would be crazy to expect such wonderful guidance at every juncture of life, but a guidance optimist thinks that it can be had in some important contexts.

The guided hike example brings the values of guidance to a proximal focus on one day's action, but in any such case, one can sense the farther horizons of our curiosity (charging matters as "interesting") and our quest for justification (charging matters as "important") in confiding ourselves to guidance. The invitation of the park brochure is embedded in the inviting presence of the park, the park system, the government, the literature on wilderness, and my circle of friends sharing that interest. The commands of the ranger are typical expressions of a relationship that I have learned to be responsive to in a certain way – that is, "dealing with an official," which is a species of respectful yet collegial interpersonal coordination. The explanations of things in the park belong to a fabric of science and history. The ranger's appealing personal example of a manner of living with other people and with the wilderness implicitly speaks to a long-term interest in having a compass to follow always, as opposed to a single map. In all of these respects, I come to the hike already guided, presently guidable, and destined to participate in further development of the occasion's farther-reaching guidance.

It is not to be expected that someone else will come to an occasion of guidance looking for the very same reward as I did or that we will equally click with a particular guide. The very factors that most interestingly make us different people virtually assure that our criteria of successful guidance will differ in some interesting way. But our desires and experiences overlap a good deal and in some areas are strongly constrained by ideal consensus (as in a scientific or religious community) so that we can generalize and agree about good guidance.

Best-case guidance balances an impressive power in one who helps (the sagacity of the ranger) with the respected power of one who is helped (the reasonably vigorous and intelligent hiker). This balance is not automatic, though we experience something close to automatic balancing in normal conversation. In guidance relationships, we are constantly losing balance and liable to get stuck in positions of lost balance. To avoid the extremes of being captured and dominated, on the one hand, or left dangerously alone, on the other, we would like to know any and all practicable patterns of maintaining the balance of healthy guidance, and we have a vital shared interest in instituting ideally consensual directives as our *nomoi* (our practical allowances by custom or law) in the dimension of real interaction, as well as *logoi* (reasons) in the dimension of thought and argumentation.

The patterned conduct postulated by *nomoi* is a necessary support for what we regard as intelligent or responsible agency. The Easily Led Actor who invariably conforms to direction is not *following* that direction in any meaningful sense; such an actor is merely a wheel turned by other wheels. At the opposite, self-directed extreme, the Easily Lost Actor who freely decides at every moment whether to fall in with an available directive does not have a directive-following disposition and may even lack pattern-following competence.[12] Such an actor *could* be responsive to the guidance of any momentary inspiration, and we might have biological or psychological reason to predict that such

---

[12] Wittgenstein emphasizes the requisite *Technik* and *Praxis* of rule following; see, e.g., *Philosophical Investigations* §§198–224.

responsiveness will indeed be observed at times, but we cannot demand and count on it practically.

Once we put ourselves on the road of intelligent and responsible shared life by submitting in principle to the guidance of *nomoi* – as we surely will, for we are guidance optimists – the dilemma of other-controlled vs. self-controlled action comes back in relations an actor can have to the *nomos*. Our terms "heteronomy" and "autonomy" refer to this dilemma, but not straightforwardly. The original application of the terms is to communities, which have the power to generate *nomoi* commonly applicable to their members. Thus a politically "heteronomous" community has its *nomoi* imposed from outside, as by a conqueror or higher level of government, while an "autonomous" community is allowed and expected to determine its own *nomoi*. It was a conceptual stretch when Kant, inspired by Rousseau, adapted these political terms to express individual practical stances. An individual, unlike a community, cannot be responsible *for nomoi*, because *nomoi* are transsubjective in principle. An individual can, however, be responsible *to nomoi* either by uncritically going along with imposed *nomoi* or by freely choosing which available *nomoi* to follow and in what spirit.[13] Kant asserted that rightly oriented individuals freely accept a perfectly reliable, universally applicable *nomos* generated by pure practical reason.

There are rival reasons for championing individual heteronomy or autonomy based on authoritarian vs. liberal values. Under the aegis of Enlightenment, the liberal option prevails, seen not as a dangerous extreme of willfulness but as the most authentic form of personal responsibility. (The willful extreme is not called "autonomous"; we call it "autocratic" or "libertine.") According to the autonomy ideal, the *nomoi* themselves are defined and instituted by reasonable collectives, hence with consistency and authority, but they are also freely adopted and honored by the individual agent, hence with personal responsibility and sincerity. This is the individualist turn of guidance optimism, now a formidable rival to communitarian and traditionalist alternatives.

The autonomy ideal should be regarded with caution. If autonomy really is the solution of a guidance problematic, it must embody a

---

[13] Kant's influential conception of heteronomy is different. The *nomoi* of moral interest are realized in the individual's mind, but these *nomoi* are heteronomous or autonomous depending on whether their formulation has been determined primarily by nonrational factors (such as selfish passion or someone else's say-so) or by reason itself. *Groundwork of the Metaphysic of Morals* Ak. 4:440–444.

balancing of powers, a collegiality in interdependence. An agent who exercised self-directive freedom by choosing not to follow standards of community life would be rejecting the very premise of shared standards for shared action and with it an entire genre of guidance that is constitutive of normal humanity. In the case I have offered as paradigmatic, the ranger's guidance, though fallible, is constitutive of that hike; it would be inconsistent and disruptive to go along on the hike while disobeying the ranger, continually reminding him of your self-directive sovereignty. The *nomos* element in the autonomy ideal commits you to striving for a socially intelligible consistency in your conduct, whether with or apart from the ranger, much as logic commits you to ideal consistency in your thought.

Of course, you may quite legitimately want to strike out on your own. You may want to navigate the terrain based solely on your own knowledge, to prove your own expertise (though hardly without having consulting external sources of knowledge previously, without responding to perceptual guidance from the physical environment, or without obeying basic rules of good conduct and coherent thought). You may want to be free to "wander," simply for relaxation or in the hope that interesting or important unprogrammed experiences may come about. You will enjoy your self-determination while remaining on a tether to *nomoi* you did not make by yourself.

The presumption for attending to guidance is so strong, given our interdependent mode of life – and for attending to guidance as controlled by the particular community of a language – that it seems nearly miraculous that we have enshrined an ideal of a mentally free individual sufficiently disembedded from social custom to make his or her own lucid decisions regarding *nomoi*. This ideal is first culturally supported in an explicit, systematic way in the philosophical and religious texts of the so-called Axial Age, the pivotal time for formulating the chief enduring intellectual and spiritual ideals of literate civilizations.[14] Central appeals in these texts are formed by their candidly competing for the attention of persons who are capable of considering rival perspectives on supreme appeals (using referents like "nature" or "God" or "nirvana").

---

[14] For a fuller discussion of the Axial Age and axiality concepts, see Sections 5.1 and 5.3. The "Axial Age" notion comes from Karl Jaspers in *The Origin and Goal of History* (trans. Michael Bullock, Routledge & Kegan Paul, 1953), chap. 1. Charles Taylor develops his closely related notion of the "disembedded" individual in *A Secular Age* (Harvard University Press, 2007).

The audience assumed by such texts can be characterized as "enlightened" or, as a way of indicating the larger cultural-historical development, "axial." The set of problems that comes with promulgating axial ideals and sustaining a community of free individuals continually rethinking their positions, revising *nomoi* according to arguable *logoi*, can be called the axial problematic. As these disembedded individuals are now guided by transcendental points of ultimate reference and rational curiosity about what *can* be thought, as distinct from received communal wisdom, the axial problematic involves not only their voluntary relation to their cultures but their ideal global solidarity with all free individuals and with all cultures to the extent that cultures help free individuals solve their problems. It is a cosmopolitanism.

A politically pointed late-modern development of the axial problematic is the problematic of "emancipation." In working through the freeing of individual subjects from the guidance disaster of being dominated by means of unjust *nomoi*, the problem of domination is seen to reach into the very formation of subjectivity so that the question of what constitutes a subject must be reopened. Tacking against axial optimism and the confidence of modern Western rationalism, there is mistrust of the supposed unity and power of the subject. *Who* then is the eventual beneficiary of emancipation? That remains to be determined – like the new men and women who will appear after class conflict is ended, according to the theorists of communism. Presumably, emancipated (or less dominated) subjecthood will sufficiently resemble autonomous subjecthood that it will be affirmable on generally the same ideal terms of freedom and reasonableness. This seems to be an inescapable constraint on any ideal that could figure as a solution in our guidance problematic.

1.6 THE PROBLEMATIC OF *THE* GUIDANCE

While we are contemplating guidance as a structural feature of our life, we should not absentmindedly overlook the preeminent practical importance of *the* guidance, whatever it may be, that is unavoidably relevant in a particular context of action.

The use of the definite article presumes something about what the listener wants or needs to have said. Floating free as an incomplete expression, "the guidance" is likely to arouse curiosity of a practically focused or anxious kind – perhaps something like how incomplete reference to "the rider" would strike horses. This is appropriate.

Starting small, suppose that I want to make a certain kind of cookie but do not know how. Fortunately, I am able to look up *the* recipe. It is a situation in which there is probably a best or at least correct way to do something that I want to do and that appropriate directions will enable me to succeed in doing. If my prospect of *the* guidance I need is clouded by the discovery of several different but equally valid-seeming recipes, I may at first feel at sea, but probably I will come around to embracing one of them as *the* guidance *for me on this occasion*. If anyone asks, I will later cite it as *the* recipe I followed. This common episodic form of *the* guidance is the notional frame for the desired and at least possible answer to any particular practical question that comes up.

Alternatively, suppose that after staring blankly at a book recipe I find an online video on how to make my cookie. Then, watching a human being perform the necessary actions, I have a much stronger guidance experience – closer to the ideal of having a competent cook actually at my side. The guidance is active in the moment of my practical need, combining understandable content with prompting I can follow. (One is reminded, as in the ranger example, why interhuman guidance is paradigmatic.)

But now raise the stakes. A robber is holding a gun on me, and the question of what to do is very urgent. It is a situation in which there *may* be a best or at least highest-chance-of-survival way of conducting myself – so I am bound to hope. As I do not instinctively know what to do, I need guidance, and not just any relevant guidance but *the* guidance in the sense of the definitively best and most trustworthy guidance – guidance to live or die by, guidance that will pierce the clouds of doubt and fear as no merely informational guidance could. Anyway, it is not possible at the moment to look anything up. I have to draw on something I already know.

In the most serious situations, one often looks to one's most seriously adopted role models, on the principle (again confirming the paradigmatic form of guidance) that the greatest guidance is provided by the greatest guide. If I am religious, I am likely to think of a saint or savior: "What would S do?" or "What has S asked us to do?" Now I am reaching out to the guidance of S as *the* guidance to live or die by. To maintain that highly trusted status, a guidance that counts as *the* guidance will probably apply comprehensively to my life, or at least *the* guidance in the present situation will be coherently connected with similarly trustworthy guidance in other situations. I would otherwise suffer from a practical uncertainty far more threatening than the chance of being disappointed by a cookie recipe and perhaps even more deeply threatening than the chance of getting shot. Looking for a linguistically supported version of *the* guidance in this sense will almost certainly lead me into at least one well-developed normative realm like law, programmatic politics, philosophical ethics, or religion.

Any member of a literate religious tradition will be able to form an idea of *the* guidance on the basis of *scripturalism* – that is, reverent attention to a canonical record including teachings and exemplary actions of a Guide. Scripture itself has the instituted status of the Guide (for Sikhs, the "Guru") or the Guidance (as the Qur'an calls itself), a set of life directives possessing a paramount authority. Christianity is a scripturalist religion, and so a Christian accosted by a robber would be likely to reach consciously for a New Testament–based view of what Jesus would do or would ask his followers to do in that situation.

What *would* a scripturally guided follower of Jesus, God, an Upanishadic sage, the Buddha, or Kongzi do? Obviously not attack, fool, or flee the robber. The only good way forward would be to somehow engage the robber in a personally meaningful exchange. If this would be the directive, as seems plausible to suppose for many (though not all) scriptural schools of thought, then scriptural Guidance would clearly be endorsing and building upon the general human presumption for communication – *the* guidance that is always happening (or if not yet happening is always expected and usually desired to happen) between interlocutors who continuously cue each other as to the direction and acceptable resolutions of their relations. *The* guidance in this sense is realized in normal communicative action.

We have now identified three significant senses of *the* guidance, or three aspects of the problematic of *the* guidance: (1) the immediately relevant information and timely prompting that one wants in a particular context of action, assuming that one can reach out in that smart communicative way that opens up prospects of success in everything from baking a cookie for the first time to dealing with mortal threats and enemies; (2) the ultimately definitive answer to a practical question – which can only stand up in reflection if it fits with a comprehensive rightness; and (3) a recorded set of utterances instituted as the Guidance, to be reverently respected as members of world religions tend to respect their scriptures or as a literary canon or body of law is analogously respected.

The guidance in a fourth sense is the whole linguistic system of meanings, necessarily normative inasmuch as every possible linguistic act is a successful or unsuccessful contribution to an intersubjective world-representing and world-shaping project. "The guidance" is "the language" we speak, operationally (the good-enough English in this case, I hope), and, underlying any language, our human orientation to work together linguistically.

There may be a fifth sense to discern also, if reflection can tie these ontic realizations of guidance to an ontological enabler and unifier of them all, a guidance inherent in being – *the* guidance in *everything*. It could be the teleological drive of Aristotelian Nature or the reaching out of divine Love or the calming or opening of Emptiness. Presumably we would choose and verify one such vision of universal guidance by connecting it with the most useful-seeming pieces of guidance for concrete situations. The character of the supreme ordering might seem to fulfill the interpersonal style of guidance that we normally treat as our paradigm, or it might seem to transcend that paradigm without violating it.

All the senses of *the* guidance presume a need for guidance in a situation. If there is anything to be realized about *the* guidance for human beings generally, some account is needed of the general situation. Are we subjects of guidance simply because we are at liberty? Because we share the world with fellow actors? Because our powers are limited? Because our mode of life is interdependent? These are the structural considerations that philosophy fills in and that we are embarked on filling in now. But there might also be a historical consideration that we have arrived at a time of opportunity to live more successfully by accessing guidance, in an auspicious phase of a long quest – or that we have strayed or degenerated or even that we have gotten turned around into perverse enmity toward our own true interest so that negative elements in our present way of living need to be offset by a positively helpful power. We might get this kind of situation report, offered as *the* report as part of *the* general guidance, from a scripture.

1.7 ORGANIZING GUIDANCE, OR *DAO*-ISM

We know from some of the earliest of all writings that guidance itself is a major theme of literate discussion. (Not that it is a brand-new idea; oral cultures, too, have terms for such discussion.)[15] Principles of cosmic order

---

[15] Roy A. Rappaport discusses the Sioux concept of *Wakan-Tanka* and analogues in other nonliterate cultures in this connection. *Ritual and Religion in the Making of Humanity* (Cambridge University Press, 1999), chap. 11.

such as Ma'at, Asha, Rita, and Dike are proclaimed as ultimate directives and sanctions of good conduct. In early literature, there is an exultant perception of the great fact of the order – how all the beings actually are in harmony precisely insofar as their existence and action conform to a pervasively appreciable pattern.

> The rivers stream truth [Rita]; the sun stretches through the real.
> (Rig Veda 1.105.12)[16]

And normative significance is readily derived:

> The path that is yonder, belonging to the Adityas, made as
> something to be proclaimed in heaven –
> it is not to be overstepped, o gods.
>
> (1.105.16)

> Honey do the winds [blow] to the one who follows truth [Rita];
> honey do the rivers stream.
> Honeyed be the plants for us.
>
> (1.90.6)

A subtheme of growing importance is the value of the mental realization of this pattern – its profound intellectual interest and its power to solve difficult spiritual problems for individuals.

> Of truth [Rita] there exist many riches. The vision of truth smashes
> the crooked,
> and the signal call of truth bored open deaf ears ...
> Of truth the buttresses are firmly fixed ...
> [Whoever] holds fast to truth, just he wins truth.
>
> (4.23.8–10)

The people who think about the great scheme of harmony become increasingly sensitive to their own participation in that order as voluntary and salvific (separating them from many of their erring neighbors), which gives rise to major idioms of critical thinking such as Heraclitus' philosophy of Logos. Now the principle of order has become unmistakably an issue, and there are ideological rivalries about it. The discussion reaches a point where the very premise of guidance is rigorously questioned, as by the Greek skeptics and the Daoist philosophers – although virtually all thinkers agree that guidance should be drawn from a wise perspective more comprehensively aware and less selfish than ordinary practical reckoning.

---

[16] Rig Veda translations are from *The Rigveda*, 3 vols. (trans. Stephanie W. Jamison and Joel P. Brereton, Oxford University Press, 2014).

The classical Chinese debate about guidance is now a world classic due to the fame of the key Confucian and Daoist texts especially. The Confucians were very diligent in organizing guidance. In the *Lunyu* (known in the West as the "analects" of Kongzi/Confucius), we find a beautifully balanced discussion of better and worse ways of handling diverse life situations in relation to a small set of unifying practical principles, with teasing hints that one supremely trustworthy principle may rule them all – perhaps benevolence, perhaps understanding, perhaps filial piety. There is also a minimal but effective grounding of guidance in an ancient Chinese principle of cosmic order, Tian or Heaven – possibly originally a royal ancestor whose will for everything has been rationalized as an ideal or even naturally prevalent concurrence of all things, a normative Nature. The sage Kongzi is represented as taking his cues from Heaven; in a bold approximation to royal status, he is a protégé of Heaven (*Lunyu* 7:23, 14:35).

The ethical aspect of the Chinese guidance discussion may be foremost now for most readers, but the political aspect was originally of great importance and remains so in principle. The *Lunyu* shows us the chronically unemployed scholar Kongzi in a professional transition from counseling rulers on their exercise of power to showing the best way for any conscientious individual. He is embarrassed by his separation from politics, for he knows that human well-being depends heavily on a governmental organizing of guidance. One can take personal refuge in the idealized "government" of the sage-kings setting the example of virtue and so weather the tough times of bad government in the actual world. But it is recognized that such times can be very tough.

The Confucians try to set the scene properly for the availability and use of guidance. They are assembling a textual guidance system that will work as scripture, but their project is also a prototype for what today can be called transcendental pragmatics. The goal is to secure a platform for all moral and political reasoning by identifying the necessary conditions for undistorted social fellowship.[17] The many forms of guidance on which we depend cannot simply be left to chance and improvised. Their content must be intelligibly and usefully patterned and benevolently oriented, and their occasions must be anticipated by role and attitude specifications for guides and guided – so that rulers and subjects, for

---

[17] See Jürgen Habermas, "What Is Universal Pragmatics?" in *Communication and the Evolution of Society* (trans. Thomas McCarthy, Beacon, 1979), pp. 1–68.

example, can expect to receive complementary kinds of politically crucial guidance from each other.

The Confucian project arouses a Daoist counterproject for which the most important concept to use rightly is *dao*: way. Any reader of the *Lunyu* and *Mengzi* gets a clear sense of the Confucian *dao*s or guidances as organized by a definite practical style – "If you lead along a straight way, who will dare to go by a crooked one?" (*Lunyu* 12:17) – and a philosophical principle, a super-*dao*. But two fundamental objections may be raised to the Confucian *dao*-ism. The practical objection is that the Confucian *dao*s are not really effective in straightening things out. To define and enforce virtues is paradoxically to estrange oneself further from real commonality and harmony by taking in hand and meddling with what can hold only at a more basic level (*Daodejing* 19), where there is no dividing of "do this" from "don't do that,"[18] and which is manifest at times in a more "crooked" and useless way than conventional ethicists would like (*Zhuangzi*, chap. 1 [HY 1/42]).[19] The theoretical objection is that the claim to define or at least indicate a super-*dao* is impossible to fulfill inasmuch as "the *dao* that can be named is not the true *dao* " (*Daodejing* 1). The primal source of what is graspable, the original opening for grasping, cannot itself be graspable (21).[20]

The practical objection shows lack of trust in the probing and balanced conversation among thoughtful persons that we expect to correct any errors in guidance – the sort of conversation that Kongzi and his followers model for us in the *Lunyu*. The classic Daoist discourse is in a drastically different style, relying on odd sages' paradoxical affirmations of an action that is nonaction, a teaching that is wordless, a self that is no self, and a way that is no named way. If a Daoist paradox properly enters one's

---

[18] See Koji Tanaka, "The Limit of Language in Daoism," *Asian Philosophy*, 14 (July 2004), 191–205.

[19] HY citations refer to chapter and line number in the Harvard-Yenching text (ed. Charles Sturgeon, ctext.org/zhuangzi, 2006–2018).

[20] Hansen argues that the Daoists pull not toward a mystical Dao-being but away from ontological foundationalism altogether toward the language game of *dao*ing. "Daoism is a *dao* about *dao*: it discourses about discourse, prescribes about prescription. It is a series of theories about *dao*s ... The striking new insight of Daoism is that our discourse is the *real* authority, not nature. Nature was a universal shield behind which philosophers hid what they were really doing. Nature is neutral in the disputes between moral philosophers." Chad Hansen, *A Daoist Theory of Chinese Thought* (Oxford University Press, 1992), p. 210. Tanaka agrees: "It is philosophically fallacious to hold the view that the Daoists are concerned with mystical reality, the Dao. Instead, the Daoists provide 'theoretical' treatment of the guidance 'Don't be guided by any guidance!' and its paradoxical nature" (191–192).

mind, it knocks one off the paths of normally constrained optimistic purposiveness and into an open field of "free and easy wandering" (*Zhuangzi*, chap. 1 title). (A similar Buddhist ideal of nonattachment to directions is declared in the Heart Sutra: "There is no wisdom, and there is no attainment whatsoever.")[21]

From one point of view, there is a maximal liberation from *nomoi* in this. (Not a perfect liberation – one continues to live as a human being.) From another point of view, the Daoist derives his or her own distinct *nomos* from a personal partnership with the untamed Source of all. This is arguably the peak of "autonomy," uniting the self-direction of an exceptionally free agent who has thrown off all conventional constraint with the profound consistency and true commonality to be found in the Source. (Compare the strangely behaving Hebrew prophets, partnering with Yahweh, and Indian forest sages, partnering with Brahman.) Daoist autonomy is supported by the theoretical objection to conceptualizing the supreme Way, which secures the most authentic recognition of what simply Is and is Common, by refusing to frame it.[22] (A similar deference may be found also in Parmenides, Spinoza, Schleiermacher, Heidegger, and Tillich, all of whom resolve the guidance problem by espousing an extraordinary super-norm – Tillich calls it "theonomy" – of attunement to primal Being.)[23]

Daoism is obviously impractical. I imagine that if I were assigned a Daoist ranger instead of the high-tech ranger of my original guidance problem, I would not have to worry about moving in lockstep, but on the other hand I could easily be disappointed by not covering the ground I expected to cover. Of course, it could be a wonderful hike, going with and bringing out a grain in that country that conventional guidance and perception would miss. But I do not know that that will happen, for I cannot assume that any graspable principle of guidance will be employed. Given the uncertainty but also the distinctive potential benefit

---

[21] *The Prajna Paramita Heart Sutra* (trans. Lok To, Sutra Translation Committee of the United States and Canada, 2000), p. 113.

[22] Or, alternatively, recognition of the irrelevance of any conception of Being (see note 16).

[23] Tillich specifies "theonomy" as follows: "Autonomy asserts that man as the bearer of universal reason is the source and measure of culture and religion – that he is his own law. Heteronomy asserts that man, being unable to act according to universal reason, must be subjected to a law, strange and superior to him. Theonomy asserts that the superior law is, at the same time, the innermost law of man himself, rooted in the divine ground which is man's own ground ..." Paul Tillich, *The Protestant Era* (trans. James Luther Adams, University of Chicago Press, 1948), pp. 56–57.

of Daoist guidance, the best of all solutions perhaps would be to hike with a mischievous Daoist at one time and a conscientious Confucian at another.

A harmony of Confucian and Daoist guidance in some measure will be supported by two premises they share with each other and with many other classical schools of thought: (1) that the basis of good guidance, the superguidance or Ur-guidance, must already somehow be extant to be *found* by the rightly oriented inquirer; and (2) that the practical direction of human life on the ultimate ground of good guidance must nevertheless actively be *formed* by rightly oriented thinkers and communicators.

Confucians and Daoists differ sharply on how relation to the Ur-guidance is to be achieved. Confucians bank as much on tradition and social-role authority as on reason and abstract principle; one gives oneself a chance to be on the right path in a particular domain by looking reverently to the enshrined examples of sage-king behavior and taking well-programmed cues from one's ruler, father, elder brother, or husband. The classical Daoists champion free perception and thought; they also recognize, however, that ordinary conventions are in force, and they think there is a higher Guidance to be engaged. From a Confucian perspective, what the Daoist surmises about that Guidance needs traditional and social discipline. But the Confucian appeal to the ordering of Heaven brings it into agreement with Daoism about a suprahuman origination of Guidance.

Most importantly, both Confucianism and Daoism are schemes for unending critical reflection and reason-giving conversation. (As philosophies, they consist purely of such schemes; as religions or elements of cultures, their ideas and characteristic ways of discussing them are woven into instituted systems of practical observance, including scriptural devotion.) The Daoists make fun of the Confucians for their busy regulating, but the Daoists are busy in their own way, confronting us with strange questions and propositions that we must stretch to interpret. In an optimal Chinese-style guidance system, Confucian traditionalism would helpfully keep everyone attentive to the rationales for existing social arrangements and the value of consistency while Daoist iconoclasm would encourage our free questioning and reconcile us with "crooked" results.

*

The guidance power of words was taken very seriously in classical Chinese thought. The Mohist and Confucian program of a "rectification of names" is a manifestation of this (*Lunyu* 13:3; illustrated by "Let the prince be a prince, the minister a minister" [12:11]). It is a philosophically optimistic response to the perceived unreliability of discourse.[24]

At the highest level, Kongzi takes it for granted that Heaven simply does not speak (*Lunyu* 19:3),[25] and Laozi says about the Way, "Listen for it and there is nothing to hear" (*Daodejing* 35).[26] There is no close Chinese analogue to Heraclitus' Logos philosophy identifying the principle of reality with the vehicle of communication.[27] Kongzi and Laozi both set the interhuman guidance of their philosophizing out to the side from their prime points of orientational reference in Heaven and the Way. In refusing to say that Heaven or the Way guides us in a paradigmatically interpersonal way, they implicitly take a humanistic position on the formulation of guidance. The guides in this scene are the language users – we humans who strive to be well informed and rightly oriented.

Let us now examine how guidance, with its promises and hazards, comes into speech.

---

[24] It is typical of Kongzi and Laozi to express distrust of speech: *Lunyu* 4:24, 5:5, 8:19, 9:24, 10:1, 11:25, 12:3, 15:5, 15:27; *Daodejing* 1, 2, 5, 14, 16, 21, 23, 25, 32, 35, 37, 40, 43, 56, 81.

[25] He does, however, refer to "decrees of Heaven" (2:4).

[26] *Daodejing* (trans. Roger T. Ames and David L. Hall, Ballantine, 2003), p. 132.

[27] Heraclitus' conception of ultimate appeal and response seems un-Chinese in the important respect that he calls on us to *listen to* the *logos* (DK 50), which though hidden from vulgar thought (DK 123) is not inaccessible. On the other hand, the Heraclitean *logos* metaphor might need to be interpreted as rising above intellectualism and anthropomorphism, indeed above anything that Heraclitus or anyone else *says* ("listening not to me but to the *logos* ..." DK 50, to whatever an attunement to the One of All (no ordinary "listening"!) requires. Trans. G. S. Kirk, in *The Presocratic Philosophers*, 2nd ed. (ed. G. S. Kirk, J. E. Raven, and M. Schofield, Cambridge University Press, 1989), p. 187.

2

The Speaking Problematic

Our acts and artifacts of communication often seem adequate for our purposes, and some are cherished as especially powerful and trustworthy. When communicated guidance seems acceptable, a number of uncertainties and hazards of relationship must have been successfully negotiated. We shall consider now uncertainties and hazards confronting all language users in what we may call the speaking problematic.

2.1 STARTING TO SPEAK

In one sense, no one can really start speaking. Whenever speech occurs, a working set of linguistic meanings and procedures has already been instituted and there are historical precedents of things already said. Speaking always has the character of entering back into speaking and using some of its given potentialities. But it is true at the same time that speaking always needs to be started and always has the character of an intervention. Speaking occurs in episodes that must be initiated and in phases that must be carried through. Accomplishments of speaking depend on contingencies of intention, performance, and circumstances, all attended by issues of appropriateness.

Speaking cannot start if no one is or could be listening. One cannot grab the reins of guidance if the reins are not attached anywhere. Speaking is comportment in a communicative partnership. Therefore, if speaking has started, the action is shared.

At many moments, one is not speaking. What makes it a question of whether to start? There are many different scenes in which the question might arise, each already framed by goal-serving, risk-managing social conventions.

Suppose you and I sat down together on a bench, sharers of a public space for the nonce. Why would we say anything? What would be wrong with *not* saying anything? Does the mere fact that we are speakers, members of Team Communication, oblige us to check in with each other in case one of the normal reasons for helpful speaking applies?[1] Neither of us knows if we have information or emotional support wanted by the other until some clue is given. But we may be under an urban norm of buffering between lives, or we may be claiming an entitlement to rest sometimes from the exertion of speaking. Or we may be intimidated by the risks.

A man sat on a bench next to me in the Underground on a hot July day. When a train went by the other way, he said, "That breeze really helps!" Why did he speak? Perhaps only out of a habit of making pleasantries or due to a belief about social norms. But perhaps in that moment he consciously wanted the results that did obtain: we made eye contact, smiled at each other, and put our sharing of the space and occasion on a positive footing, making a place of community. Thanks to his directing attention to the breeze that had just gone through the station, we shared an experience both sensorily, in the moment, and philosophically, con-templating a model of how life is, conjuring up in an encouraging way awareness of much that has happened and much that has already been said. That was nice! Thinking back on this, I am reminded of my basic optimism about communicative action and spurred to think more about how communicative partnerships enrich our existence.

But what if he had gone on to say, "Hot enough for you?" and more empty things of that sort? – Disappointing.

Or what if he had babbled self-contradictorily, or with phony sophis-tication had mocked the meaningfulness of things that other people say? – Discouraging.

Or: "I saw that [term of contempt for a category of people] bothering you"? – Disgusting, or threatening. (Worse, suppose he had said, "Men like us, we know what to do with those [term of contempt]"?)

---

[1] According to the anthropologist Bronislaw Malinowski, "to a natural man, another man's silence is not a reassuring factor, but, on the contrary, something alarming and dangerous ... To the primitive mind, whether among savages or our own uneducated classes, taciturnity means not only unfriendliness but directly a bad character." "The Problem of Meaning in Primitive Languages," "Supplement I," in C. K. Ogden and I. A. Richards, *The Meaning of Meaning*, 7th ed. (Harcourt Brace, 1945), p. 314.

Or: "How do you know you won't be spending eternity in Hell? Do you know the Word of God?" – Alarming.

If the stranger had indeed spoken further, beyond a pleasant checking in, probably my most important general measure of satisfaction with his speech would have been the interest for me of the kind of guidance he was offering. For an ideal of relevant and respectful guidance is in force in any communicative situation, specified for me by my own criteria of relevance and respect. The bad continuations I have imagined fall to either side of that ideal: the time-wasting kind of talk that can make no difference to my life, on one side, and the presumptuous, pushy kind of talk that tries to affect my life too strongly, on the other.

The stranger who spoke evidently had his own resolution of issues that still face me if I am wondering whether I should start speaking. Arguably I ought to sense tremendous opportunity and a significant pull of propriety whenever the common impediments to striking up conversation are removed. If for no other reason than the practical prudence of developing and testing my own grasp of how the linguistic community operates, I should be active in that network. But listening or reflecting might help me more than speaking. What decides me to take the lead and speak?

For someone who is extensively exposed and entangled in communicative interaction, the advantages of limiting further exposure might seem great. Speaking exposes one's intentions, which always have some strategic significance for Team Communication's future and for competitions within the Team; one may not wish to show any more of these cards. Speaking also encumbers one with responsibilities: whatever one says, one represents henceforth ("According to you, X . . .") and holds down as the starting point and direction of a program ("But you *said* that Y . . ."). To the extent that one is playing a guidance role, one is of course obliged to speak effectively as a guide. But one may understandably wish to give away nothing more.

The balance of risks and opportunities looks very different when one is not exposed enough. To someone who has been lost in the wilderness, for whom the question is not how to continue but rather how to restart communication, the sight of another human being (unless a dangerous foe) will virtually compel speech – to plug in again to the network, activating the interdependence of communicators, and make known the need for help.

The wilderness scenario is not as exceptional as it might first appear, for what constitutes being lost in the wilderness is subjectively relative – some of us are lost in the crowd or even in interpersonal relationships, shut out from meaningful connection (and whose connections are *fully* meaningful?). Also, there is a fascination and a rhetorical excitement in acting as though we are just now espying each other in the wilderness of all that *could* be said and done and making a fresh communicative start, poetically or philosophically or politically. Whether or not we reap benefits on this premise, it is never an irrelevant premise.

"Hey!" – or however the sound of speaking begins, announcing the speaking event in advance of any content, and guidance in advance of any indicated direction – hails the other, dispelling the other's oblivion of your interest or your current plan of action. Hailing would indicate a willingness for a particular kind of interaction on a particular occasion even if one were calling only to a turkey; if the summons is to a genuinely communicative relation, then it must be recognized in that character as a kind of word, an open gate on a path to response. If the gate is marked for a particular hearer, then the summons is a name.

It seems fair to say generally that calling a name evinces optimism about a communicative partnership, for even very diffident or very imperious name users (up to the limits of grotesque name abuse) open up to being spoken to – that is, to being guided in return, believing that good will come of this. To call a name is to acknowledge someone as a charter member of a team within the Team – a working group that has for present purposes a significant portion of the linguistic community's whole action. To respond to one's called name ("Yes?" "Here I am") evinces responsibility, accepting that what one's existence amounts to is bound to the actions of others.

If communicative partnership is to be realized at that juncture in compliance with that stimulus, the necessary complement of hailing is hearkening. The hearer, too, starts something, provisionally as a willing receiver of the speaker's locutionary and illocutionary direction. As the irruption of hailing preceded saying anything, the hearer did not have a choice about suffering the perlocutionary effect of the summons coming when and as it did; if the communication goes well, it will reconcile the hearer to that takeover of attention.

At the hailing/hearkening moment, the hearer accepts communicative partnership without yet knowing a number of things about the upcoming venture:

What sort of communication will it turn out to be – informational, invitational, negotiational? What opportunities for response will the hearer be given, and in what veins of response?

Are the speaker's intentions benign? (Despite old acquaintance, the speaker may have a different character or agenda now; acquaintance is always being newly forged.) How will the speaker's speaking relate to the rest of what the speaker is up to?

Is the speaker psychologically competent, able to coherently relate experiences to intentions and intentions to utterances? Will our relationship prove tenable on those levels?

Is the speaker epistemically competent, able to coherently relate utterances to experienced and knowable states of affairs? Will the speaker's locutions, however they might be intended, be understandable in an ultimately helpful way?

Is the speaker socially and linguistically competent? Will the speaker be a tolerable guide in the presumptive areas of knowledge and practice, neither useless nor overbearing? Will the speaker appropriately relate newer utterances to older utterances for the sake of a coherent larger conversation?

Problems in these areas are not rare. It speaks impressively of our investment in communicative interdependence that on the whole we give ourselves so trustingly to new ventures of speaking. Even if our primary socialization did not hold us in this pattern, we would have a very strong motive to plunge ever and again into communicative partnership insofar as all our substantial thoughts, including our doubts and disillusions, require the framework of speech for their articulation and evaluation. Our guidance issues are essentially matters that speakers speak of, matters that cannot be addressed otherwise than by locutions and debates.

We know that the framework is unavoidable. We also know that anything an interlocutor comes to say *could* prove to be *very* valuable. (One must speak very tediously indeed to neutralize this expectation.) We also know that we depend on conversation to learn a stream of things concerning ourselves that are determined exclusively by uses of "I" and "you" – including some things of great moment, as in "You're scaring me" or "I love you."

2.2 THE LISTENER'S DOUBTS

As speaking gets underway, the hearer may gladly fall into a partnership that seems entirely congenial. But if the hearer is conscious of the new beginning in the speaking – perhaps because a poetic or philosophical or political speaker has deliberately activated the sense of new beginning – then a variety of doubts will tacitly if not explicitly qualify the early steps taken by the hearer in response to the speaker's guidance.

Speaker S is saying P for the sake of offering guidance G to hearer H – for example, telling H that "a dangerous-looking E," a specimen of a certain ethnicity, is in the street so that H may consider whether to risk encountering E – but what locution other than P could be said for the sake of G that could be truer or more practically adequate, or what guidance other than G could be more practically auspicious or could simply put S and H on a different path? What is S not saying that S could say? In other words, what does H risk missing insofar as H attends to and builds on S saying just P?

What is the cognitive load of P? Is P supposed to be a straightforwardly public fact being fairly reported, or a "realization" that S is earnestly recommending to H, or an "as-if" figure offered for H's elective adoption?

Even if there is a clear "natural" understanding of what S is saying, what is the true purport of what S is saying? What does S really mean in the communicative venture to which saying P belongs, or – putting the focus more on the listener's opportunity and work of understanding – what is ultimately to be gathered from S's communicative venture to which saying P belongs? In saying P, what is S playing at? (Keeping S and H together indoors, perhaps? Why?) In construing P, what is H playing at? If one can surmise what S or H is playing at, what will be involved in playing that out?

What is the true audience of S's speaking? Is it really meant for H, and if so, is it meant for certain others as well, and subject to what assumptions and expectations? For example, if S means to derogate a class of people, must H renounce certain future partnerships with people of that class and embrace certain partnerships with antagonists of those people in order to go forward in conversation with S? Or if S's appeal simply fails to recruit other listeners, what will the effect of H's rapport with S be on H's relations with the others?

What backing does S have? Who else, with what standing and what interests, does S represent in saying P? Might S be imitating others? What is S's authorization? The same question can be raised about P's authorization within the economy of things S has said or might say: Is S actually in a position to know what P asserts?

We can sum up all of these uncertainties by saying that H cannot know everything that might be important to know about where S's inauguration of communication will lead. At the start of a communicative episode,

H can have at best only a preliminary evaluation of the possibilities. The ideal of a trustworthy speech source, which often plays a crucial role in religious epistemology, addresses these doubts but can hardly banish them. Communicative trust can stand lucidity about the hazards in following a speaker only with a commensurate degree of courage in the listener supported by a sturdy norm.

2.3 ORDINARY POWERS OF SPEECH AND IDEALS FOR THEIR EXERCISE

Whoever begins to speak and whoever listens are optimistic that speaking will succeed, producing presences that would otherwise not be present and gatherings that would otherwise not be gathered. A general assumption underlying this optimism is that agents just in speaking and listening exercise sufficient power to attain important ends in dealing with beings – at least, some of their characteristic ends under normal circumstances.

What is our conception of "power" in this context? As with the concept of guidance, and with the same justification of catering to our keenest interest, I suggest that the best choice for a paradigm of power is an agent whose self-determination determines changes in the conditions or prospects of other beings. Let us say that, in a given set of circumstances, S has the power P to bring about result R just in case S can voluntarily act in such a way that R results. The range of possible results and S's freedom and uncertainty in relation to them determine the problematic of S's power P. A broad natural definition – say, that entity E has a power P to bring about result R if, in a given set of circumstances, E completes a set of sufficient conditions for R – may at first seem to capture an equally original and stable sense of power. But this sense is not really original or stable, because a power that is not elective is not really owned by its supposed possessor. Does the earth *have* the power to pull us downward? I feel "its" pull; on consideration, however, I can see that the earth is one node in a larger system conditioned throughout by attractions of mass. To think of the earth itself acting through gravity is shorthand for considering how the universe works in our neighborhood, the earth being our prime centripetality for many practical purposes. So it is with any physical thing as such, even a volatile one: we think that a volcano has the power to destroy a nearby city because we judge that a destructive eruption *could* occur – we have to watch out for that happening – but it is the earth-at-the-volcano, or rather the-universe-at-the-earth-at-the-volcano, that does what the volcano does. And the universe is not demonstrating to us that it has the power to do this. It is just being the process that it is.

Tool-power is a logically stronger sense of power than the natural sense because it is attached directly to the power of voluntary agents. A chainsaw is a powerful tool for cutting up trees; a jeweler's screwdriver is a powerful tool for getting into watches. Tool-power is manifested and measured by the results it makes attainable by an agent.

Tool-power seems a relevant way to think about the power of language in the sense of our linguistic resources – the psychological machinery of our linguisticality and the vocabulary and grammar and heritage of expressions we can draw on in using that machinery. There is a button-pushing aspect of language use. If I say "Stop!" to you in a normal occasion of English use, I take advantage of the command's psychological and semantic linkages to bring about your stopping. This button pushing is necessary for all communication. But more is required. If only I really could make you stop before you step into traffic! If only you were so well trained! My "Stop!" is actually much more likely to make you *think* of stopping than to make you stop. I have put you in the resulting condition of having heard me say "Stop!" which involves to some extent your *understanding* me to be ordering you to stop (although there are variable fillings-in of the hearer's understanding that cannot be directly determined by a speaker's action);[2] produced with that condition is the *prospect* before you of possible imminent danger if you do not obey my command. I assume or hope you will respond appropriately to this prospect. I am acting for the sake of that continuation of our coordinated life. My most interesting speaker power in this "Stop!" case is my power of affecting your agenda by bringing before you that daunting prospect of

---

[2] An elucidation of communicated meaning on the basis of the interlocutors' understanding of each other's intentional states can get very complicated, since understood content cannot be assumed to be constant throughout the chain of "A understood B, B understood that A understood B, B understood that A understood that B understood," etc. There can be important variations at each level of understanding. To use an example in which this possibility is very obvious, we may suppose that B understands that A understands that B intended to avow love for A by saying "I love you" in a normally intelligible use of that expression, but we may not suppose that B's understanding of A's psychology and the general psychology and spirituality of love is identical to A's understanding of B's psychology and the general psychology and spirituality of love, and differences of understanding will ramify importantly up the chain of understandings. The standardness of meaning content assumed by Gricean analysis and by most everyday interpretation holds these variations at bay.

danger – perhaps a real danger of walking into harm, certainly a danger of falling out of communicative accord with me.

Thus, while it is true that there are great results of coordinated thought and action that agents can attain only by communicating linguistically, it is highly misleading to say that we attain these results by using language as a tool. It is not normally the case that we produce desired effects in listeners just in the unilateral causal way that a tool user produces effects; nor do we normally set about influencing listeners by electively picking up language as our advantageous device. We are already in language. There are instrumental aspects of speaking, to be sure: we do choose among available linguistic moves, in an available language, in the medium of linguistic existence, and we do act for the sake of bringing about changes in the world. But the fact that self-definition and intersubjective communion are always at stake in "using" a linguistic move makes it decisively unlike the ordinary sort of tool that is entirely subordinate to the manipulative intent of its user. While it is not wrong to say that we use the resources of language, it is overridingly more appropriate to say that we conduct and express ourselves linguistically. Saying that speakers and listeners "use" language has the oddness of saying that birds use flight (although birds do use flight to travel and to hunt) or that musicians use music (although musicians do use music to set a pace or a mood). Birds fly; musicians play; people talk.

The "powers of speech" are therefore best understood as our powers as speakers. To take this position conceptually does not entail a strong thesis that speakers' acts are formally prior to the language they speak. For it may also be acknowledged that linguistic action is necessarily shared action, never a purely private or new initiative, and that this action must be shared in a fundamentally linguistic way, structured by an already-acquired linguistic comportment, a preexisting vocabulary and grammar, and a communicative history.[3] Our powers as speakers must be exercised in concurrence.

Let us see how the chief powers and associated problems of communicative action become manifest in the carrying through of speaking.

---

[3] I see this as the core of a proper pushback to Davidson's dissolution of the premise of an existing common language in favor of a myriad of specific and mutable individual speaker and hearer understandings. See Donald Davidson, "A Nice Derangement of Epitaphs," and Michael Dummett, "'A Nice Derangement of Epitaphs': Some Comments on Davidson and Hacking," in *Truth and Interpretation* (ed. Ernest LePore and Donald Davidson, Blackwell, 1989), pp. 433–446 and 459–476.

(1) *Expressing intention.* With the first intelligible sound, the speaker steps out into the space of communications, inserting the physical presence of the sound and the sound's intentional qualification and thus realizing the presence of the speaker, the presence of a possible respondent to the speaker, and whatever the speaker succeeds in representing or channeling, including a positive or negative disposition.

The speaker strikes an intentional pose that can be noticed, commented upon, and reacted to. Under more or less self-control, the speaker will also be somewhat exposed as more or less skillful with words, more or less mentally healthy, and more or less culturally normal. The speaker's public biography may well contain this speaking. A foundation is being laid for later possibilities of saying "I said X" or "I meant Y." (Down the road, something will have to be done about the problem that hearers will not remember or take into account anything one has said unless they seize on it for their own reasons.)

Hearers will have learned from their own experience as speakers that utterance can never be assumed to represent the speaker's intention adequately. (Further, a speaker's intention can never adequately answer for how it plays in the interintentional field, in the gap between "What did she mean by saying that?" and "What does saying that mean?") The practical hazard for hearers is that a deceptive, whimsical, or weak-willed speaker will not act consistently with the implications of the intention he or she announces. The public ideal, accordingly, is that the speaker will be sincere and consistently able to show and confirm this sincerity to hearers, saving them from doubt; the gap between intention and utterance will not be the undoing of the communication.

The hazard for the speaker is that an important aspect of what is intended will not be understood because the linguistic announcement fails to convey it. The speaker may intend something infinite or paradoxical that can only be hinted at by using words in an abnormally cryptic way. Or the speaker may simply intend to provoke us or disengage from us by speaking mysteriously.

(2) *Naming.* Even without explicit self-naming, the speaker introduces or refreshes his or her status as an undeniable object and subject of responsibility (for that is what one's "name" means metonymically) and also the status of the summoned hearer. Whatever the speaker chooses to name is spotlit in the theater of beings that are to be reckoned with. The dramatis personae have begun to be assembled, each with a stipulated identity and an actual or virtual presence for the communicators.

Now there are possible objects of praise and condemnation; so too there are possibilities of misdirecting praise and condemnation.

(3) *Convening an actively communicating community.* The first sounds of speaking will be in the mode of a certain sonic and emotional appeal pregnant with implications for what will follow – ordinary plaintalk, military bellowing, beguiling singing, ritually constrained chanting, secretive whispering, piteous wheedling – presuming a favorable mood and circumstances for a desired communicative episode and promising to sustain the right mood.

If the proposed communication is to get anywhere, probably its community will be circumscribed by the particular language the summoning speaker employs. For a language has developed not only to facilitate communication but to separate networks of communicators – perhaps for the ultimate reason of distinguishing those who normally cannot be mortal enemies from those who may be.[4] The speaker will automatically enjoy a measure of freedom within his or her default community in using linguistic means instituted by that community and is positioned to enjoy the benefits of participation in that community's actions; but the speaker may also have learned a different community's language and so may experience freedom from the fate of belonging to just one social organism.[5]

Once a speaker has summoned listeners, a team has been formed (drawn from the presupposed larger Team of possible communicators) to carry out one or more specific initiatives. The team operates in an intentional place created by the communication within the broader space

---

[4] For the modern cosmopolitan, it is hard to understand or accept this condition of structural antagonism between communicating communities. "Time and again, linguistic differences and the profoundly exasperating inability of human beings to understand each other have bred hatred and reciprocal contempt," writes George Steiner in *After Babel* (Oxford University Press, 1975), p. 56. His own explanation of language plurality emphasizes an individual bias toward private and intimate communication, although he does evoke the society-level issue with his reference to "treason": "The psychic need for particularity, for 'in-clusion' and invention is so intense that it has, during the whole of man's history until very lately, outweighed the spectacular, obvious material advantages of mutual comprehension and linguistic unity ... there is in every act of translation – and specially where it succeeds – a touch of treason" (232–233).

[5] Steiner: "Through language, we construct what I have called 'alternities of being'.... To move between languages, to translate, even within restrictions of totality, is to experience the almost bewildering bias of the human spirit towards freedom. If we were lodged inside a single 'language-skin' or amid very few languages, the inevitability of our organic subjection to death might well prove more suffocating than it is" (473).

of the world. The summoning speaker is the team captain. The captain's followers accept respondent roles, looking forward to a communicatively coherent future.

Good captain or bad captain? At the point of starting a communicative episode, the two central issues are likely to be these: What gives the speaker standing in the community that is called for by the speaker's initiative such that we would be willing to listen? And what makes the current beginning-of-speaking an apt intervention?

The ideal for granting standing ought to be the fullest possible acquaintance with the speaker to the extent that acquaintance and knowledge of circumstances found trust and whatever sort of deference the situation calls for. (Acquaintance and knowledge of circumstances can cause lessened interest due to the speaker's predictability or bad track record.)

The ideal for apt intervention can be defined from the perspective of the ideally knowledgeable and well-intentioned participant in the communicative episode. Simply to be worth listening to, receiving due respect, the speaker must at least not threaten to pull us out of productive or safe activity we are currently engaged in; better, the speaker must draw our communication in a plausibly promising or reassuring direction. In communication that is wholly in gear – as when a good wilderness guide successfully leads a hike – the speaker is a sort of messiah at each moment, saying precisely the needed thing for the optimized situation. Although the messiah of the moment is not automatically an acceptable guide in other situations, satisfaction with leadership in one context can optimistically expand in a sort of nimbus of approval, encouraging the accepted leader to speak whenever he or she can provide relevant help – implicitly encouraging the speaker to take fully as much initiative as he or she helpfully can, so far as this is compatible with others doing the same. Ideally, speakers should provide neither less nor more than the guidance they can helpfully provide. This ideal will shape what counts as a well-formed linguistic expression with respect to sufficiency.

The ideal of apt intervention implies a problematic of allocating guidance roles properly. We need a system to minimize disrespect and inefficiency in our continually changing allowances of authority in our conversations. Since a culture is constituted partly as a working resolution of this issue – since being American or being Japanese involves knowing when and how to speak – a culture can easily be blind to human problems in its communicative style, and it may be richer or poorer in internal resources for improvement in that dimension. (Is American culture rich or poor in resources for addressing the tendency of men to interrupt women in conversations?)[6]

In the exceptional case where a speaker is regarded as the Messiah or the Prophet or the Buddha, the one who starts the decisive rectification of everyone's life in the world, then all history backward and forward must be interpreted on the premise that the speaker's communicative venture is the supremely apt intervention of all time. (But even this supremely pivotal guidance does not cancel the assumption of teamwork among guides and between guides and the guided.)

(4) *Projecting a prospect.* A speaker seems to be starting *something* in the coordinated activity of the convened community. If I shout "Hey!" to a stranger, I prefigure at least that we will go on to talk about some mutually interesting aspect of life-in-the-world – unless this is just the "Hey!" said lightly in passing to affirm our sharing of existence. The power of speaking in this aspect is to signal an aim for some portion of Team Communication's activity, indicating somehow who is involved and whether the practical focus will be found in play, work, ritual, political deliberation, or loving intimacy. An ideal for a language is to be well equipped for such projection with instantly appreciable phrases, whether open-ended wide-scope ones like "What's up?" or task-oriented ones like "As you will recall ..." or invocations of consensus like "As we know ..." The rhetorical ideal for the projecting speaker is to match the gambit to the occasion properly and effectively: "Friends, Romans, countrymen ..."

The hazard of being misled attends all the instituted devices of guidance. A speaker who projects a friendship prospect by saying "Friends ..." may wish to exploit or harm me. On the other hand, a well-meaning speaker runs the risk of failing to satisfy the expectations raised by addressing "friends," which may weaken his or her own position and the power of the "friend" gambit. (Many such gambits are undoubtedly kept afloat, despite abuses and disappointments, by their social utility.) The community will be interested in canonical cases as references for when gambits go well or badly. The would-be speaker can gain needed courage from aligning with good precedents and can be significantly handicapped by not knowing a good precedent.

---

[6] One reason to answer this question optimistically is that the tendency is extensively documented by American academic researchers and extensively discussed in American mass media, with a new term, "manterrupt," coined just for this purpose.

(5) *Deciding the structure of guidance.* Guidance will be delivered in a certain way. The language used locates the guidance within the practices of a community. More specifically, the speaker can determine a plan for guidance by framing it with certain expressions. "As I said ..." puts guidance into a temporal frame; the speaker is suggesting that the fullest benefit of guidance will be received by attending to the consistency and governing precedents in his or her speaking as it accumulates, its structure distilled and made salient by well-chosen and well-timed expressions. "As Aristotle wrote ..." similarly puts guidance on a schedule but with much larger consistencies and weightier precedents to heed. The hearer is now addressed as a listener, a studious follower of guidance. And the hearer may be required to recall what was said and a certain order among things said – putting a command with the force of a constitutional provision ahead of a command with the force of a statute, for example.

What is the right schedule? When is it proper to offer guidance as a momentary inspiration? When should we void guidance of any notable content or rhythm so that it can serve as mere ongoing reassurance of the presence of one's fellows, as in purely phatic communication, or refrain from providing guidance in one area so that the audience's attention will move to other, more productive areas? When is it proper to fortify guidance against inattention or disagreement? How is the form of a proffered guidance fitted to the form of the practice it directs? A parent may feel that guidance needs to be secured by as many guy wires as possible against the winds of a child's waywardness: "How many times have I told you not to X?" This parental remonstrance is famous for showing its own futility, but the greater significance of "How many times?" is that it nudges the hearer toward the needed premise of a rule – that is, a guidance for all situations of a kind, not merely an inducement or an intimidation at one juncture. A rule is a structure tying experiences of success or failure together; to learn a rule is to grasp that consistency.

With scheduling and rule formation of guidance comes the problematic of proper authority, constraint, and application. Must we, in our present or projected area of concern, hearken to Aristotle's dicta? Does good guidance in our situation necessarily involve relating our acts to Aristotle's proposals? Are we best advised to think of ourselves as *playing off* a momentarily inspiring Aristotle, finding new consistencies, or as *working out* an Aristotelianism, anchoring ourselves in a known consistency? On a larger view, what is the most fruitful setup of guidance combining fundamentally enabling rules that are to be faithfully worked out with permissive openings to new rules? When is guidance best served by the structure of a text-like closed canon and when by a conversation-like open canon ("Moses said X, but I say Y")?

(6) *Articulating content: the locutionary power.* Now we arrive at the Austinian dimensions of speech acts.[7] The power to say P may be called locutionary. By locutionary power, a speaker brings a hearer to consider that something obtains (perhaps thrillingly present) or does not obtain (perhaps hauntingly absent) in some way in a world that they commonly address – often something that can be reconsidered later as well, held constant by its linguistically instituted identity but also always subject to linguistic reframing at the discretion of the speaker. Available linguistic expressions enable a speaker to direct a hearer's attention to infinitely many different items ("meanings" as well as worldly particulars) and classes, relations, and qualifications of things. Moreover, one can say P just on one's own, as someone else's deputy, or as a representative of the community.

What matters most about locution, generally, is recognizing acting beings and constraining forms and saying what their actions and constraints are or are not. Our speaking and thinking belong to the basic work of getting the interplay of actions and constraints into satisfactory shape. Epistemology is messy: how we "believe" or think we "know" the purport of locutions or "understand" their content is highly variable according to person and context. But very often we do not have to subscribe to the exact same cognitive loading of utterance to be able to go forward with a sufficiently shared orientation.

The intrinsic problematic of locution has to do with speaking truly and relevantly. Any actual or possible locution may be false or, even if not false, displaceable by a nonequivalent alternative. A locution (by which I mean any member of the set of expressions that are equivalent in a given context, having the same meaning of interest) must be secured for truth and preeminent relevance if its content is to play an essential role in guidance.[8] The locution must be drawn from an authoritative source, or it must be the product of an accepted method; this requirement applies to the speaker's choice of linguistic expression as well as to his or her

---

[7] J. L. Austin, *How to Do Things with Words* (Clarendon Press, 1962).
[8] I admit that there are cases of tutelage or duress where a spoken falsehood may give the best guidance, even knowingly accepted in its false character – as when a battlefield medic says "You'll be OK!" to a gravely wounded soldier.

understanding of the matter to be conveyed. Fortunately, any known expression in our language enjoys the authority and the methodical testing of past usage, which is sufficient security for being able to make oneself understood with that expression in normal circumstances. To satisfy the requirements of a particular practical context of guidance, however, additional validation will usually be needed, such as a basis in the speaker's and hearer's experience or in a communally instituted guidance.

The most important of all validity conditions for locution is its fit with the totality of what is known and felt. Neither the signified content nor the proposed truth or practical value conveyed by what one says ever stands by itself. To issue a locution is to make one more contribution to our immense project of building and maintaining a shared working model of life-in-the-world – a map of what is (that may pick some things out distinctly while purposely leaving others blurry)[9] and a choreography for dealing with what is. It is like hanging another picture or adding another walkway in the Museum of Accessible Experiences. Its cognitive import is a vector sum of its relationships with the values of all the items in the Museum.

There is a certain variability of epistemic inflection in locution that speaker and hearer must resolve. Content is always *figured* by the speaker and *entertained* by the hearer, but entertainable content is not necessarily *asserted* or *accepted* as true of actuality or the real world or even as true possibility. It may be floated as a fiction or notion. We can transact a lot of intentional business or simply enjoy ourselves in a purely virtual world of fictions and notions. Nevertheless, there is an abiding centrality of assertion insofar as our pretending and questioning lead us around an imaginary world to which certain items and states of affairs do belong (such as a world in which the smallest unicorns *are* always purple), much as by true assertion we find our way about in a more fully shared world; and the felt import of that imaginary world stems in part from whatever

---

[9] Malinowski on what I have called blurring: "When moving with savages through any natural milieu – sailing on the sea, walking on a beach or through the jungle, or glancing across the starlit sky – I was often impressed by their tendency to isolate the few objects important to them, and to treat the rest as mere background. In a forest, a plant or tree would strike me, but on inquiry I would be informed – 'Oh, that is just "bush."' An insect or bird which plays no part in the tradition or the larder would be dismissed '*Mauna wala*' – 'merely a flying animal.' But if, on the contrary, the object happened to be useful in one way or another, it would be named" (331).

virtue it possesses of representing objects of true assertion (as small unicorns may represent physically existing small children).

Another kind of locutionary inflection is worth noting here. I have been using the expression "fully shared world" to distinguish the physically existing world from subjectively varying worlds of dream and imagination, but the most proper sense of that expression would combine physical and subjective experience with our experience of established, inescapable ideals that are not physical entities but are not merely individual experiences either. In filling out an inventory of a culture's "fully shared world," we should include all the terms that would be acceptable to capitalize in print: Justice, Truth, and even Unicorn (as an essence). I think we can regard this kind of guidance as an ordinary power of nominalization, though it is much involved in extraordinary meanings.

(7) *Coordinating relationship: the illocutionary power.* Wittgenstein used the notion of "language-games" to call attention to the diversity of basic types of linguistic collaboration. The game model seems apt to the extent that communicators normally accept role definitions and follow a set of procedural rules. But most communicative episodes are unlike most games in that they are not designed to produce winners and losers. And while many communicative episodes can, like games, be characterized as "pastimes," many others cannot; they are freighted with pragmatic importance in the most fully shared world and look more like instrumentally justified tasks than enjoyable games.[10]

The illocutionary power of speaking is the intralinguistic part of the practical setup for playing a communicative game or shouldering a communicative task. My diction, syntax, or rising or falling tone indicates to you what I am doing or trying to do *in* speaking to you – for example, that *in* leading off with the words "Could you ..." I am *asking* you something, or alternatively that *in* starting off with "You could ..." I am *telling* you something about your own capability. In a serious tone, I could be pressing you to conform to a shared feeling or action; in a playful tone, I could be encouraging you to respond impulsively; in a dreamy tone, I could be inviting you to entertain some imaginative content. Whichever way I am speaking, I exert the speaker's illocutionary power to summon

---

[10] For a review of disanalogies between games and ordinary language use, see Rush Rhees, *Wittgenstein and the Possibility of Discourse* (Cambridge University Press, 1998), pp. 60–62 and chap. 5. Rhees lays most weight on discussion as a central, ungamelike use of language.

up the prospect of an upcoming segment of communicative action in which we fulfill already-understood roles such as asker and asked-of, teller and told-to, singer and singer-with, or political representative and represented.

Austin called the illocutionary tenor of a speech act its "force" – as in, "Her statement had the force of a demand." Even though it is crucial to distinguish the prospect-summoning power of speech acts from the phys-ical-effects-producing power that the word "force" might suggest, there are several auspicious implications of the metaphor of force. One is that force is interestingly indeterminate; it affects probabilities of occurrence but produces particular results only via the particular actions or omis-sions of action that we call causes ("pressure" bursting a pipe where it does, for example, via the impacts of energized molecules on the weakest point in the pipe). So too, as Austin pointed out, the illocutionary force of an utterance is specified in a particular way depending on how the speaker means the utterance to be taken and how the hearer takes it.[11] As a metaphorical communicative pressure, the illocutionary intent embodied in an utterance, however polite, really does *impose* on its audience; the speaker is forcing (though in a not fully determinate way) the communi-cative action into a desired pragmatic format, tilting the probabilities of outcome in a desired direction.

In serious speech, illocutionary force intensifies a serious relationship between subjects. When I convey a truth to you, I prompt us both to be witnesses of what is the case; when I convey a moral imperative, I stipulate that we are both obedient executives of the right; when I praise something, I figure us both as enthusiasts for the thing praised or the terms of praise. In frivolous speech those relationships are attenuated.

The pragmatic clarity provided by illocutionary indicators may be relatively more helpful to the hearer or to the speaker. For instance, saying "I order you to go!" instead of "Go!" may help the hearer to make a good decision whether to obey. For the speaker's purposes, the "order" may increase the force of the order by disclosing or highlighting assumptions that support it (as in a military context there will be the generally accepted necessity of obeying orders from superiors) and by sheer emphasis of intent, with implied bad consequences later if that intent is not honored. (Compare "You must go!" or "Go now – I mean

[11] Austin, p. 32.

it!") Students of rhetoric will find illocutionary vocabulary useful in clarifying how actual utterances embody intent. But some guiding utterances of great importance may be resistant to a narrow specification of illocutionary force, particularly when (as is common in scriptural guidance) they invite a free involvement of their audience in determining the upshot of the guidance.

(8) *Achieving effects: the perlocutionary power.* Still following Austin, we may say that *by* speaking (as distinct from illocutionary force *in* speaking) we sometimes exert the perlocutionary power of effecting changes in the world. This occurs in four quite heterogeneous ways.

(a) One is the "button pushing" by which speech elicits attention and produces awareness of linguistic material. Sometimes we consciously take the psychological power of speech into account in deciding to whisper, shout, sing, or insistently repeat a motif. More subtly, we can choose relatively unfamiliar or comfortable words for effect.

(b) We can directly effect changes in the social world of instituted practices by expressing agreement or making avowals: for example, saying "I will" at the altar makes me married, and my boss saying "You're fired" cancels my employment. Austin called such utterances "performatives." They have the illocutionary aspect that they draw their results from definite collaborative setups, like that of being subject to the boss's authority.

(c) There is also a much broader array of effects in the world that are mediated by speaking and listening: for example, along with my *advising* you to shut the door *in* saying "The door won't stop rattling till you shut it properly," in the case where you comply, I have *persuaded* you to shut the door *by* having said that. The cases Austin is most interested in here are psychologically and narratively intelligible hearer effects like being convinced, surprised, or mollified – all sharing the property that one could confidently (though not infallibly) expect to produce such a result in one's hearer and thus reasonably intend to do it and think of it as the object of one's action, even though one could at no point say "I hereby convince (or surprise or mollify) you in saying X."[12]

(d) Finally, I might bring about the shutting of the door, without any idea of producing that result, by saying something unintentionally

---

[12] Austin, p. 117.

suggestive or irritating. Note that in these latter two kinds of case, I cannot say that I accomplished an effect *by saying* P – I do it only *by having said* P, and only when the effect came about as a *presumed* result of my having said P. The presumption is that my speaking occasioned, perhaps facilitated, someone else's decision.

Perlocutionary power is typically doubtful, or at least susceptible of different evaluations, because it is mediated by free agents determining their own actions. (Did Iago bring about Desdemona's death by what he said to Othello, or must we blame Othello's ravening insecurity?) Nevertheless it is a tremendous, potentially monstrous power. (Many of today's cities exist because someone said "This is the place.") It is also eerie and intimidating because a high percentage of the effects of speech, rippling outward from the immediate intended and unintended effects of each speech event, are beyond the foresight and control of the speaker.

We try to exercise perlocutionary power in all persuasive speech. Our everyday coordination of practice depends on it; our political capability depends on it. There are many, many situations in which the attractive showing of an advantageous or honorable course of action will very probably be followed by the audience choosing that action, or in which an aversive showing of something awful will very probably be followed by the audience rejecting it. But the effects of speaking can never be perfectly programmed. Indeed, a major part of political or social responsibility is staying in place to cope with unwanted and difficult consequences of what one has said.

In archaic times it might have been maintained that our religious capability depends on our perlocutionary power, seeing that much of our received religious language is framed as persuasion of gods; but a general reinterpretation of religious language that has been broadly dominant in the world religions has put those urgings and entreaties on a footing of spiritual self-cultivation, thus avoiding perlocutionary embarrassment.

We have been making all along a global perlocutionary claim that communicative action builds and maintains an interesting and useful shared model of life-in-the-world. The effect is both intended and real – it is what we strive to achieve and what we have achieved. We serve the inclusive purpose of developing our linguistic life-in-the-world model *by* every act, insofar as we act linguistically; turning the "by" relation around, we can also say that everything we do, insofar as it is done linguistically, is done *by* speaking in service of the inclusive guidance purpose. (The corresponding global illocutionary claim is that *in* telling, advising, warning, requesting, pleading, and so on, we are always providing guidance.)

(9) *Silence as speaking.* Much that can be done by ordinary speaking can also be done without words in a situation informed by communicative intention. The audience can infer a content or a relationship or be prompted to do something. The ambiguity and suspense in registering a speaker's silence can become an extraordinarily interesting or motivating experience, manifesting a special power of language (such as in amorous or religious invocation).

*

In the study of language, we sometimes evaluate utterances merely to improve our view of how they work, assuming that they do; we ferret out the conditions on which they depend and identify their essential invariants and variables, such as the locutionary, illocutionary, and perlocutionary powers of speech. But sometimes we withhold the assumption that utterance provides guidance as desired, as needed, or as advertised in order to figure out the conditions under which an utterance of a given sort *would* fulfill ideal sense and justification requirements. In the present study, we are headed toward that critical sort of evaluation of a kind of religious utterance.

What can we say generally about standards of acceptable utterance merely from contemplating the general powers of speech?

It appears that a speech act would be irreproachable if it consisted of a relevantly informative and true locution issued in the framework of a fully collegial speaker-hearer relationship with patently benign net results (so far as results can reasonably be linked with speaking) in real lives. In that optimal case, all speech values are realized. In suboptimal cases, however, it is often hard to tell how different speech values interact and how the trade-offs should be weighed. The interdependence of the powers of speech is evident and inescapable yet not deductively rigorous like the relations between the sides and angles of a triangle. It is quite possible, for example, for an army to be ordered not by its authorized commander but by an imposter, telling them a gross falsehood about enemy strength, to attack, resulting in victory. Is such a speech act acceptable, in view of its effect? Many would approve; in wartime it is hard to discount military success. But many others would disapprove due to an overriding concern for the integrity of military practice or of truthful speech generally.

Or think of the grim scenario where someone conscientiously refrains from falsehood in answering a would-be murderer and thus helps to bring about a wrongful death.[13] Can the locutionary standard of truth and the illocutionary standard of collegiality be upheld at the expense of perlocutionary disaster? Can the perlocutionary horizon be minimized by reasoning (as Kant did) that speakers never actually control the outcomes of their speech? All that can be determined from an overview of the powers of speech is that it would be wrong simply to disregard any of these powers or their interdependence.

The virtuous speaker – intelligently truthful, earnestly collegial, and tactically skillful and responsible with regard to the foreseeable consequences of speaking – always assumes risks of not being understood or understandable, not receiving or earning needed cooperation, and not having desired effects, all in the shadow of this great structural hazard of possible conflict between ideal demands in speech situations. And the ideal demands themselves are contextually variable. When might telling a specific truth actually upset the hearer's good understanding? ("I saw her go into his apartment last night.") When does needed initiative overwhelm needed deference? ("I'm *telling* you ... !")? When does the risk of a bad effect, like the perlocutionary disaster in the murder example, require making an exception to a generally defensible strategy?

The two fundamentally different modern ways of relating ethical standards to speech are to position speakers as intelligent respondents to nonlinguistic facts of pleasure and displeasure, in the manner of classical utilitarianism, or to derive ethical standards from standards of worth and value inherent in the speaking project itself, in Kant does (and Habermas in his discourse ethics).[14] A limitation of the Kantian approach, arguably, is that it is blind in principle to the gravitational pull of pleasure and pain on all our deliberations and to the true significance of the unhappiness we have rationalized. In the case of the would-be murderer seeking a victim,

---

[13] Immanuel Kant, "On a Supposed Right to Lie from Altruistic Motives," in *Critique of Practical Reason and Other Writings in Moral Philosophy* (trans. Lewis White Beck, University of Chicago Press, 1949), pp. 346–350.

[14] Jürgen Habermas, "Discourse Ethics: Notes on a Program of Philosophical Justification," in *Moral Consciousness and Communicative Action* (trans. Christian Lenhardt and Shierry Weber Nicholsen, MIT Press, 1990), pp. 43–115, and "Remarks on Discourse Ethics," in *Justification and Application* (trans. Ciaran P. Cronin, MIT Press, 1993), pp. 19–112.

I want to say that *of course* we should lie to save a life, *especially* if the life belongs to someone we care for. Kantians either deny the reality of that motivation or devise their own imperfectly relevant rationales for the lying that the situation demands.[15] On the other side, an arguable limitation of a utilitarian construal of situations of moral choice is that any such situation is already mediated by language use and thus by ideals inherent in speaking. Because I am *speaking* to the would-be murderer and the other is *capable* of speaking to me in return, I am immediately required to treat him or her as a communicative colleague and not simply as an object of strategic action; the endangered person I should want to defend is not merely a "life" in the sense of a site of experience but a *sharer* of the status of membership in a communicating community, his or her material interests already having been subordinated to the holding of communicative rights by all members.

I do not think it is necessary to take one side or the other in this basic disagreement to accept that the teleology of guidance is definitive for linguistic existence. The guidance claim convenes utilitarians and Kantians on central affirmations they ought to share. That humans vitally depend on a constant supply of intersubjective world-representing guidance, so that obtaining adequate language-grade guidance is bound to be a constant top-ranking object of our practice; that our need for guidance is grounded in irremovable natural and social needs; that our response to these needs will in the best cases be intelligent; and that the cultivation and exercise of our intelligence depends on good linguistic practice – none of these points should be in dispute.

What can be in dispute are historical stage settings of action, ethical rankings of values, and designs for the intelligent leveraging of our capabilities. The basic guidance thesis brings a conscientious pragmatism to bear on discussion of these matters. It seems that no viable position can be dismissive of these values sustained by the powers of speaking:

(1) A content value: the speaker's message or order or request should be substantial in its cognitive content and perspicuously centered in its relevant context.

(2) Backing: our confident collaboration with a speaker normally requires that the speech act have a relevant authorization, whether

---

[15] For example, with the theory that the would-be murderer has forfeited the right to be told the truth under universally valid rules setting preconditions for truth telling. While this idea is not irrelevant, it does not seem to respond squarely to the moral claim of the endangered life.

from a generally accepted information source or precedent, the speaker's own experience, or whomever the speaker represents.

(3) Completeness: a speaker should say all that needs to be said for the purposes of a communicative endeavor, with nothing relevant kept secret or overlooked.

(4) Respect for interlocutors: although illocutionary setups and purposes of communication strike widely varying balances of privileges, interlocutors should always really be deferred to somehow.

(5) Tact and timing: a speaker should speak aptly, steering participating agents and their communicative projects in an arguably right direction. We should not let a general formalism or empiricism make us overlook the moment of tactful and tactically successful speech.

2.4 SPECIAL POWERS OF SPEECH AND IDEALS FOR THEIR EXERCISE

The idea that one might use language in a *specially* powerful way does not come out of the blue; it comes from a recognition of the power already exercised in ordinary speech and of farther horizons of its possible exercise. With the possibility of announcing intention comes the possibility of intimating incomprehensible or otherwise overwhelming intentions. With the practice of giving names to things comes the possibility of naming something unheard of or some ineffably distinctive personal or group attribute. With the practice of putting things in noun categories based on everyday perception comes the possibility of creating vast rosters of things with imputed affinities ("clean" vs. "unclean," "organic" vs. "inorganic"). With quantification and comparison comes the possibility of declaring something the "only" or the "greatest." With subject-verb and subject-adjective conjunction comes the possibility of striking metaphors. With the practice of relaying messages from others and agreeing with others on statements comes the possibility of claiming an exceptional authorization. And so on. This is a family of ideas that will surely be acted upon.

The human reliance on specially powerful language is as obvious as the fangs on a tiger and one of the most important facts about human culture. The principal manifestations of our interest in exercising special linguistic powers belong to familiar categories of high accomplishment – art, politics, religion, science – which shows that the extraordinary has become, in a way, ordinary, yet the domesticated extraordinary usage manages to maintain its distinction from the ordinary, retaining high value.

In reviewing the special powers of utterance and their associated ideals, we should keep an eye on the meaning of power in the changed context. Does the ordinary paradigm for meaningful power still hold – namely, the capable worldly agent – or does a new paradigm, something like spirit possession perhaps, displace it?

(1) *Poetic speech.* Going further than the ordinary use of rhyme and rhythm to make utterances memorable and usual, the poet ventures to use words in a lastingly unusual way to occasion an extraordinarily stimulating experience in the audience. The poet's discourse is subjectively intense due to the license it takes in summoning before our attention something that is not ordinarily present – a supernatural being, an epic theme, an obscure or vagrant subject – and due also to its novel combinations and schematic placements of words. The audience is amazed by the freedom of the expression and the intensity of the registered meaning. The audience may have been enabled to grasp a state of affairs intuitively that no definition of terms could capture.

Typically the greatest meaning gain from poetic speech is not in disclosing items in the world informatively but rather in discovering new ways for a subject to move in the world while registering the presences and absences of things in multiple arrays. The subject-world relationship gets complicated and more complexly charged, like a growing neural net.

Poetic speech expands the repertoire of linguistic guidance and does so continually, breaking out all over, so that we perceive a progressive, developmental aspect of our guidance project. As a result our long-range optimism is increased as well as our optimism about having striking locutions on hand for upcoming occasions. The emboldening cognitive adventures of fresh metaphors and other tropes are energy cells renewing this optimism.[16]

A modicum of courage is required to speak poetically, departing from what hearers expect, but anyone can do it. Those who do it successfully are, at the very least, recognized as persons of distinctive capability. Is the experience so impressive that one wants to say more about the power

---

[16] As far as Google search reveals at the time of writing, no one has ever previously written "metaphors are energy cells."

involved? Is the poet "inspired," drawing power from a greater source? If we want to say "inspired," what could we think about the source of inspiration? One natural thought is that the poet has lit upon possibilities given in our language; but language itself does not forge metaphors and assemble couplets. Language itself is a power holder only when we entertain the stimulating poetic conceit of a personified language. That could be a god (the Indian Vac, the Egyptian Ptah).

If poetic power does come from a god, we have one powerful kind of answer (to be elucidated in another category of special power – that of inspiration) to a serious question about the poet's backing. The poet significantly affects our perception of life-in-the-world – especially of that which we are prepared to honor. Is there good reason to believe this influence to be trustworthy? Insofar as we think of poetry bubbling up freely from inspiration or genius, there can be no justification of a poetic production, except that it turns out to be coherent with the culture that receives it.

(2) *Narrative*. The original "story" is just a report informing a hearer about an occurrence the hearer did not witness. But the scope of narration enlarges as occurrences are elaborated or newly conceived and as additional means are used to spotlight the most interesting and important touchstones in the narration – notably the capacities of the actors involved, striking turns and reversals in the practical situation as it unfolds, and the mythic recognizability of types of action and situation. No clear line separates reports from works of narrative art. As consumers of reports, we are students of life-in-the-world, keeping track of what happened and how it happened so that our practical understanding of our own situation is fuller. As consumers of stories, we are likewise students of life-in-the-world, cultivating our practical understanding, except that we have embarked on an exploration of possibilities so that our interest is now held by the desires and trials of imagined life.

A report or story can assemble expressions from diverse, even irreconcilable points of view. The premise is that the hearer can judge what to make of the whole affair, having been given something interesting to go on. The most passionately rhetorical storytelling cannot override the hearer's evaluative discretion, since for the hearer, the storyteller is as much on stage as the story's characters.

Generally storytelling differs from sober reporting in striving for a maximum of impact. The *great* story discloses a fully satisfying life (a narrated segment of life being treated as decisive for the quality of a whole life) that a subject can lead imaginatively. The *great true* story, if there is one, discloses a great life led in the fully shared world by subjects who are fully active imaginatively and fully responsible practically. We can imagine a great true story coming about either by a credible report of occurrence that generates maximal imaginative satisfaction or by a thrilling imaginative exercise that is able to gather real-world credibility. The appeal of an evangelical religion like Buddhism or Christianity may register initially in the first way, but as its testament shifts over time from the category of news to the category of literature, its appeal will accordingly come to center in its imaginative power, catering to "our craving for a perfect story which we feel to be true" (Stanley Hauerwas).[17]

The special power of narrative is the captivating cogency of its presentation of life to imaginatively active students of life. A story can charter and sustain a community by establishing an arrestingly vivid, practically instructive, anxiety-reducing, loyalty-inspiring model of how action is shared.[18] The fact that speaking can be composed so elaborately, imposing so much attentional and intentional constraint, makes narrative all the more impressive to those who reflect on it.

(3) *Magical speech.* As the extraordinary power of storytelling grows naturally out of the ordinary power of reporting on occurrences, the extraordinary power of magical utterance grows out of the ordinary power of getting things done by asking, ordering, or otherwise cognitively positioning people to do them. Magical speech comes into its own distinctive power, as storytelling does, just where there is a break between strictly realistic occurrence and imagined occurrence. There is a kind of maximum of optimistic storytelling when purely imaginary happenings are achieved by the exercise of purely imaginary powers. We pull back from that height of fantasy by giving our serious storytelling some representational realism for the sake of relevance to life. Something similar happens with magic. We pull back from an utterly fantastical optimism concerning our worldly goals and acts by embracing a measure of realistic

---

[17] Hauerwas is drawing on remarks by Reynolds Price to explain the status of Christian scripture: "It may be asked, why these texts? My answer is simply: These texts have been accepted as scripture because they and they alone satisfy what Reynolds Price has called our craving for a perfect story which we feel to be true. Put briefly, that story is: 'History is the will of a just God who knows us.'" "The Moral Authority of Scripture," in *From Christ to the World* (ed. Wayne G. Boulton, Thomas D. Kenney, and Allen Verhey, Eerdmans, 1994), p. 44.

[18] This is a Malinowskian point about the function of myth in oral cultures (see note 23 in Chap. 3); on the political relevance of the Israelite epic in the Hebrew Bible, see Seth Sanders, *The Invention of Hebrew* (University of Illinois Press, 2009).

practicality. Magic lives in a balance between an extraordinary extension of perlocutionary power, on the one hand, and our ordinary powers of speaking to our fellow agents together with our ordinary powers of dealing with physical entities and monitoring the results, on the other.

I am disagreeing with the view that magical speaking is based on naïvely thinking of language and reality as so solidly correspondent that reality could not fail to respond to the right word as intended.[19]

Does magic "work" by generating a purely virtual, make-believe addition to our existence that coheres appropriately with other fictions we entertain? Or by producing actual results in the fully shared world? Or in the manner of ritual, guiding shared action to assure a certain structuring of community life? Or as a helpful periodic confirmation of a global sense of the connectedness of all powers? In a culture in which magical practices are instituted, magic appreciably works in all of these ways.[20] The proper uses of magic may be extensive and fully ingrained in a culture's common sense about how to get things done, but they must indeed be "proper" – they are invariably marked as extraordinary, restricted to particular occasions, techniques, and practitioners, and they usually manifest a proprietary linguistic weirdness, the "abracadabra" factor, which separates the specially empowered speaking self of magic from the ordinary speaking ego.[21]

Magic is ambiguous in what it presupposes about its environment and medium. Is it necessary to believe that the world fabric is such that properly focused intentions can produce desired outcomes much as one's own thoughts can produce one's own bodily actions? Or that a breathlike "force" running all through things can be steered by word sounds emitted by a qualified person? Or that entities in the world have in their own natures a spiritual susceptibility to influence by speech? Or that powerful spiritual agents produce the desired results by hearing, understanding,

---

[19] Robin Horton, *Patterns of Thought in Africa and the West* (Cambridge University Press, 1993), p. 226.

[20] One of the best combinations of thorough study of a magic-using culture with thoughtful discussion of issues in evaluating magical language use is Bronislaw Malinowski's work on the Trobriand Islanders, *Coral Gardens and Their Magic*, vol. 2: *The Language of Magic and Gardening* (Indiana University Press, 1965), part VI. The fruitful central question for Malinowski in this work is how to translate magical language. Another central anthropological work arguing for the reasonableness of magic in its cultural context is E. E. Evans-Pritchard, *Witchcraft, Oracles and Magic among the Azande* (Clarendon Press, 1937).

[21] Malinowski writes in *Coral Gardens* of a "coefficient of weirdness in the language of magic" (218–233).

and complying with the magical utterance? Explainers of magic do not typically plump for just one of these ideas.[22] Nevertheless the most important premises are common to them all: the optimistic expectation that speaking can be adjusted to exert an even greater perlocutionary power than it ordinarily displays, supported by an optimistic view of the world as responsive to speaking, ready to participate like a fellow subject in the forming of shared intentions and actions – not merely a causal mechanism.[23]

On the border of magical speech are religious modes of speech that serve the formation of an ultimately desirable world-transcendent state of being rather than the production of any worldly result. The *nembutsu* of Japanese Pure Land Buddhism, for example, is a strange short phrase chosen to express complete trust in the compassion-power of Amida Buddha, "*Namu Amida Butsu* " (derived from a Sanskrit phrase meaning "homage to Amitabha"); the devotee repeats the phrase to achieve pure concentration on salvation. The koans of Zen are logically odd riddles and anecdotes that sometimes allow the hearer's mind to slip sideways, so to speak, out of the natural meshes of thought into sudden enlightenment.

The case of cursing or blessing is like magic to the extent that it seriously prefigures a desired effect of speaking, but it is distinctive in being centered on the power dynamics of a personal relationship. The special power involved is an extension of interpersonal dependence: the recipient of a blessing is advised to expect to do well as though greatly aided by the one giving the blessing, even at places and times in which the blesser is absent. Cursing and blessing can be interpreted as purely expressive behavior more naturally than magic can. What is expressed is a will to realize a practical consequence of the authority the one cursing or blessing claims to have over the recipient, thus making that authority more real.

The promiscuous cursing of things is a parody either of quasi-magical cursing or of invocational cursing calling on a higher power.

---

[22] Apparently there can be no clear adjudication of whether Trobriander magic depends on the collaboration of spirits, as Mosko argues against Malinowski. Mark S. Mosko, "Malinowski's Magical Puzzles: Toward a New Theory of Magic and Procreation in Trobriand Society," *Journal of Ethnographic Theory*, 4 (2014), 1–47.

[23] The controversial and still ambiguous idea of a predominant "participation" mentality in magic-using cultures was advanced by Lucien Lévy-Bruhl – *How Natives Think* (trans. Lilian A. Clare, Allen & Unwin, 1926), p. 76 – and revived by Stanley Tambiah in *Magic, Science, Religion, and the Scope of Rationality* (Cambridge University Press, 1990), p. 105.

Almost all scholarly interpreters of magic have taken for granted that magic does not work as it purports to. Tylor allows that the practitioner of magic might sincerely believe in it and so is "at once dupe and cheat."[24] But Frazer insists that successful magicians are "arrogant." "The sorcerer who sincerely believes in his own extravagant pretensions is in far greater peril and is much more likely to be cut short in his career than the deliberate impostor."[25] Magical utterance on this view is intrinsically in violation of the general norms of truthful locution, collegial illocution, and responsible perlocution. We are in tune with Frazer when we regard "mumbo jumbo" as one of the paradigmatic overreaching misuses of language.

Magic scares me. I am disturbed by the seemingly toxic cultural effects of witchcraft belief in societies where such belief is prevalent and, in my own society, by individuals dabbling in occult power as a way of putting themselves above regular human responsibilities. But I grant that magic is not science and therefore cannot be invalidated for failing scientific tests, and I see that logic- and science-oriented critics have attacked the imaginative discourse of poetry and narrative, too, for treacherously making our expectations of life less realistic – an attack that is alarmingly small-minded. I also suspect that the border between magic and invocation, between the intention to compel desired results and the intention to position oneself appropriately in relation to ideally good results, is often indefinite. It seems reasonable to suppose that if magic is a mainstream practice in a viable culture, it will usually be directed and checked in generally beneficial ways, even though it will sometimes misfire and be abused like any other mainstream practice.

(4) *Invocation.* Frazer argues that the Age of Magic was bound to end because of the inefficacy of magic but that there had to be an Age of Religion before the Age of Science could take over. In the Age of Religion, the magicians shifted their ground and became priests. Their extravagant pretension now was not to compel results in magical fashion but to intercede propitiously with superhuman agents who do have the power to compel results. The true magicians are the gods and spirits. But because our fulfillment now depends on personal relationship with superhuman agents who have moods and complicated agendas similar to our own, the priests are not embarrassed by disappointing outcomes. They can always claim that the gods move in mysterious ways, that the people's intentions

---

[24] Edward B. Tylor, *Primitive Culture*, vol. 1 (John Murray, 1871), p. 121.
[25] James George Frazer, *The Golden Bough*, abridged ed. (Macmillan, 1922), pp. 60, 53.

toward the gods are defective, or that the people are still being punished for past sins. Eventually, says Frazer, as humans learn more about natural regularity, it becomes sufficiently evident that priestcraft, too, is fallacious.[26]

Whether or not based on a false belief, the priestly concentration on relationship with gods led historically to major ethical formulations of justice and virtue on which cultures still depend. A high god had to be approached like a very powerful person, carefully and with the best possible reasons for interpersonal leverage: Is not the action we ask from You what a truly, indeed, maximally benevolent agent *would* do, and would do to benefit *all* in the community You rule, fairly according to their deserts or forgivingly in spite of their offenses? In accounting for ourselves before a god, must we not report on our own imperfections much more thoroughly and mercilessly than a normal child would self-report to a parent? In this way, the god one figured as an ultimate object of personal appeal became the ultimately appealing personal god, a supreme ideal of intentional-discursive life.

The mode of utterance that reaches beyond ordinary speaking with the optimistic intention of establishing relationship with a higher power may be called *invocation*. The one invoked could be a higher human power with extraordinary authority, such as a king, or a beloved as holding extraordinary power over one's happiness, or a power that is present only in being imagined. The invoking move involves acting as though the one invoked, visible or invisible, can be brought down on the initiative of the one invoking to the plane of ordinary interpersonal conversation where (now incongruously) the powers of communicators are balanced. The one speaking is daringly making a crucial move *for* the one spoken to – "Hear my plea!" – more presumptuous than the ordinary summoning or inform-ing or ordering of a human colleague.

The language of invocation is "O my king/queen!" or "O my God!" That these two expressions are close in spirit is an important consider-ation for the development of invocation. During the age of monarchy, the language of invocation *had to be* usable, since on many serious occasions there was no other way to communicate properly with a royal leader. With the practical necessity of invoking sublime authority came a disciplined refinement of the language and an increased confidence in using it. Then, with the maturation of world religions, the rank-and-file

---

[26] Frazer, pp. 824–825.

members of the community would gain access to the language and the confidence. All would be priests.

Invocation is second-personal at an amazing pitch. One dares to be "I" to a "You" who transcends the ordinary accessibility of "yous"; one takes it wholly upon oneself to maintain the convivial tension of two persons being present to each other (although in prayer it may be essential that one understands the Other to be inalterable).[27] The problem of this pragmatic transcendence is distinct from the cognitive problem of a transcendent referent. One will find a solution of the cognitive problem in Aquinas's discussion of the names of God; God can be *characterized* as good or powerful by *analogy* with the creaturely realizations of those qualities that are within our ken.[28] But Aquinas's doctrine of analogy does not tackle the pragmatic problem involved in calling "O my God!" in the first place just as if one were calling "O my brother/sister!" The practical validation of the invoking move can consist of nothing other than the persistence of the invoker. An external observer might be led by appearances of prospering or suffering to think more or less favorably of the premise that the invoker is in a real, active relationship with the one invoked – but there could always be different explanations; after all, it is within the invoker's discretion to interpret prosperity as a trial and suffering as a mark of favor.

Swearing by is a third-personal way of invoking. If I swear to something "by Heaven," I am boldly telling my audience that I do have a real relationship with Heaven and that they can count on me not to dishonor it, either because I am so deeply confirmed in that relationship that I just wouldn't or because I stake so much on my hopes for that relationship that I wouldn't dare.

(5) *Political speech.* As invocation is marked by an extraordinary You, political speech realizes an extraordinary We. The ordinary possibility of speaking for plural subjects embraces both innocuous reporting scenarios, as in "We were out picking berries," and relatively precarious and risky declarations of shared intention, as in "We won't let you have any of our berries!" spoken for one group against another. Here the assumed or required group backing is temporary, and even in the moment of utterance the group might not agree. The extraordinary political possibility is to speak with a sufficient collective assurance that the group can be counted on to support what a speaker says on its behalf. The political speaker need

---

[27] D. Z. Phillips, *The Concept of Prayer* (Routledge & Kegan Paul, 1965), chap. 3.
[28] Thomas Aquinas, *Summa Theologica* I-I Q. 13 Art. 5.

not be given the sublime royal authorization (though one sees the road of strengthened political assurance leading to Leviathan); nor are we automatically ushering in ethical discourse (though with another strengthening of collective assurance, there will be talk of what is obligatory for all humans). The essence of the venture of political speaking is to speak for a "we" and to have it count as the "we" having spoken, putting a backable shared intention into play in a larger communicative action that includes other political speakings. (Expansive optimism and responsibility will push this venture toward a problematic ideal of "the people" or "the public" in whom conflicts of political groupings would be superseded.)

An ideal of political responsibility attends political speaking: one cannot expect to have the backing of a community if one's speaking is not geared to the fulfillment of one's constituents' wishes. The community may maintain special standards of political speech, such as a sloweddown dialogical format,[29] to assure this. The necessary theme of political talk is group success. The political speaker, in that character, is a group instrument. Political speech's definitive perversion is the demagoguery or decree hurling of one who makes the group an instrument of his or her own fulfillment.

(6) *Profanity* is the ugly foil to political speech. It, too, embodies a shared intention, but at the level of id. Passionately hostile, subpersonal attitudes toward life-in-the-world are vented from underneath the ordinarily acceptable formats of linguistic communion. The hearer is given the choice of submerging in the id talk and giving up a degree of normal personal control of the situation, fighting the submergence, or fleeing it.

(7) *Legal discourse* is related to political speech in expressing a communal will to stabilize the community's action. From the ordinary possibility of giving orders and turning some of these into remembered rules of thumb, legal discourse develops an extraordinary fixity, precision, logical pursuit of consistency and completeness, and impersonal application of orders so that the members of a community live inside its laws as one lives inside a house – a house like a geodesic dome with all its structural elements open to view. Of course writing will be needed to fulfill the legal project. But rulings can be issued (as edicts) and remembered and brought to bear in an oral culture. Recitable laws as well as poems, narratives, proverbs, and invocations regularly confront nonliterate people as dicta with guiding force even

[29] As do the Kuna people of Panama in their "chief language" (also called "God language"), according to Joel Sherzer in *Kuna Ways of Speaking* (University of Texas Press, 1983), pp. 49–51, 57–60, 74–98.

without being assignable to a present guide. (The mythic lawgiver like Moses or Manu is a *virtually* present guide.) Recitable guidance forms a major portion of the meaning of writing and reading texts.

(8) *Scientific discourse.* It is hard now to imagine scientific discourse without the support of literacy, but we can make out a base for it in a way of speaking. The extraordinary linguistic reach of scientific discourse is in its abstract generality and impersonality. The ordinary generality of referring to "crows" and "birds" that have "life" is developed into the extraordinary generality of referring to "the crow," "the bird," and "life" as such[30] and then to decomposable "organisms" and "bodies" that have measurable "mass." The ordinary causal explanation of citing agents and quasi-agents as the instigators and constrainers of change leads to the extraordinarily impersonal mode of explaining events and things by characterizing processes in which they are embedded. This reach toward a more abstract comprehension expressed in a more abstract, fluidly adjustable, seemingly perfectible language requires a reflective turn and a certain detachment from personal participation in events. Along similar lines, some of those who practice magic reflect on its broader patterns of efficacy and failure and draw technical conclusions about the properties of a basic force, *mana* perhaps; certain priests reflect on dealings with the gods and draw theological conclusions about divinity and virtue.

(9) *Inspired speech* is an important category of speaking power that does not have a defining quality or purpose other than to expand our view of how content or intention may reach the actual production of speech. An entranced or spirit-possessed or divinely prompted speaker speaks as the mouthpiece of another speech source, perhaps adapting for our benefit a higher language we could never understand. An illocutionary partnership is thereby formed with the speaking's true source that may be thought highly valuable even in the complete absence of useful speech content, as in glossolalia. Or valuable content may be delivered that could come from no ordinary living human subject: word from the dead about the past, revelations from divine mind about the future, illuminations of the true basis of existence by the vibrating core of reality.

Inspired discourse is linguistically remarkable only in that it offers a scenario in which nonsensical utterance might be highly meaningful. Otherwise, if inspired discourse is to make sense, it must do so in

---

[30] See Bruno Snell, "The Forging of a Language for Science in Ancient Greece," *Classical Journal*, 56 (1960), 50–60, for a unique attempt to trace the development of scientific sense using resources of the Greek language.

linguistic formats we have already identified. It may be thought to do this in its own eminent way; for example, the Qur'an, delivered by a divinely guided Muhammad, is thought by Muslims to be supremely credible and beneficial partly because of its poetic intensity, and yet it cannot be classed with human poetry. Inspired discourse is *epistemically* remarkable in that it can purport to offer information with the backing of an extraordinarily qualified speech source (such as an omniscient deity) and with extraordinary prospects of confirmation (such as at the end of the world), but that is another set of issues than what we are considering here.

Wittgenstein raised a problem about rule following that applies to inspired discourse: if we are to understand a speaker, we must be able to follow the speaker's uses of language. But it seems that either we *can* get hold of the logic of what an inspired speaker is saying, so that the inspiration premise becomes unnecessary, or we *cannot* follow – the speaker seems to be speaking just as mysterious promptings come to him or her – so that the speaker remains cognitively separate from us, in his or her own privileged relation with the source of inspiration, and in the most important sense fails to speak meaningfully.[31] If inspired speech gets over this hump, it must be because either (a) the inspiring source is not simply transcendent but rather is already engaged in the followable consistencies of ordinary communication, though more wisely or energetically than hearers had thought humanly possible; or (b) the inspired speaker manages to wrestle the mysterious promptings of a transcendent provocateur into a new followable discourse. Either God or Muhammad is doing a great job of making human sense.

*

Now what can we say about what generally makes for acceptable exercise of extraordinary powers of speech? (I say this "we say" *philosophically*, leaving in suspense whether agreement, if we achieve it, is ordinary momentary agreement as we reflect or has an extraordinary social-historical solidity in common with political and scientific speech.)

Sometimes extraordinary speech needs an extraordinary justification, but often not. I do need a working relationship with an extraordinary speech source if I am to be the vessel of inspired discourse. I do need to be specially qualified if I am to speak magically with any hope of effect. I do need to be in the right relationship of a high degree of practical

---

[31] Ludwig Wittgenstein, *Philosophical Investigations* §§143–238.

interdependence with someone I am cursing or blessing – but the relationship will be an ordinary one. To use a trope or tell a story, I need no justification beyond general linguistic competence. I become qualified to speak politically simply by rising to an occasion of speaking properly for a group (although for larger-scale and more durable political authority, I will need to be anointed for the role within an accepted scheme). I become qualified to engage in legal or scientific discourses merely by being observant of how those discourses work. As for profanity, its point is precisely that it is unjustified.

The overall impression one gets in surveying the extraordinarily powerful uses of language is not that the speakers become superheroes – although the magician and the fully empowered political leader may approach this status – but that enterprising uses of language allow greater complexities of life-in-the-world to become factors in our communicative guidance project. The typical effect of hearing extraordinarily powerful language is not to get knocked off one's base but to become enlightened. Even people influenced by political speech are enlightened about the situation and will of the group, except in pathological cases.

We also see recurrently that the relevant validation of an envelope-pushing use of language lies in the speaker's and audience's ability to go on. Our culture filters out the failures and builds on the successes.

I see no reason to think that any of the standards for acceptable ordinary speech are suspended in principle for extraordinary speech. Magic is the apparent outlier; to manipulate other persons magically is inherently antithetical to respectful communication. But that kind of magic is normally proscribed as "black magic." I propose a normative compliance thesis: *Extraordinary speech must comply with the standards of ordinary speech in order not to be disqualified as overreaching and excessively dangerous.* The additional standards for each type are determined by its distinctive goal and conditions of feasibility. The added standards may create significant tensions – as the impersonality of good scientific discourse, for example, is in tension with the personal candor of good speech generally. But it must be possible to manage such tension humanely.

2.5 THE QUESTION OF THE BASIS
OF EXTRAORDINARY SPEAKING

We assume about an ordinary speaking situation that I say to you what I wish to say to you, that you hear what I say and on that basis directly form an understanding, probably adequate for both your purposes and mine, of what I wished to say to you, and that you understandingly grasp not only the semantic content of what I said but for what reasonable purpose I said it (that is, at least one reasonable purpose among many that might be in play) and on what basis I felt able to say it (at least one reasonable basis). A communicative relationship is unproblematically functional when these conditions are satisfied.

When special powers of speaking are exercised, the chances of satisfying all these conditions are reduced. In the very worst case, I seem to be talking as an instrument of another speech source that is inscrutable, so you can gather nothing about the intention animating my speech or its backing; I am using incomprehensible expressions, and I have given you no account of why I am lending myself to speaking in this weird way, nor is there any instituted context for it. In the best possible case, the content of my speech is clear, and my intentions, purposes, and warrants in speaking are readily and confidently grasped, thanks in part to a supportive social and cultural context, while a great benefit is derived from my exercising one or more of the extraordinary powers of speaking – as when a political speech uses poetically or religiously stimulating means to rally one's nation to a great cause. (Many Americans will think of Abraham Lincoln's Gettysburg Address or Martin Luther King Jr.'s "I Have a Dream" speech as exemplary.) Even in the best possible case of extraordinary speaking, however, there is some uncertainty about what is going on communicatively. It may be an enlivening uncertainty, suggestive of the power of a benign spirit attending the communicative performance. Or it may be alienating and doubt-provoking.

To better understand and evaluate a communicative performance, we may ask two key questions. The first is this: What is the typical *character* of this kind of speaking – what are its essential constituents, and how is it supposed to come about and to play out? In our exploration of the powers of speaking, we have been gathering ideas about the character of genres of speaking. The second question, connecting linguistic variables with epistemic and moral variables, is this: What is the *basis* of this speaking? For example, if it is an ordinary report of information, how did the speaker acquire the information in the first place? If it is an extraordinary summons of political will as in the Gettysburg Address, how was the speaker authorized to set a course for the nation, and how does the speaker know or have enough confidence to claim that the proposed course is the right course?

Extraordinarily powerful speaking is precarious in its basis. In contrast, the general practice of ordinary speaking is automatically acceptable. That is the normative aspect of its ordinariness. It is firmly established as our general strategy and technique for sharing a view of life-in-the-world on the unchangeable basis of humanity's intelligent interdependence. Its limitations can be noted, but it can be rejected only in a difficult act of mystical self-isolation. The same cannot be said of extraordinary speech, which in virtually all cases *can* be rejected – not as incomprehensible, but as lacking an acceptable basis.

The precariousness of extraordinary speech is part of its distinctive strength, however. Because its acceptableness cannot simply be taken for granted, it must actively hold its own in relation to the other powers at play in human life; it must sufficiently appeal to subjects who are free in relation to it, who might very well demonstrate and enjoy their freedom by rejecting not only a poet but poetry, not only a priest but religion, not only a politician but politics. Thus a relevant teleological definition of poetry, religion, or politics would be the discourse that organizes exercises of the extraordinary power of speaking poetically, invocationally, or politically in such a way as to maximize its chances of being accepted and influential in the present and in the future.

Do we attain a more helpful view of life-in-the-world when we hearken to extraordinary speech? It depends on whether we are fortunate in the extraordinary speech we are offered, which is largely outside of any human being's control, but it also depends crucially on how we take it. So long as there are arguably better and worse ways of taking the speech in each sort of case, the linguistic community cannot pretend to have an adequate basis for following extraordinary speech if it does not allow for the fullest possible critical discussion of that basis. The practices of writing and reading will make themselves indispensable in support of this needed discussion.

3

The Writing Problematic

We, my possible readers and I, are literate: written guidance is densely woven into our shared life. What can writing and texts add to communicative action? What are their pragmatic hazards?

3.1 FREE-FLOATING UTTERANCES

That written utterances are independent of live speech occasions is hugely important for the logistics of archiving and disseminating linguistic content. But this independence is not a peculiarity of writing. It is integral to utterance.

Utterance involves a presentable linguistic expression (a signifier) and a thinkable sense (a signified). The linguistic expression is a guide marker for the sense, and the sense is a guide template for intentional positionings in the world we model in communication. Considered as guides to the world, real or figured, senses serve the purpose of "reference." But senses are interesting in their own right. We entertain them, tweak them, and tout them to explore how they might apply. *Pace* Ricoeur, it is for this more fundamental reason, not because a written text has been detached from physical ostension, that understood sense "intercepts" real reference;[1] but texts do make this independence of sense much more appreciable.

---

[1] "In living speech, the *ideal* sense of what is said turns towards the *real* reference, towards that 'about which' we speak. At the limit this real reference tends to merge with an ostensive designation where speech rejoins the gesture of pointing. Sense fades into reference and the latter into the act of showing. This is no longer the case when the text

Whether referring or not, the senses marshaled in a saying compose a thing-said, a meaning. Given that whatever one says is evidence of the quality of one's saying in general, it might be expected that speakers will always carefully choose just the expressions that will establish the most satisfactory things-said. But that is not what happens. Often our main purpose in using speech is not to refine our shared model of life-in-the-world but rather to manage our immediate positions and feelings with respect to each other. Thus particular forms and contents of speech stream by ephemerally, quickly chosen without much thought, relying heavily yet loosely on familiar conventions; and the intent is often to give information vaguely or ambiguously. What is advantageous in this is that the speaker stays on top of the communicative flow and avoids becoming caged by things-said. Sometimes a speaker becomes confused or irritated if asked about his or her utterances as if there were more to them than ephemeral vague signals. If there is to be backtracking scrutiny, the question that is more reliably acceptable than "Why did you *say* X?" is "What did you *mean*?" which can now be refreshed or corrected by saying whatever else the speaker wants to say. We are open to a new formulation because we understand that X, the something-said, is likely to represent the speaker less well the more definitely we pin it down as an objective utterance. We respect the mobility of the one who is meaning, the meaner. "Meaning" as verb trumps "meaning" as noun.

The great exception to this rule is when the speaker wants the meaning of X to be unambiguous and remembered because the point of saying it is to determine something specific in the subsequent behavior of the audience. The giver of a cooking instruction wants the hearer to add precisely a teaspoon of salt right after the flour is mixed in. The giver of law wants hearers not to kill animals of specified kinds. Let us call such utterances decrees. These speakers want their decrees to be taken seriously as definite things-said because they intend specific consequences and because they know they cannot stay constantly with their hearers to repeat their meaning as needed. The hearers must be able to act on their own on the basis of the received guidance. But this means that the decree, too, must stand on its own, its sense detachable from its original oral delivery. If the cooking instruction to add salt only guides me when I recall my instructor Julia actually telling me this, if I am capable of making the right move

takes the place of speech. The movement of reference towards the act of showing is intercepted ..." Paul Ricoeur, "What Is a Text?" in *Hermeneutics and the Human Sciences* (ed. John B. Thompson, Cambridge University Press, 1981), p. 148.

with the salt only when I remember myself hanging on Julia's words, then I am a poor pupil; I have not gotten what I was supposed to get, a meaning still present in the words issued by Julia when Julia herself is absent. If I refrain from killing a protected animal only by recalling that Ashoka commanded me on that subject (Pillar Edict 5), I do not yet really understand the command in its intended meaning as a law. The status of being a cognitively competent person by virtue of having gotten proper instruction or of being a political subject capable of collaborating with others under the rule of law depends on the enduring meaning of decrees.

Writing promotes the independence of utterances generally and makes decrees much more effective in certain ways, yet oral culture is already profoundly affected by utterances that float free from events of saying and particular speakers. One sees this most clearly in sayings that are framed by "They say . . ." such as rumors and proverbs, but *any* accepted word or phrase in a language participates in this "They say . . ." or "How does one say . . . ?" detachment of sense from any actual speaking. Linguistic competence requires intelligent participation in this detachment of sense.

The meaning of an utterance need not be traced back to what someone actually meant, notwithstanding that the status of most actual utterances depends on some assumption about their origin. An utterance that is intelligible at all has at least the authorization of communal use of the elements and procedures with which it is composed such that any of us *could* have said it intentionally, whether or not correctly. At that level of sayability, the authorizer is the inclusive "they" or "one." At the more discriminating level of epistemic or moral authorization, no community is so naïve as to assume that anything that has been repeated is necessarily true and right, but communities differ from each other and differ internally about how to check on this. The axial tendency is to expect the hearer to validate an utterance rather than to confirm validity by tracing it to an authoritative originator. But whether the route to validation goes via an authoritative source or via efforts of the hearer, communal validation remains ultimate inasmuch as "true" means "to be accepted in thought *by us* (shareably)" and "right" means "to be accepted in practice *by us* (shareably)." The sense of a significant utterance is released from its speaker at the start and received as meaningful by the whole community at its end.

The detachment of sense from speaker can be overtly marked in an utterance where the aspect of impersonal objectivity is important. For example, proverbs tend to be pithier and more musical than utterances that could plausibly be ascribed to an individual on an actual occasion.

Magical spells, ritual incantations, and laws tend to be more elaborate and require more memory work than ordinary sayings. And we have the powerful expressive procedure of recitation – speaking with the clear intention of repeating rather than originating utterance – and the recording device of writing.

3.2 MARKS

One can begin to "write" by composing words in one's head, but generally composition counts as writing only because it gets inscribed. Inscription, on the other hand, is not necessarily destined to communicate. Much as speaking begins with a sound that may or may not submit to linguistic discipline, inscription begins with a marking that may or may not become an act of linguistic guidance.

The Altamira cave in Spain, famous for its beautiful Paleolithic images of animals, also contains a few hash marks inscribed in a wall for an unknown reason, not obviously in a symbolic pattern. They make one wonder about the inherent meaningfulness of the act of making a mark.[2] Mark or no mark – what were and what are on the two sides of that disjunction? How could the marker have conceived the significance of the options of marking and not marking and the distinction the mark would create? (The binaries then compound: Bent mark or straight? Solid line or broken line? Separate lines or paired? The *Yijing* shows the rich possibilities of attaching meaning to such differences.)

The mark stands out from the stream of occurrence, becoming one of the permanent things. It happened, like everything else that really happened, but now it is something else. The mark accomplishes overtly in the physical world what a serious utterance would like to accomplish in the stream of communicated meaning. While we can broad-mindedly affirm that any utterance is, in principle, a historic intervention in the totality of communication, we must admit that only a few intentionally crafted and conserved utterances play that role appreciably. With physical marks in durable media, the odds are much different. Any mark cut into a rock will probably last for a long time relative to a human life. It will prove that the mark-making agent is a world changer, no mere hanger-on, and it will do this not in the widely variable way that *any* physical action upon the

---

[2] I observed these myself in the Neocueva at Altamira. I have not found any published discussion of them.

world proves the existence of an agent, or in the hopelessly dubious way that a memory attests that something happened, but rather as the purest and surest manifestation of intent to have an effect on the world, announcing one's efficacious presence at a time and place. Even before we consider the power of the mark to communicate with other subjects or to represent facts or ideas, then, we can see that it realizes a connection between the marking subject and the world in which the marking subject has a prominent position along with the stubborn mark.

The mark is also a social initiative proving that "Kilroy was here," compelling its audience to recognize the marker's precedence in the construction of shared action.[3] The audience must adjust to a position of building on what the marker has already done.[4] As fait accompli, the mark is an apt symbol for everything that ought to be acknowledged as already in place; for that reason, if for no other, the writing of law, perhaps God's carving in stone tablets, aptly expresses the force of law; the ultimate direction for life is aptly said to be *inscribed* in our souls; and the notion of a still-relevant oral law in a literate community is purposely provocative. (These are three elements of the Jewish law tradition.)[5]

The mark has a native authority and prestige in its own space, wherever that is. If I come upon a mark in a cave, I understand that the marker navigated or inhabited that cave before me and succeeded in imposing his or her intentions on the physical setting. There is some of this effect in encountering any inscribed text anywhere. The text must be reckoned with just because it has received a physicality. Most texts are perishable, however, so they keep us busy: we know that if the densely woven fabric of the text world's signified meanings is to last, it must continually be reasserted by physically conserved, perceptible marks.

The text, as mark, gives an order as a performance script; its reader may encounter its recorded utterance as what-is-to-be-uttered, considering that the writer of the script may have chosen the words with great care

[3] I am compelled by information found online to admit that the Australian "Foo was here" preceded the American "Kilroy was here."

[4] What does it mean that images in cave painting frequently have other images painted over them? It is either a sign of deliberate displacement or a sign that respect for precedent is not an issue in this context. More to the present point, there is no doubt that Akhenaten's successors intended the most profound disrespect by effacing his inscriptions.

[5] To wit, the tremendous event of the delivery of the written law at Sinai; the axial prophet Jeremiah's "new covenant" written in the heart; and the rabbinic oral law (ultimately given a written form in Mishnah and Talmud yet preserving crucial orality standards) claiming original authority on a par with that of the written Torah. As is known also from Indian and Iranian traditions, orally propagated precedents can be fully authoritative.

and a great purpose. Not in all cases but in many, it seems an important consideration at least preliminarily that the writer of the text may have taken advantage of time, discretion, and other resources to get the utterance *right* in form or content, working it up, revising, affected by the thought that only one expression can be the best. (One can never assume that a written text exactly reproduces a spontaneous outburst, although celebratory hymns and love letters may try to give this impression.) Both for the sake of receiving good guidance and for the sheer possibility of performing the script, "Recite after me:" is always the text's implied beginning. For the same reasons, exegesis of the text will be in order, and once interpretation is launched, the text will show its opposite aspect, not commanding like a present speaker but lying on the table as "indecidable" material for any number of envisionings.[6] Unable to answer for itself when questioned, the text is silent and enigmatic.[7]

The precedence of any mark – most suggestively the hash mark, simplest of all marks – can be understood to represent ideal precedence itself, considered apart from any particular manifestation or confirmation. I may not understand what the ultimate precedence of logical forms or moral ideals involves, but if I put a mark into the world, and the meaning of my gesture is not exhausted in self-assertion (as in merely carving my own personal sign), I point to that precedence, which puts all self-assertion in a corrective context.

Paradoxically, that-which-ultimately-precedes (a problematic but unavoidable thought) is necessarily prior to any actual inscribing and so *cannot* be identified with any particular mark or script, even if the mark uniquely arouses the thought.[8] The serious-minded marker always comes too late. Realizing that fact becomes part of the meaning of marking and the interpretation of marks. It will enter into any ordering of multiple guiding texts – for example, we will rely on a Platonic text judged more philosophically adequate, more mature, to control the interpretation of

---

[6] "Indecidable": Hugh J. Silverman, *Textualities* (Routledge, 1994), p. 80.

[7] Plato, *Phaedrus* 275e.

[8] Daniel A. Madigan concludes from the Qur'an's references to "book" (*kitab*) that the most important factor in the constitution of the divinely guiding book is divine decree at a deeper level than writing: "Thus there are two kinds of writing. One consists in putting mnemonic marks on paper (or some other material); the other is a much more significant activity, the exercise of divine authority and knowledge, for which writing functions as a metaphor or a symbol rather than as a simple description. The Qur'ân reserves the verb *kataba* almost exclusively to cases of the latter." *The Qur'an's Self-Image* (Princeton University Press, 2001), pp. 122–123.

texts Plato wrote earlier because of our surmises about what ultimately takes precedence – namely, the truth Plato was tracking.

The mark is a notable self-assertion by the marker almost any way we look at it, but at the same time it is a great convenience for an audience, making guidance permanently available and thus serving the larger communicative project. If you could mark the turns on the forest trail, then the rest of us could find our way even when you cannot guide us in person. If you could write down the recipe for that cake, I could make it on my own. If you would be so gracious, O King, as to list the protected animals on a rock pillar, I could remind myself or others of the law whenever necessary.

The mark is of great service also in embodying a judgment of where, how, and why to mark. If marks proliferated too much, they would become meaningless, like the spray-painted figures on abandoned buildings. Where marks matter, there has been an implicit filtering of possibilities of marking, just as our vocabularies reflect a filtering of naming possibilities. The *Yijing* has a uniquely important position in Chinese tradition partly because it so explicitly addresses the guidance of that which has ultimate precedence as represented by just two indispensable written marks (sometimes called "exemplary images" and taken to be the seeds of all written characters).[9] The hexagrams of its core text exhibit possible combinations of unbroken and broken lines determined by the casting of yarrow stalks. In the old Imperial Court, particular answers elicited by divinatory questioning were recorded and studied by historians along with the events to which they pertained; indeed this appears to have been the origin of historical writing in China. But the *Yijing* hexagrams hold significance also in the genre of general wisdom, for with their two main layers of attached interpretations, they organize a world of

---

[9] According to Mark Edward Lewis, "Xu Shen['s] history of writing [begins] with an extended quotation of the 'great Tradition' account of Fu Xi's examination of the 'images of Heaven' and the 'models of Earth.' This concludes: 'Thereupon he first made the eight trigrams of the *Yi*, in order to hand down exemplary images.' Thus the trigrams are not only copied from images, but they in turn furnish images for the later development of graphic signs. [Then he] narrates the invention of written graphs by Cang Jie. 'He observed the footprints of birds and beasts, and recognized that meaningful patterns could be distinguished. For the first time he created graphs and tallies ... When Cang Jie first made graphs, he relied on categories and the imaging of shapes. Therefore they were called *wen* ['patterns'; simple, nonanalyzable graphs]. Later the 'form and sound' graphs increased ... '*Wen*' are the roots of all images of things." *Writing and Authority in Early China* (SUNY Press, 1999), pp. 272–273.

cosmological, anthropological, and ethical meanings. Anyone can enter this world to take bearings by these means.

With the dissemination of the detachable meanings of repeatable utterances, we plunge deeper into the problematic of diverging interpretations and the vital need of a communicating community to harmonize disagreement rather than squelching it (supposing that no human community can afford the stagnation of total interpretive conformism). With reliance on inscription, we enter an additional problematic of organization. Where do these inscribed meanings end up? Can they all be put on steles in public places? Do they get listed and dumped in archive boxes from which specialists can retrieve them if anyone feels the need? Do they fall into a strange new order that confuses us?

Zeus ordered Hermes to write down the misdeeds and unjust acts of men severally on shards and pile them up in a chest close by himself, in order that, after examining them, he might exact the penalty from every man. Since the shards lie heaped up one upon another awaiting the time when he can examine them, some are late to fall into the hands of Zeus, others more prompt. We must not, therefore, be surprised if some evil doers who were quick to commit crimes are late to suffer for them. (Babrius)[10]

Or is it feasible to incorporate all of the most important utterances into well-integrated compound utterances? The layered *Yijing* shows how scripture can be an elegant solution.

3.3 LITERACY AND LITERATE COMMUNITIES

An oral culture has its own means of fostering variety in interpretation and organizing the results. Literacy is a cultural game changer not by suddenly introducing this level of shared action but by further empowering it. An instructive aspect of the Axial Age textual collections is that many of them manifest within themselves the evolution of increasingly systematic oral teaching into a harmonized crossfire of texts.

Anthropologists of literacy debate what literacy consists of and how it affects a culture. There is the Goody/Havelock/Ong thesis that literacy is a definable constellation of practices occasioning major social and cognitive changes, notably in creating an objectively informative, corrigible, and systematically filled-out shared knowledge bank that fosters an

---

[10] Fable 127, "The Mills of the Gods Grind Slow," in *Babrius and Phaedrus* (trans. Ben Edwin Perry, Harvard University Press, 1965), p. 165.

impersonal point of view and a more rapid, intelligently guided progress of arts and sciences. Pushing back, there are counterclaims that writing and reading occur in many different patterns of social practice.[11] This discussion is freighted with rival views of the social value of literacy: on the one side, that it is an important and mostly benign human progression, and on the other, that it is often an instrument of oppression by elites who enforce certain patterns of written communication to preserve their own privileges.[12]

The prestige of literacy is so great that one may seem to show contempt for whole cultures and groups of nonliterate or less literate people if one ascribes a distinctive power or value to literate communication. There is also a risk of underestimating the presupposed and still-preserved orality in textual discourse. On the other hand, if one analytically blurs or normatively denounces literacy, one risks missing the significance of some of the greatest historical changes, cultural differences, and intellectual issues. So it is important to determine what can properly be said about how the powers and problematic of writing go beyond the powers and problematic of speaking.

Like speaking itself, literacy is not a skill merely but a distinctive communicative strategy. We write and read for the sake of participating in a shared life in which important parts of life guidance have been shifted from face-to-face encounters to easily and widely disseminated recorded utterances representing an all-encompassing range of contexts. The literate agent is very differently guidable, by virtue of operating in a world stocked with texts of various types and vintages, and is extraordinarily empowered to offer guidance – paradigmatically by performing and interpreting great texts. Since indefinitely many texts either extant or coming online *could* provide relevant guidance, perhaps even unavoidably applicable guidance, for a high proportion of the literate subject's life

---

[11] The Goody/Havelock/Ong thesis that writing and reading are typically associated with important cultural changes has been attacked and qualified but not overthrown. For the original claims associated with Goody, see Jack Goody and Ian Watt, "The Consequences of Literacy," *Comparative Studies in Society and History*, 5 (April 1963), 304–345, and on the controversy, David R. Olson, "Footnotes to Goody: On Goody and His Critics" (barthes.ens.fr/articles/Olson08.pdf, 2008). For more on the thesis, see Jack Goody, *The Interface between the Written and the Oral* (Cambridge University Press, 1987); Eric Havelock, *The Muse Learns to Write: Reflections on Orality and Literacy from Antiquity to the Present* (Yale University Press, 1986); and Walter J. Ong, *Orality and Literacy: The Technologizing of the Word* (Methuen, 1982).

[12] For critique of literacy ideology, see Brian V. Street, *Literacy in Theory and Practice* (Cambridge University Press, 1984).

choices, the capacity to sift, discern, and judge the import of texts and of all guidances together with texts is at a premium. Thus the most meaningful sense of "literacy" incorporates our self-formative ideals of "critical thinking" and "historical consciousness."

Literate people still need oral competence in presentation and discussion of text-based thought. There must be a dialogical appropriation of any really meaningful guidance. From the perspective expressed by Plato in the *Phaedrus* (274–275), the text is all too likely to defeat the purposes of literacy by becoming an alienated semblance of knowledge, unable to explain itself or substantially benefit its user; the defense against this is to cultivate in philosophical practice a personal apprehension of truth or at least a clear view of the pathways to truth. From the perspective of the Qur'an, the religious institution of Scripture or the Book is corruptible, as may be seen in how Jews and Christians have used their scriptures to prove clashing partisan views of the requirements for salvation; the remedy is provided in the uniquely close relations between divine reality, the divine Messenger, and the recitation brought by the Messenger orally to the godly community on the basis of revelatory oral instruction.[13]

A notorious pitfall of text use is a kind of inversion of critical discernment, an inability to see actuality because it is blocked by complacent book learning, as with the Aristotelians who would not look through Galileo's telescope, or by romantic book enchantment, as with Don Quixote and Emma Bovary.[14] The ideal of literacy cannot, therefore, be an ideal of receiving guidance exclusively from texts; the inscription of textual utterance upon the soul should not interfere with the soul's other powers. In a regime of literacy, texts generally enjoy a preliminary entitlement to make their appeals, but their guidance power has to be earned

---

[13] "The Jews say, 'The Christians stand on nothing,' and the Christians say, 'The Jews stand on nothing,' though they recite the Book . . . Never will the Jews be content with thee, nor the Christians, until thou followest their creed. Say, 'Truly the Guidance of God is guidance'" (2:113, 120). Ary A. Roest Crollius discusses Qur'anic evidence that Muhammad, after early appeals to the corroboration of Jewish and Christian scriptures, more strongly resisted demands for another "Scripture" in the sense of another Heaven-sent complete Book by insisting on the one hand on the universal scale of God's revelatory activity and on the other hand on the unique character of God's live, ongoing revelation of the Qur'an. *Thus Were They Hearing: The Word in the Experience of Revelation in Qur'an and Hindu Scriptures* (Gregorian University Press, 1974), chap. 2.

[14] "There is an old enmity between books and reality. What is written pushes into the place of reality, making its categories and guarantees superfluous . . . ever and again leading to a weakening of the authenticity of experience." Hans Blumenberg, *Die Lesbarkeit der Welt*, 2nd ed. (Suhrkampf, 1983), p. 17 (my trans.).

by successful appeal to discerning subjects and must stand up to continued critical examination. This is true even for the texts of paramount authority in scripturalist religious traditions, insofar as scripturalism involves literacy.

The literate have literate ways of making mistakes: reading the wrong texts (for relevant guidance purposes); knowing too little about the circumstances of a text's origination or its purpose; making too much or too little of an author's intentions; placing wrongly focused "meanings" of texts into wrongly chosen or fallaciously assembled systems of meaning; choosing the wrong portion or aspect of a text or set of texts to guide the interpretation of the whole; making unwarranted assumptions about how the text refers to the fully shared world; assuming wrongly that the audience of a written allusion will take it as intended. The literate agent needs a kind of guidance that cannot come strictly from reading another text – a superguiding cultural *tradition* that has sifted out unhelpful ideas and procedures over time, or a present testing of meaning in a *forum* of the fullest possible questioning and answering. With the motto "Trust the conversation," one could invoke the community's protection with either the tradition or forum scheme in mind or both. (Some will insist on a higher-level solution such as "Trust God" because human solutions are all fallible. As we will see, scripturalism can claim to fill *all* of these prescriptions for superguidance.)

Literate subjects are typically excited by the opportunities for expanded experience and subtle conversation that texts afford, and in eagerly searching out texts and interpreters, they may simply take for granted or fail to notice that the actual community of literate communication is restricted in humanly important ways. There are naturally given differences of inclination and mental character between people who want to live on an enterprisingly literate basis and people who (though capable of reading and writing in the most common modes) prefer to live on the basis of oral guidance. Crosscutting that kind of difference, there are social and economic barriers to participation in literacy; as we moderns might put it, some people who should go to the university cannot, while some go who might as well not. Thus the strategy of getting maximum benefit from texts must incorporate a strategy for dealing responsibly with lesser literacy within the community. This is a vital daily concern for professionals providing literacy-based guidance to semiliterate or nonliterate yet morally autonomous clients.

The fully literate community will part company with most of the less literate in drawing guidance from semantically and poetically ambitious texts that set benchmarks for fulfilling the powers of language and are properly appreciable only with keen wits and hard work. Some of these texts will be historically somewhat alien and hard to interpret. A text that effectively serves the more and less literate at once, resonating in both frames of reference – a great song or political speech, for example – will play a specially important role in holding the larger community together. Texts of both sorts can be faithfully transmitted as "classics." According to Michael Nylan, some of the songs in the Chinese *Classic of Odes* were believed in classical times to be spontaneous compositions by peasants, which meant that by mastering that material a literate person would gain an ethically and politically desirable awareness of the commoners' perspective.[15]

The fully literate community is always a subcommunity, even in Iceland; nevertheless, there is an important difference between the ancient guise of literacy, where the users of texts are a tiny guild proud of their special intellectual and spiritual advantages, and its modern version, in which the benefits of literacy are supposed to be accessible to everyone through a universal education scheme.[16] Although we still have a literate elite and there are still limitations on the reach of fully literate guidance, the literacy agenda is fully mainstreamed in most contemporary societies. In this important way, textual guidance has just lately fully come into its own.

3.4 THE BOOK

I had better never see a book than to be warped by its attraction clean out of my own orbit, and made a satellite instead of a system. – Emerson[17]

I do not think that the sense of "text" is too much strained by the notion of "oral texts." We know from surviving scriptural traditions that highly refined and systematically arranged utterances can be passed down through many generations by memorization and accessed when needed by recitation. The Vedic/Brahmanical tradition is a spectacular case in point.

The *book*, however, surely demonstrates a distinctive and persistently extraordinary power of writing. We see the value of the book in the

---

[15] Michael Nylan, *The Five "Confucian" Classics* (Yale University Press, 2001), p. 97.

[16] On the practices, ideals, and social realities of ancient scribal culture, see David M. Carr, *Writing on the Tablet of the Heart* (Oxford University Press, 2005).

[17] Continuing: "The one thing in the world, of value, is the active soul." Ralph Waldo Emerson, "The American Scholar," in *The Complete Essays and Other Writings* (ed. Brooks Atkinson, Modern Library, 1950), pp. 49–50.

expectation of leverage that early book users express. For instance, a biblical writer repeatedly backs up prescriptions to the Israelites by saying "as is written in the book of the teaching of Moses" (Joshua 9:30–35, 23:6) and ends the story of Joshua commanding the sun to stand still "as is written in the Book of Jashar" (Joshua 10:12) – evidently a solid validation.[18] A book is where you *would* find the necessary information and where anyone *would* want a claim inscribed ("O that my words were ... inscribed in a book!" [Job 19:23]). A book is what ought not to be missing from a good library.[19] In Plato's dialogues, Socrates and his friends refer frequently to so-and-so's book, evidently prime fuel for their conversational fire, and Socrates tells us that a great intellectual turning point of his life came in an encounter with a book of Anaxagoras (*Phaedo* 97) – foreshadowing our own encounters with the arch-guidance of Socrates in Plato's books. Some civilization heroes are rescuers of older wisdom in the format of books: the priest Hilkiah, who found the Book of the Law during temple repairs in Josiah's reign (2 Kings 22); Ezra, who brought the Book of the Law from Persia (Nehemiah 8); Kongzi, who compiled the Chinese Classics; and Dao'an and Xuanzang, who played a comparable role in bringing Indian Buddhist scriptures to China.

If we know of a book that is no longer extant, like the Book of Jashar, we are still haunted by it. Any book has invaded the world and taken a place not merely as an episode of utterance but as a concrete fact of what has been uttered that could be encountered anywhere, anytime, like a thread running throughout the fabric.

Books can be easily collected: in Athens, everyone knows you can buy one cheaply in the marketplace (*Apology* 26), and in Jerusalem, there are apparently too damn many of them (Ecclesiastes 12:12). Yet a single book

---

[18] Hebrew Bible translations are from *Tanakh: The Holy Scriptures* (Jewish Publication Society, 1985). Note also the self-accrediting intimation that you can trust the book you are reading (i.e., Joshua) to distill what you need to know out of the older book.

[19] There are multiple stories of kings sending their librarians out to collect all existing books for a central library. In the 2nd c. BCE Letter of Aristeas, we read: "Demetrius of Phalerum, the president of the king's [Ptolemy's] library, received vast sums of money, for the purpose of collecting together, as far as he possibly could, all the books in the world. By means of purchase and transcription, he carried out, to the best of his ability, the purpose of the king. On one occasion when I was present he was asked, How many thousand books are there in the library? and he replied, 'More than two hundred thousand, O king, and I shall make endeavor in the immediate future to gather together the remainder also, so that the total of five hundred thousand may be reached. I am told that the laws of the Jews are worth transcribing and deserve a place in your library'" (ed. R. H. Charles, www.ccel.org/c/charles/otpseudepig/aristeas.htm, 1913).

has content that can occupy endless discussions. There is a presumption of fullness of relevant articulation. In offering the whole of some desired guidance, a book can be compared with the speech transcript that Phaedrus carries around (*Phaedrus* 228) or the Kshatriya's teaching that astounds the Brahmins (Chandogya Upanishad 5.3), but a book has the advantage that it can incorporate more ingredients in a more elaborate and telling order. If a speech is a pavilion, a book is a castle. One can live in it and defend it.

The ideal of a great book is of inscribed guidance so clearly gotten right and so convincing a unification of virtual or prospective experience that one does want to live in it, making it a sort of headquarters (though not to the exclusion of living in other headquarters at the same time). This ideal place is like a castle also in that one cannot very well live in it alone. Even if it is fiction, the great book makes claims that must be tested in shared life, if they are indeed of book-level importance, and the articulate book forms meaning complexly, generating interpretive challenges that must be addressed collaboratively. One latches on to a great book as a personal asset, but not as personally owned or mastered; one is impelled to discuss it with others, hoping that their responses will be complementary.

Here we run into a prime problem in determining the meaning of book utterance. An interpretation is needed to get the benefit of a great book, but such a book will not submit to a single interpretation. Its elements can be ordered variously; the very identification of elements will change with different readers and contexts; there is too much possible meaning to be crystallized in a single Gestalt. Thus any interpretation of a great book is *forced*, if it is held to be *the* right interpretation, and this is true, awkwardly, even for a book like the Qur'an purporting to give *the* guidance for life. A community of interpreters can agree on boundaries separating unacceptable from acceptable interpretations – indeed, the community will define itself partly by this very boundary drawing – but that agreement is always subject to renegotiation.

Enriching the analogy, a great book is a castle headquarters not only for contemplating the things that are presented by the book but for looking at everything else in its light or along its lines, functioning as a sort of observatory. The enthusiastic reader rejoices in access to this vantage point, appreciating it as one of the best available opportunities for guided viewing. (Sometimes the vantage point is identified with the author rather than the book, viewing the author as the intentional principle of the book and related writings. One can contemplate life profoundly from the perspective either of *The Trial* or of Kafka.)

The book can be defined as a fully articulate whole of guidance. Impressive in what it can contain between two rollers or covers, the book makes an apt symbolic container of a person's whole life, or of everyone's life (as in the biblical Book of Life) once everything has happened. That the book has been written strongly implies that everything most relevant to its topic has been presented; there is no suspense about what the writer has not said or could yet say, in contrast to our lively sense of an oral speaker's power to hold content back. For why would a book be written if not to complete its surveys, its categorizations, its explanations, its rhetorical gambits?

But while "the Book" may notionally represent a complete unification of experience and a full locution, the usual format of a book corresponds to *an* experience and its articulation; no book can be the whole of guidance, and so we have larger formats. The strategically inclusive *encyclopedia* is an ideal of providing at one site the most important cognitive guidance in all areas. Beyond that there is the *canon* ideal of a complete collection of crucial textual guidance in a given area of concern. A *curriculum* will organize our dealings with the canon's contents for best results, promoting study of semantic, expressive, and historical relations among the key books. Finally, the *library* ideal gathers together all texts that might be needed for any reason. One lives in a book at a time of one's life, enjoying its rewarding view; one lives in a canon throughout one's life, sharing it with fellow recipients of a certain education; one shares a library with everyone else, the readers of *Sports Illustrated* and *Consumer Reports* as well as the readers of all the works of Balzac and all the world's scriptures. What constitutes an adequate encyclopedia, canon, or library can be proposed by an individual but ultimately must be decided by a community, for an individual cannot be the guarantor of guidance on so large a scale. Only from a poet's or theist's exalted God's-eye view or as an ambitiously programmatic statement by a scientist can the whole world order be pictured as a single Book.[20] Only from an obsessive Borgesian perspective can a library of diverse books be construed as meaningfully interdependent in every possible respect, converting the practical arrangement of a library into a fully hypertextual

---

[20] Poet: Goethe writes to Merck, "See, nature is a living book / Uncomprehended, but not incomprehensible," quoted by Blumenberg, p. 217. Theist: Dante, *Paradiso* 33.82–90, in *The Divine Comedy* (trans. John Ciardi, New American Library, 2003), p. 892. Scientist: Galileo on the "Book of Nature," *The Assayer*, in *Discoveries and Opinions of Galileo* (trans. Stillman Drake, Doubleday, 1957), p. 237.

network of utterance data – a perspective worth noting, because some mystical interpreters of scripture have felt authorized or obligated to take it by their conception of scripture.

In one obvious sense, books are primarily for the literate, who are best positioned to study their meaning and get their benefit. The less literate may believe, with good reason, that some of the most important truths and judgments are written in books, which places them at an unfortunate distance from one of the main venues of communicative action. This creates a magnetic attraction between the more ambitious of the less literate and the more considerate of the more literate – a propulsion of education.

3.5 TEXTUAL GENRES: THE CHARTER

In speaking, I can make all sorts of adjustments on the wing. I can say something very awkward and then save the situation by announcing that I am joking. Written texts are detached from this possibility, except when presented by an active interpreter. They must be labeled properly, incorporate sufficient cues in their chosen words, or simply be entrusted to a foreseen interpretive stance of their likely audience if they are to have a good chance of being communicatively successful.

Once a genre is established, communicators have permission to define the purpose and method of their guidance along certain lines. The genre of jokes allows me to put things lightly and mischievously, though perhaps not on solemn occasions or with social superiors. My jokes join a continuum of everyone else's jokes and may be appraised by comparison with a selection of remembered classic jokes. If a genre of humorous *writing* is established, a *literature* of humor arises. Study of the literature will produce detailed knowledge of the genre's structures and variations, its relations with other genres, and various implications for thought and communication. On the basis of written texts, it will be possible to focus and discuss very precisely the part of the whole work of guidance that communication in a genre carries out – how humor can reinforce or undermine social discriminations, for example. The master of a genre becomes a canonical cultural guide (like Mark Twain).[21] The ensemble of master works reveals

---

[21] The eminent humorist Twain is actually the most quoted American writer in *The Yale Book of Quotations,* according to its editor, Fred R. Shapiro (blog.yupnet.org/2006/12/19/most_quoted_aut/, 2006).

the contours of an area of perennial concern and the shapes of perennial expressive opportunities for addressing such concern.

With the endless elaboration of discourse made possible by writing comes a great elaboration of distinct sets of interpretive expectations of utterance, and with that come multiplied occasions of ambiguity and error.

On the bright side, a writer can innovate at the level of genre without being tightly constrained by the ordinary procedures of speech and conversation. The writer offers a new contract to the audience: this will be the goal, these will be the standards (in my *Vita Nuova*, in my *Commedia*).

The genre itself may be the message; that is, the most important meaning conveyed by writing in a proposed genre may be the general implications of such a genre being practicable (such as the coordination of poetry and philosophy in *La Vita Nuova* or the collision of irreconcilable perspectives on life serving Kierkegaard's "indirect communication" in *Either/Or*). Or a transposition of genre framings of a text may be the main event (as in demythologizing the New Testament or mythologizing a Faulkner novel).

The basis of a genre is a power of language. The *charter* is a type of text worth examining in its connection with a distinctive power of collaboration in writing. Oral culture's texts are sculpted by multiple subjects as well, to be sure; indeed it is harder for one speaker to hold any sort of patent on utterance in an oral culture than it is for a writer in a literate culture. But with text writing comes the possibility of explicitly negotiated collaboration on the content of a text. In the genre of the charter, this is essential and a plus; part of the special helpfulness of charter guidance is that it records agreement. It might have been drafted by Solon or the Duke of Zhou, but its communicational genius is that it can be hammered out by multiple contributors and will in any case be approved by some sort of committee, thus representing communal action at an auspicious juncture of founding or newly norming the practices it guides; and it can be revised at later times by authorized writers and editors, thus representing communal action diachronically in historical coherence. Like a core course syllabus at a university, it may be so extensively and continuously revised that it can no longer be said to have been "composed" by anyone.[22]

---

[22] The analogy between syllabus and scripture can be strong: "It is probably wrong to think in terms of a composition of the *Documents* text [the Chinese *Shujing*], as some passages at least must represent a loose synthesis of shared truths about the past continually reformulated over centuries." Nylan, p. 132.

A charter's guidance function is most overt when it is written in a political or legal idiom, but the charter genre cuts across all other genres. A Romantic poetry circle could adopt *Lyrical Ballads* as its charter, claiming solidarity with Wordsworth and Coleridge. A Christian movement could adopt four stories of the life of Jesus and a bundle of pastoral letters by the movement's leaders. Malinowski points out that oral cultures use their myths as charters for communal life.[23]

The distinctive problematic of the charter is generated by its ongoing representativeness. Any serious interpreter of a charter is intentionally engaged with fellow members of the chartered community and so with the political problematic of defining the community's membership and the members' shareable intentions. What ultimately matters is neither what the original authors intended by the language in a charter nor how brilliant an idea the present interpreter can form about it but rather securing for the chartered community the direction the community arguably needs and can collectively follow.

As the chartered community's internal debates continue to brew and its practices evolve, it must walk a line between the opposite pitfalls of fatally undercutting the authoritative charter, on the one side, and allowing a biased interpretation or revision of the charter to give advantages to momentarily stronger parties, on the other. A strong charter shows resiliency, surviving losses of faith and partisan manipulations. It realizes a pragmatic ideal of a text meeting a community need, an *adaequatio scripti ad communitatem*. Scripturalists believe that scripture supremely realizes this ideal.

3.6 NON-TEXTS THAT REALLY ARE NOT TEXTS: THE BOOK OF NATURE, THE BOOK OF HISTORY, AND HUMAN ACTIONS

In fine, do we want to know what God is? Search not the book called the Scripture, which any human hand might make, but the Scripture called Creation.
– Thomas Paine[24]

Discerning and exploiting guidance is so powerful a human interest that we tend to be quite happy to construe any sort of phenomenon as direction-giving in a way that is significantly analogous to utterance – from a bird flying overhead taken as a warning to our whole environment

[23] Bronislaw Malinowski, "Myth in Primitive Psychology," in *Magic, Science and Religion* (Doubleday, 1954), pp. 93–148.
[24] Thomas Paine, *Age of Reason* (Michigan Legal, 2014), p. 25.

viewed as the Book of Nature. The analogy is not arbitrary; our direction taking as hearers is in fact rooted in our direction taking as perceivers. Nevertheless, it must be remembered that nothing that is not an utterance can have all of the important communicative attributes of an utterance (except figuratively), and so there must be significant tension and risk of error in seriously treating any non-utterance as an utterance equivalent.

An utterance is someone's figuring of some portion of the world or life therein. Its guidance meaning incorporates the existence, situation, and agenda of the speaker or writer as well as its detachment from physical actuality as a memorable message. Thanks to its lingering presence in memory and citation, we can remain aware of what an utterance represents, what practical relationship it proposes, and what effects it promises or threatens, and we can play off of these meanings. By design, utterances haunt our lives, which is why pseudo-utterances (like the bird flying overhead) are also haunting, though less properly so. Whereas a book haunts us as a benchmark unified vision of life-in-the-world, the existing world does not haunt itself with any particular booklike envisioning, nor even with timelessly instantiable types of thing and laws of occurrence, except insofar as these meanings are inscribed in a Book of Nature that we ourselves write or imagine being written. Nature itself is pressure and process, not a discourse. Its unity is not intelligent and its forms are not theses until we render them so (posing as nature's scribes). Natural facts and regularities often have great relevance and a desirable reliability for guidance purposes, yet the hope for objective, neutral, or fully real *book* content in a *Book* of Nature fits poorly with the utterance expectations of locution, illocution, and perlocution. What (subject's) perspective, what (interintentional) partnership, and what (social) prospect are offered here?

Can a Book of History be sufficiently personal as a supposed Book of Nature cannot? The great theme of history is community formation conceived as the upshot of actions. We can and do write large histories to place our ventures meaningfully in the largest context of action, but the vast, complex, and ambiguous shared action of history in the sense of what has really transpired is not in itself anyone's figuring of anything, and history identified too closely with anyone's figuring becomes falsely encouraging or falsely constraining. To conceive American history, for example, as "George Washington's book" would be grotesquely inappropriate (though possibly a productive literary conceit). It may be thought that conceiving the whole of history or the red thread of salvation history as "God's book" is acceptable and even mandatory for monotheists, given that God is the universal Creator and an authorized account of world history is offered by a scripture, but the same problem obtains here: a book is one author's action, while any real history is an extensively shared, maddeningly yet instructively muddled action of which it is necessarily true that no one uniquely valid account could be given.

As for regarding human actions as textlike, in line with a "hermeneutical" approach to the social sciences (on which Ricoeur, among others, has written helpfully),[25] it is true that human action is expressive in a social context and so is always at least latently communicative and meaning-generating. All intentional action is susceptible of interpretation to establish how it might fit into an intelligible way of living in the world. Usually it is easy to represent intentional conduct by interpretive utterance because they have corresponding forms of reference and organization (although the forms of the conduct as it occurred should not be uncritically assumed to be identical to the forms of an account of the conduct).[26] In interpreting utterance *as utterance*, however, and more specifically a text as a text, we endeavor to establish *the* envisioning of life-in-the-world that it *proposes* to its hearers (whatever else might be true of the speaker's *action*). When actions leave a quasi-written trace, they do so not merely by expressing or manifesting intention but by *messaging*. For the most part, the traces of our action, though "legible," are not textually unified.

3.7 WRITING AS TRANSCENDENCE OF THE WRITTEN: THE WRITER AND THE UNWORKING WORK

No Scripture can be of any help to us ... The Book is no longer ... as we ought to know since Mallarmé and Joyce, Blanchot and Derrida. – Jean-Luc Nancy[27]

Following the heroic exploits of Enlightenment writers as social opinion leaders, the prestige of writing and the written work rose to a new high for

---

[25] Paul Ricoeur, "The Model of the Text: Meaningful Action Considered as a Text," in *Hermeneutics and the Human Science* (trans. John B. Thompson, Cambridge University Press, 1981), pp. 197–221.

[26] To the end of interpreting human actions as quasi-texts, Ricoeur seems justified in asserting that actions are like texts in having world reference, illocutionary and perlocutionary force, and an open field of possible future meanings, but we must not run the necessarily more mysterious meaning of actions themselves together with their clarification by interpretation. This would be another version of the error of identifying history as it happened with history as told.

[27] Jean-Luc Nancy, "Divine Places," in *The Inoperative Community* (ed. Peter Connor, University of Minnesota Press, 1991), p. 135.

the Romantics: "If the spirit makes it holy, each authentic book is a Bible" (Novalis).[28] "Every man that writes is writing a new Bible" (Carlyle).[29] The great Writer might be a social leader like Voltaire or Hugo but might also be a sublime individual, a Flaubert or Mallarmé, benefiting from a presumption of originality (a fecund solitude) and cultural perspicacity (from a disembedded vantage point). The futurist or modernist Writer might even create a world-unto-itself Text completely outside the power of regular human speech.

But then these inflationary modern views of writing gave way to a thorough postmodern attempt to scrub writing clean of any pretense of ruling or creating a world. Nancy's remark that "the Book is no longer" reflects the new common sense of postmodernism.

In the same span of time, the printed environment of human life, like its built environment, expanded and filled in; newspapers, magazines, and cheap books became as prevalent as paved roads. Ironically thwarting the Enlightenment, the omnipresent guidance of mass media content came to seem just as hypnotically "mythic" (as Barthes now deployed that term) as the campfire guidance of oral culture.[30] Textuality was now a trap: How could anyone challenge the coercions of this print world except by writing a good book with good sales?

Sartre is an interesting borderline figure in the late modern use of the Writer's communicative position. He is as serious as he could possibly be about being a Writer, no less so than Flaubert or Mallarmé, but rather than produce an added world of textual artifice, he insists on engaging citizens' issues without any pretense of accomplishing something privileged or enduring in his writing. The Writer can play a leading role in exposition of issues, but the responsibility of Writer and reader alike is pegged firmly to the present juncture of communicative action.[31] Since the text created by the Writer is ideally transparent to a successfully negotiated partnership of freedoms, the situation of Writing is highly fluid, and the idea of a text

[28] Quoted by Blumenberg, p. 275.

[29] Thomas Carlyle, 1832 journal entry, in *A Carlyle Reader* (ed. G. B. Tennyson, Cambridge University Press, 1984), p. 25.

[30] Roland Barthes, "Myth Today," in *Mythologies* (trans. Annette Lavers, Hill & Wang, 1972), pp. 109–159.

[31] "The writer has chosen to reveal the world and particularly to reveal man to other men so that the latter may assume full responsibility before the object which has been thus laid bare ... all literary work is an appeal ... the writer appeals to the reader's freedom to collaborate in the production of his work." Jean-Paul Sartre, *What Is Literature?* (trans. Bernard Frechtmann, Harper & Row, 1965), pp. 18, 40.

that has made a permanent mark or holds canonical authority becomes almost oxymoronic; in "offering itself to the free judgment of all men, the reflective self-awareness of a classless society . . . literature is, in essence, the subjectivity of a society in permanent revolution."[32] Instead of the truly *original contribution* of a *creative* Writer who lives to advance the art of Writing, we are to look for the truly *honest intervention* of an *engaged* Writer who lives for the full humanization of our shared life.

The difficult proposition that the appropriately ambitious Writer is bound to be opposed to the Written has a certain political and culture-war relevance in Sartre but can serve other agendas as well. Purely for the aesthetic interest of maximizing the interesting yield of writing, the Writer or astute reader may privilege the freely connecting, shape-shifting, never-finally-arriving writing process and the "text" as its spirit or trace over any guarantee of supposedly unified and enduring meaning offered by either the "work" or the "author"; or the literarily serious "work" may be interpreted as an "unworking."[33] Contrary to the premise that writing imposes an advanced order on life, the Writer and reader together can take advantage of the writing opportunity to enter "the vast play of language," a flux among fluxes.[34] Or, purely for the intellectual interest of pondering how to comport oneself on an uttermost human frontier, the Writer can deepen the immediate practical experience of facing a blank page (much blanker than the face of any interlocutor, more perplexing than any speaker's charged silence) into the metaphysical experience of facing the chaotic aspect of pure possibility with an accompanying total uncertainty.[35] The Writer is an adventurer who gives indications of the abyssal darkness of that place of reconsidering what thought and expression might have to do with, including what Else there is than any guidance

---

[32] Ibid., pp. 152–153.

[33] "Text" vs. "work": Roland Barthes, "From Work to Text," in *Image Music Text* (trans. Stephen Heath, FontanaPress, 1977), pp. 155–164. "Work" as "unworking": "To write is to produce the absence of the work (worklessness, unworking) ... writing as unworking [*désoeuvrement*] (in the active sense of the word) is the insane game [mentioned by Mallarmé], the indeterminacy that lies between reason and unreason." Maurice Blanchot, *The Infinite Conversation* (trans. Susan Hanson, University of Minnesota Press, 1993), p. 424.

[34] "Vast play": Michel Foucault, *The Order of Things* (Vintage, 1970), p. 307. Flux among fluxes: Gilles Deleuze with Claire Parnet, *Dialogues* (trans. Hugh Tomlinson and Barbara Habberjam, Columbia University Press, 1987), p. 50.

[35] Blanchot on the "extreme situation" of what Mallarmé calls "the sole act of writing": "Whoever goes deeply into poetry escapes from being as certitude, meets with the absence of the gods, lives in the intimacy of this absence, becomes responsible for it, assumes its risk, and endures its favor" (38).

we know how to follow. This Writer may be prompted by a realization of the absence or nonnecessity of what communicators have hitherto wanted or needed to assume: a knowable cosmos, an ordered society, a progressive conversation. Or the Writer may be undergoing a moral crisis, living in the aftermath of a Disaster and seeking an adequate articulation of that unbearable situation as an abject rather than self-possessed subjectivity.

So understood, the radical freedom of Writing is at great risk of coming to naught. Will the Writer leap off the precipice into pointless unintelligibility? Or merely write capriciously or spitefully like Dostoevsky's Underground Man? Or abdicate to the unconscious or some other unknown Beyond in a fling of automatic writing, like the surrealist Breton? If the Writer steps back from the precipice, will that not reaffirm historical stabilities of communication after all? A radical new beginning, even if actually made, cannot be shared as such in an understandable utterance.

Blanchot's ideal of the "work" does involve radical beginning, but beginning obtains in a different dimension than understandable content.[36] What counts is that the reader enter with the writer into the supreme difficulty of serious writing.

Communication of the work lies not in the fact that it has become communicable, through reading, to a reader. The work is itself communication. It is intimacy shared in struggle by reading's demand and writing's; by the work as form and measure, constituting itself as power, and the same work's measureless excess, tending toward impossibility. (198)

Despite their lack of cognitive moorings, writer and reader have a strongly guiding experience insofar as they experience

the agonistic struggle which is the character of the work's very being. The work is the *violent liberty* by which it is communicated, and by which the *origin* – the empty and indecisive depth of the origin – is *communicated* through the work to form the brimming resolution, the definiteness of the beginning. (204)

Ultimately, an alienated shareable guidance is derived from this experience:

The reading which initially projected itself into the intimacy of the work, only to fall out of it the better to maintain it and to fix it in a monumental immobility, finally projects itself outside and makes of the work's intimate life something which can no longer be realized unless it is displayed in the world and filled with

---

[36] These page references will be to Blanchot, *The Space of Literature* (trans. Ann Smock, University of Nebraska Press, 1982).

the world's life and with history's ... That which had neither sense nor truth nor value, but in which everything seemed to take on sense, becomes the language which says true things, says false things, and which one reads for instruction, for increased self-knowledge, or to cultivate the mind. (205)

Blanchot is using an ideal of serious literature to stage the question of the radical origin of guidance itself. All communicators face this question whether they use writing or not, but writing, especially in the format of the book, makes it acute by maximizing room for independent initiatives by the participants in communication. The question gets its radicality and difficulty from the assumption that individual communicators face life with an unprogrammable subjective freedom to construe, value, and speak however they will while nevertheless being bound to share with others their construing, valuing, and speaking, enmeshing themselves in social facts. Blanchot projects the dialectical interplay between free initiatives and sharing as the engine of the work, which neither abdicates from sharing (for it narrates and argues intelligibly) nor complacently resolves into a meaningful message. "The work is not the deadened unity of repose. It is the intimacy and the violence of contrary movements which are never reconciled and never appeased – never, at least, as long as the work is a work" (226).

Blanchot's conception of the work yields a formula for the supreme guidance, that of divinity: "The work bespeaks the divine, but only inasmuch as the divine is unspeakable. The work is the presence of the god's absence, and in this absence it tends to make itself present" (231). Evoking the Christian metaphysics of Christ, Blanchot claims that "through the work there takes place in time another time, and in the world of beings that exist and of things which subsist there comes, as presence, not another world, but the other of all worlds, that which is always other than the world ... the work ... is *the* event of history itself" (228). We follow the intimations of the work as the mediator between ourselves and this Other. "Even if truth be drawn from the work, the work overturns it, takes it back into itself to bury and hide it. And yet the work says the word *beginning* ... It is the dawning light that precedes the day. It initiates, it enthrones" (229).

In religious thinking, a Savior figure like Christ or the Buddha may be seen as the principal emissary of the world's eternal Other and therefore the decisive clue for right relationship with this Other. Thanks to an effective Other-mindedness, this fellow being is able to engage in ultimately rectificatory acts such as forgiving enemies or realizing the implications of all past lives. The abstract dilemma of Otherness – that the Other must be absent and uncomprehended in its authentic presence and identifiability as Other – is practically solved by the Savior's mediation. How, then, does the Writer's work mediate between us and the Other? There must be as many mediations as there are works and readings of works. Rather than any churchlike community strongly guided by identified meanings, there must be a loose association of members of an advanced literate community whose lives are teased by the deepest uncertainty that does not collapse into simple ignorance or confusion. What their deep uncertainty substantively *concerns*, beneath the variously important subject matters of the texts, can be elucidated ontologically or ethically, but on the plane of communication it can be explained in terms of two intersecting dialectics: one between free expressive initiative and stable linguistic form in the writer's creation of the work, the other between individually free interpretation and social agreement in the work's reception.

The ultraserious view of Writing brings us to a quasi-religious view of its guiding power. The Other makes a supreme appeal. But religious language is a genre of its own, or a family of genres, and needs examination for its own sake, as we will undertake in the next chapter.

*

What generally makes for acceptable exercise of the powers of writing? The same as the standards for speech, one would like to say, except that because the written text has been detached and distanced from the self-correcting speaker who could guide us in person, we have high expectations that the text be properly laid out and complete and that it play scrupulously by the rules of its genre. It must be a working model of an understandable kind, serving the epistemology of history or law or fiction. It must not set a trap for us as we bring these expectations to it: the good text is candid about its limitations. At the same time, the impersonal communication of books and other mass media leaves it to us to determine a text's illocutionary proposal and perlocutionary prospect; there is no stopping someone from turning a shopping list into Scripture (as in Walter Miller's *A Canticle for Leibowitz*).

A full answer to the question must take account of a major wrinkle in the history of literacy. The status of writing in a broadly literate society like ours is very different from its status in a society of restricted literacy. Today we think of the book as a means of expanded communication, not as a hidden record or magical inscription. But some of the most important books in our library originated in whole or in part in societies of restricted and mystified literacy. The Qur'an, for example, though clearly a book geared to expanded communication, contains reminders of a "heavenly tablet" tradition that assumes that ordinary people depend on priests and prophets to reveal the most important written content.[37] The Qur'an is negotiating a passage between two phases of literacy; by claiming its own divine derivation, it takes advantage of this passage to glorify its content.

We see the Heaven-to-earth idea in the Romantic notion that a new book is like a new Bible, a message brought forth from a pure and esoteric state in the writer's soul to an exoteric state of imperfect yet world-redeeming sharing, and we see it again, inverted, in the postmodernist assertion that the Book must be defunct because experience cannot be perfectly unified as we had supposed it must ideally be. The staying power of the Heaven-to-earth view of the book is due to a reciprocal charging between the esoteric principle of Distilled Perfect Utterance – not guaranteed, of course, but *symbolized* by the unseen labor of the author and the relative immutability of the written record – and the exoteric principle of disseminated, variously usable meaning. We continue to look to writing for both kinds of fulfillment. The greatest books – classical Scriptures, Romantic works of genius, postmodern works of anguish – inflame and gratify this complex desire.

---

[37] "Heavenly tablet" in Qur'an: 56:77–80, 85:21–22. On this kind of tradition, see William A. Graham, "Scripture," in *The Encyclopedia of Religion* (ed. Lindsay Jones, Macmillan, 2005), pp. 8195–8196.

4

The Religious Language Problematic

In the days before psychological analysis was possible the evidence for a special world of words of power, for *nomina* as *numina*, must have appeared overwhelming. – C. K. Ogden and I. A. Richards[1]

The language of religion towers above the languages of science, art, and law-giving. It is the crown of languages because it leads the dance of the three grammatical persons, of the jubilance of "we's," of the humility of "you's," of the amazement of "they's." – Eugen Rosenstock-Huessy[2]

4.1 THE RELIGIOUS AMPLIFICATION OF LANGUAGE

To begin as relevantly as possible: *Om.* When people pray or chant or make exalted statements of purpose or appreciation, it is evident to themselves that they are using language in a specially focused way, and it is evident to an observer with comparative perspective that they are doing this in somewhat typical ways. Thus religious language stands before us as an object of study. *Amen.* The special focus has to do with ultimacy. The religious move is to go all the way, to make contact with either the true ceiling of life, exulting in what we may attain, or the true ground, anchoring what we hope to retain. But it is probably best not to say much more than this about the religious purposing of language, for

---

[1] C. K. Ogden and I. A. Richards, *The Meaning of Meaning*, 7th ed. (Harcourt, Brace, 1945), pp. 26–27.
[2] Eugen Rosenstock-Huessy, *Practical Knowledge of the Soul* (trans. Mark Huessy and Freya von Moltke, Argo, 1988), p. 41.

there does not seem to be a more definite element that invariably determines religious intent. Religious speakers may or may not be addressing a supernatural being, reinforcing their sense of identity or commitment to their traditions, expressing a most-profound need, or grappling with a most-profound question. They may or may not be using a specialized vocabulary as a magician would, intense wordings as a poet would, or the stern language of royal edict; or telling or citing a very comprehensive story; or exhibiting a model of how the universe works. But these are all elements that commonly lend themselves well to the ultimacy-oriented communicative moves that people make in virtually all cultures, and they are abundant, though not predictable, in developed canonical utterances such as liturgies, hymnals, and scriptures.

We should be cautious about treating any particular specimens or defined kinds of language use as paradigmatic for religious language, for several reasons. Descriptively, we should be open-minded about phenomena that might be interesting in this connection, and we should not preempt questions and insights concerning the relations among kinds of language use as they overlap or blur or flow into each other.[3] To divide "political" speech from "religious," for example, interferes with recognizing how political and religious uses of language share their means, such as the language of edict, and their ends, such as the preservation of community, and how they may influence and depend on each other. Insofar as we are allowing religious language to register with directive force, we should not favor one model of religious utterance so much that we preempt its contestation or complementation by different models, even within a single tradition. For example, the parabolic teachings of Jesus and the Buddha are prominent in their respective traditions and are formally comparable, but they are not the only utterances that might be regarded as providing decisive guidance in their traditions, nor are they wholly alike in form and function.

It may seem sensible to designate "the religious" objectively as having to do with ultimate practical goals and commitments while leaving the subjectivity of religious guidance a free variable. There is wide variation in religious subjectivity, certainly, yet a basic issue of subjectivity should not be ignored. Suppose that in a time of drought two farmers offer prayers for rain to their community's supernatural Lord. One prays in a matter-of-fact prudential way, the other in an anxiously soul-searching

---

[3] Ann Taves is persuasive on this subject in *Religious Experience Reconsidered* (Princeton University Press, 2009).

way. In a clear sense these are equally cases of religious utterance, if both farmers are sincerely addressing community survival in a cosmic context; both are realistic about the world figured by religious thought. But in another clear sense the soul searcher is more religiously intent, reaching for an inner ultimacy of perception and commitment to match the outward ultimacy of the issue of the community's viability. And the soul searcher's prayer is more likely to inspire earnest or awed feelings in others. If we did not see that the soul searcher's prayer is more religiously saturated, we would not understand what religious teachers are often striving to achieve with their audiences and what regular members of a community often take to be a representative religious act or person.

Religious language in the broadest sense consists of all language that is used for religious purposes, including the matter-of-fact farmer's prayer that takes religious reference points completely for granted. But if we are on the lookout for amplifications of linguistic power in accordance with religious intentions, we shall be particularly interested in language that advances an interest in exploring or expressing the ultimacy of an intention or state of mind vis-à-vis an objective ultimate, as in the passionate complaint of a righteous person suffering injustice; or in language that devoutly advances an interest in exploring or proclaiming the ultimacy of a belief system's objective reference points, as in the analytical discourse of a theologian or the elaborated praise of a hymn. Indeed, a matter-of-fact farmer's prayer will very likely be *phrased* in a devout and theologically articulate way – otherwise the words would not seem right – which points back to a sponsoring intention for the language that is more actively religious.

Since language is always guidance, whatever else it consists of or accomplishes, serviceability for guidance must be taken into account in assessing the meaning of any utterance or model for utterance. We may suppose that religious language is always (whatever else is going on) religiously guiding in one or both of two senses of that phrase: guiding with respect to the ultimacy of the objects of religious affirmation – saying perspicuous things about Brahman or Emptiness, for example – and guiding in accordance with the subjective ultimacy of religiosity, that is, modeling or effectively expressing a stance of faith, love, or piety.[4] It is always at least latently *the* guidance, the life guidance one

---

[4] My argument for forward-looking faith, backward-looking piety, and present-minded love as primary forms of devotion is in *Appeal and Attitude* (Indiana University Press, 2005), chap. 8.

ideally cannot avoid and indeed cannot avoid prioritizing. Sometimes it presents itself in this aspect very pointedly, asserting that the time is *now* to withdraw the poisoned arrow of ego-centered craving or to expect the Kingdom of God.

Let us examine the characteristic linguistic expressions of the religious push toward ultimacy in the three Austinian dimensions of speech acts: locutionary articulation of what is the case, illocutionary position taking in communicative relationship, and perlocutionary pursuit of effects. Each dimension features a part of the religious promise of followable guidance and a corresponding part of the problematic of religious language. Whereas a theologian might give a top-down definition of divine guidance in terms of divine speech acts that are sui generis, uniquely real and powerful, we are approaching the possibility of divine guidance from the bottom up and so must think in terms of religious amplifications of human linguistic guidance.

4.2 RELIGIOUS LANGUAGE AS INFORMATIVE

The locutionary part of guidance is to clarify which beings are in our world, what they are like, and how they relate. As religious language serves a maximal optimization of life that goes beyond finding food and shelter, it characteristically provides extra vocabulary to populate a larger world than the world of ordinary experience by naming entities, properties, actions, and relations that are not observable and trackable in the way that the objects of ordinary language are (though not necessarily regarded as outlandish, either). Further, religious teachings and interpretations rely on locutions that purport to assert, possibly with truth value in their own frame of reference, certain ways in which all relevant things, ordinary and extraordinary, really come together. Manifesting a religious attitude or affective reaction may be of locutionary help in establishing the sense and credibility of what is figured. Extraordinary items may be designated by metaphor or metonym, by new nominalizations (Sanskrit *deva* and Latin *deus* are "shining ones"; Germanic "god" is "the invoked one"), by appropriation of foreign words, or simply by saying an ordinary word with special scruple, giving it the distinction that in printed English is shown by capitalization. If I say "breath" with religious emphasis, for example, I mean a breath-of-breath or breath-beyond-breath, a primally or transcendently animating and communicating breath: "Spirit."

For the religious speaker, meaning "Spirit" by a breath word is a *reach* beyond ordinary affairs into the extraordinary, and yet the word functions as a *name* for an item regarded as present or potentially present, the same as anything else's name. (For the moment let us think only of a name's referential function, not the appellative function of personal names.) The ingenuous speaker is not guessing at what *might* exist corresponding to the term. But someone else who does not take the speaker's thus-expanded world for granted, an outsider to the usage or a doubter, will ask for an explanation of how a term for something invisible can be meaningful. That will require a negotiation to determine how the speaker wants or needs to affirm continuity and discontinuity in the relation between the term's shareable conception and its extraordinary referent.

The key idea for the religious conception might be *analogy*: Spirit is present in "something like" the way breath is – or, more optimistically, in a way that is "a good deal like" the way breath is – plausibly enough like it that one feels one is (or, weaker, "could well be") aimed in the right direction by the ordinary clue.[5] Or the idea might be *symbol*: the experience of breath seems to "participate in" the reality of Spirit so that in using a breath word with the right emphasis, struck by what it vividly evokes for us, we seem to move into active relationship with that invisible being or mode of being.[6] Or the idea might be *metaphor*: highlighting the transcendence of the invisible target, the word for breath and its associations conjures up a challenging mixture of "is" and "is not," of possible similarity and evident dissimilarity with the target reality.[7] Religious metaphor is an invitation to an ongoing adventure of trying to see the extraordinary X in some sort of telling association with its graspable vehicle Y.[8]

This is a core problematic of religious locution. Just where religious speakers locate themselves between the modest confidence of analogy, the

---

[5] "A good deal like" – Nicholas Wolterstorff, *The God We Worship* (Eerdmans, 2015), p. 92.

[6] "Participate in" – Paul Tillich, "The Meaning and Justification of Religious Symbols," in Sidney Hook, ed., *Religious Experience and Truth* (NYU Press, 1961), p. 4.

[7] "Is" and "is not" – Sallie McFague, *Metaphorical Theology* (Fortress, 1982), pp. 14–19; cf. Paul Ricoeur on the "semantic impertinence" or "contradiction" in metaphor in *Interpretation Theory* (TCU Press, 1973), p. 50.

[8] Discussion of these options is usefully summarized by Dan R. Stiver in *The Philosophy of Religious Language* (Blackwell, 1996), chap. 6. For a thorough analytic discussion of positions on metaphor, see Michael Scott, *Religious Language* (Palgrave Macmillan, 2013), chap. 13.

devout attachment of symbolism, and the anxious audacity of metaphor seems to depend on the degree to which they feel optimistic or secure in living in their religiously expanded world – depending, in turn, on how effectively religious locutions have structured that world – and the degree to which their conversation includes questions about the intelligibility of religious talk. Analogy, symbol, and metaphor are all strong conceptual attractors for a religious speaker's self-explanation. It can be argued that metaphor is the strongest attractor in our modern situation, where we are bound to undertake literate examination of religious options at a time of stronger-than-ever epistemic and moral challenges from rival perspectives.[9] But the dominant model for religious speakers themselves when they offer religious locutions is simply one of naming what they speak of and characterizing what they name and the situation in which they are dealing with it. In theological or philosophical mode, they can discuss critically how the notion of ordinary breath relates to an extraordinary referent, but more importantly for themselves, they *do* have occasion to say things like "The Spirit is working among us!" or "No one knows where the Spirit goes!" that they take to be descriptively true.[10] And they can agree on the presence or potential presence of their powerful referent even while varying in how they conceive it – one perhaps thinking of the Spirit on the model of a living person, another on the model of a more abstract esprit de corps.

The religious and nonreligious can agree that a word like "Spirit" is dangerous because of the power in the extraordinary reach of its reference. To speak of something beyond what people see and handle – how is that not reckless, overbearingly pretentious, or hopelessly oblique? If such a word is to have a respectable use, that use must be appropriately configured and constrained so that it makes reliable sense. The Wittgensteinian idea that a word's normal use belongs to a "language-game" addresses part of this challenge: we need to know how utterances fit into a learnable system of "moves" that have definable effects on a developing shared situation, as in a game. One can contemplate how a religious locution is a makeable game move within the charmed circle of a theological discourse ("the Spirit proceeds from the Father and the Son") by

---

[9] McFague makes this claim (10–14).

[10] Janet Soskice would prefer to say that "'God is Spirit' denominates rather than describes God, or, more precisely, it denominates the source of thousands of experiences which Jews and Christians have spoken of, using the descriptive language at their disposal, as the working of the spirit, and which they take to be God." *Metaphor and Religious Language* (Oxford University Press, 1985), p. 154.

reading a sufficiently rich religious literature, or by consulting a good anthropological description like Evans-Pritchard's account of the many ways in which the African Nuer speak of Spirit (*kwoth*).[11] But the language-game idea does not get us all the way to the felt realism and serious teleological import of religious talk. For that, we also need the idea that linguistic communication constructs a life-world that communicators inhabit together. It is because one understands that there is no other life to live than one's own life and no other world to live in than one's own world that life-world-constructing moves are occasions of the most serious acceptance or rejection.

The question of how religious locutions can successfully refer seems to be defused by noncognitivist theories that construe religious reference as the projection of an attitude or intention.[12] The noncognitivist idea is that the religious speaker seeks to establish an orientation needed for a nobler or more bearable life by *positing* a world infused by Spirit and *resolving* (and perhaps at least implicitly calling on others to similarly resolve) to live *as though* we have that extraordinary being to deal with for important purposes. Utterances that seem descriptive are really coded policy or value affirmations.

Noncognitivists are right to look for a specification of the religious speaker's religious attitude, since it is true that whatever is said religiously is said in announcement and reinforcement of the optimistic project of living in a religiously expansive life-world. But noncognitivism has a glaring general weakness in its denial of a real referent of religious locutions: it either fails to consider or only arbitrarily settles the question of what a "being" might be in an extraordinary frame of reference. Mature religious speakers do not take the prime referents of religious locution to be beings that are concrete in the same way that the objects of ordinary experience are (although they may complement their literal religious assertions with extensive make-believe in religious narrative and imagery, and they may make serious claims of *linkage* between extraordinary being and ordinary being, as in divine incarnations). They always assume *some* epistemic and semantic distance between extraordinary and ordinary referents – whether cautiously bridged by analogy, creatively stirred by metaphor, or subject to the extreme check of apophaticism where the arch-extraordinary is concerned (God or

[11] E. E. Evans-Pritchard, *Nuer Religion* (Oxford University Press, 1956), chaps. 1–5.
[12] For helpful evaluation of different ways in which noncognitivism can be applied to religious language, see Scott, op. cit.

Brahman or nirvana or the Dao). Otherwise there would be no specifically religious cognitive gain in religious guidance. But there cannot be a religious cognitive gain if religious referents are not beings about which there can be knowledge (negative as well as positive). Moreover, if the religious venture lacks a cognitive component, it cannot have a main kind of communicative rigor, a standard of substantiality and consistency in what is said. Reflecting both of these considerations, a great deal of religious discourse evidently means to be genuinely *informative* in a *religious way* – that is, correctly identifying and characterizing points of reference in a religiously expanded world.

A religious discourse dedicated to apophaticism or pragmatism may take the approach of minimizing its locutionary purport and so may have little concern with locutionary standards. That is a choice that is relatively uncommon in religious history but not freakishly rare. The opposite choice, common but not standard, is to make locutionary content the central and decisive aspect of religious utterance. The claim in its boldest form would be that a supreme religious locution (such as "God is the world's Creator" or "Everything is Self") puts hearers in cognitive contact with That by which all things ordinary and extraordinary come together – the precious knowledge of That grounding and lifting hearers so that they can live in an expansively responsible and optimistic way. The most important aspect of religious utterance, so regarded, is its truthfulness. Orthodoxy rules.

The ideal of truthful religious language is haunted by a transcendence dilemma. If we understand the content of the great locution too well, it is too familiarly human, and we cannot be in touch with the saving extraordinariness of the objective Ultimate. But if we do not understand it well enough, there is little point in claiming that the locution makes it accessible. One strategy for overcoming this difficulty emphasizes the meaning of what is said religiously in a highly mobile, flexible campaign of saying relatively apt things; another places its trust in the very saying of sacred words with full affirmation of their extraordinariness.

An example of the first strategy is the "models" approach advocated by Ian Ramsey. The objective Ultimate, God for Bishop Ramsey, is impossible to see clearly or whole, but there may be various modelings of God that support a central Christian interest in knowing God.[13] (For Ramsey, knowledge of God is a matter of working out an adequate

---

[13] Ian T. Ramsey, *Religious Language* (Macmillan, 1957).

interpretation of what has been realized in odd yet climactic "disclosure experiences" of "something more" in our situation than what is empirically obvious, experiences that get completed in a commitment embraced by the subject.) Modeling God as "infinitely good," for example, uses the qualifier "infinite" to direct our attention beyond particular instantiations of goodness to the cap of all goodness.[14] But any graspable model has only a limited positive capacity to represent the Ultimate and may also have dangerously wrong associations that must be checked, so we must "use as many models as possible, and from these develop the most consistent discourse possible" while never closing the door to new models.[15] Thanks to the rich locutionary content of our religious discourse, drawing on our own and everyone else's disclosure experiences of the depth of what we find most strikingly meaningful in our lives, we come to the best possible understanding of the structure of the best life in the world. In a Ramseyan religious conversation we will never be freed from uncertainty or disagreement, but we will have ample opportunity to enrich and support each other's understanding nonetheless, and locutionary optimism will be sustained.

A very differently oriented pair of approaches, yet similarly confident about the capacity of language to give us access to divine truth, are taken in classical Hindu theories of language.

The premise of *shabdapramana*, "word as source of knowledge," is that certain important truths can be learned only by being told something. In ordinary life, one could never come to know the details of unrepeatable happenings experienced by others if one did not find out by their testimony.[16] In religious matters, one could never learn from experience or by rational analysis how to perform a correct sacrifice, as the ritual-oriented Mimamsakas point out. Nor can one learn from experience or by rational analysis what one's own true status in the scheme of things is. The "tenth man" parable evokes this point: one member of a traveling party of ten is

---

[14] "Cap" meaning that God is not just the greatest instantiation of goodness but stands out from the scale of goodnesses in something like the way a circle stands out from the scale of regular polygons with ever more sides. Ibid., pp. 75–80.

[15] Ramsey, "Words about God," in *Words about God* (ed. Ian T. Ramsey, Harper & Row, 1971), p. 210; cf. Ramsey, *Models and Mystery* (Oxford University Press, 1964). On problems and remedies at the level of models like God the Father, see also McFague, chap. 5.

[16] R. I. Ingalalli, "Independence of *Shabdapramana* (Testimony as Autonomous Source of Knowledge)," in *Shabdapramana in Indian Philosophy* (ed. Manjulika Ghosh and Bhaswati Bhattacharya Chakrabarti, Northern Book Centre, 2006), p. 95.

required to count his party and can only count nine until a stranger comes along and tells him, "You're the tenth!"[17] Nor can one arrive teachably in the *neighborhood* of the imperceptible, incalculable religious truth without direction by words.[18] Granted that the words conveying knowledge in such scenarios do not work in complete independence of the hearer's experience and reasoning, the words are nonetheless indispensable.

Another premise, obviously indebted to the highly developed priest-craft attested in the Vedas, is that we can go further than merely accepting canonical religious language as our authoritative information source about the gods and Heaven, or as effective in guiding our ritual address of the gods: we can amplify our acceptance of this language by honoring those very Sanskrit words and phrasings, provided that they are correctly pronounced and understood – even just the one supreme syllable-word, *Om*, the "very soul" of all meaning[19] – as the actuality, the very vibration, of the objective Ultimate. On this view, it is credible that the Ultimate can be participated in by vocalization because the ultimate apprehensible character of Actuality *would* be the intelligent articulating of vibration – the realizing of primal energy as structure or primal structure as energy – and vocalization is the human action that is most concordantly participant in that lucid vibrancy and so most apt for uniting subjective with objective ultimacy. It is further credible that Sanskrit would be the medium of optimal participation, as Sanskrit is of

[17] Shankara, *Upadeshasahasri* 1.12.2–3, 1.18.172–174; Purushotta Bilimoria, *Shabdapramana: Word and Knowledge as Testimony* (Kluwer, 1988), p. 285; see also Section 6.3. On the concept's more tenuous presence in Buddhism, see José Ignacio Cabezón, *Buddhism and Language* (SUNY Press, 1994), pp. 99–107.

[18] Shankara says that the cognitively accessible referent of claims about Atman is the intellect, which is not the Atman but a "reflection" of it, like a mirror reflection of a face. "In the [bearer of the 'I'-notion] there is the reflection [of the internal Seeing], and words referring to the former could indicate the internal Seeing indirectly, [but] never designate It directly." *Upadeshasahasri* 1.18.29, in *A Thousand Teachings: The Upadeshasahasri of Shankara* (trans. Sengaku Mayeda, SUNY Press, 1992), p. 175. There is a related Advaitin analogy of directing attention to the brighter star in a double-star system, where the true target is the star that is hard to see (Arundhati, also known as Alcor). Anantanand Rambachan, *Accomplishing the Accomplished: The Vedas as a Source of Valid Knowledge in Shankara* (University of Hawai'i Press, 1991), p. 68.

[19] On *Om*: Chandogya U. 1.1 (union of essential meanings, signification of Yes), 2.23.2–3 (principle of all speech and of whole world); Taittiriya U. 1.8 (indicates ritual compliance); Shvetashvatara U. 1.13–14 (means of perceiving Self); Mundaka U. 2.2.3–4 (Om the bow, Self the arrow, Imperishable Being the target); Prashna U. 5.1–7 (object of meditation); Maitri U. 6.5 (focus for worship); Mandukya U. 1–12 (comprises the four quarters of Self); "very soul," Bhartrihari, *Vakyapadiya* I.17 (trans. K. R. Pillai, Motilal Banarsidass, 1971).

all known languages the most perfected. (One could similarly exalt any language one experiences as supporting actual closeness with the divine.) The transcendence dilemma is thus overcome by the fortunate possibility of speaking and hearing words that are intrinsically supermeaningful.

It is not thought that anyone could casually deploy these words and attain knowledge of divinity. They must be handled in the right way, which requires the right preparation and attitude. The Rig Veda speaks of a joint birth of mortal and immortal meanings of speech (1.164.38) and subsequently of four divisions of speech of which three, known only to the Brahmins, are closely bound to eternity, causing no motion, in contrast to the fourth, which is ordinary speech (1.164.45). At least one important Hindu writer, Mandana Mishra, claims that the original seers of the Vedas discoursed at the next-to-highest level, beyond which we can only speculate about a supreme speech (*para vac*).[20] Admitting "levels" will of course prompt discussion of how different sorts of knowledge might be accessible on the different levels – a discussion that is hard to avoid in any developed religious hermeneutics but not one we need to enter at this point.

Is there any protection against superstitious delusion in placing a privileged language or vocabulary on a supposed higher plane of meaning? There may be a reassuring persistent testimony that in the proper saying of these words one dwells in a maximally serene and luminous place. A stabilized practice through time gives some assurance that the reach toward divinity on these terms does not clash with other humanly important commitments. The most superstitious uses of sacred words stand out from religiously well-regulated uses in being comparatively whimsical, even desperate, and divisive. If we take the view that Vedic language is authorless, then we deny the possibility of deceit or misunderstanding originally skewing the religiously crucial utterances; alternatively, we can trust the communal tradition to have filtered out all inherently untruthful wordings.[21] However, it seems that guiding locutions *about* the sacred language from outside it – whether from one's guru in being initiated into religious meaning or from scholarly study of issues in construing and validating religious meaning – are an indispensable

---

[20] On Mandana Mishra's scheme and its implications, see Harold G. Coward, *The Sphota Theory of Language* (Motilal Banarsidass, 1980), pp. 128–133.

[21] On the principal arguments for authorlessness, see Prabal Kumar Sen, "Some Alternative Definitions of *Shabdapramana*," in Ghosh and Chakrabarti, pp. 54–55. The Nyaya and Yoga schools claim to get the same assurance of a reliable sacred text by identifying it with the speech of God, who is perfect.

auxiliary for coming to the language in an acceptable way.[22] And these pieces of auxiliary guidance will be more directly subject to ordinary human cautions and measures of wholesome guidance.

Some high views of sacred language mount up even higher to a supra-locutionary position corresponding to one or more of the initial phases of speech we identified earlier – the first sounding, the first convening, the first offer of order. The main interest is in the event of existence rather than in dependent verbal representations of that event. But any version of the high view that claims that *what* the sacred language says is religiously crucial can be counted as locutionary.

High views of sacred language are in tension with our general locutionary assumption that the value of language depends on its semantic content, for the following reason.

Generally, a word signifies something, and the distinction between the word (in the sense of the sound or mark) and what it signifies entails that one could use a different word or phrase to make the same signification. An important exception to this rule is call names, which are sounds or marks that have the function not of indicating or saying something about a referent but of asserting a restricted relationship: the uniquely named being will respond as desired only if addressed by the name. When we say loosely that "words are names for things," we fudge the difference between referring and calling upon, and we do this for a reason – namely, that as we exercise our unrestricted, relatively unproblematic power of referring to things by their "names" third-personally, we have lurking hopes for the privilege and power in relationships that may be realized through the second-personal use of call names. We love the idea that Adam, who named all the animals (Genesis 2:19–20), could call them all.[23] And it is a central appeal of a religious tradition that it offers a call

---

[22] Here is an example of the sort of advice that a contemporary academic Vedic scholar, in this case a liberal, can give: "Vedic mantras contain both higher and lower ideas. Profound and eternal metaphysical and psychological truths and ethical intuitions of unsurpassed and perennial value as well as baseless beliefs and untenable ideas are to be found in it; and while it describes spiritual techniques of the highest order, it also elaborately deals with practices and performances fit only to be undertaken by credulous, insensitive and indiscriminating persons. A Puranic text says there are three meanings in all the Vedas [i.e. the well-known Agni, Fire, etc.; the One God within those beings; and the spiritual]. Let us concentrate on the adhyatmika [spiritual] meaning of the Veda – its spiritual essence." K. Satchidananda Murty, *Vedic Hermeneutics* (Shri Lal Bahadur Shastri Rashtriya Sanskrit Vidyapeetha, 1993), p. 12.

[23] Significantly, we read in the episode's conclusion that Adam did *not* form great relationships with the animals – "no helper was found" (Genesis 3:21).

name for one whom we could otherwise only refer to categorically as Creator or the Highest. It is only thanks to this ambiguity that we can treat names as words; without their referential capacity they would be in a different category altogether, like exclamations.

The notion that speaking an unsubstitutable holy language, text, verse, word, or syllable involves one in the holy life of its source is closer in its logic to call naming than to referring. But call naming is closer to music than to language. Like birdsong, its locutionary import is just the signature announcement of someone's availability for active relationship with another. (Or perhaps we should say "proto-locutionary" in consideration of Staal's idea that mantras, like song, are older than language.)[24] Indeed the musicality of holy language is fully embraced in the traditions that idealize Nada-Brahman, divinity as sound. In these traditions, mantras are token realizations of the melody, harmony, and rhythm of eternal being. It is a fully valid religious practice to recite mantras without knowing what the words say, since what the mantras say on the plane of human semantics is not their point;[25] they provide their life-optimizing orientation in a more basic way (perhaps in accordance with a user desire to be controlled rather than guided).

Yet sound divinity cannot be wholly separated from word divinity. For if the enactment of ritual is not to be mindless, or if the activation of eternal wholeness and bliss is not to be merely temporary, there must be an understanding of the situation that bridges all such episodes together with the rest of life, and this understanding must be bound somehow by the meanings of the eternally valid Vedic words, or else we would be at the mercy of proliferating and dubious human interpretations of the Vedic words and our practice. Thus the semantic content of Vedic

---

[24] Frits Staal, "Mantras and Bird Songs," *Journal of the American Oriental Society*, 105 (July–Sept. 1985), 549–558.

[25] This is a debated issue. See Frits Staal, *Rituals and Mantras* (Motilal Banarsidass, 1996) and Harvey L. Alper, "Introduction" to *Understanding Mantras* (ed. Harvey L. Alper, SUNY Press, 1989), pp. 10–13. According to Guy Beck, "it is only in the Yoga, Tantra, and music traditions wherein Shabda-Brahman [Word-Divinity] is recast as Nada-Brahman [Sound-Divinity] that the idea of 'pure cosmic sound' detached from linguistic meaning emerges ... From within the context of the Vedic ritual, which utilized these highly charged 'magazines of sound' to facilitate the ritual action, the notion of 'properly pronounced' language as power, or Shakti (Vak, the goddess of speech), emerged during the Vedic period." *Sonic Theology: Hinduism and Sacred Sound* (University of South Carolina Press, 1993), p. 34. On the intellectual and moral uses of mantras, see also Harold Coward and David J. Goa, *Mantra* (Columbia University Press, 2004), pp. 17–18.

utterance is not irrelevant – the high view is protected from superstitious distortion by its locutionary support – and we can interpret the high view as locution-centered insofar as referential meanings of words are required to deliver the divine

On either of these Hindu views, Vedic utterances are regarded as eternal and authorless.[26] It is argued a priori that if a human being had authored them, they would not have their unquestionable validity.[27] (More modestly and plausibly, I think, and with broader application, one could argue that insofar as sacred utterances are regarded merely as humanly authored, they cannot have the fullest religious relevance.) A posteriori, the Vedas are recognized as that subset of all language of which it is true, as shown by extensive and limitless experience, that one acquires crucial knowledge for optimizing life by hearing it or that one participates in divinity by saying it, and the successful transmission of the Vedas through time supports the idea that human linguistic production is informed by eternal meanings.[28]

*

If you are hungry, you need to know what is edible and inedible and where edibles are. If you are at war, you need to know where your enemy is and with what capability. If you are in love, you need to know where your beloved is and how disposed toward you and others. Truths, falsehoods, credibilities, incredibilities, unknowns, and unknowabilities in

---

[26] According to the Mimamsa Sutra, the eternal meanings of words are *manifested* in different utterances, not *produced* variously by speakers (1.1.6 et seq.), and we know that the Veda is (at least conceivably? or imaginably?) not the work of any person, because there is an unbroken tradition of the text among the students of the Veda (1.1.27 et seq.). Mimamsa Sutra of Jaimini, in *A Sourcebook in Indian Philosophy* (ed. Sarvepalli Radhakrishnan and Charles A. Moore, Princeton University Press, 1957), pp. 487–498.

[27] Kumarila presents it as a metaphysical point: that which is eternal cannot be caused. *Shlokavartika* 1.41, in Radhakrishnan and Moore, p. 498.

[28] Thus, in disagreement with the Mimamsa position, it can be denied that words as such are eternal while still affirming their eternal meaning. Vacaspati writes, commenting on Yoga Sutra 1.27–28: "Although a word does become one with the *prakriti* [material force] along with the [divine] power, it comes back into manifestation along with the power; as earth-born creatures becoming one with the earth on the cessation of the rains, come back to life on being wetted by showers of rain water. Thus God makes a convention similar to the convention which indicated the former relation. Hence on account of the eternity of the succession of similar usage [in the Vedas], due to simultaneous knowledge, the relation of word and meaning is eternal. Independent eternity is not meant." Quoted in Beck, p. 87.

such matters vitally affect you and give you strong motivation to get adequate cognitive guidance in identifying them. The religious amplification of locutionary content and truth ideally responds to a profound need that can be modeled as an amplification of hunger, enmity, and love. The need is met by identifying the higher Sustenance, the radical Enemy, and the final Beloved.

Like a guided walk in a wilderness park, religious guidance has the fundamental elements of a prospect of specially desirable reward, a need for access and passable pathways, and a healthy preference for true guidance that does not tip over into laissez-faire advice on the one side or dispossessing control on the other. The healthy balance ideal can guide our evaluation of different views of religious locution.

The Ramseyan "models" approach is representative of intellectualist approaches that run relatively close to the pitfall of leaving guidance seekers to figure things out on their own as best they can. Reading Ramsey, one acquires the idea that a divine goodness lies on the far side of ordinary instantiations of goodness as a "cap" on the series. But the religious attractor itself (for a Christian, God's generosity embodied in Christ) is not present in the notion of a cap. If the "infinite goodness" locution does succeed in stabilizing a cognition of divine goodness, it does so only by cooperating with another religious experience (say, faith in Christ provided by divine grace). The idea of a transcendent goodness and the conative attachment to a perceived inordinate generosity might be well matched in being similarly superoptimistic and mutually supportive. But the idea all by itself does not pick out what is religiously crucial.

The high Hindu view of religious language as making present the very substance of divine life runs toward the opposite pitfall of dispossession. On this view, Vedic language fulfills its sacred purpose by completely imposing its extraordinary cognitive structure on the subject who pronounces it. But if I am not to abandon the very premise of guided life in the religious context, I must insist that *I* am cognitively inflecting the presence of divinity when I participate in the sacred language – if only in the way that a comet tail inflects the sun's presence. And given that the comet tail of an intelligent being includes thinking, my thinking about the meaning of Vedic utterance is crucial to my liberation.[29] Vedic language can inform my thinking but cannot supersede it.

---

[29] According to Shankara, the oneness of the Self is clearly shown only when scriptural testimony together with reasoning demonstrates it; the meaning of scriptural texts should

4.3 RELIGIOUS LANGUAGE AS APPELLATIVE

If one has grown up with theism, one might think that truths concerning transcendent matters are accessible to us only because a transcendent Speaker speaks them to us. How else could they have been made known? If supposedly authorless sacred texts are credited as the source of transcendent truth, as in the Mimamsa Vedic tradition, must not the texts themselves be understood in effect as the Speaker, the supreme Guide?

But no speaking God or God equivalent is needed as a supplier of transcendent truth. It might simply be the case that we have found that certain of our ideas and expressions function as windows or lenses through which transcendent truth becomes visible. Even theist ideas and expressions could be regarded in this way. A savvy old biblical prophet might reveal in his memoirs, deflatingly yet not cynically, "Of course I was merely working in a certain rhetorical tradition when I said 'Thus says the Lord' and 'The Day of the Lord is a day of darkness, not light,' but that intense language got me thinking about what life is all about; it drew me toward an ultimate question of rightness and a corresponding higher righteousness; I found extraordinary truth in it."

The reason that a wise prophet would frame an address to the Israelites as a summons from their superhumanly powerful yet discontented Lord is that this approach would joltingly get their attention and give them their best chance of improving their spiritual position. Confronting them with their superior Other, the "Highest," and warning of wrong relation with that Other would maximally amplify their sense of being accountable for their choices and actions. The chief prophetic concern is the extraordinarily serious accountability that one must avow vis-à-vis God, not the cognizable presence or nature of God. There is a cognitive component in this positioning, to be sure: one must appreciate that the Judge is just, the Overseer is wise, and the Ruler is powerful; one must think that the Other in all these aspects is real (not merely a parent projection, a fantasy, a morbidly feared Nemesis, etc.); and one must face the Other in a bearable form (a Lord, for instance, rather than an abstract infinite demand). But it is quite possible that everyone's conceptions of the Other are faulty. (For example, what if the Gnostics are right and all who speak of God as this world's creator are mistaken?) And different views of the Other will be seized upon no matter how the Other is presented.

be explained and tested in the light of arguments (see *Brihadaranyaka Upanishad Bhasya* 2.4.5; 4.5.6; 3.1.1) (Murty 32).

(For example, the God called Father may be understood as a supreme force or beauty or possibility.) In any case, the issues of believing or not believing in, making correct attributions to, or adopting an appropriate attitude toward this Other would not be *serious* unless there were in the first place a Call, arousing the intention to be responsive in *that* relationship and at the same time bringing to a head the practical issue of one's positioning amongst one's fellow communicators. The paramount significance of belief in the Other is the positioning it sponsors rather than its role in explaining the world.

The Call from the ultimate Caller poses the ultimate version of the problem of justification – that is, the problem of arriving at an acceptable position in a relationship the standards for which are not under one's control. We say, for example, that making an upsetting truth claim is justified if one's relevant evidence and logic are sound or that illegally speeding to the hospital is justified in an attempt to save someone's life, because a notional jury of all reasonable people would accept these acts. But the irruption of an extraordinary relationship creates an additional, extraordinary question of acceptability, the standards of which are mysterious (though not completely so, given that communication is occurring). If this happens, it may come as a shocking surprise, or it may have been something that we were always thoughtful and morally sensitive enough to have been looking out for, at least implicitly (as Karl Rahner argues).[30]

The religious guidance that acts primarily by establishing an extraordinary relationship among communicators may be called appellative inasmuch as a divine call has priority. There will be a telltale illocutionary operator in presenting such guidance or in clarifying what is happening: an announcing, summoning, warning, commanding, inviting, or beseeching; in print, an exclamation point. Such utterance will be a "source of knowledge" (*pramana*) that one is in a relationship. Emphasis on a dynamic relationship-creating call is characteristic of the style of religious communication called prophetic that dominates core portions of Zoroastrian, biblical, and Islamic scriptures. It is not found only in so-called prophetic religions, but we may be sure of finding concerted attention to it

---

[30] "It belongs to our nature to stand before the unknown God, before the free God, whose 'meaning' cannot be determined in function of that of the world or of us. A positive, clear, and definitive relationship between God and us cannot be established by starting from us. God alone can establish it. Thus we must always keep in mind the possibility of a revelation of this God." Karl Rahner, *Hearer of the Word* (trans. Joseph Donceel, Continuum, 1994), p. 9; cf. pp. 52–54.

there, and we may pick it up in that fascinating historical period in which prophetic and mystical branches of Indo-Iranian religion seem to split apart, Zarathushtra on one side and the Upanishads on the other.

The ancient hymns of Zarathushtra make continual reference to the "truth" or "doctrine" concerning divinity but put remarkable energy into the staging of the hearer's choice to hearken to that truth and join the good side – in Zarathushtra's world, the side of respectable farmers in their struggle with cattle thieves.

And now I will proclaim to you who draw near and seek to be taught the truth of Him who knows all things; the praises that are for Ahura [Mazda], and the sacrifices that proceed from the Good Mind, and likewise the wholesome meditations inspired by Righteousness ...

Hear then with your ears; see the bright flames with the Better Mind. It is for a decision as to religions, man and man, each individually for himself. Before the great effort of the cause, awake to our teaching!

Thus are the primeval spirits [Ahura Mazda and Angrya Mainyu] who are famous as a pair, and each independent in his action. They are a better thing and a worse, as to thought, as to word, and as to deed. And between these two let the wisely acting choose aright. Do not choose as the evil-doers!

... When vengeance shall have come upon these wretches, then, O Mazda! the Kingdom shall have been gained for Thee by Good Mind. For to those, O Living Lord! does that Good Mind utter his command, who will deliver the Demon of the Lie into the two hands of the Righteous Order. (Yasna 30:1–3, 8)[31]

There is some reminiscence here of a mythically framed knowledge of supernatural beings and how they have acted, but substantially no other guiding truth is suggested about divinity than that it is Good, and no other quality of life is demanded than loyalty to the Good. That loyalty divides the community of truth from the community of falsehood.

The cattle have already set the example, choosing fellowship with well-settled citizens rather than thieves:

Thine, O Ahura! was Piety; Thine, O Creator of the cattle! was understanding and the Spirit, when Thou didst order a path for her [the cattle]. From the earth's tiller the cattle goes, or from him who was never tiller. Of the two she chose the husbandman, the thrifty toiler in the fields, as a holy master endowed with the Good Mind's wealth. (Yasna 31:9–10)

Among the Brahmins in India, meanwhile, a priority of relationship may be found in the Vedic Hymn to Speech (Vac):

---

[31] Adapted from the text in *The Zend-Avesta*, in *Sacred Books of the East*, vol. 31 (trans. L. H. Mills, Oxford University Press, 1887).

O Brihaspati, (this was) the first beginning of Speech: when they (the seers) came
forth, giving names.

What was their best, what was flawless – that (name), set down in secret, was
revealed to them because of your affection (for them).

When the wise have created Speech by their thought, purifying her like coarse
grain by a sieve,

in this they recognize their companionship as companions. Their auspicious mark
has been set down upon Speech.

Through the sacrifice they followed the track of Speech. They found her having
entered into the seers ...

They say that another is stiff and swollen in his companionship: him they do not
spur on at all in the competitions ...

Who has abandoned the companion joined (to him) in knowledge, for him there is
no share in Speech at all ...

When, in the mind's quickness that is fashioned in the heart, Brahmins perform
the sacrifice together as companions,

then they leave behind some by their knowing ways.

(10.71.1–3, 5–6, 8)[32]

"Speech" seems to be functioning here as a call to friendship, perhaps not
as a mere auxiliary to the high realization of the true meaning of divine
speech but as the very substance of that realization.[33]

The Bhagavad-Gita is steeped in Vedic and Upanishadic teachings
concerning the nature of the Real, but the "highest word" of the Gita
and a highlight in its well-known pivot to the way of devotion (*bhakti
yoga*) comes in Krishna's call to a love relationship:

And now again give ear to this my highest Word, of all the most mysterious: "I
love you well." Therefore will I tell you your salvation.

Bear Me in mind, love Me and worship Me, sacrifice, prostrate yourself to Me:
so will you come to Me, I promise you truly, for you are dear to Me ...

Never must you tell this word to one whose life is not austere, to one devoid of
love-and-loyalty, to one who refuses to obey, or to one who envies Me.

[But] whoever shall proclaim this highest mystery to my loving devotees,
showing the while the highest love-and-loyalty to Me, shall, nothing doubting,
come to Me indeed. (18:64–65, 67–68)[34]

---

[32] *The Rigveda*, vol. 3 (trans. Stephanie W. Jamison and Joel P. Brereton, Oxford University
Press, 2014).

[33] According to Biderman, "the driving force behind [the Vedic seers'] creative activity is
intimate friendship." Shlomo Biderman, *Crossing Horizons* (trans. Ornan Rotem,
Columbia University Press, 2008), pp. 95–97. I think the most natural construal is that
the hymn celebrates the specifically priestly fellowship that is enabled by the seers' gift.

[34] *The Bhagavad-Gita* (trans. R. C. Zaehner, Oxford University Press, 1966). Crollius
remarks, regarding 18:67–68: "The injunction to transmit the message to others is
given with the personal election and vocation to a mission we do not hesitate to call

As with the Hymn to Speech, Krishna's appeal to Arjuna can be seen as auxiliary to enlightenment, an emotional facilitation of full mental adherence to the Real. But the fellowship of divine love can equally well be seen as an end in itself, and Krishna's appeal can serve as a charter text for the love-centered *bhakti* movement that gathers strength for centuries thereafter in the postclassical world.

Appellative religious guidance is intensely personal. This is both a strength and a weakness for guidance purposes – a strength in taking full advantage of the overriding cogency of interpersonal appeal, a weakness in its unsecured cognitive content and uncertain pragmatic consequence. Because of that strength, a perspective that is not primarily appellative can gain intensity from an appellative touch, as in this comment by Dogen, the Soto Zen patriarch, on reading scripture:

"To read Scriptures" means that we collect together every single, solitary Ancestor of the Buddha and read a Scripture through their Eye. At this very moment, in a twinkling, the Ancestors of the Buddha become Buddhas, give voice to the Dharma, give voice to Buddha, and do what a Buddha does. If it is not an occasion for this kind of "reading Scripture," the Head, Face, and Eye of the Buddha's Ancestors do not yet exist for you.[35]

*

The core religious sense of appellative guidance is the "Oh my God!" pang of finding oneself actually in a particular relationship with its particular contours of possible rectification. Worship as pure acknowledgement is likely to be the act that makes the most religious sense in this dimension. The core benefit promised by the appeal is that the hearer will live in an interintentionally challenging relationship rather than by self-direction. The appellative sense is most robust religiously when it is richly suggestive about how thoughts and actions would comport better or worse with the instituted relationship and when it coheres with other optimizations of life. It is thin when it is invoked arbitrarily or pro forma. It is useless when it suggests nothing about how to live.

There is an obvious danger here of attachment to a demonic Other. We can be caught up in the profound drama of justification with whoever

---

prophetical. " Ary A. Roest Crollius, *Thus Were They Hearing: The Word in the Experience of Revelation in Qur'an and Hindu Scriptures* (Gregorian University Press, 1974), p. 237.
[35] Dogen, *Shobogenzo* (trans. Hubert Nearman, Shasta Abbey, 2007), chap. 20, p. 238.

seems to be addressing us as the supreme Other. A plausible supreme attitude ideal offers some protection by prescribing an appropriate character to the experience of the Call and the language of response to it. Is our Called-for comportment tranquil or rather fearful? Is it loving or rather discriminating or hating? Is it open to knowledge or rather bigoted or reductively fundamentalistic?

Individuals may hearken to the divine in wildly different ways, and so the biblical tradition sets great store by specific covenants given by God to cope with the disorders of worldly life, frequently citing the Abrahamic, Mosaic, and Davidic covenants. The Qur'an, too, invokes covenant (*'ahd, mithaq*). Covenants provide some practical consistency in the communities they charter. But communities of different covenants will be stuck in intractable and unedifying disagreement with each other so long as each insists on its given covenant and associated Lord, unless their members also engage in intellectual study of divinity and pragmatic study of religious conduct. A discourse of pure summons and hearkening cannot generate by itself all the content and correctives it needs.

4.4 RELIGIOUS LANGUAGE AS PRAGMATICALLY EFFECTIVE

All guidance is supposed to be helpful somehow, but some forms of guidance have a primarily instrumental aspect that is valued apart from any intrinsically rewarding aspects they may also have. An example of intrinsically rewarding guidance is a dancer leading another dancer in a successful dance. An example of instrumental guidance is a piece of advice on dancing ("For this waltz, count one-*two*-three"). A religious example of instrumentalism would be a mantra that is said to be good for purging karmas that obstruct Liberation.[36] Religious utterance may be regarded as an extraordinarily *effective* means of making progress toward optimal existence. It is then validated insofar as it can be seen or believed to deliver those results. It may also, unlike an ordinary dance guide, be thought to be unsubstitutable.

One can find instrumentalist views of sacred utterance in any tradition, along with critiques of such views.[37] Some of the most seriously maintained instrumentalist views will be found among Buddhists and the

---

[36] Coward and Goa, 12.

[37] Here is an example of Christian critique of the popular notion that the Bible is "an instruction manual for life": Jared C. Wilson, "The Bible Is Not an Instruction Manual" (www.crossway.org/blog/2015/08/the-bible-is-not-an-instruction-manual/, 2015).

classical Daoists, for several reasons: a dominant desire to attain mental peace rather than a state of belief; an interest in looking beyond the signified content of utterances to a more extraordinary realization that the utterances cannot represent, although they can help the seeker to move in that direction; and a deep skepticism about the permanence or value of any specifiable order, including the order of a language – especially a supposedly perfect language.[38] The Buddha said, pragmatically:

> Of whatsoever teachings, Gotamid, thou canst assure thyself thus: "These passions conduce to passions, not to dispassion; to bondage, not to detachment; to increase of (worldly) gains, not to decrease of them ..." of such teaching thou mayest affirm, Gotamid, "This is not the Norm. This is not the Discipline. This is not the Master's Message." But of whatsoever teachings thou canst assure thyself (that they are the opposite) – of such teaching thou mayest with certainty affirm: "This is the Norm. This is the Discipline. This is the Master's Message."[39]

Dogen calls Buddhist scriptures "the tools of the Great Truth."[40] Some of the most devoted of all scripturalists are Buddhists, and one of the Buddhist texts that has received the most concerted devotion is the Lotus Sutra; yet the Lotus's famous self-deabsolutizing teaching is that the cosmic Buddha-nature may employ quite different "expedient devices" of expression at different times and places to promote spiritual progress.[41]

---

[38] The Sanskrit-wielding Brahmins in India portrayed the Buddhist writings as linguistically inferior. Very different Buddhist counterclaims arose: (1) that no language or scripture can escape the delusory snares of worldly structures; (2) that the Pali canon is in fact the uniquely great written guidance; and (3) that everything in the cosmos utters Buddhist truth, if one is alive to it. On Shingon founder Kukai's *hosshin seppo* teaching in this latter vein, see Fabio Rambelli, *A Buddhist Theory of Semiotics* (Bloomsbury, 2013), chaps. 1–2. In this perspective, the canonized writings are but brief abstracts of the cosmic scripture. Because of a magical Tantric interest in assuring results, Kukai circles back to the very high view of religious language with which the Veda is so often honored: "Tantrism transformed language from its status as expedient means, employed in order to convey meaning or induce certain actions, to an absolute and unconditioned entity, something that could not be translated without losing its essential character. Kukai believed that the Indian phonemes and script were endowed with a unique nature" (Rambelli, 13). See also Luis O. Gómez, "The Whole Universe as a Sutra," in *Buddhism in Practice* (ed. Donald S. Lopez Jr., Princeton University Press, 1995), pp. 107–112, on the *Sutra of the Coming Forth of the Tathagatas*.

[39] Vinaya Pitaka 2.10, in *Some Sayings of the Buddha according to the Pali Canon* (trans. F. L. Woodward, Oxford University Press, 1925), pp. 278–279.

[40] Dogen, p. 611.

[41] In the Parable of the Burning House (chap. 3), a father anxious to lure his children out of a burning house promises each child the toy that seems most compelling to him or her. About Buddhist scripturalism, Cabezón remarks: "Even in a tradition that finds anathema the kind of dogmatism that allows for the possibility of scripture as a source of proof, we find that, in practice, the authority of scripture is held sacrosanct. This fact,

The Smaller Pure Land Sutra is known for its promised pragmatic benefit. The text leads with an enchanting description of a blissful world (*Sukhavati*) where "the sources of happiness are innumerable":

And again, O Shariputra, in that world Sukhavati there are lotus lakes, adorned with the seven gems, viz. gold, silver, beryl, crystal, red pearls, diamonds, and corals as the seventh. They are full of water which possesses the eight good qualities, their waters rise as high as the fords and bathing-places, so that even crows may drink there; they are strewn with golden sand. And in these lotus-lakes there are all around on the four sides four stairs, beautiful and brilliant with the four gems, viz. gold, beryl, silver, crystal.[42]

But this language is not meant to describe a place one would wish to live in for its gratifications, as we live in the ordinary world; that would miss the clue that the discourse locates us in a different world and would be contrary to the Buddhist endeavor to be free of craving. Rather it serves as a frame of symbolic pointers to excellence supporting a concentration of mind upon the holy compassion of Amitayus (Amitabha, Amida), who, as we are told in the Larger Pure Land Sutra, is committed by a perfect intention to the salvation of all sentient life. The spiritual result is the main concern. It comes about differently than many would expect:

Beings are not born in that Buddha country ... as a *reward* and result of good works performed in this present life. No, whatever son or daughter of a family shall hear the name of the blessed Amitayus, the Tathagata [who rules this country], and having heard it, shall keep it in mind, and with thoughts undisturbed shall keep it in mind for one, two, three, four, five, six or seven nights – when that son or daughter of a family comes to die, then that Amitayus, the Tathagata ... will stand before them at the hour of their death, and they will depart this life with tranquil minds. After their death they will be born in the world Sukhavati, in the Buddha country of the same Amitayus, the Tathagata. Therefore, then, O Shariputra, having perceived this cause and effect, I with reverence say thus, Every son and every daughter of a family ought with their whole mind to make fervent prayer for that Buddha country.[43]

The "tranquil mind" is Buddhist liberation, for which "born in Sukhavati" is a figurative expression.[44]

---

we might suppose, is invariant from one tradition to the next because of some very basic quality of religious texts and of religious people" (111–112).

[42] The Smaller Sukhavati-Vyuha Sutra (trans. F. Max Müller), in *Buddhist Mahayana Texts* (ed. E. B. Cowell, Dover, 1969), part 2, pp. 93–94.

[43] Ibid., pp. 98–99.

[44] Here is a representative modern interpretation of the discourse on the Pure Land: "Why did the Buddha speak of a land 'to the west'? Why a westward country? One reason is again to do with concentration of the mind. If the Buddha had said that the land is

Zen master Ekai (Mumon) used Zen's sacred koans like disposable bricks, we are told in the preface to his koan collection:

In the year 1228 I was lecturing monks in the Ryusho Temple, and at their request I retold old koans, endeavoring to inspire their Zen spirit. I meant to use the koans as a man who picks up a brick to knock at a gate, and after the gate is opened the brick is useless and is thrown away. My notes, however, were collected unexpectedly, and there were forty-nine koans, together with my comment in prose and verse concerning each, although their arrangement was not in the order of the telling. I have called the book "The Gateless Gate," wishing students to read it as a guide.[45]

This is the typical self-deprecating instrumentalization of Zen guidance. Its extreme expression is the saying attributed to Linji: "If you meet the Buddha, kill him." What counts is moving forward on your path toward enlightenment; to embrace a doctrine or Savior is to be blocked.[46]

The classical Daoists similarly undermined confidence in cognition, pushing back against the ethical and ritualistic system building of the Confucians; yet the Confucian position as modeled by Kongzi in the *Lunyu* is not dogmatic. One of Kongzi's main emphases is perpetual learning. To be sure, his reverent mind is informed by sacred prototypes in ancient rituals and texts, and as for appellative guidance, it is not too much to say that Kongzi feels Called by his supremely virtuous predecessor, the Duke of Zhou (3:14, 7:5).[47] But Kongzi's ultimate confidence

---

everywhere (which it is), then our mind, already scattered and dispersed in its daily confusion, could not concentrate its vision. 'Everywhere' pulls too hard at our mental limitation. But when the Buddha says 'Western country,' our thought goes at once in that single direction. Of course many will think that this Pure Land is really situated in the western quarter. According to a person's capacity, he believes what he believes ... even though we are now truly in the Pure Land, human illusion prevents us from seeing it so. Therefore Gautama Buddha couches this teaching in terms of an immensely desirable country – an offer no one could find unattractive." Hosen Seki, commentary, *Buddha Tells of the Infinite: The "Amida Kyo"* (Japan Publications, 1973), pp. 15, 49.

[45] Transcribed by Nyogen Senzaki and Paul Reps in *Zen Flesh, Zen Bones* (ed. Nyogen Senzaki and Paul Reps, Tuttle, 1985), p. 124.

[46] We should not take the advice to kill too lightly. In the biblical book of Deuteronomy, there is a divine command to kill one's relatives if they worship a different god than Yahweh (13:6–11); in its Israelite context, that is not purely metaphorical advice, and later biblically guided communities have emulated the Israelites (see Calvin's argument for imposing the death penalty for idolatry in his Commentary on Deuteronomy 13). Neither is it purely metaphorical when Jesus says he comes to divide families (Matthew 10:34–39); Christian faith really does divide families. Religious pragmatism can be harshly extreme.

[47] Kongzi's invoking of the Duke of Zhou can be seen as an idealization of customarily prescribed encounter with one's hierarchical superiors. According to Mark Edward

seems to be placed in the process of *getting it right* through study and conversation. The *Lunyu* begins: "The Master said, To learn and at due times to repeat what one has learnt, is that not after all a pleasure?" (1:1) and returns to the theme: "The Master said, He who by reanimating the Old can gain knowledge of the New is fit to be a teacher" (2:11).[48] "It is better to learn" [than to spend time merely thinking] (15:30).

There is a place for holding up a model of perfection, like the sublime sage-king Yao (8:19), but Kongzi does not claim to provide perfect guidance. He expects his followers to find for themselves the unifying thread of his teachings (4:15). It may be said that he is adapting for the spiritual aspirant the Chinese ideal of a ruler who must be a student of changing times in order to make the most appropriate rulings.[49] Only later, when Kongzi is a canonized sage and proclaimed "the equal of Heaven,"[50] can his writings can be credited with having *gotten* their subject matter *just right, infallibly*, on a higher plane than the edicts of worldly rulers:

The *Spring and Autumn Annals* examines the principles of things and rectifies their names. It applies names to things as they really are, without making the slightest mistake. Therefore in mentioning [the strange event of] falling meteorites, it mentions the number five afterward [because the meteorites were seen first and their number discovered later], whereas in mentioning the [ominous event of] fishhawks flying backward, it mentions the number six first [because six birds were first seen flying away and upon a closer look it was then found that they were fishhawks]. Such is the care of the Sage (Kongzi, its author) to rectify names. [As he himself said], "With regard to his speech, the superior man does not take it

---

Lewis, "[the] model of administration through a hierarchical series of staged personal encounters was fundamental to Warring States government. It was also a version of the formalized confrontations of superior and inferior that formed the Confucian theory of ritualized order, a theory that itself developed from the staged encounter of man and spirit in the performance of divination and sacrifice." *Writing and Authority in Early China* (SUNY Press, 1999), p. 28.

[48] *Lunyu* translations are taken from *The Analects of Confucius* (trans. Arthur Waley, Vintage, 1938).

[49] The Qin text *Lüshi Chunqiu* says, "Those who do not dare discuss the laws are the masses. Those who defend the laws to the death are the officials. Those who change the laws in response to the times are the rulers." Quoted in Lewis, pp. 39–40. Lewis comments further: "The sage wrote only in response to the conditions of the age. In this way, the actions of the ruler as legislator paralleled those ... in the [sage's] cosmic 'rectification of names'" (40).

[50] "The equal of Heaven": *The Doctrine of the Mean* (trans. James Legge, CreateSpace, 2016), p. 46.

lightly" [*Lunyu* 13:3]. His statements about the five meteorites and the six fish-hawks are good illustrations of this.[51]

But even here, if we think we are hearing perfect discourse, our focus can be on a practicable method of rectifying names rather than on a fixed form or sublime appeal.

The Confucians place the highest priority on working toward an actual social harmony, which makes the pragmatically helpful aspect of guidance its most important aspect, but it should be noted that they are also very appreciative of the beautiful cognitive formations of *li* (rite, principle) and sagely models of excellence. A Confucian would not say, "If you meet the Master, kill him." A Confucian would not throw the burden of pragmatic discernment so heavily onto the individual inquirer by saying, "Of whatsoever teachings thou canst assure thyself ..."[52]

*

The sense of pragmatic religious guidance can be thought of as a gateway to expanded happiness. It is filled out and verified later, when the aspirant actually makes progress or arrives at the desired ultimate state. The guidance indicates what may come by giving us a foretaste of the relevant happiness, as with Kongzi's conversations with his followers, or by pushing our response buttons strangely – figuring jewel-adorned lakes or a "gateless gate" – with the grounding of a comprehensible supreme appeal of optimal subjectivity, such as love or freedom from attachment.

Pragmatic religious guidance might be expected to make the most satisfactory sense by balancing well-understood ideals and procedures with mind-expanding, habit-loosening provocations. The Confucians and Buddhists take positions on opposite sides of this mean – the Confucians by strongly affirming traditional values and a code of conduct, the Buddhists by wrenching individuals free from family and self-reality. In China's postclassical religious history, the two teachings are often (not always) pitted against each other.

Most provocative of all, perhaps, the not-guiding guide Zhuangzi goes out of his way to say that he does not know the Way: "I go nowhere and

---

[51] Tung Chung-Shu, *Luxuriant Gems of the Spring and Autumn Annals*, in *A Sourcebook in Chinese Philosophy* (ed. Wing-Tsit Chan, Princeton University Press, 1963), p. 273.

[52] There are important passages in the *Lunyu*, however, that draw attention to a nontextual ultimate criterion of valid guidance: "The superior man bends his attention to what is radical. That being established, all practical courses naturally grow up. Filial piety and fraternal submission – are they not the root of all benevolent actions?" (1:2).

don't know how far I've gotten."[53] This makes him a borderline case of religious guidance. His judgments skip along next to an abyss of nihilistic caprice or mischief. Yet they have a preliminary guidance credibility insofar as we immediately feel delight in looking at things in Zhuangzi's unanchored, unresolved way ("Did I dream of being a butterfly, or did a butterfly dream of being me?").[54] If we embrace his noncommittalism as a form of religious guidance, we risk becoming disoriented, in trying to work out a coherent life shared with our fellow beings, or becoming complacent, if we conclude from the absence of a definite higher principle that the ideals we grew up with are no better or worse than anyone else's. Alternatively, we may embrace his text as a challenge to the very idea of religious guidance – opening an escape gate on the side of a sanctified Path so that one can get off it. This may provide relief from overbearing, dangerous Guidance.

4.5 TRANSCENDENCE OF LANGUAGE

There are powerful reasons in any religious perspective to draw a line beyond which language cannot express an important truth. It is a way of confirming the maximal expansiveness of the religious intention, and it can reinforce the ultimacy of the doctrinal suggestion that anchors a particular view. But it generates a contradiction between being oriented to the sublime divine and giving up on followable guidance.

For theists, the ultimate Being, God, is the Source of all, the Creator, and so must be in real continuity with the forms and existents that depend on God, including the words that count as divine guidance. If the existing world and the holy Word are indeed creations of God, both nature and revelation may be regarded as ladders dropped down by God; but we cannot mentally climb either ladder to find God, since the Creator of everything we can think of cannot be among thinkable things. Thus God is "this One, this Source of all unity, this supra-existent Being ... mind beyond mind, word beyond speech," according to Pseudo-Dionysius.[55]

---

[53] Zhuangzi, *The Complete Works of Chuang Tzu* (trans. Burton Watson, Columbia University Press, 1968), chap. 22 (HY 22/49), p. 241. HY citations refer to chapter and line number in the Harvard-Yenching text (ed. Charles Sturgeon, ctext.org/zhuangzi, 2006–2018).

[54] Ibid., chap. 2 (HY 2/94–96), p. 49 ("But he didn't know if he was Zhuangzi who had dreamt he was a butterfly, or a butterfly dreaming he was Zhuangzi").

[55] Pseudo-Dionysius, *The Divine Names*, in *Pseudo-Dionysius: The Complete Works* (trans. Colm Luibheid, Paulist, 1987), 588B, p. 50.

Scripture is most informative about God in saying or implying that God is not captured by reference.[56] Authentic awareness of God is an "unknowing."[57] But this is not the ordinary kind of ignorance in which we happen to be missing an opportunity to face something; it is an unknowing vis-à-vis the Source of all, which *does* engage that Source to the extent of being experienced as an illumination by it and an enabling of the most rewarding relationship with it.

For Pseudo-Dionysius, the ideal relationship with God is an ecstatic one.

> The human mind has … a unity which transcends the nature of the mind through which it is joined to things beyond itself. And this transcending characteristic must be given to the words we use about God. They must not be given the human sense. We should be taken wholly out of ourselves and become wholly of God, since it is better to belong to God rather than to ourselves. Only when we are with God will the divine gifts be poured out onto us.[58]

His mystical ideal of becoming wholly of God implies that he must leave the guide-guided relationship and the whole guidance arena of "salvation" behind.[59] The ladder of words, even if dropped by God, must be kicked away. *On* the ladder, still using words, we kick them, qualifying their meaning ecstatically: "Be exalted, O God, above the heavens!" (Psalm 57:11). Pseudo-Dionysius daringly says that God is "drunk" (as in Song of Solomon 5:1, "drunk with love"), standing outside of all good things.[60]

Apophatic theology has its own manifest articulacy supporting its effort to realize transcendence – whether in linkage with affirmative theology and the superlative "beyonds" of Pseudo-Dionysius or in Maimonides' more strictly negative mode of denying all attributes to God.[61] But it perplexes religious guidance by placing its "unknowing" affirmation of God on a different plane entirely than the plane of

---

[56] Pseudo-Dionysius also affirms that Scripture is richly informative in praising God for being responsible for all things in creation (596C–597A, p. 56) and in specifying primary noninterchangeable differentiations of divinity such as the Persons of the Trinity (637–640, pp. 58–61).

[57] 872A, p. 109. [58] 865C–868A, p. 106.

[59] "Salvation, benevolently operating for the preservation of the world, redeems everything in accordance with the capacities of things to be saved and it works so that everything may keep within its appropriate virtue." 897A, p. 114.

[60] Letter Nine, 1112B–C, p. 287.

[61] Moses Maimonides, *Guide of the Perplexed*, part 1, §§53–59. For Pseudo-Dionysius's own execution of the *via negativa* see *Mystical Theology*, chaps. 2–5.

canonical events and teachings. It gives reason to be a theist, or a Source-ist rather (since the notion of a personal deity is anthropomorphic), but no reason to be a Zoroastrian or Jew or Christian or Muslim except to show gratitude to the tradition within which one came to one's orientation to the Source, or just insofar as a tradition offers a practicable way of living as a Sourceist. Sourceists may well belong to a theistic, revelation-guided religious community, but they will have a divided mind about that community's ideology, philosophically negating it while pragmatically affirming it; that will be the Sourceist kind of religious reasonableness. Sourceists are bound to be at odds with the appellative guidance in that community that traces the relationship-instituting Call of the divine Other to an unsubstitutable divine transmission or incarnation. (Pseudo-Dionysius clearly regards Christian scripture as unsubstitutable, and yet no essential reason binds him to it; to a historically informed reader he seems to be using what he calls "the Divine Scriptures" as a convenient corroboration of his Neoplatonic emanationism.)[62]

Locutionary apophaticism was decisively shifted by Karl Barth into an appellative key in his early "crisis theology."[63] Barth named God "the Wholly Other" to open up a theological horizon beyond all human self-affirmation, the radical problem of justification of humanity and its religion. By the logic of the radical problem of justification, descriptive language can point to God only negatively, and pragmatic language can be used only supertentatively. "The road is most strangely defined almost entirely in negatives: but it is named the 'incomprehensible way of love'

---

[62] The priority of Pseudo-Dionysius's Neoplatonic conception is confirmed by what he says when he makes a theme of a divine call: "Beauty (*kallos*) bids (*kaloun*) all things to itself" (*Divine Names* 701D). The Divinity is the universal Final Cause toward which beings are drawn by desire. "One gets the sense that Dionysius, despite his dependence on a host of biblical passages [in *Divine Names*], represents a tendency to atomize the biblical text in the service of an overriding systematic concern." Bernard McGinn, *The Foundations of Mysticism* (Crossroad, 1991), p. 162. McGinn is among the scholars who argue that Pseudo-Dionysius succeeds in Christianizing Neoplatonism by affirming the immediate dependence of all beings on the One, but this idea is important in Plotinus also. Michel Corbin argues that "*Jesus is not a particular case of the naming of God, a contingent figure of a naming that would be conceived independently of him, but rather it is in and through him that any naming of God occurs. 'We see every hierarchy end in Christ'* (Pseudo-Dionysius, *The Celestial Hierarchy* 505A)" – quoted in Thomas Carlson, *Indiscretion* (University of Chicago Press, 1999), pp. 174–175. Still, it might be truer to say that Christ centers the Dionysian hierarchy because the hierarchy is presented as Christian than that the hierarchy is Christian because Christ centers it.

[63] See Karl Barth, *The Word of God and the Word of Man* (trans. Douglas Horton, Harper & Row, 1957) and *The Epistle to the Romans*, 6th ed. (trans. E. C. Hoskyns, Oxford University Press, 1933).

(1 Corinthians 12:31). Can this rightly be named a road? It is no road – which we can observe or investigate or even enter upon."[64] But in order to orient Christian theology to the Other's own Call as distinct from a speculative or mystical conception like the Neoplatonic One, Barth found it necessary to identify the Other with God's humanly effective self-revelation in Jesus Christ as attested in Christian scripture. It is *that* "Word" "which we do not say to ourselves and which we could not in any circumstances say to ourselves ... that smites us in our existence."[65] "The real experience of the man addressed by God's Word is the very thing that decides and proves that what makes it possible lies beyond itself."[66] While the divine Source of all, purely as such, cannot be equated with a human person or text, the Source's sense making or *unifying* of all (to borrow Neoplatonic language again) is concretely apprehensible uniquely and decisively in the scriptural Jesus Christ. That is the premise on which theology develops its distinctive insights and so guides the extraordinary Christian life. The division between abstract and concrete elements of guidance still forces an intellectual stretch, but the stretch is now made within a religious community's position, rather than creating a divided mind about that position.

The same principle seems to be at stake in a classic Islamic controversy about the Mu'tazilite thesis of the createdness of the Qur'an. Ibn Hanbal stood up to punishment from a caliph to affirm on the basis of the Qur'an's own language, in which God speaks first-personally, that the Qur'an is coeternal with God.[67] While Ibn Hanbal may come across as a dogged literalist in this episode, it is not so much literalism that is vindicated here as the principle that God's own guidance must be unique and unsubstitutable. "God's word is not separate from Him."[68] This is a way of preventing the detachment of theism from concrete revelations. If the Mu'tazila were right in treating the Qur'an as a case of God creating a speaking, then any speaking at all could be counted as God's speaking,

---

[64] *The Epistle to the Romans*, p. 239.

[65] *Church Dogmatics* I/1 (trans. G. W. Bromiley, T&T Clark, 1975), p. 141.

[66] Ibid., pp. 220–221.

[67] Ibn Hanbal's position is the majority Sunni position; the Mu'tazila affirmed and Shi'a still affirm the createdness of the Qur'an. Many Sunnis distinguish the created "utterance" of the Qur'an in Arabic from its uncreated meaning basis, a move that Ibn Hanbal did not accept. On this debate see Rein Fernhout, *Canonical Texts: Bearers of Absolute Authority* (trans. Henry Jansen and Lucy Jansen-Hofland, Rodopi, 1994), pp. 124–145.

[68] Ahmad ibn Hanbal, "Creed," in *Judaism, Christianity, and Islam*, vol. 2: *The Word and the Law and the People of God* (ed. F. E. Peters, Princeton University Press, 1990), p. 47.

and the real guidance of our designating one or another speaking as God's own speaking would come from our own conception of what God would say. Instead, the religious mind should unite the abstract and concrete elements of divine appeal in devotion to the Qur'an and its allied Jewish and Christian revelations, regarding them as both heavenly and human.

A good example of pragmatic apophaticism will be found in the Mahayana approach to the ultimate state of affairs – namely, *nonduality* as between positives and negatives and as between the ordinary and extraordinary worlds. The following passage from the Vimalakirti Sutra is set up by the stellar layman Vimalakirti having earlier demonstrated unrivaled spiritual insight and eloquence, leading us to expect at this point a climactic doctrinal takeaway:

> When the various bodhisattvas had finished one by one giving their explanations, they asked Manjushri, "How then does the bodhisattva enter the gate of nondualism?"
>
> Manjushri replied, "To my way of thinking, all dharmas are without words, without explanations, without purport, without cognition, removed from all questions and answers. In this way one may enter the gate of nondualism."
>
> Then Manushri said to Vimalakirti, "Each of us has given an explanation. Now, sir, it is your turn to speak. How does the bodhisattva enter the gate of nondualism?"
>
> At that time Vimalakirti remained silent and did not speak a word.
>
> Manjushri sighed and said, "Excellent, excellent! Not a word, not a syllable – this truly is to enter the gate of nondualism!"
>
> When this chapter on Entering the Gate of Nondualism was preached, five thousand bodhisattvas in the assembly were all able to enter the gate of nondualism and to learn to accept the truth of birthlessness. (Chap. 9)[69]

The sutra that is guiding us, though not silent, indicates Vimalakirti's silence, which points to the higher orientation; it is an open gate on a path of letting go of attachments and distinctions. (According to the Mandukya Upanishad, one can speak and yet leave syllables behind on the basis of the uniquely right syllable: in the prescribed four-part pronunciation of *Om* as *A-u-m-*, the fourth part is a silence.) Silence promises a blessed state. We are not there yet, so the meaning cannot be confirmed. But in following the guidance, we are headed there.

---

[69] *The Vimalakirti Sutra* (trans. Burton Watson, Columbia University Press, 1997), pp. 110–111.

PART II

PROBLEMATICS OF SCRIPTURE

5

What Is Scripture?

The Lord's City of Righteousness has virtue for its ramparts, fear of sin for its moat, knowledge for its gates, zeal for its turrets, faith for its pillars, concentration for its watchman, wisdom for its palaces. The *Basket of Discourses* is its marketplace, the *Supplementary Doctrines* its roads, the *Conduct* its court of justice, and earnest self-control is its main street. – Questions of King Milinda 5.5[1]

5.1 THE PHENOMENON OF SCRIPTURAL RELIGION

The premise of a supreme Text providing supreme Guidance has crucially informed the development within the last several millennia of a new, globally dominant version of religion that is commonly called "world religion." In a broad sense, all world religion is scripturalist; to use Wilfred Cantwell Smith's term, all world religion is in crucial part the product and continuation of a long-term collective activity of "scripturalizing."[2]

How does scripturalizing begin, and what is driving it? Some of the oldest components of existing scriptures show that early in the use of writing a religious thought process has already moved deeply into ritual and theological rationalization. There may not yet be scriptural canons, but priests and scribes are certainly gathering hymns, prescriptions, and oracles into collections. They are then in a position to form synthesizing

---

[1] In *Sources of Indian Tradition*, 2nd ed., vol. 1 (ed. Ainslie T. Embree, Columbia University Press, 1988), p. 113. The texts mentioned are the three "baskets" of the Theravada Buddhist scripture.

[2] Wilfred Cantwell Smith, *What Is Scripture?* (Fortress, 1993).

thoughts, as in the Rig Veda's relatively late creation hymns (late second or early first millennium BCE):

The sacrifice, which is extended in every direction by its warp threads and
    stretched out by a hundred and one acts of the gods –
these fathers who have traveled here weave that. They sit at the warp, saying,
    "Weave forth, weave back."
A man extends [the warp] and pulls it up (with the heddles); a man has extended it
    out upon the vault of heaven here.
Here are their pegs; they sat down upon their seat and made the saman-chants the
    shuttles for weaving.
What was its model, its image? What its connection? What was its melted butter?
    What was its frame?
What was the meter? What was the Praüga-recitation, what the hymn? – when all
    the gods offered the god [as the Sacrifice].
The gayatri meter became the yokemate of Agni. Savitar has united with the
    usniha meter
and Soma with the anustbh meter, gaining greatness through the hymns. The
    brihati meter helped the speech of Brihaspati.
The viraj meter is the full glory of Mitra and Varuna, and the tristubh meter is here
    Indra's portion of the (sacrificial) day.
The jagati meter entered the All Gods. According to this did the seers, the sons of
    Manu, arrange (the ritual).
The seers, the sons of Manu, our fathers, arranged (the ritual) according to this,
    when the sacrifice was born in ancient times.
Seeing with my mind as my eye, I think of the ancient ones who offered this
    sacrifice.
The courses (of the ritual were) joined with the praise songs, joined with the
    meters. The heavenly Seven Seers were joined with the model (of the rite).

(10.130.1–7)[3]

Along with synthesizing thoughts, there are deepening and distilling thoughts:

The non-existent did not exist, nor did the existent exist at that time.
There existed neither the airy space nor heaven beyond.
What moved back and forth? From where and in whose protection? Did water
    exist, a deep depth? ...
What existed as a thing coming into being, concealed by emptiness – that One was
    born by the power of heat. ...
Who really knows? Who shall here proclaim it? – from where was it born, from
    where this creation?

---

[3] Rig Veda quotations are from *The Rigveda*, 3 vols. (trans. Stephanie W. Jamison and Joel
    P. Brereton, Oxford University Press, 2014).

The gods are on this side of the creation of this (world). So then who does know
 from where it came to be?
This creation – from where it came to be, if it was produced or if not – he who is
 the overseer of this (world) in the furthest heaven, he surely knows. Or if he
 does not know ... ?

$$(10.129.1, 3, 6-7)$$

The hymn to the indeterminable One may be a compiler's reflection on
the implications of a body of tradition; it may be a passionate articulation
of responsible relation to the eternal, wrought with literary care; at
the same time, it may be a competitive sense-making proposal in a
discussion among colleagues working with the same data, an intellectual
winning move.

By the middle of the first millennium BCE, we see explicit competition
among proposals of ideal ultimates in all the civilization centers of the Old
World – most notably among prophets in Persia and in the Israelite
kingdoms, among early philosophers in Greece, among Brahmins and
Kshatriya intellectuals in India, and among classical Chinese thinkers.
Texts produced in this competition become core norming texts for the
world's leading scriptural and philosophical canons because they articulate reflectively unsurpassable conceptions of divine being – the monotheist God, Nature, Brahman, the Way – and life-unifying attitudes of
response – fidelity to ultimate righteousness, theoretical rationality,
unshakeable personal tranquility, constant social considerateness.

Karl Jaspers proposed to call the mid–first millennium the "Axial
Age," arguing that the true "axis" of humanity's spiritual history is not
the birth of Christ exclusively, as Hegel had said, but is shared by multiple
civilizations commonly arriving at a stage of formulating ultimate intellectual and spiritual ideals that become unavoidable guidance for any
thoughtful person.[4] (This sort of guidance is fascinatingly "axial" also in
the sense of offering a vantage point at the center of the turning wheel of
temporal experience. The Buddha said in his sermon at Benares that the
truth is the immoveable axle of salvific teaching.) Combining the ideas of

---

[4] Karl Jaspers, *The Origin and Goal of History* (trans. Michael Bullock, Yale University
Press, 1953), chap. 1. Jaspers took the term "axis" and its equivalent expression "origin
and goal" from Hegel's lectures on philosophy of history, signifying "the point in history
which gave birth to everything which, since then, man has been able to be, the point most
overwhelmingly fruitful in fashioning humanity" (1). See G. W. F. Hegel, *The Philosophy
of History* (trans. J. Sibree, Prometheus, 1991), p. 319. Hegel's word is "*Angel*," however,
rather than Jaspers's "*Achse* " – more the idea of a hinge or pivot.

Enlightenment and Classical Age, Jaspers emphasizes the insightful experience of the axial thinkers:

Man becomes conscious of Being as a whole, of himself and his limitations. He experiences the terror of the world and his own powerlessness. He asks radical questions. Face to face with the void he strives for liberation and redemption. By consciously recognizing his limits he sets himself the highest goals. He experiences absoluteness in the depths of selfhood and in the lucidity of transcendence.[5]

Jeremiah and Heraclitus and Kongzi, for example, all speak of a lonely but fatefully illuminating personal relationship they have with a principle that rules the universe (God, the Logos, Heaven). In the profound Indian debate that emerges at this time, the Upanishadic sage's indications of Brahman-absoluteness in the depth of Atman-self arise on the one side, and the Buddha's lucid transcendence of selfhood arises on the other. In China, the founders of philosophical Daoism, Laozi and Zhuangzi, ask the most radical questions conceivable about what can be named and known.

The new themes and methods are fostered by a new communicative situation. Although classical thinkers operate from a base in small countercultural groups and still with a very restricted audience, they capitalize on expanding literacy by offering textually recorded claims about the nature of reality, the world, and the human good on the premise that a mentally free individual can weigh the merits of any such claim against others in a competitive market for such proposals.[6] In the classic texts that represent this period, debates and discoveries are staged to acknowledge and reinforce this premise, sometimes opening fresh consideration of issues with the dramatic intervention of a prophet who is "no prophet, nor a prophet's son" (Amos 7:14) or a Kshatriya who teaches what no Brahmin knows (Brihadaranyaka Upanishad 6).[7] Partnership between humans and the divine is now anchored in the

---

[5] Jaspers, p. 2.

[6] The extent to which religious cultures actually sustain a competitive "marketing" of religious options varies considerably. For an illuminating use of this model in the Roman Empire, see John North, "The Development of Religious Pluralism," in *The Jews among Pagans and Christians in the Roman Empire* (ed. Judith Lieu et al., Routledge, 1992), pp. 174–193, and for tests of the model in multiple contexts, see *Religion and Competition in Antiquity* (ed. David Engels and Peter van Nuffelen, Latomus, 2014).

[7] All Hebrew Bible quotations are from *Tanakh: The Holy Scriptures* (Jewish Publication Society, 1985).

conscientious individual as such rather than in the ancestor or ruler (Jeremiah 31:33, Zhuangzi 4).[8]

The classical thinkers' individualism is in considerable tension with the communitarian agenda of traditional religion. Henceforth the appeal of religious teachings can no longer be merely traditional or ethnic or based on personal charisma. The new axial ways begin to divide into the genres we call "philosophy" and "religious teaching," with the philosophers focusing on free rational analysis and justification of views while the religious writers focus on directly proclaiming and explaining the ultimates or reflecting on actual experiences of them. The religious approach will be associated with stronger assertions of communal authority, but both approaches use the gambit of offering the mentally free individual, positioning him- or herself in relation to other mentally free individuals, a necessarily abstract but sufficiently articulated supreme appeal – a single attention-centering conception of ultimate Reality or Bliss or Righteousness, for example – and a cogently specified ideal for a sovereign attitude – a single life-centering orientation like Reason or Faith or Detachment.[9] While a scripture may contain much material that does not deal directly with such points, it will be thought (by those who think with it seriously) to center on material that does. For the individual, the supreme appeal is the end of the road of religious thoughtfulness. (For the community, in contrast, it is only one of the ends, along with other elements of organized religious life.)

To sum up, let us state a thesis on axiality: *In a historically revolutionary way, thought leaders have successfully appealed to mentally free individuals with reflectively ultimate life-guiding ideals concerning what to be oriented to (supreme appeal) and how to maintain the best orientation (sovereign attitude), thus capitalizing on expanded literacy and creating a long-lasting new regime of communicative action in which we still*

---

[8] "For this is the covenant that I will form with the house of Israel after those days, says the Lord: I will place My law in their midst and I will inscribe it upon their hearts, and I will be their God and they shall be My people" (Jeremiah 31:32). "By being inwardly direct, I can be the companion of Heaven. Being a companion of Heaven, I know that the Son of Heaven [the emperor] and I are equally the sons of Heaven." *The Complete Works of Chuang-Tzu* [Zhuangzi] (trans. Burton Watson, Columbia University Press, 1968), chap. 4 (HY 4/18), p. 56. HY citations refer to chapter and line number in the Harvard-Yenching text (ctext.org/zhuangzi).

[9] I develop this idea in *Appeal and Attitude* (Indiana University Press, 2005). Like Jaspers's conception of the Axial Age, it is anticipated by Max Weber's account of a formative rationalization process in the world religions. See Weber, *The Sociology of Religion* (trans. Ephraim Fischoff, Beacon, 1993).

live. Let us state also the corollary that *the new format of communicative action generates a difficult social problematic: to sustain a practically sufficient intellectual and spiritual consensus among mentally free individuals who are aware of multiple cogent options of commitment.* This is the postclassical problematic of "Christendom," the *ummah*, the *sangha*, and of community of belief in all world religions – and for some the problematic of multiscripturalism.

For communicative beings like ourselves for whom nothing important is resolved apart from guidance, optimism about identifying a supreme appeal and a sovereign attitude spills over into the strongest possible expectation of an ultimate Guidance on the strength of which these ideals would be realized. Thus a triple thesis is motivated about an ultimate Guidance, either in a confident mode or in a conditional hopeful mode: that it *exists* (or could exist), that it is (or would be) *accessible*, and that it is (or would be) *full*. This teleological thought is best unpacked in reverse order.

The Guidance must be *full* to be sufficiently powerful and reliable. It must provide all needed theological and anthropological information for the rectification of life. If it is textual, it must consist of a very rich set of texts offering directives that make sense for beings with our emotional and intellectual needs, and it must allow generations of interpreters to address newly experienced aspects of the human situation. It must hold the answers to all relevant questions.

The Guidance must be *accessible* to us so that we who attend to it, together with whoever else we are responsible to, can participate in this guidance relationship understandingly. If it involves "revelation" of otherwise inaccessible thoughts or facts, this revelation must be communicated in a way that is humanly appreciable – say, by divine accommodation to human limitations, and perhaps by the allegorical presentation of higher truths beneficial to those who have ears to hear them. (To assure fullness and accessibility, a scriptural culture typically maintains three bodies of sacred text: a primary scripture thought to contain all essential data, a secondary scripture thought to provide all necessary solutions in principle for interpretive problems raised by the primary scripture, and a supplementary literature of commentaries, doctrinal codifications, theological analyses, and classic expressions of spirituality.)

Supposing that the full and accessible Guidance could actually *exist* has important implications when we try to think through the conditions of that possibility. A scripturalist would ask: *How else* than by scripture could all the theological and anthropological information needed for the ultimate rectification of life be rendered accessible to everyone, to different people differently according to their capacities and needs, in an axially reasonable religious community? An individual might claim to have received an ultimate life orientation from falling in love, reading an evocative poem, having conversations with a wise elder, or observing what plants and animals do through the seasons, but such a claim could be adequately explained and defended in a religiously communicative community only if it could be seen to tally with benchmarks established by a historically well-developed, rigorously curated conversation on the great religious issues concerning supreme appeal and wholesome attitude. What we call "scripture" is the accessible record of precisely those benchmarks. (This line of thinking will be developed further in considering the scriptural mediation of religious concepts in Section 5.5.)

5.2 THE AXIAL BREAK AND SCRIPTURAL LAYERING

Because axial ideals are extraordinarily abstract and are retailed by a dramatically direct appeal to individual hearers, a shift between axial and preaxial thinking occurs very noticeably within the older scriptural collections. Notwithstanding that the Vedas, the Hebrew Scriptures, and the Chinese classics all embody a commitment to long-term continuity overriding the axial/preaxial difference, the relationship of materials from different regimes of communicative action is an unavoidable axial concern in these and other scriptural traditions.

Tzu-lu asked how one should serve ghosts and spirits. The Master said, Till you have learnt to serve men, how can you serve ghosts? (*Lunyu* 11:11)[10]

A strong discontinuity thesis about axiality would assert that once axial ideals appear, *they* alone are the intellectually and spiritually relevant ideals, and it is strictly *their* cogency for diverse audiences over time that accounts for the continuing ideal relevance of an intellectual or spiritual tradition. Preaxial material is a backdrop of merely historical interest; nonaxial thinking is either irrelevant or antagonistic (at best, a useful foil) to axial thinking. Philosophy that does not conceive itself as religious presumes discontinuity, claiming the axial revolution for itself. (Plato encourages this stance in his harsh rejection of Homeric theology – not,

---

[10] *Lunyu* quotations are from *The Analects of Confucius* (trans. Arthur Waley, Vintage, 1938).

though, in his reworking of myths for his own purposes.) To the contrary, a continuity thesis about axiality would assert that axial ideals are cogent for a historically old, mentally diverse community because they can be harmonized with preaxial practices and perspectives. Generally the continuity thesis is supported by religious philosophers and by the scriptures themselves. It is also a strong proposal in religious history (Bellah's "nothing is ever lost").[11]

Another way to state the issue is in terms of two nearly opposite meanings of "revolution." The axial "revolution" can be seen as an overturning and replacement, but it can also be seen, more in keeping with the rationalized traditionalism of most of the scriptural Axial Age thinkers, as a coordination of older commitments with newer prospects allowing all our cultural assets to revolve around a stable central axis.[12] This axis might coincide with the intellectual and spiritual position of scripture; scripture might play the functional role (not uniquely or exclusively but characteristically) of the axle needed to maintain this kind of revolution – the axle of axiality. On that supposition, whoever decides to break entirely with older cultural commitments, as on the radical wings of the ancient and modern enlightenments, must oppose not only particular traditions but the very premise of axial revolution in the sense of an inclusive cultural harmony.

Axiality understood as a strategy of continuity would also support the idea that the power of spiritually impressive ideals depends on their imaginative and emotive rootage in historically older sources – Brahman as everything's living Reality derived from brahman as priest-managed

---

[11] One of Robert Bellah's main theses of intellectual-spiritual history is that human capacities and orientations corresponding to every important stage of human history, from small nomadic bands through the archaic state and into literacy and modernity, are demonstrably conserved in the fabric of our life. *Religion in Human Evolution* (Harvard University Press, 2011), p. 267. It is a separate question, explicitly raised by Bellah, whether or under what conditions all these elements can work together to our satisfaction. "The Heritage of the Axial Age: Resource or Burden?" in *The Axial Age and Its Consequences* (ed. Robert Bellah and Hans Joas, Harvard University Press, 2012), pp. 447–467.

[12] "While the axial age certainly produced many of the foundational 'isms' that have since shaped the world, and in many ways must be seen as 'revolutionary,' what characterizes axial thought is at the same time something very different: a respect for and indeed a return to 'tradition.' What unites such diverse figures as Lao-Tse, Confucius, Buddha, Socrates and Plato – besides the fact that they more or less lived in the same period – is their search for the unchanging, and their insistence that human beings cannot, and should not, create everything anew ... the spirit of axial thought was deeply antirevolutionary, and involved a personal conversion away from the excess [of greed and hate in] ... the ecumenic [imperial] age." Bjorn Thomassen, "Anthropology, Multiple Modernities and the Axial Age Debate," *Anthropological Theory* 10 (2010), 337.

power, Tian (Heaven) as the cosmic law derived from Tian the royal "great man," Zion as communal perfection derived from Zion as the central strong point Israel took from the Jebusites and lost to the Babylonians.[13]

We can see something of how this works in scripture by comparing shift points in the Vedas and the Hebrew Scriptures that exhibit the reorienting power of the axial proposals. Both involve revision of the ideal of sacrifice.

Sacrificial ritual, a linchpin of religion in preaxial agriculturalist societies, is elaborately described and rationalized in some of the older layers of the Vedas and in the biblical book of Leviticus. The conscious purpose of sacrificing is to do the best that can be done to attain the greatest attainable well-being for sacrificers and their community, "that you may live upon the land in security" (Leviticus 25:18).[14] It is the highest prudence. When the Mundaka Upanishad takes up the topic, the unwary reader may at first feel reassured that the system works:

Here is the truth: The rites that the wise poets saw in the Vedic formulas,
Stretched in many ways across the three Vedas –
Perform them always, you who long for the Truth;
That's your path to the world of those who correctly perform the rites.
When the flame flickers after the fire is lit,
Then let him make his offerings, between the two pourings of ghee ...
"Come! Come!" say the oblations shining bright, as they carry their offerer on the sun's rays of light.
They praise him, telling him flattering things: "This is yours, this *brahman*'s world [*svarga*, 'heaven'], built by good deeds and rites well done."

(I.2.1–2, 6)[15]

---

[13] Paul Ricoeur followed this linkage in axiality in attacking Rudolf Bultmann's disjunction between meaningful "kerygma" and no-longer-credible "myth": "Cosmic symbolism does not die but is instead transformed in passing from the realm of the sacred to that of proclamation. The new Zion prophetically inverts the reminiscence of the sacred city, just as the Messiah who is to come projects into the eschatological future the glorious royal figures of divine unction ... the existential breadth of this [salvific ethical] decision is preserved against all the insipidities and banalities that its profane transcription threatens to produce only if, at the same time, the older symbolic depths of death and resurrection, of the return to the maternal womb and rebirth, are reactualized. Would the word 'conversion' continue to signify anything if we absolutely lost sight of what was expressed in these symbols of regeneration, new creation, and the advent of a new being and a new world? I think not." "Manifestation and Proclamation," in *Figuring the Sacred* (trans. David Pellauer, Fortress, 1995), pp. 66–67.

[14] On religious sacrifice in general see R. L. Faherty, "Sacrifice," in *Encyclopedia Britannica*, 15th ed., vol. 16 (Encyclopedia Britannica, 1974), pp. 128–135.

[15] Upanishads are quoted from *Upanishads* (trans. Patrick Olivelle, Oxford University Press, 1996).

So far, so good: the sacrificer gains a heaven (or is "flattered" to think so). Suddenly a different view rears its head:

> Surely, they are floating unanchored, these eighteen forms of the sacrifice, the rites within which are called inferior.
> The fools who hail that as the best, return once more to old age and death …
> Deeming sacrifice and gifts as the best, the imbeciles know nothing better.
> When they have enjoyed their good work, atop the firmament, they return again to this abject world.
> But those in the wilderness, calm and wise, who live a life of penance and faith, as they beg their food;
> Through the sun's door they go, spotless, to where that immortal Person is, that immutable self.
> When he perceives the worlds as built with rites, a Brahmin should acquire a sense of disgust – "What's made can't make what is unmade!"
>
> (I.2.7, 10–12)

The text has now asserted a new Upanishadic ideal of supreme tranquility realized in a supreme immutable Self. Priestly sacrifice is surpassed – yet not completely rejected. Traditional guidance is modulated to a new key. Rather than give up a goat or a horse for the sake of higher goods and enjoyment, one should give up desire itself; rather than give up shorter-term for longer-term happiness, one should detach oneself from the whole temporal pursuit of happiness and dwell only in the imperishable.

A similarly profound critique of sacrifice occurs in the prophetic book of Amos, long recognized for its early statement of ethical monotheism:

> [Thus says the LORD to Israel:] I loathe, I spurn your festivals,
> I am not appeased by your solemn assemblies.
> If you offer Me burnt offerings – or your meal offerings –
> I will not accept them; I will pay no heed
> To your gifts of fatlings.
> Spare Me the sound of your hymns,
> And let Me not hear the sound of your lutes.
> But let justice well up like water,
> Righteousness like an unfailing stream.
>
> (5:21–24)

The sacrificial cult is not simply thrown out in this context, either, but its positive meaning is made conditional on a more fundamental requirement of righteousness, sometimes portrayed by the Hebrew prophets as the fruit of an inward sacrifice that reconstructs the self:

> With what shall I approach the LORD,
> Do homage to God on high?
> Shall I approach Him with burnt offerings,

With calves a year old?
Would the LORD be pleased with thousands of rams,
With myriads of streams of oil?
Shall I give my first-born for my transgression,
The fruit of my body for my sins?
He has told you, O man, what is good,
And what the LORD requires of you:
Only to do justice
And to love goodness,
And to walk modestly with your God.

(Micah 6:6–8)

A conspicuous power of the ideal of Immutability or of Justice is that you or I could lift it out of the text that presents it and apply it as we see fit. But the continuity thesis speaks for the specifically scriptural cogency of the axial ideals being embedded in their cultural context with their historical precursors. To be a disciple of Upanishadic tranquility is still to be required to go to one's guru with firewood for sacrifice in hand (Mundaka U. I.2.12–13). To be a disciple of the ethically demanding God of Israel is still to be embedded in the festivals and solemn assemblies of the people. The sacrificial cult is accepted as part of the route to the axial realizations, both as a historical reality of membership in a community's shared action and as a pedagogical strategy for arriving at the crucial understanding in the best way.

Axial formulations have the same "broken" yet continuous relationship with the older narrative material of myths and folktales. For example, there is testimony in Vedic and Hebrew scriptures alike to a dragon-slaying chief god who makes the world habitable – Indra in the Vedas, Yahweh in the Bible.

Now I shall proclaim the heroic deeds of Indra, those foremost deeds that the mace-wielder performed:
  He smashed the Serpent. He bored out the waters. He split the bellies of the mountains. (Rig Veda 1.32.1)

Thou didst crush Rahab like a carcass, thou didst scatter thy enemies with thy mighty arm. (Psalm 89:10)

But the portrait of the conquering god is variously adjusted in later texts for axial purposes. In Chandogya Upanishad, Indra becomes the student of a more authoritative figure, Prajapati, for the sake of developing a spiritual lesson.

Prajapati said: "That is the Self, this is the immortal, the fearless, this is Brahman" ...

Now Virokana, [the bad student,] satisfied in his heart, went to the Asuras [demons] and preached that doctrine to them, that the self (the body) alone is to be worshipped, that the self (the body) alone is to be served, and that he who worships the self and serves the self, gains both worlds, this and the next ...

But Indra, [the good student,] before he had returned to the Devas [gods], saw this difficulty. As this self (the shadow in the water) is well adorned, when the body is well adorned, well dressed, when the body is well dressed, well cleaned, if the body is well cleaned, that self will also be blind, if the body is blind, lame, if the body is lame, crippled, if the body is crippled, and will perish in fact as soon as the body perishes. Therefore [he said] I see no good in this (doctrine). (Chandogya Upanishad 8:7–12)[16]

In the book of Job, Yahweh's relation with the monster Leviathan is set on a different plane than mythical combat – "though the sword reaches it, it does not avail" (41:26) – in order to contemplate, via the extended metaphor of the crocodile, the supremacy of God in a world where evil is structurally inescapable and functional:

> Can you draw out Leviathan with a fishhook,
>   or press down its tongue with a cord? ...
> Any hope of capturing it will be disappointed;
>   Were not even the gods overwhelmed at the sight of it?
> No one is so fierce as to dare to stir it up.
>   Who can stand before it?
> Who can confront it and be safe?
>   – under the whole heaven, who? ...
> Its heart is as hard as stone,
>   as hard as the lower millstone.
> When it raises itself up the gods are afraid;
>   at the crashing they are beside themselves.
> Though the sword reaches it, it does not avail ...
> On earth it has no equal,
>   a creature without fear.
> It surveys everything that is lofty;
>   It is king over all that are proud.
>   (Job 41:1, 9–10, 24–26, 33–34)

The book of Job has a takeaway idea that can be stated without reference to Yahweh or Leviathan, but the layering of axial over mythic content is obviously essential to the meaning of the text as received by an audience for whom Yahweh, the personage dominating Israelite history, is the

---

[16] Similarly, in the Buddhist *Dhammapada*, Indra is made an exemplar of *appamadena*, awareness or earnestness (2.10).

accountable core of the monotheistic God, who is in turn the accountable core of reality. Less obviously, the layering may be essential even to the generally appreciable ultimate sense of the takeaway idea. If there had not been an imagining of the contest between powers for good and bad at the highest level of agency – think also, in this tradition, of the liberation from Egypt – would rational reflection have been forced to discern a structural economy of good and evil in the world?

In comparison with the Vedic and Hebrew scriptures, the Confucian classics seem to have filtered older material more severely for the sake of teaching matters of political and ethical principle. We are shown the great powers as conquerors by virtue rather than force, ideal patterns to emulate, especially King Wen and the Duke of Zhou in their classic transfer of the Mandate of Heaven from the Shang dynasty to the Zhou. But stories of conquest are presupposed nonetheless, centrally that of the Zhou:

> King Wen is on high,
> Oh, he shines in Heaven!
> Zhou is an old people,
> but its Mandate is new.
> The leaders of Zhou became illustrious,
> was not God's Mandate timely given?
> King Wen ascends and descends
> on the left and right of God.
>
> August was King Wen,
> continuously bright and reverent.
> Great, indeed, was the Mandate of Heaven ...
> Was [the number of Shang royalty] not a hundred thousand?
> But the High God gave his Mandate,
> and they bowed down to Zhou.
> (*Shijing* [Classic of Poetry] 235.1, 4)[17]

Kongzi celebrates an older legendary king by almost completely neutralizing his physical action:

The Master said, Among those that "ruled by inactivity" surely Shun may be counted. For what action did he take? He merely placed himself gravely and reverently with his face due south; that was all. (*Lunyu* 15:4)

The layering of axial over older narrative content seems essential here too. If all we knew of Shun were that he faced south, he would be an arbitrary

---

[17] Trans. Burton Watson in *Sources of Chinese Tradition*, 2nd ed., vol. 1 (ed. William Theodore de Bary and Irene Bloom, Columbia University Press, 1999), p. 38.

sign of an ideal of hierarchy or rectitude or tranquility. Since we have heard of his great actions, including his work in mythic time with China's flooding problems, the extra move of reducing his rule to facing south is more potent.

The younger scriptural traditions that begin with axial teachings do not dispense with mythic support; they fill it in from older sources, as the Qur'an fills in its own versions of the biblical creation and flood stories and as Buddhist and Daoist scriptures appropriate holy sites and divine agents and miracles from Indian and Chinese lore. The layering may frame a new realization about an older authoritative point of reference, such as in realizing a local god as God or a bodhisattva or in moralizing a flood myth; or it may simply serve to provide the interesting imaginative grip on transhuman parameters of action that myths had always been providing, as flood myths had placed human life in the larger natural cycle of dissolution and regeneration.[18]

I propose an ideal model of scriptural layering, loosely inspired by the apparent facts of historical sequence of composition in the major traditions, to highlight principal aspects of the guidance work that each layer does:

(1) *Powers.* Any community's traditional stories figure the greatest good and evil powers in the world. This is a primary cosmic theme of what we call myth. Scripture takes over myth's function of clarifying who and what we have to deal with, reading a world order out of their relations. Because scripture is a text that can be studied and questioned critically (despite all the exalting and mystifying treatment a scriptural text may have received), a premium is placed on coherence – for example, the coherence of reducing gods to one God or placing divine beings in a celestial hierarchy or organizing the people's constituent tribes in a sacred genealogy. Even the historically compressed Qur'an was obliged to work through an issue at this level in the affair of first affirming and then denying the intercessory "daughters of Allah" enshrined in the old Kaba.[19]

(2) *Principle.* This is the layer of the axial breakthrough, with statements of general principle focusing supreme appeals and sovereign

---

[18] See Mircea Eliade, *Patterns in Comparative Religion* (trans. Rosemary Sheed, University of Nebraska Press, 1996), §72 "Deluge Symbolism," pp. 210–215.

[19] The "Satanic verses" speaking positively of Lat, 'Uzza, and Manat as intercessors are said to have been deleted from 53:19–22.

attitude ideals. Its main effect is to rationalize the scene of life and guidance in a boldly simplifying (and thus profoundly issue-raising) way. Ultimate religious *conceptions* like the Abrahamic God and the Chinese Heaven are metaphysical transmutations of personalities that had earlier been mythicized. Comprehensive and deep, they are not ostensible beings at all (or they become ostensible only in extraordinary circumstances that are not rationally explicable, as in the Christian Incarnation).

> The True One pervadeth all things.
> All things come to pass as the Lord ordaineth.
> He who hath understood the Divine Will
> Recognizeth only the One Reality
> And he alone is what man ought to be.
>
> The Lord, being Unknowable, cannot be comprehended.
> But the Guru hath given me
> A sweet joy of His Presence.
> Kabir saith: My doubts have departed from me.
> In all things I have recognized the Taintless One.
> (Guru Granth Sahib, *Rag Prabhati* 24)[20]

(3) *Community development.* Building on the mythic and axial heritage, later additions to scripture will show how to provide fully for the cognitive and pragmatic needs of the scriptural community. Within the Qur'an we can place the practical rulings of the Medinan surahs in this layer.

Insofar as historical layering combines older with younger texts representing multiple genres, serving purposes of tradition maintenance and popular education together with advanced guidance for reflection, scripture can be said to acquire a "polyphonic" fullness of guidance.[21]

[20] In *Selections from the Sacred Writings of the Sikhs* (trans. Trilochan Singh et al., Allen & Unwin, 1960), p. 215.

[21] On biblical polyphony see Paul Ricoeur, "Naming God," in *Figuring the Sacred* (trans. David Pellauer, Fortress, 1995), pp. 223–228. To appreciate the polyphony, it is necessary to "put in parentheses the properly theological work of synthesis and systematization" – "Toward a Hermeneutic of Revelation," in *Essays on Biblical Interpretation* (ed. Lewis S. Mudge, Fortress, 1980), p. 92. Karl Jaspers objected to the ideal unification of the Christian Bible, locating the spiritual power of the Bible in its diversity of perspectives and contradictions. *Philosophical Faith and Revelation* (trans. E. B. Ashton, Harper & Row, 1967), p. 333.

5.3 THESES ON AXIALITY

I submit that the major ideas of Axial Age thinkers are inescapably interesting and relevant to us – to anyone who might read these words – because we too find ourselves in the communicative situation of literate cosmopolitans. We conduct ourselves as though each of us is mentally available to be persuaded by the best available world- and life-organizing ideas, and these ideas reach us through published, discussable, adoptable, portable proposals. At the same time, we are positioned and funded cognitively by historical communities. Thus we are embroiled in the difficulties inherent in sustaining a partly voluntary community of individuals whose free choices must be compatible and whose historic basis for concord will certainly contain not only great principles but also troubling legacies from the past like sexism, classism, and cultural chauvinism. These are the main dimensions of the axial situation.

The supposed new quality of axiality seen in the ideals of the Axial Age has been the subject of widely varying interpretation and debate.[22] Is its key element reflexive self-awareness? Critical thinking? Theoretical world modeling? Post-magical "disenchantment"? World-rejecting transcendentalism? Is any such element definitely present across multiple cultures or in one or more distinct phases of human history?[23] These issues form an extensive agenda for scholarly discussion that will be relevant to the general phenomenon of scripture and the characters of the different scriptures. But the basic principle of axiality that is most broadly helpful in orienting our consideration of scripture here is just the premise of literate cosmopolitanism, presupposing an expansion of elite literacy beyond the craft of temple and palace scribes and of commoners' literacy beyond everyday pragmatic uses. The axial proposal in essence is that there can be a literate, fully informed, freely critical address of what is of overriding importance for life that is carried out on a basis of inclusive communal consensus.

The idea of axiality is connected to the general idea of an itinerary of cultural development incorporating some sort of enlightened classical

---

[22] John D. Boy and John Torpey, "Inventing the Axial Age: The Origins and Uses of a Historical Concept," *Theory and Society*, 42 (2013), 241–259.
[23] See the papers in *The Origins and Diversity of the Axial Age* (ed. S. N. Eisenstadt, SUNY Press, 1986), and in Bellah and Joas. A good discussion of China issues is David L. Hall and Roger T. Ames, *Anticipating China* (SUNY Press, 1995).

phase. For our purposes it does not matter whether axial thinking first appeared in the middle of the first millennium BCE, as in Jaspers's account, or where it first appeared. It may have begun in the second millennium BCE (as Jan Assmann argues for Egypt), and it may still have been brewing up in the time of the Qur'an and farther into the Common Era.[24] The extent to which axiality has a standard profile is subject to study; I think we should admit that it has assumed significantly different forms with different philosophical and social implications, no one of these manifestations being uniquely full or decisive for world history (contrary to what has been claimed by Havelock and others for Greek culture).[25] It does matter greatly for our understanding of axiality that we view it as a potential development of the communicative situation in any linguistic community, which gives plausibility to Jaspers's important contention that axiality is a multicultural creation and asset rather than one culture's brilliant imposition on the world.

Axiality is not the whole essence or explanation of scripturalism. The phenomenon of scriptural religion is a large complex of sociocultural formation and literary and intellectual development, both active and reactive, and scriptural components have widely different assumptions, styles, purposes, and circumstances of origin. Nevertheless, the recorded debates and teachings of the Axial Age prophets, sages, and philosophers are of specially great interest in making sense of the scripturalism phenomenon, partly because they and their later analogues have in fact exerted a magnetic power necessary for generating and sustaining this form of religion and partly because they are central in the phenomenon's ideal relevance to *us*, as shown by our continuing experience of what powerfully informs an argument or enlivens a discussion. *We* are most likely to take a religious proposal seriously if it is in the axial form; *we* are

---

[24] Jan Assmann, "Ancient Egypt and the Theory of the Axial Age," in *From Akhenaten to Moses* (American University in Cairo Press, 2014), pp. 79–94; Josef van Ess, "Islam and the Axial Age," in *Islam in Process* (ed. Johan P. Arnasson et al., Transaction, 2006), pp. 220–237.

[25] See, e.g., Eric A. Havelock, *The Muse Learns to Write: Reflections on Orality and Literacy from Antiquity to the Present* (Yale University Press, 1986). Havelock credits the Greek alphabet with "providing the sole instrument of full literacy to the present day" – "The Oral-Literate Equation: A Formula for the Modern Mind," in *Literacy and Orality* (ed. David R. Olson and Nancy Torrance, Cambridge University Press, 1991), p. 26.

most likely to take ancient stories or laws seriously (or indeed any stories or laws) if we can see a connection with ideas of the axial type; *we* are most likely to use or play off of scriptural forms when we want to make a resonating point.

That in brief is the rationale for an axiality thesis about the scripture phenomenon. Such a thesis can be maintained independently of many other possible theses concerning the form and causation of axiality. The main axiality thesis will be worth considering in several different aspects:

(1) As a genetic factor, the mode of literacy we call "axial," involving overt intellectual competition and individualized critical thinking in awareness of major intellectual and spiritual options, was a necessary condition for the rise of scriptural religion, as was also the need and desire for cultural benchmarks that could be respected as classical or axis-defining.

(2) The axial orientation and content of core scriptural texts is necessary for their ideal relevance. Their supreme appeals and ideals are convincing conclusions in thoughtfully addressing our life situation, including its extraordinary dimensions.

A third, sociocultural form of the thesis recognizes the destabilizing powers of classical teachings and of individual literacy:

(3) In referring to what I have called the axial situation, "axiality" names a cultural problematic in which literate communities are obliged, on the one hand, to reconcile their evolving views and practices with classical touchstones and, on the other hand, to harmonize the ever-varying views and practices of their individual members, all while the appeals of generally accessible classical writings reinforce the mental independence of some of their most influential members. Individuals are kept on the same page by their community's scripture, but scripture contains many pages and supports many readings. The composition and conduct of the more actively literate community within the larger literacy-influenced community are subject to continual negotiation. That we are caught up in this problematic ourselves is one of our strongest reasons to try to come to terms with what scriptures manifest and imply about axiality.

A specific version of the sociocultural axiality thesis was memorably formulated by Ibn Rushd to make sense of the fact that no society is axial in the sense of being wholly on the same intellectual and spiritual level as an axial thinker. Ibn Rushd asserted that in society as he knew it, and by implication in every postclassical society, there is a philosophically minded class that works to meet the axial challenge, an ideological class that is satisfied by persuasive arguments, and a nonintellectual class that forms its beliefs by imagination rather than reason.[26] (The Qur'an itself frequently appeals to "people who understand," implicitly discriminating between those who go for the rational kernel of a teaching and those who are content to hold a shell.)[27] That these three classes arrive at formally different understandings of religious matters is an important consideration in determining what scripture says, since a defensible interpretation for philosophers (concerning the Qur'an's promises of heavenly bliss for believers, for example) may be unworkable for dogmatic theologians and incomprehensible to the masses. And yet a world-religion community is viable only if its three constituent classes are in meaningful consensus.

Many contemporary societies have a much better system of universal education than Ibn Rushd could have expected to see, but even with broadened access to the most enlightened education, it is foreseeable that any human community will be stratified in something like the way Ibn Rushd described. Unless a strong selection filter has been applied, even a population of smart college students will be stratified in something like this way, indicating that the differences are not caused only by socioeconomic factors or intelligence levels. This may be a species misfortune or a salutary natural diversification of human sensibilities. Be that as it may, a community informed by axiality must continuously deal with this harmonizing challenge. Ibn Rushd would say that scripture plays an indispensable role in keeping the philosophers, ideologues, and common people in religious union, because it provides suitable directives compatibly to all three classes. He gets crucial help here from the theory of allegory, first developed for Abrahamic monotheism by Philo and Origen, which posits that scriptural texts present truth often on more than one of several different planes of meaning – literal, rational, and spiritual – corresponding to the human powers of ordinary perception, rational

---

[26] Averroës (Ibn Rushd), [*The Decisive Treatise*] *On the Harmony of Religion and Philosophy* (trans. George Hourani, Gibb Trust, 1961).

[27] E.g., at 2:164 and 10:24. Qur'an quotations are from *The Study Qur'an* (ed. S. H. Nasr et al., HarperCollins, 2015). The "kernel/shell" language comes from Ibn 'Arabi in *The Meccan Revelations*, quoted by William C. Chittick, "Ibn al-'Arabi's Hermeneutics of Mercy," in *Mysticism and Sacred Scriptures* (ed. Steven T. Katz, Oxford University Press, 2000), p. 166.

reflection, and religiously formed insight.[28] A text about eating fruit and meat in Heaven may not make literal sense to one reader, who must derive guidance from a rationally deciphered or religiously transfigured meaning, while another reader may receive compatible guidance from the same text in an utterly literal-minded way – the crucial common-denominator idea being that respect for the world-unifying divine makes for the highest happiness. Or so an optimist about axial harmony would suggest.

5.4 TOWARD AN ADEQUATE GENERAL CONCEPTION OF SCRIPTURE

In the happiest cases of comparative study, we find that in thinking back and forth between things that seem to be members of a class, we reach a new and improved understanding not only of our comparands but of our very terms of comparison. Thanks especially to W. C. Smith's framing of the global "scripturalization" phenomenon, we are in a position to reap such rewards now in the category of scripture.

For English speakers, the Latinate word "scripture" designates a special category of authoritative writings. The authority of these writings will be sufficiently tamed for purposes of examining them comparatively, I think, so long as we distinguish little-s "scripture" and "scriptures" from the capital-S "Scripture" that would refer just to one tradition's revered Text. We may let the Latinism of the term remind us of the fact that a scripture can be sequestered in a language of privilege not

---

[28] This version of allegory theory comes from Origen, *On First Principles* (trans. G. W. Butterworth, SPCK, 1936), 4.2.4: "One must portray the meaning of the sacred writings in a threefold way upon one's own soul, so that the simple man may be edified by what we may call the flesh of the scripture, this name being given to the obvious interpretation; while the man who has made some progress may be edified by its soul, as it were; and the man who is perfect and like those mentioned by the apostle: 'We speak wisdom among the perfect; yet a wisdom not of this world nor of the rulers of this world, which are coming to nought; but we speak God's wisdom in a mystery, even the wisdom that hath been hidden, which God foreordained before the worlds unto our glory' (1 Corinthians 2:6–7) – this man may be edified by the spiritual law, which has 'a shadow of the good things to come' (Hebrews 10:1). For just as man consists of body, soul, and spirit, so in the same way does the scripture, which has been prepared by God to be given for man's salvation" (275–276). Origen did not always apply the same scheme; see Henri de Lubac, *History and Spirit: The Understanding of Scripture according to Origen* (trans. Anne Englund Nash, Ignatius, 2007), chap. 4.

understood by many who are subject to its regulation – a major unhappy irony on the normative world-religion conception of scripture.

Because of the pervasive problem that Western cross-cultural scholarship tends to construe its objects and define its terms in ways that impose Western conceptions, often by privileging a normative style of literacy, it may be objected that "scripture" is a fatally biased category. (A similar objection is made to "religion" and "world religion.") But there are good reasons to continue to use the term "scripture" in comparative studies despite the danger: (1) there is, in fact, growing acceptance of a genuinely generic meaning of "scripture" that includes many significant ingredients shared across traditions; (2) we do not have a better alternative than "scripture" in an English-speaking context, as the denotations of "canon," "sacred text," and "classic" are variously too broad; and (3) we should not disguise the live issue of ultimate life guidance by avoiding the term's strong religious charge.[29] There is also the linguistic advantage that the terms "scripturalizing," "scripturalism," and "scripturalist" turn out to be very useful in exploring various dimensions of the phenomenon.

The phenomenon of scripture really is multicultural. The categories of Veda, sutras, and *jing* are not projections or echoes of Western "scripture," despite their often being framed that way in Western or Westernizing venues; they are robust counterparts. Consequently, our understanding of the Bible or the Qur'an must be informed by how they resemble or fail to resemble their non-Abrahamic counterparts so that we can appreciate how each is a particular version of scripture, not the patent-holding prototype. Comparative perspective is enlarging and humbling, not automatically leveling and imperialistic. (Yet no comparison can be absolutely fair. There is no "View from Nowhere.")

It is widely known that each of the so-called world religions has its own scripture. With our expanded use of the category of scripture comes, on the one hand, a horizontal enlargement of our awareness inflecting our general notion with ever more anthropological difference but, on the other hand, a vertical heightening of our awareness of the Guidance issue, encouraging the philosophical expectation that what any of these scriptures says will be *worth* pondering, given its presumed power to direct human life. As a supreme kind of religious classic, a scripture has a universal interest that accredits its sponsoring religion as a "world"

---

[29] Miriam Levering, Introduction to *Rethinking Scripture* (ed. Miriam Levering, SUNY Press, 1989), p. 6; William C. Graham, "Scripture as a Spoken Word," in Levering, p. 140.

religion more meaningfully than the simple demographic fact of having a large number or wide distribution of adherents. In the large literate world, any scripture is globally relevant – relevant somehow to each of us, and to each of us positioned in relation to everyone else, in the dimension of life guidance despite our varying temperaments and circumstances. How it *should* be relevant is a matter for rational evaluation and thus for philosophy. But philosophers who accept the challenge of determining the ideal relevance of scripture face a complex challenge of reasonable construal in view of the different possibly viable strategies of interpretation and justification of scripture in each tradition.

Without sufficient comparative learning and critical testing, the category of scripture can be badly misconceived. Paradigms drawn from sources that happen to be more familiar to us can lead us astray. For example, the popular Christian assumption that scripture is the word of God would be hugely distorting if applied to the nontheistic Confucian scriptures, while the Confucian idea that scripture transmits the virtue of ancient sage-kings could be applied to only a small part of the Bible.[30] Once such differences are pointed out, we properly become more cautious about generalizing. Yet the general phenomenon remains, as does the human situation at its base. To ignore the category of scripture would be to refuse to recognize important differences writing and reading are typically associated with in religious life[31] and generally would insulate received understandings of scriptures from being challenged by new comparative hypotheses.

On the descriptive side of religious studies, a notion of scripture is needed that is broad enough to register functional and spiritual similarities between the Bible, the Qur'an, the Vedas, the Guru Granth Sahib, and the various canons of Buddhists, Jains, Daoists, and Confucians, along with any other textual mediations of religious life that appear to follow much the same pattern. We want the fullest possible specification of that pattern, and we want to see its range of instantiations through space and time. For this purpose, our general definition should not be too narrow (as in "word of God"), but neither should it be so broad ("sacred text") that it misses the historical emergence of scripture as an

---

[30] Within a religious perspective that is committed to conceiving divine revelation as the word of God, there may be compelling *theological* reason to construe all divine guidance in this way; see Jacques Dupuis, S.J., *Toward a Christian Theology of Religious Pluralism* (Orbis, 1997), pp. 244–253, on how non-Christian scriptures may be regarded as containing a non-plenary, non-decisive "word of God."

[31] See Section 3.3, note 11.

intellectually and spiritually decisive religious asset for a relatively large community, a major new vector taking over some or all of the traditional power of holy persons and rituals to relate ordinary people compellingly to an Ultimate. There are a host of significant descriptive questions about scripture that our definition should not foreclose but rather should set us up to discuss, both specific and general. For example: Did the New Kingdom Egyptians have scripture?[32] When and how did the Torah begin to be scripture?[33] Is the Yoruba Odu Ifa on a path of global publication and authoritative use comparable to other scriptures?[34] When Buddhists characterize their sutras as linguistically ordinary and pragmatically instrumental, in deliberate contrast with a Hindu exaltation of divine Vedic scripture, are they varying the concept of scripture, or are they challenging the very premise of scripture?[35] When Hindus prioritize holy sound over semantic meaning, are they (intentionally or not) removing the Vedas from the category of scripture?[36] Are there replacements for scripture in modern culture?[37] How have core religious concepts – divinity, God, Brahman, nirvana, Heaven, the Way, soul, karma, faith, love, piety, righteousness, church, *sangha*, tradition, scripture itself – been conditioned by their scriptural formation?

We cannot feel reasonable confidence that we are asking the right questions about the right data, however, until we have clarified our

---

[32] Jan Assmann, *From Akhenaten to Moses.*

[33] Bernard M. Levenson, "The Development of the Jewish Bible: Critical Reflections upon the Concept of a 'Jewish Bible' and on the Idea of Its 'Development,'" in *What Is Bible?* (ed. Karin Finsterbusch and Armin Lange, Peeters, 2012), pp. 377–392.

[34] Maulana Karenga, *Odu Ifa: The Ethical Teachings* (University of Sankore Press, 1999).

[35] José Ignacio Cabezón discusses how Buddhists can take the special spiritual utility of their scriptures very seriously without looking to them for a peremptory "inspired" validation of religious claims. *Buddhism and Language* (SUNY Press, 1994).

[36] "In the oral transmission through recitation sound is all that counts. The words have to be handed down in exactly the same form in which they have been heard. There is no tradition for the preservation of meaning, a concern regarded as a mere individualistic pastime. The Brahmins' task is more noble: to preserve the sound for posterity, maintain it in its purity, and keep it from the unchecked spread and vulgarization which attaches to the written word." Frits Staal, "The Concept of Scripture in Indian Tradition," in *Sikh Studies* (ed. Mark Juergensmeyer and N. Gerald Barrier, Graduate Theological Union Press, 1979), p. 122. See also William A. Graham, *Beyond the Written Word* (Cambridge University Press, 1987), chap. 6, and Barbara A. Holdrege, *Veda and Torah* (SUNY Press, 1996), pp. 220–221, 414–416.

[37] Wesley A. Kort argues that in Western modernity, scriptural reading was extended to nature, history, and literature, each competing with and then supplanting the Bible. *"Take, Read": Scripture, Textuality, and Cultural Practice* (The Pennsylvania State University Press, 1996), chap. 2.

evaluative interest. What counts as a significant similarity or difference depends on what we want to find. What then is at stake for us in what we make of scripture? Both for honesty's sake and to support discussion of the ultimate meaningful attractors and standards of reasonableness in the study of religion, our definition of scripture should also reflect our thought that any scripture at least in part lends itself to a construal that might seriously engage any reader anywhere in the vein of ultimate life guidance. A philosophically useful definition will build on the prima facie interest scriptures hold for any reader and will open doors toward ideas worth considering about why and how scripture holds such interest. The axiality thesis regarding scriptural content is a clarifying idea on this front.

To advance our preliminary characterization of the field of reference, I will now offer a minimal list of essential features of scripture. The stipulations are not uncontroversial, but I believe they usefully pick out issues and ideas that deserve cross-culturally descriptive and rationally evaluative attention.

(1) As regards form, scripture (from Latin *scriptura*, "a writing")[38] is fixed, published, and communally enshrined utterance. It is firmly in place, awaiting all comers like a temple – a temple made of language that you and I, the interpreters, can enter anywhere, anytime.

In practice, a scripture does not exist solely in the space of ideas; its subscribing community is obliged to renew its oral and aural presence regularly.[39] But the large, diverse, potentially universal community associated with scripture is possible only because scriptural content does lodge in the minds of individuals. Scripture capitalizes to the greatest possible extent on the capacity of texts to guide the thought and practice of individuals as well as communities. Although communal rituals assure its transmission and standing, it can affect lives in many other ways on many other occasions because it has been released to individual receivers.

I refrain from defining scripture as "written" in consideration especially of the Vedas, which are thought to have existed on a purely oral basis for most of their career. The oral processes that produced the Vedas were evidently not inferior to scribal processes in developing and fixing

---

[38] On the semantic history of *scriptura* and related words, see William A. Graham, "Scripture," in *The Encyclopedia of Religion*, 2nd ed. (ed. Lindsay Jones, Macmillan, 2005), pp. 8196–8197.

[39] On the oral and aural aspects of scripturalism, see Graham, *Beyond the Written Word*.

content and sustaining critical reflection on content.[40] Thus our focus should be on the properties of a corpus of repeatable utterance regardless of whether it is written down.[41] We should be mindful, too, that the Brahmins had weighty religious reasons not to write scripture down lest it be reduced to mere information and released to faulty interpretations.[42]

Nevertheless, there is a real tension in the notion of "oral scripture." One can pertinently ask whether the oral Vedas would be better viewed as pre- or proto-scriptural rather than as a full-fledged example of scripture, given that they were closely held by a literate elite. (In the first millennium BCE, Sanskrit was a specialized priestly language.)[43] Should they count for us as priestly lore rather than scripture, given our world-religion conception of scripture as a platform for a diverse community? Should we accept the argument made in certain Puranas (officially considered secondary scripture, *smriti*) that they are more important than the Vedas

---

[40] For reasons to think that writing played an important role in Vedic composition, see Jack Goody, *The Interface between the Written and the Oral* (Cambridge University Press, 1987), chap. 4. For a review of recent scholarship pointing mostly the other way, see Paul Griffiths, *Religious Reading* (Oxford University Press, 1999), pp. 34–39.

[41] Even the Qur'an's great emphasis on "writing" and "book" as formats of revelation does not necessarily refer literally to a written version of scripture, argues Daniel A. Madigan in *The Qur'an's Self-Image* (Princeton University Press, 2001).

[42] See Graham, *Beyond the Written Word*, pp. 73–74, and Thomas B. Coburn, "'Scripture' in India," in Levering, pp. 104–105. Because the Zoroastrian scriptures were not written down for many centuries either, W. C. Smith speaks broadly of an oral/aural "Indian and Iranian mode of what the West has called scripture," influencing the Qur'anic tradition of oral recitation as well (49–50). On priestly resistance to writing down the Zoroastrian scriptures, see Mary Boyce, *Zoroastrians* (Routledge & Kegan Paul, 1979), p. 50; on why "the Veda" as knowledge should not be turned into "the Vedas" as texts, see C. Mackenzie Brown, "Purana as Scripture," *History of Religions*, 26 (August 1986), 69–73; on classical rabbinic misgivings about the "decoding written text" type of reading or "informational reading" as distinct from memorized recitation with validation by a written text, see Rebecca Scharbach Wollenberg, "The Dangers of Reading as We Know It: Sight Reading as a Source of Heresy in Early Rabbinic Traditions," *Journal of the American Academy of Religion*, 85 (September 2017), 709–745; on resistance to writing down oral Torah because it should remain proprietary to Israel, see Steven D. Fraade, "Concepts of Scripture in Rabbinic Judaism: Oral Torah and Written Torah," in *Jewish Concepts of Scripture* (ed. Benjamin Sommer, NYU Press, 2012), p. 39; and on early debates about writing down Qur'an and hadiths, see Madigan, pp. 27–28, and Gregor Schoeler, *The Oral and the Written in Early Islam* (trans. Uwe Vagelpohl, Routledge, 2006), pp. 111–141. Aleda Assmann and Jan Assmann note a common pattern of delaying the use of writing in handling culturally definitive traditions – "Schrift," in *Historisches Wörterbuch der Philosophie*, vol. 8 (ed. Joachim Ritter and Karlfriend Gründer, Schwabe, 1992), p. 1418.

[43] On the history of the use of Sanskrit in India, see Sheldon Pollock, *The Language of the Gods in the World of Men* (University of California Press, 2006).

in our darkened age because they are written down and thus able to reach and help many more people?[44] I think it is an important fact that the Upanishads of the mid–first millennium BCE display a cast of participants in discussion significantly expanded beyond Brahmins to include certain women and Kshatriyas, implying a more public Vedic appeal. But is it even more telling that many centuries later we find Shankara still maintaining a ban on sharing Upanishadic wisdom with the Shudra class – a ban that to this day is upheld by many orthodox Brahmins?[45] However we answer these questions, by now the Vedas have become undeniably one of the benchmark scriptures in our world, thanks to cogent interpretation of the Rig Veda and Upanishads and the supplements provided by popular non-Vedic texts.

(2) As regards content, the distinctive power of scripture lies in providing guidance embraced by a community, guidance of the most profound practical interest and unlimited practical relevance in that community. This Guidance is taken as commanding, exhorting, advising, inviting, even teasing, but in any case *decisive* – in some way necessary and in some way sufficient – for ultimate human success.[46] (Whether the texts must be viewed as *perfect*, and whether such perfection can be insisted upon without causing distortive interpretation, is debatable.[47] But some sort of completeness claim is inherent.) A scripture-embracing community sponsors for the generality of its members a textually guided conversation about right thought and action in relation to the best human outcome and

---

[44] Brown, "Purana as Scripture." Brown notes that the claim is implied also in a late passage of the Mahabharata (76). The written revolt against Brahminism may have been instigated by Buddhists (78–79).

[45] Commenting on Uttara Mimamsa Sutras I.3.33–39. See Francis X. Clooney, *Theology after Vedanta* (SUNY Press, 1993), p. 138.

[46] Depending on how they are specified, these presumptions of necessity and sufficiency may force a conflict between scriptural guidance and general demands of reason. A complacently exclusivist necessity thesis stops interreligious conversations before they can start: members of other communities cannot have the crucial clues. An undiscerning sufficiency thesis leads to John Wyclif's frightening limitation of the horizons of all research: "I do not think it is right for us to admit any science or conclusion to which Scripture does not bear witness." *On the Truth of Holy Scripture* (trans. Ian Christopher Levy, Medieval Institute, 2001), p. 129.

[47] Nicholas Wolterstorff argues that inerrantists are bound to make a "wax nose" of the scriptural text, subverting the Guidance of divine discourse as they bend its meaning however seems necessary to save its truth on the level of the appropriated human discourse. *Divine Discourse* (Cambridge University Press, 1995), pp. 227–229. Cabezón notes a suspect flexibility in Buddhist reconciliations of scriptural texts on the premise that divergent texts must variously be using "skillful means" to advance readers to enlightenment (95).

sponsors for those of its members who are so inclined a scripturalist mode of devotion in which performing and pondering Scripture is a primary way of relating to the divine and attaining the best orientation in life.

Guidance is an advantageous central notion in a general account of scripture for several reasons. (a) Recognizing scripture as the Guidance places it perspicuously in the development and economy of human linguistic guidance as one of its most ambitious realizations. (b) The commonly held notion that scripture establishes a "worldview" is framed in an appropriately religious way: a religious worldview is not simply *in place*, like the modern worldview, or simply *available*, like Romanticism, but solicits the world-viewing mind as the *possibly requisite* view for self and community. The believer holds that view not simply on its ostensible merits but *as Guided*.[48] (c) The notion of guidance is broad enough to accommodate scripturalists whose focus is on ritual or moral practice together with those whose focus is on true representations or a dialectic of interpretations; it works equally well for those who suppose they are hearkening to a personal Guide who communicates by means of the text and those for whom some other sort of reality, perhaps just the text itself, is the ultimate shaper of Guidance; and it works for those whose attention is captured by an extraordinary numinous quality in their scripture together with those who regard their scriptural directives pragmatically as the best available textual helps toward the best living. (d) Recognizing scripture as guidance puts the center of our thinking right where the action of thoughtful religious life is, in experiences of appeal and deliberations of response. Students of the text can acknowledge the scriptural appeal's significance as a live option without taking a devotional plunge. (e) As a bonus, "guidance" is the preferred self-categorization of the self-consciously scriptural Qur'an, which W. C. Smith regarded as the culmination of a major scripture-defining phase of religious history.[49]

(3) The actual community of scripture, though historically and culturally specific, is conceived as expansive and potentially universal. A guiding text relevant only to a small, homogenous, or fixed group would count merely as a manual or charter for that group. Thus the

---

[48] On scripture as establishing a worldview, see Biderman, pp. 81–85. Biderman's way of recognizing scripture as Guidance is to argue that fact and value meanings are consistently "entangled" together in religious texts (89–96); see Section 6.6, pp. 232–234.

[49] E.g., 2:2, 2:185, 3:138, 16:64. The Qur'an also frequently refers to its special benefit of "making clear" (e.g., 16:64, 16:89, 26:2). The concept of guidance can apply to both admonition and explanation. W. C. Smith's judgment: *What Is Scripture?* p. 47.

covenant recorded between the ancient Israelites and their god YHWH is a type for a Jewish version of scripture only because the Israelite scheme has become interpretable as a model of righteous comportment with directive force that anyone can feel. (This is not to say that any scriptural community must proselytize – only that any scriptural community can make compelling sense of its spirituality to any audience.)

Negatively, it seems possible and desirable to keep certain other features out of the definition.

(1) Although scriptures are often associated with supernaturalist beliefs about the origination of the component texts, the quality of scriptural text, the effects of heeding it, or the subject matter to which it gives privileged testimony, they need not be.[50] Naturalism is a mainstream option in Confucian scripturalism and cannot be excluded in many other traditions. Scripturalists are conceptually required to take cues somehow from past cultures represented in their texts but not to believe in supernatural beings or miracles that were formerly believed in.

(2) Scriptures can serve as the paramount recordings of Guidance in their communities without being the sole or supreme authorities in those communities. The general notion of scripturalism can be distinguished from a narrower, polemically pointed *sola scriptura* program; even enthusiasts for *sola scriptura* may insist that their Guide is not actually the scriptural text but rather a divine being for whom scripture serves as a uniquely valid instrument of communication. The role of scriptures in religious life may be dictated by rituals or other vectors.[51] The religious guiding force of other, non-scriptural texts may be more important in certain situations.

---

[50] From a history of religions perspective, Gustav Mensching claims that scriptures are always believed to be of divine origin (*Das Heilige Wort* [Röhrscheid, 1937], p. 71), but the justification of that claim would have to be circular – to wit, the many old forms of Indian and Chinese scripturalism that do not make that assumption would have to be disallowed. (Mensching's book almost completely ignores Confucianism and Daoism.) In any case, the issue of greater interest here is whether divine origin is a necessary assumption for a scripturalist now. Admittedly there is a sense in which any text that counts as Guidance must be informed by divinity.

[51] Kendall W. Folkert distinguished a "Canon I" pattern in which scriptures are vectored by other religious elements and a "Canon II" pattern in which scriptures are more independent, sometimes acting as a primary vectoring element. Both patterns are exhibited in Christianity. "The 'Canons' of 'Scripture,'" in Levering, pp. 170–179.

(3) Nor is a scripture necessarily regarded as uniquely valid. South and East Asian scripturalists often express great respect for scriptures not their own.[52] The Qur'an, though famously "matchless," claims to be continuous with prophetic revelations all over the world and to be closely associated with Jewish and Christian scriptures.[53] In making some scriptural comparisons, it may not be appropriate to ask which among their "conflicting truth-claims" could be true, because not all scripturalists claim to receive truth in that conflictable sense in their guidance from scripture.[54]

(4) Scriptures are always given the form of canons, for the sake of knowing where the requisite Guidance is to be found, but scriptural canons are not necessarily closed in principle, despite the advantages of being able to delimit the Guidance and to solve all interpretive problems by exegeting a limited base of information.[55] Nor are canons uniformly prescriptive. Readers of scripture commonly make strategic decisions about what within the larger body of scripture will function operationally as their Guidance.

---

[52] Gandhi is a famous example of Hindu appreciativeness of other traditions – not uncontroversial among Hindus, but not out of the mainstream either: "I regard my study of and reverence for the Bible, the Koran, and the other scriptures to be wholly consistent with my claims to be a staunch *sanatani* [orthodox] Hindu ... I find the Hindu scriptures to satisfy the needs of the soul. My respectful study of other scriptures has not abated my reverence for or my faith in Hindu scriptures. They have indeed left their deep mark on my understanding of the Hindu scriptures" – *Young India* 9/2/26, quoted in K. L. Seshagiri Rao, *Mahatma Gandhi and Comparative Religion*, 2nd ed. (Motilal Banarsidass, 1990), p. 134.

[53] The Qur'an's statements on its own uniqueness (e.g., 11:13, 17:88) are tied to the immediate struggle to accredit Muhammad's revelations as divinely authentic and decisive for their audience in a way that other Arab poets' and soothsayers' utterances were not (69:40–43). The Qur'an often asserts continuity with earlier Abrahamic revelation (e.g., 3:3, 4:135, 5:48).

[54] For an analysis of the "conflicting truth-claims" aspect of religious pluralism, see John Hick, *An Interpretation of Religion*, 2nd ed. (Yale University Press, 2005), chap. 20. Jan Assmann argues that Abrahamic traditions are informed by an absolutist conception of supreme appeal, a "Mosaic distinction" between true religion and paganism first formulated by Akhenaten (*Of God and Gods* [University of Wisconsin Press, 2008]). Assmann worries that the Jaspersian conception of axiality as a privileged true consciousness uncritically repeats this universalist move with its intolerant implications. "Cultural Memory and the Myth of the Axial Age," in Bellah and Joas, pp. 366–407.

[55] On the sometimes strong interest in a manifest completeness of scripture, see Johannes Leipoldt and Siegfried Morentz, *Heilige Schriften* (Harrassowitz, 1953), chap. 4; on canon-based exegesis see Jonathan Z. Smith, "Sacred Persistence: Toward a Redescription of Canon," in *Imagining Religion* (University of Chicago Press, 1982), pp. 36–52.

(5) It is true that strong claims are made in certain traditions for the unique excellence of scriptural language, but in historical and comparative perspective, one sees no linguistic quality that could be considered necessary in a scriptural text.[56] If one wants to say with W. C. Smith that scripture is a distinctive mode of language, the distinction must be located in scripture's *function* – according to Smith, the function of supporting human "involvement in transcendence."[57] Scriptures are composed out of preexisting textual materials of various qualities and genres that in many cases were not conceived as scriptural when they were first produced.[58]

The question of scripture's genre is important, as genre determines appropriate expectations of a text. I think the notion of supreme textual religious guidance puts us in a position to say more about it than Smith says in his very abstract proposition about transcendence. But Smith is right that scripture's genre determination is orthogonal to the kind of genre distinction we make between poetry and prose, even though it takes advantage of the genre-specific powers of its constituent texts.

5.5 THE SCRIPTURAL FORMATION OF AXIAL CONCEPTS

It is a fact of cultural history that the perceived meaning of scriptures depends on axial concepts. There is arguably a related truth of equal importance concerning the essential scripturality of the axial concepts – namely, that their commanding intellectual and spiritual interest and their cultural and transcultural negotiability are inseparable from their scriptural formation. The concepts can be taken seriously and can do serious work for us because they have been baked in a scriptural oven. Much as a good chef understands how oven-baked items differ from boiled or fried, a student of religion should understand how scripturally formed notions differ from notions formed by other means.

The ideal relevance of the historical preparation of a key concept is appreciated by scholars in their disciplines. Consider the concept of

---

[56] Surveying the wide variety of texts considered scriptural, Graham concludes: "The 'scriptural' characteristics of a text belong not to the text itself but to its role in a community. 'Scripture' is not a literary genre but a religio-historical one" ("Scripture," p. 8195). But see Section 5.5, p. 168 on Northrop Frye's claim regarding the application of certain powers of language in the Bible.

[57] W. C. Smith, p. 231.

[58] See the excellent discussion by John B. Henderson in *Scripture, Canon, and Commentary* (Princeton University Press, 1991), chaps. 1–2.

subjectivity in philosophy. "Subjectivity" is a word in the dictionary that anyone can use, but a philosophically serious treatment of the concept must be cognizant of its development from Descartes's "I think" forward, with a number of major idealist enrichments and counter-idealist challenges. This development is canonical, which is a short way of saying that a claim addressing or implicating the nature of subjectivity will be seen as most likely to be worthy of consideration in philosophical research (the current conceptual research we think most likely to inform future conceptual research) if the conception it uses has been tested by the relevant major arguments of modern philosophy. We might call this the dialectical formation of the concept. When we take a concept to be the product of the most developed relevant dialectic, we suppose that it is, for now, charged with the right content and inescapably relevant in whatever discussions it might properly come up in.

Scriptural concepts are dialectically formed as well. Earlier, I picked out a couple of highlights in the intrascriptural development of the concept of sacrifice; we could have looked also at logically earlier and later elements.[59] As in the philosophy example, the dialectic is created partly by the accumulating contributions of writers working with the ideas of earlier writers and partly by later teachers and editors who arrange textual selections into a normative itinerary that serious thinkers are guided to adopt as part of the infrastructure of their thinking. (Scriptures vary a good deal in how this shaping process takes place and how it is represented in the text. Compared to the largest canons, the Qur'an is a sudden blast of a single thought – and yet the Qur'an is famous for having been revised by the removal of unacceptable verses.) The most serious religious discussion, much like the most serious philosophical discussion, repeatedly verifies the results of the scriptural dialectic by rehearsing it.[60]

Intertwined with the dialectical development of key concepts, a scripture might also incorporate rhetorical discoveries permitting distinctly powerful ways of identifying a supreme Appellant or involving the

---

[59] Earlier in the development would be, for example, sacrifice as a deal-sealing rite in agreements between individuals or groups (see, e.g., Genesis 15:7–21); later would be sacrifice as the self-surrender of the fully devoted lover (see, e.g., *Bhagavad-Gita* 9:29–31).

[60] There are paradigms of such discussion within scriptures – for example, the review of the debate between the Mosaic and Davidic conceptions of God's covenant with Israel in 1 Kings 9:1–9; the progression toward a personal conception of the Real in Shvetashvatara Upanishad I.1–3; the *Mengzi*'s encapsulation of the development of the concept of Heaven in V.A.5.

audience in relation. To use that language, whether or not in conscious loyalty to a scriptural tradition, is to think scripturally insofar as scripture remains its paradigmatic deployment. Even the brief expression "Oh my God!" (Psalm 22:2) depends on two crucial linguistic developments in the Bible noted by Northrop Frye: metonymic use of the term "God" to refer to an Appellant understood as transcending all possible concrete description,[61] and a proclamatory idiom of existential concern. Despite conveying little in the way of ordinary content, saying "Oh my God!" summons up important aspects of an evolved consideration of human and superhuman reality. A deity that cannot be addressed by this expression will fail a crucial test for theists. Anyone trying to gauge the meaning and viability of this expression had therefore better be aware of its scriptural genesis and refinement.

Another way in which scripture can set benchmarks for a serious discussion of a religious topic is in representing the experiences that most strenuously demand consideration. This point can be illustrated with the association of the concept of God with the so-called problem of evil.

In my own religious culture, "God" is a standard topic to the extent that I can enter into a reasonable conversation with nearly anyone about whether a "supreme being" exists (or intervenes or has particular concerns). Nearly anyone I meet is likely to have his or her own view concerning the existence or nature or conduct of a personalizable supreme being. This view need not have been gleaned from a scripture. A religiously uneducated person might have picked up the notion of God simply by osmosis, having heard people mention God in various real and fictional contexts; a thoughtful person might have formed an understanding of "God" by reflecting on the causation of the universe or the authority of values. No matter: the concept has a connection with scripture in the *prospects* for a conversation about God – where that conversation can go and with what seriousness of results. Admittedly such conversations often go almost nowhere, remaining conceptually vague and lacking significant support or application. God can be summarily affirmed or denied simply as a way of expressing a general optimism or pessimism about life, or (reversing the values) as a way of limiting or expanding the horizons of natural science. In a more serious conversation, however, the concept will be seriously tested.

---

[61] Northrop Frye, *The Great Code* (Harcourt Brace Jovanovich, 1982), chap. 1.

Often the reality of evil is brought up with the understanding that it is the most serious or one of the most serious of all tests of the very thinkability of God. It is stipulated that a God worth discussing must be powerful, wise, and good to such a degree that the undeniable evil in our world makes God incredible. Theism depends, then, on being able to make sense of God's engagement with an evil-ridden world.

What should count as the kind of evil that makes this a serious discussion? Pain, death, inhumane treatment? What *should* disturb us that much, in that way? One can turn to a theist scripture at this point and be taught how to specify both God and evil. The Hebrew Bible points out murder and persecution as primary evils; moreover, its historical dramatization of the relationship between God and humanity offers understandings of God and evil tested by experiences of intense suffering. In my culture, a serious discussion of God is very often drawn into the biblical formation of the meanings of God and evil (especially in the collective ordeals of the Israelites and the personal ordeals of David, Job, and Jesus) because biblical material, to those who know it, seems unsurpassably relevant to the development and testing of our understandings of these points of reference.[62]

But suppose the God discussion stays clear of biblical material because the discussants are ignorant of the Bible, or actively want to disconnect from a biblical framing they see as unhelpful (as in rejecting the term "the Holocaust"), or are more interested in non-biblical points of reference such as modern experiences of sexist and heterosexist oppression. A well-informed listener would still judge the discussion by biblical benchmarks. It would seem serious in part because it either converges with the biblical terms of discussion or appears to match those terms. For example, a feminist repudiation of God would seem serious to a well-informed listener only if it premised a supreme causality not less worthy of consideration than the biblical God and an evil not less disturbing than murder and persecution as biblically condemned.

One might object that scriptural religion, though undeniably of great influence de facto in the cultures in which most of us are raised, cannot be granted cultural authority de jure, given that one can step clear of any religious tradition, precisely for the sake of thinking as seriously as possible, and construct a rationally purified religious ideal. Is that not

---

[62] For a very conscious reckoning with biblical touchstones in contemporary philosophy of religion, see Eleonore Stump, *Wandering in Darkness: Narrative and the Problem of Suffering* (Oxford University Press, 2010).

just what Plato and Aristotle did? I deny, however, that Plato and Aristotle stepped or could have stepped entirely clear of traditional religious utterances while having their theological proposals register as worthy of religious consideration. For they, too, were necessarily subject to the listener's test of comparative relevance and depth; their conceptions, too, had to engage recorded traditional wisdom concerning human failure and unhappiness.

Another reason to deny that Plato's and Aristotle's works exist outside of a scriptural context lies in their own textual accomplishment. By assiduously publishing their newly powerful, revisionary conceptions, the leading Greek philosophers turned out to be the climactic scripturalists of classical Greek culture, supplying in texts the supreme ideals by which everything else in their tradition would henceforth be evaluated.

5.6 SCRIPTURAL AUTHORITY

Enshrined by a community as Guidance, scripture possesses an authority over its devotees that might be seen through a Durkheimian lens as a textual implementation of the community's power to control the minds of its members. That Jürgen Habermas viewed social evolution through a Durkheimian lens in his *Theory of Communicative Action* may help to explain why he granted scriptures no role whatever in his account of the "linguistification of the sacred," a historic shift from archaic social norming by collectively maintained myth and ritual to modern social norming by the communicative action of reflectively self-conscious actors freely pursuing mutual understanding.[63] This is an odd omission given that literacy, understood in a strong sense as the active use of individual mental independence supported by reading and writing, is at the heart

---

[63] Jürgen Habermas, *The Theory of Communicative Action*, vol. 2 (trans. Thomas McCarthy, Beacon, 1987), pp. 47–62, 77–111. See also his paper "Toward a Reconstruction of Historical Materialism," in *Communication and the Evolution of Society* (trans. Thomas McCarthy, Beacon, 1976), pp. 130–177, where he cites Jaspers's Axial Age (151–152) and sketches a break between "early" and "developed" civilization based on the appearance of "postconventional legal and moral representations" (157). Habermas later expresses a positive view of the Axial Age civilizations as supporting moral autonomy in *The Future of Human Nature* (trans. Hella Beister, Max Pensky, and William Rehg, Polity, 2003), p. 40, and by implication acknowledges a "wider semantic potential" of scriptural content in public reasoning in Habermas et al., *The Power of Religion in the Public Sphere* (Columbia University Press, 2011), pp. 28, 115.

of the modernization of consciousness and culture that Habermas is concerned with; literacy is an essential ingredient of scripturalism; and scripturalism is a major historical agent in expansions of literacy. To relegate scripturalism to archaic groupthink would be to miss a main part of the linguistification story.

It is true that scriptural religion can operate much in the style of preaxial religion when the intentional community of believers coincides with the local or ethnic community. Scripture can be taught repressively and studied in a completely conformist spirit. But that is not the only form of scripturalism that obtains historically, and it is certainly not the scripturalism that would be a live option for a rational inquirer now. Any use of reading and writing that lacks critical thinking, that provides no remedy for heteronomy and the colonizing of minds, will seem to us a sadly stunted realization of literacy. On the axiality thesis concerning scripture, free questioning is essential to scriptural devotion because scripturality is constituted in part by the published text's affirmation of the mental freedom of individuals. Thus scripturalism cannot be deemed essentially "authoritarian" with the usual negative implications of arbitrary imposition and blind compliance.

But scripture is understood to be eminently authoritative in some sense. What then is its authority, best construed, and how does it possess and exercise this authority?

Scripture possesses outstanding axial *interest*, on the present account, because its content and mode of presentation support supremely responsible encounter with a supreme appeal. But scripture is also more than a reliably powerful "classic" (in the usual Western sense of that term) or "great book."[64] A translation of the *Daodejing* might be life changing this week for a particular reader whose life was changed last week by Daniel Quinn's *Ishmael*; such a reader can respond to the *Daodejing* as a classic or great book without being minded to respect its instituted scriptural status. Yet that sort of instituted status gives the *Daodejing* a distinct importance in principle such that Daoists are obliged to prioritize it and literate people around the world will be obliged to take account of it throughout the foreseeable future. So our conception of scripture should include a consideration about how a religiously instituted text is not

---

[64] See David Tracy's nonauthoritarian account of scripture as "religious classic" in *The Analogical Imagination* (Crossroad, 1981), pp. 108, 160, 163, and Krister Stendahl's rebuttal (making the authority point) in "The Bible as a Classic and the Bible as Holy Scripture," *Journal of Biblical Literature*, 103 (1984), 3–10.

merely the prompt or portal for a religious experience but a commanding illocutionary act in a communicative drama.[65]

That the Hebrew, Sanskrit, and classical Chinese scriptures contain some of the oldest surviving texts in the world has long been a bragging right for those cultures.[66] While few would wish to argue today that older thoughts and statements are necessarily better ones, temporal priority in discourse is still a significant consideration in organizing communication into a whole. If we view the diachronic extension of our community's communications as a historical growth significantly like a conversation in which touchstones are continually being established for what can relevantly be said, we will want to determine which of the things said earlier are most important to keep track of for our most important purposes. Scripture speaks to this question as no other kind of text does. Scripture's conversation-framing role is foundational, like that of a political constitution or body of law, except with the special charge of governing the whole conversation about getting life right. Regardless of when they were actually uttered or recorded, scriptural utterances count ideally as the first things said, the most original Dicta, capable of warranting or correcting subsequent utterance. In a scriptural community, all religiously significant utterances can be ordered in an ideal larger conversation according to the relevance and propriety implications of such dicta.

The choice and the experience of scriptural dicta cannot be arbitrary or merely convenient for someone, obviously, but their authoritative grounding cannot be provided by the axial ideals alone, immediately interesting as they are, because they are scripture's most easily detachable element. For example, unlimited love is a compelling ideal possibility that one might encounter in the story of a monk whose compassion is so great that he vows not to enter the most blessed state except in company with all other sentient beings. Anyone can be struck by such a story, in the

---

[65] This idea is developed by Kevin Vanhoozer in "From Speech Acts to Scripture Acts," chap. 6 in *First Theology* (InterVarsity, 2002), pp. 188–200.

[66] For example, Hellenistic Jews defended the honor of Judaism by arguing that Moses not only preceded the classical Greek writers in time but was the source of their most important ideas. Clement of Alexandria (*Stromata* I.15) mentions the Pythagorean Philo, Aristobulus the Peripatetic, and several others as showing the precedence of Jewish philosophy to Greek. Cf. Josephus, *Against Apion* 2.168, in *The Works of Josephus* (trans. William Whiston, Hendrickson, 1987), p. 804. On the "argument from antiquity" more broadly, see David Engels, "Historising Religion between Spiritual Continuity and Friendly Takeover: Salvation History and Religious Competition during the First Millennium AD," in Engels and Van Nuffelen, pp. 237–284.

realm of imagined possibility. For Pure Land scripturalists, however, the great Love is a reality, and one maintains a relationship with this Love by taking Guidance from the recorded vows of Dharmakara in the Larger Pure Land Sutra and related Buddhist texts. Generally scripturalists bind themselves to their scripture as authoritative by embracing an active relationship with their supreme Appellants, the Buddha-mind or Self or God or Heaven, as sponsors of the text's prioritized utterances.

How might a scriptural text appear convincingly to be one of the right venues for relationship with the source of life-ordering utterance?

(1) *The direct presentation of First Things ("revelation").* The great Vedanta commentator Shankara asserts that even when the Upanishads seem to be rationally or empirically justifying a belief, they are in fact directly disclosing the extraordinary truth of Brahman. Thus the intellectually engaging "philosophy" of the Upanishads is really "revelation."[67] Scripturalists can make the same claim about any element of scripture, even the most incredible or banal, so long as they are apprehending it as actively scriptural. The directly presentative force of scripturalized utterance corresponds to the ultimacy of the scriptural directive. Its logical position is at the base of evaluation, where first principles must be grasped, not inferred. With scriptural presentations of ultimate rightness, the grasping of that extraordinary meaning is not primarily guided by a reasoning process or experience of the world in general (although, *pace* Spinoza, these conditions on understanding cannot be excluded) but depends on encounter with a foundationally guiding utterance proceeding from a supreme Appellant.[68]

There is a scripturalist emotion of awe in being personally close to the first principle of Guidance as opposed to simply being informed about its content. There is joy in the privilege of hearing what Eternal Being has to

---

[67] Shankara, *Brahma-Sutra Bhasya*, quoted and discussed by Francis X. Clooney in *Hindu God, Christian God* (Oxford University Press, 2002), pp. 52–53. The example is Taittiriya Upanishad 3.1.1, where Brahman is positioned as a First Cause: "That from which these beings are born; on which, once born, they live; and into which they pass upon death – seek to perceive that! That is *brahman*!"

[68] Spinoza seems to wrongly treat direct presentation of Guidance and free acceptance as mutually exclusive: "Prophetic authority does not permit participation in argument, for whoever seeks to confirm his dogmas by means of reason is thereby submitting them to the judgment of each individual for decision." Benedict de Spinoza, *Theological-Political Treatise* (trans. Michael Silverthorne and Jonathan Israel, Cambridge University Press, 2007), p. 156 (Gebhardt edition pagination). However, Spinoza claims that the Bible itself does not authorize the pious Jewish view, upheld by Maimonides, that moral laws must be obeyed as prescribed in the Torah, not directly from the light of reason (79).

say to us, different in meaning from anything any creature could say for itself. As the Guidance is in an interpretable text, however, it is not an intimidating divine *tremendum*; in the respect that it is detached from the saying of the content, it is not even as coercive as ordinary face-to-face encounter.[69] So its authority is not anti-axial.

The cumulative scriptural interpretation worked out by a large, long-term historical community gives some protection from arbitrariness and inadequacy in what individual scripturalists glean from it. To be sure, that very protection imposes a risk of being epistemically manipulated by the community as a whole or its authorized interpreters. Another risk that seems serious from the point of view of ideal religious psychology is that the dominance of the scriptural appeal over reason and experience will encourage the scripturalist to seize on the textually offered Ultimate superstitiously – impelled by hope or fear rather than in sober cognizance of how things are, or renouncing personal responsibility for the relationship: "The text chose *me*!" These risks are reduced to the extent that reasoning concurs with scriptural proposals, but only a dogmatist could be sure in advance that a scripture and a discipline of reasoning will fully concur on topics they commonly address.[70]

(2) *The occasion of authoritative experience*. Reading or pondering a scripture could foreseeably be the occasion of a realization experience that is final for the religious subject. The authoritative experience – of union or strong resonance with divine being, for example, or of

---

[69] Paul Ricoeur emphasizes the detachment of the Said of texts from the actual Saying of their authors. "What Is a Text?" in *Hermeneutics and the Human Sciences* (ed. John B. Thompson, Cambridge University Press, 1981), pp. 145–164. He claims that discourse can be "more spiritual" in being liberated from the face-to-face situation – now it is open to an indefinite number of readers and interpretations constructing a shared world. *Interpretation Theory* (TCU Press, 1976), p. 31. But scriptural traditions do often represent or refer to a real event of divine giving of scriptural Guidance, such as the writing of the Law for Israel on tablets of stone in Exodus, as a prompt to view the text as representing a special Saying and as an occasion to renew the Saying of Guidance in devout recitation and reading.

[70] The concurrence of reason and scripture may be thought to be guaranteed by their common divine formation. According to Lodewijk Meyer, a zealous Cartesian, the true philosophy "starts from principles that are immovable and known through themselves, and proceeds through legitimate inferences and logical demonstrations which are clearly and distinctly perceived. That this philosophy owes its origin to God, the Good and the Great, the father of light and the fount of wisdom, is agreed by all. For 'every good gift and every perfect gift is from above, and cometh down from the father of lights, with whom is no variableness, neither shadow of turning,' as James says in his Epistle, ch. 1, v. 17." *Philosophy as the Interpreter of Holy Scripture* [1666] (trans. Samuel Shirley, Marquette University Press, 2005), p. 105.

satori-enlightenment – must itself set the measure of reality and goodness; for *that* subject, in *that* condition, there can be no comparable or superior standard. A scripture may be identified as the ultimate help to this end among textual offers of guidance, perhaps even among all offers of guidance. Shankara exemplifies this possibility as well.[71]

(3) *The communalist premise* of scripture is that the reader is brought to the possibility of encountering the first principles of Guidance authentically – to being able to grasp the unconditionality and real relevance of the Upanishadic immutability ideal or the prophetic justice ideal, for example – by enrolling in the practice and story of an existing community. The idea that one receives guidance from divine revelation by believing in a transmission of testimony going back to certain persons who were in contact with the divine is a weak model of membership, because the guidance at the point of one's own much later reception of it is relatively faint and dubious.[72] The stronger communalist idea is that first principles are presented in their *fullness* of practical meaning by giving the individual the benefit of the community's historical experience with its essential lessons tellingly focused and dictally ordered in scriptural narratives and directives.[73] The experience of the community with these texts shows that they stand the test of time and include everything its members need to be thinking about.[74] The respondent to the scriptural appeal now has answers, beyond free-floating abstract ideals of love and respect, to spiritually vital questions: How can free individuals live together in deep agreement? To which other existents should a free individual be most actively responsible?

---

[71] The role of experience in Shankara is controversial. Anantanand Rambachan argues that experience has no role to play for Shankara beyond confirming knowledge derived from scripture study – *Accomplishing the Accomplished* (University of Hawai'i Press, 1991), pp. 109–112. Arvind Sharma argues that Shankara sometimes allows for an experience of Brahman not derived from the Vedas – "Sacred Scriptures and the Mysticism of Advaita Vedanta," in Katz, p. 172.

[72] Linda Zagzebski, *Epistemic Authority* (Oxford University Press, 2012), p. 193.

[73] Saadya Gaon, *Book of Doctrines and Beliefs* 3.5. Spinoza brings up the same point while taking a dimmer view of experience as the persuader of those who do not reason (76–77).

[74] Saadya emphasizes the diachronically confirmed trustworthiness of scripture and the dependence of human thought on cultural tradition in general (*Book of Doctrines and Beliefs* 3.5). Meyer, who strongly subordinates scripture epistemically to natural reason, concedes that without scripture we could not be sure we were thinking about everything that is most worth thinking about (239) – although scripture's "function is only to rouse its readers and to impel them to think about the matters set out therein, to look into them and consider whether the facts are as there set out" (238).

Tradition provides a foothold for the historical extension of communicative reasonableness into the relevant past. Legal tradition is one model for this; thanks to the recording of rules and precedents, we are able to go on making coherent determinations of justice. Scripture is thought to have laid down the ground rules for the best life by having published the most suitable words. In a scripturally guided conversation, the first principles of Guidance can be invoked by quoting texts: "It is written," "The Lord says," "Here is the truth," "Thus I have heard." Then, suitably reminded, the scripturalist community is tasked like a panel of judges with collectively realizing the implications of what has already been said in scripture for the decisions they now have to make.

5.7 THE PROBLEMATIC OF SCRIPTURE

The central religious task of scripture is to realize textually, so far as the textual format allows, the greatest religious amplifications of linguistic guidance. We can identify some main features of the inherent problematic of scripture with reference to main kinds of amplification we noted earlier.

(1) *Informative.* The cognitive content of scripture is established in a distinctive textual manner, partly that of a book and partly that of a library. While one can make claims about the meaning of a scripture as a whole and even construe it as a single Word, nevertheless, for any closely text-based interpretation, scripture is not a single target text but a collection of targets. The scripturalist is thus equipped with a religiously rich and helpfully self-correcting system of resources but also faced with a challenge: a responsible scriptural interpretation will normally try to achieve an equilibrium between the implications of the canon's different elements, and what constitutes the proper equilibrium will be subject to debate. Which texts form the "canon within the canon" or "high points" or "great sayings" that should determine interpretation of the whole? The axiality thesis on scripture predicts a dominant influence of texts that project a supreme appeal and a sovereign attitude prescription, to the degree that interpretation is oriented to religious reflection. But for interpretations more oriented to political, ethical, or other interests, other kinds of text could assume the greatest weight – for example, the biblical texts having to do with the territorial possessions of the Israelites, sexual or dietary laws, or apocalyptic visions. Depending on the issue, a

historian will probably see not a larger equilibrium in the community over time but rather an ever-boiling pot of rival claims.

Because scripture is supposed to be full of religious meaning, its readers will use all possible means to extract meaning from it, and two of these means are inherently problematic. *Allegorizing*, which claims to find additional meanings in texts beyond their plain sense, incurs the suspicion that it is either imposing a foreign meaning without scriptural justification (say, reading Platonic psychology into the Hebrew Scriptures à la Philo) or reductively imposing a general conception of the meaning of scripture on all its diverse elements (as in Luther's bold revival of the patristic idea that all scripture refers to Christ).[75] *Hypertextualizing* consists of freely determining the units of scriptural meaning – passages, sentences, or even single words, syllables, letters, or spaces – and connecting the units in any conceivable way to make any conceivable point. One normal mark of a master scripturalist is his or her ability to support a claim with quotations drawn from all over the canon. The broad coverage of the quotation strategy and the harmonious plain sense of the quotations reassure the audience that the speaker's interpretation is not skewed. At the other end of the spectrum, however, claims based on counterintuitively chosen units of meaning drawn from unexpected nooks and crannies of scripture are cogent only esoterically, if at all. The inherent problem here is that *any* selection of elements from scripture gets off to a fast start and wins conviction just because its elements are scriptural, which makes possible an unlimited number of stubborn if not intractable scriptural disagreements. (This problem will be restated as an objection to scripturalism in the next chapter.)

(2) *Appellative.* The scriptural text itself does not call like a prophet or answer like a guru, yet as language it speaks to us. What does listening to scripture involve us in, illocutionarily speaking? What is the pragmatic form of the communicative event? Is scripture informing us, stimulating us, commanding us, giving us moral support? Hearers will no doubt specify the illocutionary force of scriptural texts in different ways according to their temperaments and circumstances, and what one

---

[75] For an example of Philo's Platonizing, see his commentary on Genesis, *Allegorical Interpretation*, in *The Works of Philo* (trans. C. D. Yonge, Hendrickson, 1993), pp. 25–79. Luther: "Christ is the Lord, not the servant, the Lord of the Sabbath, of law, of all things. The Scriptures must be understood in favor of Christ, not against Him. For that reason they must either refer to Him or must not be held to be true Scripture." Martin Luther, "Theses Concerning Faith and Law," Thesis 41, in *Luther's Works*, vol. 34 (ed. Helmut T. Lehmann, Concordia, 1960), p. 112.

hearer takes as a suggestive parable another may take as an urgent imperative. When Augustine happened to read Paul's remarks on sensual excess in Romans 13, he received a spiritual bull's-eye hit and could not but interpret the text as prescriptive for his conduct.[76] It was not merely the Guidance for his life but immediately *the* guidance of the moment in a nearly overwhelming way. We can say generally that the appellative amplification of a supreme religious guidance imposes on any hearer the inordinate challenge of finding a right-enough position in relation to the infinitely demanding divine. Given this emphasis, an adequate specification of scripture's illocutionary force must support a realization that "here there is no place that does not see you. You must change your life" (Rilke).[77]

It may be objected that the premises of appeal and illocution assume a text expressing the communicative approach of Someone who would be performing speech acts via scripture, but in nontheist traditions ("Does Heaven speak?") and even in certain schools of thought in theist traditions, no such anthropomorphic assumption is made, and consequently no scriptural speech acts are contemplated. But regardless of what one believes about the basis or causation of the scriptural language, the fact that it is linguistic means that the issue of how it is most properly to be taken cannot be dismissed. Perhaps the nontheist will take prescriptive direction from scripture *as if* commanded by a Lord – the text will have commanding force all the same.

One inherent problem is that members of a scripturalist community will sometimes need to agree on how to take scriptural texts, yet there is no certain way to resolve such disagreements. One must wait to see if one of the possible modes of guidance proves dominant at a given juncture. More specifically, we can foresee that there will be irresolvable disagreements about whether a scriptural text ought to be taken as a decree, stringently determining our thought and practice (though without tipping over from strong Guidance into an untenable controlling relationship), or rather taken as an inviting prompt, with a maximal allowance for our own free (yet helpfully Guided) response in determining our thought and practice.

---

[76] Augustine, *Confessions*, chap. 12.

[77] Rainer Maria Rilke, "Archaic Torso of Apollo," in *Ahead of All Parting: The Selected Poetry and Prose of Rainer Maria Rilke* (trans. Stephen Mitchell, Modern Library, 1995), p. 67.

Supporting the decree paradigm, the legal model of scripture's communicative position highlights the power of scripture to *settle* questions, the *finality* of realized scriptural meaning, which might seem the very backbone of its authority and the promise of a devoutly desired elimination of uncertainty. But finality cannot be the only practical force of Guidance in an axial regime. Ideals that are axial *must* be presented not as conformist dictates of right living but as instigations of enlightened reflection and discussion on the best life – and thus not merely as an elimination of risks of error but also as an encouragement of good risks to run. The ideal of completing all possible enhancement of human life must be served by unleashing individual effort as well as by promulgating prescriptions. In this respect the teaching model of guidance is more relevant than the legal model. The free reception and fully personal realization of scriptural guidance requires initiality as well as finality in what scripture says. Identify with the Imperishable Self (Mundaka Upanishad) – or walk modestly with your God (Micah) – or adopt "consideration" (*shu*) as a life policy (*Lunyu* 15:23) – and find out what this can mean.[78] Loosen the grip of doctrines by letting the Text play with them poetically.[79] Interrupt the repetition of what is supposed to be the best guidance by floating new guidance possibilities in new ventures of exegesis. Admit one's limitations in grasping for what one needs by means of the Text.[80]

The initiality of key scriptural texts is connected to a meaning of transcendence that Ingolf Dalferth has helpfully elucidated in a recent discussion of axiality.[81] Transcendence has been a controversial part of Jaspers's formulation, as in the language I have already quoted: "[Axial humanity] experiences absoluteness in the depth of selfhood and in the lucidity of transcendence." If commitment to a transcendent *reality* were

---

[78] Trans. Irene Bloom in de Bary and Bloom, pp. 59–60.

[79] "Because *Tiruvaymoli* is good poetry, its verses and songs resist complete determination of their meaning ... it unsettles the very orthodoxy it upholds, for it always remains open to a variety of readings according to the expectations, mastery and sensitivity of its readers. Images and evocations overflow, jostling against one another ... It takes doctrinal positions quite seriously, and plays with them too: it is theologically as well as stylistically ironic." Francis X. Clooney, *Seeing through Texts: Doing Theology among the Shrivaishnavas of South India* (SUNY Press, 1996), p. 103.

[80] According to Shinran, "if the reader leaves the reading with the sense of 'now I know the answer,' the text read is not religious. The point of the religious text is to make us more acutely aware of our inadequacy, our failings, our limitations." Thomas P. Kasulis, "The Origins of the Question: Four Traditional Japanese Philosophies of Language," in *Culture and Modernity: East-West Philosophic Perspectives* (ed. Eliot Deutsch, University of Hawai'i Press, 1991), p. 219.

[81] Ingolf U. Dalferth, "The Idea of Transcendence," in Bellah and Joas, pp. 146–188.

essential to axiality, the transcendentalist religious and philosophical perspectives would be misleadingly privileged over other no less enlightened and transformative developments in classical cultures, notably the Confucian. In some cases, the "lucidity of transcendence" does involve a division between a transcendent primary Reality (Brahman or God the Creator, for example) and a less-real world we live in (*maya* or creaturehood). But this ontological transcendentalism was not definitive for Jaspers. Rather he wished to emphasize the prospect of transcending received meanings in free thought and discussion: "Man is no longer enclosed within himself. He becomes uncertain of himself and thereby open to new and boundless possibilities." According to Dalferth, transcendence in this "interpretative" sense means that we "relativize the world in which we live to a beyond, whether real or imagined, possible or impossible, meaningful or beyond meaning, that in turn prevents any closure of our life world and opens it up to what is different from it, beyond it, could be or ought to be otherwise."[82] On this view of axial transcendentalism, the axial purpose of a scripture would be defeated if it closed interpretation. Thus it can be a fulfillment of scripture's function rather than a flaw when its arguments are patently inconclusive. Accordingly, it can be part of the communalist premise that the community thrives on the new-springing of religious thought, so long as scriptural Guidance is in the mix. But this means going down a bumpy road of disagreements, navigating problematics of finality and initiality and the relation between the two.[83]

(3) *Pragmatic.* Scriptural guidance is seen as supremely relevant by virtue of its practical fruits. It provides "both food and clothing to the soul" (Yasna 55:2);[84] it gives the pattern of expanded life and points out the path of optimization. Insofar as it is dedicated to results, it must send the potentially conflicting messages that, on the one hand, its Guidance is complete and trustworthy but, on the other hand, the hearer must not dally among mere words or ideas but must work out the rectification of his or her life.

---

[82] Ibid., p. 145.

[83] Part of the problematic of finality, for instance, is that utterances can always be understood in different ways. Part of the problematic of initiality is that new interpretive ventures can always have the aspect of careless or corrupted thought as well as the aspect of sincerely constructive opening. On the problematic of the relation between finality and initiality, see Section 6.5, p. 219.

[84] *The Zend-Avesta*, in *Sacred Books of the East*, vol. 31 (trans. L. H. Mills, Oxford University Press, 1887).

[The Vedic sage Narada says:] Wandering in the vast field of the verbal Brahma (the Veda), which is difficult to traverse, men do not recognize the Supreme, while they worship him as he is circumscribed by the attributes specified in the hymns (mantras). When the Divine Being regards any man with favor, that man, sunk in the contemplation of soul [divine Atman], abandons all thoughts which are set upon the world and the Veda. Cease, therefore, Varhishmat, through ignorance, to look upon works which merely seem to promote the chief good, as if they truly effected that object, (works) which only touch the ear, but do not touch the reality ... That by which Hari (Vishnu) is pleased, is work. (Bhagavata Purana 4.29, 42)[85]

But the salvific power of the text is still strongly affirmed:

Dhundhukari ... was guilty of causing the death of his own mother and other heinous crimes, but by attentively listening to the *Bhagavata* with a repentant heart, he attained Vishnu's heaven.[86]

The fruits of scripturalism are in fact mixed. Some scripturalists are luminously serene or loving, like Sufi saints, while other followers of the same scripture are violently polemical, like jihadists. For jihadists, the great benefit in receiving guidance from the Qur'an is its clarification that the never-ending main event in earthly life is war between the orthodox righteous people and everyone else. The highest priority of the righteous must therefore be to put forth their greatest effort in fighting on God's side of that war. A pragmatic scripturalist would like to think of the written Guidance as a divine gift of effective means of rectifying human life as humans by themselves never could – but must it not be admitted that application of the Guidance is always dominated in practice by the humanly nice or nasty uses that scripturalists choose to make of it? And must it not also be admitted that many of the loving or valiant types one thinks of as closest to the human ideal were crucially influenced by one's favored scripture not at all but instead by other data and other experiences? These considerations suggest a chronically uncertain relation between scriptural study and good consequences. It is noteworthy that among the world religions, one of the strongest of all pragmatic endorsements of scripture, the Confucian, incites one of the most radical of all critiques of scriptural guidance, the Daoist.

---

[85] In *Original Sanskrit Texts on the Origin and History of the People of India, Their Religion and Institutions*, 2nd ed., vol. 3 (trans. J. Muir, Trübner, 1868), p. 35.

[86] "Bhagavat Purana Mahatmya," in the Padma Purana, related by Brown, "Purana as Scripture," p. 75n27.

Another pragmatic pitfall might be named Pharisaism, if we can borrow this term from New Testament polemics without implying anything about Judaism's own view of religious law. Jesus accused his Pharisee rivals of putting textually justified righteousness ahead of the true righteousness of divinely compassionate love; then Paul construed his own shattered Pharisaism as a vainly self-justifying works righteousness. In a typical incident in the Gospels, Pharisees would not countenance healing on the Sabbath (Luke 6:6–10), an action they took to be barred by a scriptural rule (Exodus 20:8–11). It seems that Pharisaism is a trap that the pragmatic scripturalist cannot easily escape, for what is the Christian avoidance of Pharisaism if not an attempt to follow a scripturally recorded directive from Jesus? How can the life-giving "spirit" of true religion ever displace the killing "letter" of Pharisaism (to use Paul's language in 2 Corinthians 3:6) so long as the criteria of spiritual success are textually determined?

Whether in Christianity or Confucianism, it seems that escaping the trap of superstitious confidence in a textual bargain of justification requires affirming the superior guidance of That for which scripture is understood to speak – the best life itself or its Source as *to be found* in a scripturally assisted *turn* to the holy. The Golden Rule, for example, rather than enjoining or forbidding actions, guides the hearer toward finding out what justice consists of by relating the self's own wishes to the state of the other person:

So whatever you wish that men would do to you, do so to them; for this is the law and the prophets. (Matthew 7:12)

Tzu-kung asked saying, Is there any single saying that one can act upon all day and every day? The Master said, Perhaps the saying about consideration: "Never do to others what you would not like them to do to you." (*Lunyu* 15:23)

Whereas a textually justified action is concretely finished, its merit banked, the turn to the holy is always still to be explored. Appropriately Guided individuals must pursue the turn in their own contexts in their own ways, without fully definite, clearly negotiable validation.

*

All communication is guiding, and all religious communication guides its audience in relating to the holy. Religious classics are texts of outstanding power and reliability in doing this. Scriptures are more: for the communities they charter, they are *the Guidance* in a preeminent sense, fully unavoidable for the religious. Students of religion must recognize scriptures as possibly requisite guidance for any human being and can never leave them out of account in interpreting the thought and practice of their communities, even when their influence is not direct or determinative.

Inevitably, scripture is a fetish – an object of the will to possess the greatest thing. It is made an emblem of the great history and ambition of its human sponsors. By virtue of its authority it functions as an intellectual or pragmatic utility, a machine producing final answers to questions and final choices among options. In all these respects it can be perceived as having very high value. For the devout scripturalist, however, scripture is spiritually meaningful in a way that is not captured in the category of "value." Being Guided by the Guidance is a venture into the Rectifying of life analogous to dancing with the greatest dancer – (take your pick) Fred Astaire or Ginger Rogers. As linguistic, the scriptural Guidance is interlocutory as well as interesting; as comprehensive, it mentally surrounds and surpasses the Guided; as classic, it sets ultimate benchmarks of worthy thought and expression. It is a thrillingly intimate and challenging fulfillment in the making. And yet, unlike a duet with Fred or Ginger, it is shared with everyone in principle – the ideal "everyone" being actively embodied and represented by a world religion, one of the largest and inherently least restricted of all functional human communities.

6

Evaluating the Scripture Premise

Is scripture a good idea? The question flung out without qualification obviously has no all-purpose answer and yet cannot be dismissed. Perhaps scripture as a general value proposition is like democracy, about which almost everyone in modern societies would say: Yes, it comes with many frustrations, but the good fruits, the future promise, and the fit with our best vision of ourselves all make the struggle worthwhile. Or perhaps a better analogy would be with alcohol, about which many would say: No, despite pleasant scenarios of responsible use, the costs are disastrous, far outweighing the good.

Some understandings and uses of scriptures are clearly unfortunate. In the understandings and uses of scriptures we might agree are benign, it still might not be demonstrable that the scripture premise – supreme Guidance offered definitively by Texts enshrined as authoritative by historic religious communities – is essential to what we approve of. The great scripturalist personalities, leaders, and artists might have drawn their crucial inspiration from other sources if scriptures had not been available to them. They might have done even better.

In a philosophical investigation we cannot work through the mass of evidence that would inform a substantial historical judgment on these points – a judgment that in any case could never be final. Nor can we gauge the spiritual intensity of any individual's attachment to a particular text or interpretation. We can only try to clarify the general standards and objects of our evaluative curiosity. The broadest askable evaluative question will be something like this: Under what conditions, if any, can the expectation of finding supreme life guidance in a communally authorized collection of texts be justified? We can test the depth and breadth of the apparent strengths and weaknesses of scripturalism in principle so that we are not forced to draw a conclusion or form an attitude based only on a particular experience of scripturalism, as is usually done by friends and enemies of scripture alike. (They cannot be faulted for this if they have had to embrace or fend off a particular scripturalism that was their only really available option.)

I think it will be possible to make a number of useful points about the justifiability of scripturalism using noncontroversial general notions about the justification of thought and practice. But diverse considerations are involved that are ordinarily mixed up together. We need to put these considerations into a clear order so that definite evaluative issues become discussable. I will propose some axioms of guidance and justification to provide the most basic structure for discussion, and then I will introduce some main theses for and against scripturalism.

6.1 THE AXIALIZED GUIDANCE SITUATION

On the basis of our previous discussion of guidance, I propose several axioms of serious communication. I do not see how reasoning could go forward if any of these assumptions were denied. By "guidance" I shall mean linguistic guidance in a community that is communicating at least normally.

Axiom #1: *We generally depend on guidance to act successfully and maintain our good standing in the community.* A situation in which a human individual or ensemble could act successfully without being informed by guidance would be highly exceptional. The question for us is not whether to be guided but by which offers of guidance to be guided.

Axiom #2: *We are seekers of the best guidance.* As we are at least implicitly aware of Axiom #1, and insofar as we desire to act with the most success, we desire to act on the best guidance base. In practice, we are often less attentive to the issue of guidance quality than we might be, which is often cause for regret. A main standard of justification is to have followed the best available guidance.

Axiom #3: *Guidance is offered competitively.* Any human community contains a multiplicity of speakers; for this reason alone there are bound to be options of guidance on any issue. Speakers are always at least implicitly aware of Axiom #2 and so cater to their hearers competitively insofar as they strive to speak successfully. (This point could apply also to the maneuvers of a single speaker on successive occasions of offering guidance.) We take some offers of guidance to be better than others. We can infer that any guidance that is consistently taken seriously by a number of people has won its influence by seeming more coherent, more responsible, or more advantageous than other options.

Axiom #4: *Some offers of guidance are prima facie unavoidable.* In a given situation, one or more offers of guidance may count as "the guidance." Some actual and logical conditions of successful communication normally qualify as elements of "the guidance" for any communicator. Guidance may be unavoidable because of its bearing on an object of dominant desire – for example, the latest credible report on the location of one's beloved. A main standard of justification is not to have avoided unavoidable guidance.

Axiom #5: *Some offers of guidance are untenable.* As in the example of the overly controlling park ranger, the balance of power to define shared action can be too disempowering of the recipient for the guidance to be affirmable as such, even if it happens to offer the one effective linkage with a desired result.

Suppose you desire the important result of moral solidarity with the other people living in your neighborhood, but unfortunately the only way to attain this is to submit to a brutally authoritarian religion. You would have an instrumental justification for submitting, comparable to the justification for taking a painkiller to become free of pain, but the issue of guidance would then be on another plane: just as you would consult with a doctor or WebMD about whether and how to take a painkiller, you will feel the need to consult about whether and how to submit to the locally dominant religion, and yet, in this hard case, you may be denied that help.

My view of the implications of Axiom #5 is influenced by several axiality theses that are now worth restating:

Axiality Thesis #1: *Our guidance situation has been axialized.* That is to say that the most compelling guidance addresses us as mentally free individuals. Rather than simply falling in with our peers, we may conscientiously choose the guidance that seems best. (What a guidance means for relations with my peers is generally of great importance nonetheless.) A purely authoritarian or traditionalist guidance is now untenable. Thus "the guidance that *seems best to me*" is, formally, unavoidable guidance for me; and insofar as I am attending to the ideological competition between rival offers of guidance, the credibly *ultimate* life-organizing guidance options are, materially, unavoidable guidance for me as well.

Axiality Thesis #2: *The credibly ultimate life-organizing offers of guidance are keyed to a supreme appeal (something on the order of God or Nature) and a correspondingly appropriate sovereign attitude (something on the order of faith or rationality).* A corollary is that one of the most serious and difficult questions an axial individual can face is which of multiple credible ultimates to accept.

Axiality Thesis #3 (this is the conservative interpretation of the axial shift): *The axial individual remains essentially concerned with sharing his or her being-guided with other members of a historic community – an actual community that is now understood ideally as a prototype and platform for a universal community as implied by the ultimate points of reference to which it is devoted – and with preserving and benefiting from a continuity of current beliefs and interpretations with traditionally approved offers of guidance.* As I understand it, this thesis supports the possibility that traditional scriptures are ideally relevant to contemporary people without of itself assuring that a scripture is feasible guidance for anyone.

Now I propose several axioms in the general area of what makes for an acceptable belief or practice. Informally we call for "rational," "reasonable," and "intelligent" choices with a lot of overlap in the meanings of these terms, but I will separate the three categories according to their distinct core issues associated with the locutionary, illocutionary, and perlocutionary powers of linguistic guidance.

Axiom #6: *When we have a choice of guidance that represents our situation more revealingly and coherently than alternative views we might adopt, it is more rational and so more acceptable, other things being equal, for us to follow that guidance.*

Axiom #7: *When we have a choice of guidance that positions us more responsibly than alternative positionings so that we are better able to rectify one or more relationships of concern so far as we can, it is more reasonable and so more acceptable, other things being equal, for us to follow that guidance.* The meaning of responsibility varies according to whom we are in relationship with, what the investments in that relationship are, and the stakes of our comportment. By virtue of being human, we have a general responsibility to deal fairly with all our fellow citizens; by virtue of being placed in particular relationships, we have particular responsibilities to help relatives, friends, and clients; by virtue of religious sensitivity, we may have devout responsibilities to divine and other beings.

Axiom #8: *When we have a choice of guidance that seems to give us a better chance to attain what we desire, it is more intelligent and so more acceptable, other things being equal, for us to follow that guidance.*

Axiom #9: *The best guidance is the most rational, reasonable, and intelligent.* Admittedly, we cannot calculate scores of rationality, reasonableness, and intelligence to see how the greatest sum obtains, and even if we could, our different envisionings and weighings of evaluative fulfillment would make agreement on the supposed total score unlikely. We must agree, however, that an apparent deficit of rationality or reasonableness or intelligence cannot be declared a nonissue for guidance. If we notice any such deficit, we are bound to seek better guidance as long as there seems to be any chance of finding it. This is another main standard of justification: that our choice and interpretation of guidance incorporate diligent pursuit of rationality, reasonableness, and intelligence together.

While we cannot predetermine how our attempts to satisfy these three standards will actually work out, various theses about the situation may be entertained. An optimistic thesis holds obvious appeal for an axial individual.

Optimality thesis on guidance: *To be acceptable as supreme life guidance, an offer of guidance must be discernibly the best possible guidance.*

Anyone might shrug off the question of supreme life guidance. But almost any adult member of my society would know what I meant if I raised the question. And almost anyone would see the importance of having or not having an axial view of life-in-the-world as a basis for discussing that question. Some would say they subscribe to a religion (probably to a "world religion" geared to scripturalized ideals, whether or not they pay direct attention to a scripture themselves); some would say they do not subscribe to a religion but have their own version of a religious plan for life; some would say they have a philosophy of life. Others would say, happily or ruefully, that they are figuring things out or simply enjoying or enduring life without commitment to a guided strategy. These latter are positioned as bystanders to the Guidance discussion. If the axiality theses are right, it is not possible to make a basic argument against the Guidance premise. To get any traction in an axialized discussion, one must function in some way as a guide bringing notions of a supreme appeal (even if it be the appeal of "polytheism" or some other pluralism) and a sovereign attitude (even if it be a noncommittalism) to bear on the issue. The -ism is a must.

I turn now to the standards of rationality, reasonableness, and intelligence.

6.2 *ALEPH, BET*: THE EQUIPMENT OF RATIONALITY

Most offers of guidance depend on a picture of how things are in the world in which we act. We need cognitive access and focus if we are to find our way forward; the practical issue at the core of the general standard of rationality is the feasibility of actually living in a world taken to be a certain way, with a certain roster and range of identifiable items. As members of a culture and a rational fellowship, we communicatively maintain an intentionally figured world picture to which strategically important pieces of guidance make explicit additions and corrections. If one is not sufficiently committed to any such world picture, one cannot productively or responsibly discuss life's direction with others.

Even if it is possible to transcend linguistic meaning in spiritually momentous mystical states, no one could seriously argue for a nonlinguistic guidance scheme for human beings. There could not even be a wholly nonlinguistic way of training mystics. Language is necessary cognitive equipment for life with human-grade awareness. More specifically, no one could argue that we would be better equipped cognitively if we did not tell stories, or if we did not state prescriptions or descriptions at multiple levels of generality, or if we did not have techniques for methodically studying and adding to remembered utterances.

Further, no one could expect a young person to acquire the cognitive equipment needed for a good human life without being taught by speakers of a language using the assets of a cultural tradition. Anyone who wished to object to the linguistic means used by a culture to equip its new members (as Plato objected to the Homeric myths) could not realistically propose merely to do without stories, laws, or proverbs; that person would have to propose replacements, and those replacements would have to make sense in that cultural frame.

Granting the necessity of cultural-linguistic equipment, including genres of linguistic guidance like story and law, what kind of cultural-linguistic asset is scripture? Is it one of our indispensable genres, like history? Or is it an objectionable and removable genre, as many have regarded myth?

A rabbinic story is suggestive about this issue. A man came to the great Hillel to be instructed in Judaism. He issued a fundamental challenge by telling the rabbi he could believe in a written law but not in a second, oral law. So Hillel wrote out an alphabet and asked the man to identify the first letter. "It is an *aleph*," he said. "This is not an *aleph* but a *bet*," said Hillel. "Now what is the second letter?" "*Bet*," said the man. "This is not a *bet* but a *gimmel*," said Hillel. [Pause for confusion to sink in.] "How do you know that this is an *aleph*, and this is a *bet*, and this is a *gimmel*? Only because our earliest ancestors have passed it on to us ... Just as you have accepted the alphabet on faith, so too accept the two Torahs on faith."[1]

The *Aleph, Bet* Argument, if we may so construe it, takes written scripture for granted and makes a point about our necessary trust in our human teachers and in the cultural scheme supporting their teaching – necessary to gain desired awareness and communicative competence. In the Talmudic Jewish frame of reference it is illogical to jump ship when the rabbi draws on the Oral Law as the written Torah's proper complement. We may be reminded of the Catholic argument against the Protestants that Holy Scripture never simply Guides us from itself but is always deployed and interpreted by the historic Church. By implication the appeal to *aleph* and *bet* reinforces the primary role of scripture along with rabbinic expertise. The rabbi knows his way around a teachable Jewish worldview only because the letters appear canonically in texts that support such teaching.

In one obvious way, the *Aleph, Bet* Argument is weak. The reminder that we are always already following linguistic guidance mediated by trusted guides shows only our general dependence; it does not discriminate between possibly better or worse forms of linguistic guidance that our human guides may exploit to win our attention or obedience. The point of the convert's initial challenge, after all, was to question whether Hillel himself, or his version of Judaism, was one of the better guides. Having

---

[1] *Abot de-Rabbi Natan* A15, adapted by me from the Judah Goldin translation reproduced by Steven D. Fraade in "Concepts of Scripture in Rabbinic Judaism: Oral Torah and Written Torah," in *Jewish Concepts of Scripture* (ed. Benjamin Sommer, NYU Press, 2012), pp. 34–35. On different versions of the story and their implications, see Marc Hirshman, *The Stabilization of Rabbinic Culture, 100 CE–350 CE* (Oxford University Press, 2009), pp. 99–104. There is a complementary argument in Saadya Gaon's *Book of Doctrines and Beliefs* about our dependence on tradition: "Unless there was a true tradition in this world, a man would not be able to know that a certain property was owned by his father, and that this is an inheritance from his grandfather, nor would a man be able to know that he is the son of his mother, let alone that he is the son of his father. Human affairs would be in a state of perpetual doubt ..." (trans. Alexander Altman, Hackett, 2002), 3.5, p. 110.

faith in Hillel's scripturalism is hardly on the same level as having faith in the words you first learned from your mother, the letters that all texts are written in, or the accumulated stability of word references.

In another way the argument is much too strong, in a bullying way – it says, in effect, "Given that you are being initiated into literacy by this community from *aleph* and *bet* onwards, you have no right to be skeptical of the validity of any communally instituted written guidance." The very possibility of a wholesome guidance relationship would be destroyed by the power imbalance between a rabbi acting as the community's enforcer and a hearer who is not being treated as a mentally independent adult.

Still, from the rabbi's own point of view, the cogency of the *aleph, bet* point is overwhelming. For one who is comprehensively Guided, all the elements of a literate world stance are knit together and work together. The cultural achievement of the alphabetic writing system is continuous with the achievement of the greatest literature – that is, normative religious literature; one can see, for example, that Firstness is now part of the meaning of the first letter *aleph*, as God's creative action is First for all creatures.[2]

Hillel's pupil surely wants to be treated with respect for his mental independence, but on the other hand he *has* come to Hillel for help in getting the benefit of what he evidently thinks might well be the best life guidance. He has already accepted the premise of a scriptural kind of religion. Was it *rational* for him to do so? Might Judaism as represented by a scripturalist teacher actually offer him the best prospects for enlarging and refining his capacity to identify all the important elements of the world he lives in?

It is not hard to see how *he* might come to think so. Converts to scriptural religion normally experience an exhilarating cognitive gain: there is a sacred history to learn that richly defines the historic action of the religious community, a new vocabulary to learn that maps metaphysical and moral terrain in interesting detail, and a rich array of texts with their interpretive issues to get acquainted with. And it all works together systematically. The experience for the religiously sensitive mind is like the experience of the referentially sensitive blind girl Helen Keller when she realized there are words for everything. Of course, the apparent internal

---

[2] The Zohar makes a case for the priority of the *bet* of *bereshit* ("in the beginning") and *bara* ("created") while acknowledging the presumptive priority of *aleph*. See Steven T. Katz, "Mysticism and the Interpretation of Sacred Scriptures," in *Mysticism and Sacred Scriptures* (ed. Steven T. Katz, Oxford University Press, 2000), p. 53.

unavoidability of the systematic relations among the religion's elements, anchored and coordinated by the charter texts of scripture, is not to be equated with an objective unavoidability for someone wondering whether to subscribe to the religion. But it supports an experience of cognitive optimization.

One may advocate a replacement of scriptural religion by another style of religion that is more liberal, more intuitive, or more responsive to nonhuman nature. Could such a replacement be commended specifically as more *rational*? Could there be a gain in cognitive discrimination without writing that gain down, and could religious cognitive guidance be written down for the use of a multigenerational community without getting distilled sooner or later into a text of paramount authority, a scripture? And would a new scripture not have to validate itself as no less supportive of cognitive awareness than the older scriptures, which have set benchmarks for religious rationality?

Or one may advocate a replacement of religious Guidance altogether by nonreligious guidance. There may seem to be a vast misdirection in religious rationality: yes, scriptural religion reveals and explains to its followers a wealth of things, but many of those things are gratuitous fabrications or erroneous assertions about history or the natural world. Three main areas of concern may be typified by these questions: (1) What is the good of learning the procedures for ancient rituals, the names of angels and demons, or mythical accounts of the birth of the cosmos or of a nation, as a conscientious scripturalist is often obliged to do? (2) What protects scripturalists against systematic error caused by the sort of false main organizing idea that is found in almost every scripture, such as the idea of spiritual beings or karma, pulling all analysis of human affairs into fantastical channels? (3) Assuming that an accurate and fair knowledge of human history ought to inform the most important offers of guidance humans rely upon, how could a Jewish scripturalist correct for the Jewish bias in the Tanakh's version of history (a biased selection of what to talk about and a biased valuation of what is talked about), a Christian correct for the Christian bias in the Christian Bible's version, or a Muslim correct for the Muslim bias in the Qur'an's version? Or how could a Hindu or Buddhist scripturalist correct for the disregard for empirical history that shapes their scriptural guidance?

The general defense of scriptural rationality and of religious rationality more broadly must be that it serves *religious* awareness; one learns the religious world picture in order to better know one's way about as a religiously sagacious, optimistic, and responsible agent. The religious agent intends to recognize the full depth and breadth of life, including its extraordinary aspects. Because axial religious guidance is supremely life-organizing, the religious agent enfolds all knowledge in religious knowledge, but not necessarily by excluding the claims or results of other sorts of inquiry; rather than reposing in its own separate sphere, religious knowledge can play the role of queen of the sciences or chaplain in the house of knowledge. If religion itself is productive more of error and bias than of awareness and fairness, then scripture perhaps cannot redeem it (although a thesis worth considering in that case is that scripture does redeem religion by shifting it sufficiently into a philosophical or historical or literary key). In the respects in which religion can be beneficial, scripture serves it powerfully by taking the fullest possible advantage of the resources of literacy, specifying religious claims effectively and exposing them to open, endless text-disciplined discussion.

In the more specific areas of concern:

(1) The religious picturing of life-in-the-world brings light and form to areas that are otherwise foggy. For example, the greater powers of good and evil – powers that impinge on us sometimes fatefully, as in surges of love or hostility or in constructive and destructive social movements – are, we could neutrally say, attractors of human intention. But how are we to deal with them? When we read or hear about a contest between the Buddha and Mara (*Mara-Samyutta*) or between Jesus and Satan (Matthew 4:1–11), for example, we get a practically helpful narrative grip on the struggle with evil at the level of first principles. Because the narratives are recorded scripturally, they are objects of unlimited study and questioning on a basis of linguistic engagement with the divine and communal sponsors of the text.

There is also, to be sure, a nonreligious literature on powers of good and evil – for example, historical and fictional accounts of the Nazi death camps. In that literature a classic and even canonical story (for school curricula) may emerge, like Elie Wiesel's *Night*. The analogy between such a text and scripture can be very strong when we view the text seriously as taking the measure of the powers of good and evil. The point of present interest is that scripture sets the standard here; the height of this kind of relevance is part of the concept of scripture.

(2) It should not be declared peremptorily that transempirical religious conceptions of spiritual beings or causation are fantastical. Those notions boldly go where ordinary notions do not, into the deepest and broadest framing of life-in-the-world, and the charge of fantasticality does not stick

against that very venture; it only sticks against demonstrably useless or harmful versions of it. But transempirical notions cannot be retailed without challenge, either, at least not in an axial community. Thanks to scriptural presentations of such notions, there can be theologically disciplined discussion of their meaning and relevance. Better-justified interpretations will shine in comparison with worse. One mark of a better-justified interpretation is that it prevents a religious conception from interfering with the sound formation of other sorts of knowledge. (It must be remembered, however, that on the plane of religious awareness, one of the key functions of a set of notions is to direct attention in ways that are strategically helpful spiritually, and part of that direction involves relative neglect; thus the first chapter of Genesis wants the reader to take note of "creeping things" but not of the five hundred thousand species of beetles, which would ruin the upcoming story of Noah's ark. It would be a mistake to expect a maximum of biological rationality in a religious discourse.)

(3) The issue of historical rationality seems particularly hard in defending scripture because it seems essential to scripture to put a strong twist on our ordinary understanding of history. Jewish scripture would scarcely be Jewish if it did not pay close attention to the historical fortunes of a sacred covenant between God and King David; Buddhist scriptures, on the other hand, would scarcely be Buddhist if they got bogged down in the fortunes of Buddhist kings.

There is a lurking problem here not only with the premise of scripture but with the premise of history. How can a historical account feature some agents without unfairly obscuring others? How can one organizing view of the main historical events and issues not be unfair to other views? How can a historical rehearsal of events be of any solid cognitive benefit, anyway, given the indeterminacy of large-scale shared action and the questionableness of all historical judgment of cause and result?

But let us grant that history as a professional historian tries to write it is cognitively worthwhile and that it is responsive to the ideal of maximal and fair recognition of past actions and experiences in a way that scripture characteristically is not. Let us grant also that scripture's premise of textually offered Guidance requires a strong centering of the scriptural picture of life-in-the-world that is bound to be in tension with the lateral extension of historical research and with the application of historical research to scriptures themselves.

Different scriptures may fare differently under the historical rationality challenge. Jewish scripture can be faulted for its glorification of the Israelite and Jewish experience, which has polarizing political effects throughout history and notably today in the conduct of the state of Israel, but on the other hand the passionate recording and interpreting of that experience in the Tanakh – paralleled in China by the intense scrutiny of political history that we find in some of the Confucian classics – can be credited as a main inspiration of serious historical inquiry as we know it today.

Compared with Jewish scripture, the Qur'an has a very open and spiritually affirmative view of world history. It wants to make the point that God sends prophets to remind people of their ultimate responsibility to God, especially for moral decency. It expressly states that *all* people have heard from prophets before ("There has been no community but that a warner has passed among them" [35:24]), just as all are invited now to hear the message of the climactic Prophet. In the Qur'an's view, the most important action in any historical context is the religious action of turning to God, but other sorts of action are significant as well insofar as they take advantage of the opportunity of having been created.

Buddhist scriptures stay away from historical narrative, apart from relating the discourses of the Buddha, and Buddhism has been faulted for encouraging an irresponsibly unhistorical view of life-in-the-world. A possible Buddhist response is simply to assert that historical knowledge is not spiritually decisive; enlightenment happens in another dimension entirely. The Buddha's Truth is the Truth, anytime and anywhere. A complementary response would be to point out that the demand for historical awareness will be motivated somewhere on a spectrum between trivial, distracting curiosity and serious concern for the humane quality of life-in-the-world. The sovereign attitude of compassionate solidarity with all sentient beings, persuasively presented and effectively elucidated in Buddhist scriptures, provides the best orientation for the more serious, more broadly concerned kind of historical thought. Even if historical reckoning *may* be subverted by Buddhist skepticism about the reality of self or by the swallowing up of distinct causes in the cosmic continuum of dependent origination, Buddhist pragmatism may pull the other way, using the tools of social science to find out how enlightenment is actually fostered or hindered.[3]

[3] See Joanna Macy, "To Reinhabit Time," in *World as Lover, World as Self* (Parallax, 2005), pp. 206–219.

As a further specification of scripture's ideal relevance, we may state two theses on scripture and rationality.

Thesis on the religious rationality of scripture: *In an axial religious community, scripture sets some of the supreme benchmarks for cognitive discrimination. Disregarding or underutilizing scripture is religiously irrational.*

Thesis on the general rationality of scripture: *Scripture is not necessarily inimical to rationality in any of the nonreligious applications of rationality.* The historical vindication of this thesis will lie in the practices of scripturalists like Augustine and Shankara and Zhu Xi who are exemplary in their broad rationality. (We should concede, however, that scripture is not necessarily supportive of nonreligious rationalities.)

6.3 "YOU ARE THE TENTH!": THE SUMMONS TO REASONABLENESS

We are taught to be mindful of our position vis-à-vis our fellows and to be considerate and fair from our earliest age. If all goes well, we grow up to be reasonable persons. The ideally reasonable person is one who takes as much trouble as one could expect anyone to take to act helpfully or at least non-harmfully. Since we are reciprocally dependent communicating thinkers, an essential part of reasonable action is reasonable thought and expression. If a thought is foreseeably harmful to someone else, a reasonable person keeps it to him- or herself. If a thought is foreseeably non-harmful, a reasonable person may choose to express it or not. If a thought is foreseeably helpful and can be expressed without taking undue trouble, a reasonable person expresses it. A thought having been expressed, the reasonable person is open to critical response at least to the extent that any well-meaning communicative collaborator ought to be. These general standards are inflected in relationships and situations that variously determine what counts as harm, help, and undue trouble. For example, the mutual dependence of spouses goes far beyond the mutual dependence of strangers passing each other on a sidewalk, and so marital reasonableness is far more demanding than general pedestrian reasonableness.

Most of us are imperfect realizers of reasonableness; I need to be reminded frequently that reasonableness requires *my* reasonable action in *this* relationship under *these* circumstances.

Because of its textual amplitude, a scripture can serve as a manual for the religiously responsible life. More than a resource, it becomes the unavoidable Guidance in the mode of a summons to reasonableness when it imposes on its reader or hearer an awareness of existing actually in religious relationship.

An oft-cited parable from the *shabdapramana* discussion makes the point that certain important kinds of knowledge can be acquired only by being spoken to. Whenever you are addressed, there is an interpellation effect of realizing yourself as a respondent. But you may also get more specific information about where and how you stand in the world of relationships. In the parable, ten foolish travelers cross a river and check afterward to make sure that everyone made it safely. But each member counts the others and comes to a total of only nine, concluding in anguish that someone is missing. Not until a wise passerby tells each of them, "You are the tenth!" do they realize the truth.[4] Advaitins say that with proper preparation and firm deliberation, you acquire the knowledge of the sole reality of imperceptible Brahman and that "You are that!" (Chandogya Upanishad 6.8.7) only from being told this by the Upanishadic text.[5] A comparable Christian notion is that "faith comes from what is heard" – that is, the proclamation of forgiveness and redemption in Christ (Romans 10:17).

Now it may seem that the active knowledge of one's responsible place in relationship can only be provided or triggered by a live speaker. How could the same thing happen with a reader picking up a book? Have we not recognized that the reader's detachment and freedom of initiative with respect to a text fosters the reader's mental independence?

It is true that there will be no special interpellation if a reader picks up a scriptural text in the same noncommittal way that he or she picks up an ordinary text. Even if a scriptural text happens to strike the reader as interesting or moving, the summons is still not fully scriptural. But the intentionally scripturalist reader knows that the text is supposed to work as the Guidance. The reader comes before scripture like a bride or groom coming before that personally fateful betrothed. Scripture says, "You are my disciple!"

As the wedding analogy implies, the presence of a congregation is essential to the scriptural summons. The "you" addressed by scripture is not alone. ("You are the tenth!" can serve as a reminder of this point as well.) When Jesus' disciples said, "Were not our hearts burning within

---

[4] Anantanand Rambachan, *Accomplishing the Accomplished: The* Vedas *as a Source of Valid Knowledge in Shankara* (University of Hawai'i Press, 1991), p. 60.
[5] Shankara, *Upadeshasahasri* 1.12.2–3, 1.18.172–174.

us ... while he was opening the scriptures to us?" (Luke 24:32), they were registering not only their momentary excitement in having encountered Jesus again after his death but their scriptural stimulation of responsibility as members of a historic community sustaining a textually Guiding model of life-in-the-world – a model that seemed to them to have just been dramatically enhanced. Christians hoped that Jews and cognizant Gentiles would be drawn into their movement by this stimulation.

From an epistemologically unsympathetic perspective, there could not be a gain in responsibility in becoming the follower of a scripture. It seems rather a lunge into superstition. The "burning heart" sounds like being carried away in "enthusiasm." The supposedly heightened responsibility of scripturalism draws an intolerant line against those who have not joined in – including some who may be analogously committed to a rival Guidance.

From a scripturalist perspective, however, there could not be a fully responsible life *apart* from textually available Guidance, and there is a general reason for this premise distinct from one's devotion to a particular scripture: it is not possible to invite all thoughtful persons into shared subscription to ultimate Guidance without a universally accessible Text that addresses our most important shared guidance needs, including our need for free discussion. One cannot play football without a field and a ball; one cannot play in the formulation of Guidance for a most-inclusive community without an accepted text containing interpretable ultimate directives.

A case can be made that the best text for this purpose would be a secular charter like the United Nations Declaration of Human Rights rather than a world-religious scripture. A scripturalist who has known the "burning heart" activation of maximized responsibility in the format of membership in a scripturalist community would want to apply that test to the secular alternative. Do hearts in fact burn? Is there an increase in experienced meaningful responsibility in following the guidance of the candidate text? Does following the text appropriately strengthen *following* itself, with the most important appellants in view and without an oppressive distortion of the guidance relationship? Texts that are discernibly lacking in spiritual motivation or that hamper development of the best community by their insensitivity or intolerance would be disqualified.

One can accept the ideal of textually optimized responsibility but conclude that we have not yet successfully identified an acceptable Text or that such a text has not yet been created. Or one may take the apparent absence of an acceptable Text, despite millennia of trials, as an indication that the ideal is impossible. A scripturalist might reply: I know in my own case that scripture does support responsibility. It makes me answerable to divinity in a best-informed, perspicuous way, and it enables me to respond productively to any interpretive need that arises in a global, multigenerational human conversation about the Guidance. My scripture is famous enough to summon everyone, is interesting and moving enough to hold everyone's attention, provides a wealth of material to support textually grounded nonpartisan discussion, and, most importantly, so clearly proffers the Guidance to each of us that one's heart must burn with the plunge or at least the prospect of full personal investment in it.

Thesis on the religious responsibility of scripturalism: *In an axial religious community, scripture is an indispensable platform for the religiously required maximum of responsiveness to divine and other beings.* Disregarding or underutilizing scripture is religiously irresponsible. One who is not yet a member of a scriptural community but who, in a literate context, reaches with the fullest optimism for Guidance or is ready in principle to take the fullest responsibility in receiving Guidance ought to consider whether one at least of the famous scriptures fills the bill.

A critic of scripturalism might ask: Even if we grant that there are some shining individual examples, when has scripturalism not warped the prevalent conception of responsibility in a community toward blind loyalty, reinforcing social discrimination and producing hatred of heretics and contempt of heathens?

Here is an optimistic Axiality thesis in response.

Thesis on the general responsibility of scripture: *In an axial religious community – which must be understood as an ever-axializing community – the promulgation and discussion of religious ideals can, thanks to the support of a canonical Text, inform the educational and political processes of a community in such a way that religious responsibility effectively mitigates heteronomous social conformisms and self-centered passions.*

On the optimistic view, the mixed and often discouraging evidence of scripturalism in practice reflects the struggle of scripturalism with less benign factors in human life more than it reflects inherent negatives of scripturalism. A typical, ideally inspiring scripturalist move is to "go back to scripture" or to what is perceived as the core of scripture – often the apparent personality of the religious founder and the quality of interactions in the earliest community – to peel away religious teachings that are playing out harmfully.

6.4 THE GNARLED TREE: THE TARGET OF INTELLIGENCE

We are concerned to choose more intelligent ways of living for the sake of achieving our goals. If the goal of life is to learn the most about divinity and maximally optimistic and responsible life in an explicit, discussible fashion, then following one or more scriptures is obviously a smart way to go. Scriptures are supremely rewarding study texts for religious thought, especially when bundled with their canonical supplements and commentaries – partly because of their rich and potent content and partly because of their uniquely important mandate in the scheme of religious teaching. But not every person wants to learn about divinity, and not every religious person wants to learn about divinity in a textually guided fashion. From a scripturalist point of view this is not ideal, and so the typical job description of a religious leader in a scripturalist tradition includes (1) making the case to the public, on suitable occasions, for learning about divinity on the basis of scriptural guidance and (2) making the case to the religious for learning *as much* as what scripture offers, or at least what its core offers, using communally tested methods and touchstones of interpretation.

The topic is the best life and how to attain it. Religious teaching comes forth in different guises, sometimes as a gentle amplification of desires and practical hunches people already have – as in refining the recipes for good character and stable community, healing, consoling, and tying prosperity to confidence – but sometimes as "foolishness to the wise" (1 Corinthians 1:27) or stunning paradox ("Banish wisdom, discard knowledge, and the people will be benefited a hundredfold" [*Daodejing* 19]), profoundly challenging normal practical assumptions.

There is a view of the axial shift in thought that would predict paradoxes appearing like a storm front between the mundane perspective of preaxial culture and the new transcendentalism of thinkers who have made mental contact with Being or Goodness or Emptiness and have adjusted their sense of what is real and worthwhile accordingly. Whether or not an axial teaching is ontologically transcendentalist, it does always involve a significant change of practical aim and method from communally embedded life just insofar as it offers Guidance to a free individual. This passage in the *Zhuangzi* makes multiple points about the situation:

Hui Tzu said to Chuang Tzu [Zhuangzi], "I have a big tree of the kind men call *shu*. Its trunk is too gnarled and bumpy to apply a measuring line to, its branches too bent and twisty to match up to a compass or square. You could stand it by the road and no carpenter would look at it twice. Your words, too, are big and useless, and so everyone alike spurns them!"

Chuang Tzu said, "Maybe you've never seen a wildcat or a weasel. It crouches down and hides, watching for something to come along. It leaps and races east and west, not hesitating to go high or low – until it falls into a trap and dies in the net. Then again there's the yak, big as a cloud covering the sky. It certainly knows how to be big, though it doesn't know how to catch rats. Now you have this big tree and you're distressed because it's useless. Why don't you plant it in Not-Even-Anything Village, or the field of Broad-and-Boundless, relax and do nothing by its side, or lie down for a free and easy sleep under it? Axes will never shorten its life, nothing can ever harm it. If there's no use for it, how can it come to grief or pain?"

(Chap. 1 [HY 1/42–47])[6]

The plain man Hui Tzu will not see the appeal of the Daoist "free and easy" versions of divinity and virtue until he sees both ends and means differently. To prepare the way, there is a Daoist reduction of two models of teleological efficiency – the exquisitely well-adapted wildcat or weasel having its own busy pursuit cancelled by someone else's busy pursuit and the yak having feeding limitations inseparable from its size advantage. What is ordinarily "useful" in one's life cannot be the final goal for a thoughtful subject. Finality can be found only in liberation from "use." Seen in this light, the gnarled tree and idleness are emblematic of the truly intelligent life.

Zhuangzi's striking thought could be received without the good offices of the scriptural *Zhuangzi* (although one would be much less likely to be aware of it had it not been published as a canonical text). The essential difference scripture makes to the thought is by fostering interpretive communication about it on the largest scale. For there are many questions and objections to be raised to Zhuangzi's proposal that the passage by itself does not answer: How does one combine the "free and easy" perspective with making a living, belonging to a family, helping others in need? We can align the passage with other contents of the *Zhuangzi* to work out intelligent answers that the *Zhuangzi* itself seems to support; considering other Daoist texts, we can work out still more nuanced answers and specific applications with Daoist credibility. And we can do this collaboratively with generations of Daoist writers whose concerns are the same as ours (yet with differences worth considering).

---

[6] Zhuangzi, *The Complete Works of Chuang-Tzu* (trans. Burton Watson, Columbia University Press, 1968), p. 35. HY citations refer to chapter and line number in the Harvard-Yenching text (ed. Charles Sturgeon, ctext.org/zhuangzi, 2006–2018).

One could get a piece of radically smart advice, mind-bending yet concretely helpful, from a conversation with a friend or from a lucky visit to a website. But only by drawing on a literate tradition dedicated to the interpretation of a life-guiding proposal can one participate in a culturally-historically thick realization of the idea's meaning and practical relevance – a "thick" realizing in the sense that one has arrived at concrete ways of taking many of the main variables of human experience so that they hang together in enduring support of an understanding of the situation such that one is not only well informed but well poised as a thinker and as a communicator. Such realizing is enabled by the cumulative tradition a culture possesses in its arts and sciences, history, law, philosophy, and religious teaching; but only in philosophy and religious teaching is the available guidance intentionally centered on the individual's free choice of belief, and only in religious teaching is the highest-stakes Guidance intentionally sited in a historically concrete yet maximally inclusive community. To be smartest about *that* in all *those* dimensions requires the help of scripture, the scripturalist can argue.

Thesis on the religious intelligence of scripturalism: *By virtue of its canonical synthesis of compelling core spiritual ideals and germane religious traditions, its full articulation, and its ongoing communal examination, scripture is an indispensable resource and medium of the most intelligent religious thinking and communicating.*

Critics complain that scripturalism is anti-intelligent insofar as it lays down rigid limits to acceptable thought and perpetuates old ideas that would otherwise be discredited. "At its best, religion is a set of stories that recount the ethical and contemplative insights of our wisest ancestors. But these stories come to us bundled with ancient confusion and perennial lies. And they invariably harden into doctrines that defy revision, generation after generation" (Sam Harris).[7] In the multigenerational unity of thought that the scriptural community celebrates, the critic sees stagnation and bigotry. In light of this concern, a positive thesis on the general intelligence of scripturalism cannot merely cite the powerful axial ideals and other religiously valuable resources rendered classic by the core scriptural texts; it must make something of the long-running communication about scriptural content, which in fact does not merely perpetuate old ideas but develops them in response to every sort of challenge, as the literatures of scripturalism show.

---

[7] Sam Harris, *Waking Up: A Guide to Spirituality without Religion* (Simon & Schuster, 2014), p. 203.

Thesis on the general intelligence of scripturalism: *Inasmuch as scriptures serve as platforms for unending discussion of the meaning of axial ideals and other cultural commitments that must be considered in working out the most concretely promising approach to living the best life, scriptural perspectives on life-in-the-world should be regarded as some of the most intelligent available.*

*

So far I have brought in objections to scripturalism ad hoc, as challenges to positive rationales that would be favored by scripturalists. We have not yet considered anything close to an organized full attack. I will suggest main points for such an attack in the next section, along with possible responses.

6.5 CRITICAL THESES ON SCRIPTURALISM

For each of these arguably essential or typical troubles with scripture, I think it will be generally agreed that there is much historical evidence to support the negative claim.

(1) In purporting to deliver effective ultimate Guidance in a particular package, scripturalism promotes *superstitious* belief. A superstition is an unjustified belief that if a doable X is done, a desirable Y will surely result. X is magic; Y is golden. The belief is motivated by hope or fear rather than by intelligent observation and reasoning. We see scriptural superstition not only in egregious cases of treating printed scriptures as fetishes but in the most typical kind of scripturally influenced conversation where a passage from scripture is cited to automatically center, if not conclude, a line of thought.

To probe what justifies an expectation, we may distinguish between kinds of confidence. A piano guaranteed to play beautiful music would be a magic piano – that is, a hoax; one would be foolish to start hitting the keys believing in that result. A score of the *Moonlight Sonata*, however, is not a score of beautiful music in a magic way – the *Moonlight Sonata is* beautiful music when played properly, as we know from experience, and so we are rightly confident that we will experience beauty in a performance of it. Similarly, scripturalists testify that their scripture, properly followed, *is* great guidance. But scripturalists lose the benefit of the music analogy when they claim to *know* further that their scripture is uniquely the supreme textual guidance. One could choose to dedicate oneself to following a scripture in order to lead the best-guided life possible, just as one could choose to dedicate oneself to beautiful music by playing the *Moonlight Sonata* as well as it can be played; these choices are not objectionable on their face. But positing that a scripture *in fact* causes the best life and that devotees simply take advantage of this fact is foolish or in bad faith.

The scripturalist is at risk of being trapped in a superstitious confidence in the power of a scripture as a consequence of having taken the devotional plunge of a sovereign religious attitude: *piety*, binding one to an already-determined holy reality to which one must be infinitely grateful and deferential; or *faith*, binding one to a holy prospect of optimal future life about which one must be infinitely enthused; or *love*, binding one in infinite appreciativeness and responsiveness to a holy partner in the actual present of living.[8] Scripture is an integral element in piety and faith because it explains fully and canonically what is revered or looked forward to; it is an integral element in devout love because it is at hand, open to a page, always able to be read and to keep the reader company (or the hearer, on the basis of recitation) in that profoundly response-provoking way.

A scripturalist is under pressure, then, to separate devotion from superstition. Here is one model: It is not superstitious to regard one's spouse as the most wonderful person in the world. My spouse is "the Person for me." If my scripture is "the Guidance for me" and others of like mind in just that way, no one should object. But putting the Guidance on this basis makes the axial assumption that every individual decides about it freely. The analogy is not perfect: my devotion to my spouse does not entitle me to ask everyone to adore and defer to her, yet it seems that I am not unreasonable in inviting everyone to share with me in submitting to my scripture's guidance, since a scripture, more like a political constitution than a person, is designed to govern a large, diverse community and, I might argue, has a historical track record of guiding many individuals who scrupulously avoided superstition – so at least I can argue by pointing to role models and examples of communal felicity in my tradition.

---

[8] For a rationale for this strategic definition of religious attitude ideals, see Steven G. Smith, "Three Religious Attitudes," *Philosophy and Theology*, 11 (1998), 3–24, and *Appeal and Attitude* (Indiana University Press, 2005), chap. 8.

(2) Claiming to provide complete Guidance, scripturalism promotes *fantasticality* – most blatantly so when cities of golden pavement or lands of jeweled trees are described as the believers' future abode, but always quite forcefully insofar as scriptural texts use the power of the book to define the theater of action in which readers live – just as in the powerful make-believe of fiction, except with a serious claim of realism. A scripture is not just a poem on the laudable qualities of the best life or a temporarily inspiring story. Devotion to it means treating the life it figures as real. Scriptural canons were assembled to give texts the best chance of working on their audience in this way. The mystics who claim that their scriptures *are* the reality on which the world is based may be expressing themselves more extremely than most scripturalists, but they are not fundamentally out of step with the scripture premise.

Those who live fantastically pay a toll in missed opportunities and misunderstood suffering imposed by the reality from which they have been distracted. If they persist in thinking they have made a good bargain with their inspiring alternative life, the rest of us with whom they do in fact share a real situation may justly reproach them for refusing to share with us all the responsibilities of dealing with it – such as the responsibilities of defending human rights politically or preserving ecological conditions of survival on earth.

A scripturalist might reply that the worry about fantastical pseudo-realism is overstated. We can point out the small subset of scripturalists who do intentionally live in a most-scripturally-formed theater of life; they are monastics or mystics, and they know, just as well as everyone else knows about them, that they have chosen a specialized, socially tolerable option within the larger field of scripturally guided life. Their chosen life is sustained just by their intention, not by naïve assumption or belief. They live in scripture the way conscientious married people live in marriage. Meanwhile, most scripturalists apply varying measures of scriptural guidance to life in an untamed world that is recognized as such by the wise. That recognition is reinforced by the world-religious scriptures themselves:

> [Yahweh to Job:]
> Is the wild ox willing to serve you?
> Will it spend the night at your crib?
> Can you tie it in the furrow with ropes,
> or will it harrow the valleys after you?
> (Job 40:9–10)

[Krishna-Vishnu to Arjuna:]
Gazing upon your mighty form with its myriad mouths, eyes, arms, thighs, feet, bellies, and sharp, gruesome tusks, the worlds shudder – how much more I! ... As moths in bursting, hurtling haste rush into a lighted blaze to destruction, so do the worlds, well-trained in hasty violence, pour into your mouths to undoing! ... Tell me, who are You, your form so cruel? ... what You are set on doing I do not understand. (Bhagavad-Gita 11:23, 29, 31)

Joy, anger, grief, delight, worry, regret, fickleness, inflexibility, modesty, will-fulness, candor, insolence – music from empty holes, mushrooms springing up in dampness, day and night replacing each other before us, and no one knows where they sprout from. Let it be! Let it be! ... I do not know what makes them the way they are. (*Zhuangzi* chap. 2 [HY 2/14])

It is true that some religious people construct a scripture-based alter-native reality that evades the most fully sharable world, but that perver-sion of literacy is not uniquely religious; the same split between fantasticality and realism is found in politics and government, the aca-demic disciplines, and wherever else literacy can be used well or poorly. We can reasonably demand that the virtual reality projected from scrip-ture serve as a completion of generally shared reality rather than as a replacement for it.

(3) In claiming that scripture is indispensable for contact with the first principles of Guidance, scripturalism is peremptory and *authoritarian* – jeopardizing the axial premise of a wholesome guidance relationship between mentally active participants and binding the Guidance to a contingent and questionable human vehicle.

Scripturalists do often affirm that the ultimate determinant of our orientation is just the Truth and that any argument or text has guiding authority only to the extent that it effectively represents the Truth. How-ever, the scripturalist version of "Truth" is not the still-to-be-determined object of free inquiry that one supposes in approaching truth rationally or reasonably (or in existential openness to transcendence, as Jaspers would say). The gambit of scripturalism is to impose its own idea about what the Truth turns out to be – the divine Love or Bliss or Harmony – selling that idea in its mobilization of the genres of linguistic guidance and binding the Idea to its canonized text. The texts – in practice, the top-ranking inter-preters of the texts – become tyrants.

Could anyone who takes seriously the ideal of Truth allow our access to Truth to be controlled by a particular set of utterances? That would absurdly impose on Truth the weaknesses of our linguistic efforts. The issue is least troubling in traditions that have large, relatively open canons, but even in those canons one finds texts that claim decisive importance for themselves – implying that we would be cut off from the Guidance if such a text were lost or were never rightly interpreted. For example, the Daoist *Divine Incantations Scripture* makes an urgent claim for its own unique relevance:

> The world abounds in vice and lacks goodness. The people do not recognize the truth. The Three Caverns revelations [the three main traditions in Daoist scriptures] have been spreading for a long time, but the people are benighted and fail to seek out and accept them. They bring suffering on themselves. What can be done? ...
>
> The Dao says: From now on, wherever there are Daoist priests who recite this scripture ... Heaven will allow those among the living who are ill and those with official entanglements to obtain release ...
>
> The Dao says: When Daoist priests receive the *Divine Incantations Scripture* they may not receive other scriptures at the same time. They must receive and practice this book separately. Why is this? Because there is so much divine power of the great demon kings in this scripture.[9]

According to their own traditions, the Jains suffered a major scripture loss in the fourth century BCE when a famine killed many of those who had memorized their sacred texts. Now the two principal branches of Jainism disagree about which scriptures survived and which versions of scriptures are authoritative. This is the sort of awkward and absurd predicament that scripturalists land in by yoking Guidance to their vulnerable texts.[10] Any scripturalist community must ask itself, What if we lost these texts or could not agree about which texts count? Christians may ask, What does it mean that the Gospel of Thomas was excluded from the New Testament? Sikhs may ask, What does it mean that Mirabai's song was deleted from the Guru Granth Sahib?[11] Having staked so much on the headship of the sacred text, we are liable to fall into confusion about our heading.

The Jains have carried on by combining the idea that supreme Truth obtains eternally, whether or not scriptural records of it happen to exist, with the principle that every human knower knows differently, and only

---

[9] Trans. Nathan Sivin, in *Sources of Chinese Tradition*, 2nd ed., vol. 1 (ed. William Theodore de Bary and Irene Bloom, Columbia University Press, 1999), pp. 408–409.

[10] The Jain traditions about lost scriptures may reflect attempts of Jain sects to justify their different scripture-based stances against each other. We do not know from historical evidence what happened. Zoroastrian tradition also tells of a major scripture loss due to persecution.

[11] On possible reasons for deletion, see Pashaura Singh, *The Guru Granth Sahib: Canon, Meaning and Authority* (Oxford University Press, 2000), pp. 193–195.

partially, and properly speaks only conditionally. (The parable of the blind men and the elephant is popular in Jain literature.) Evidently the orthodox scriptures and commentaries the Jains have in hand are sufficiently helpful in relating human perspectives to Truth and sufficiently compatible with other available guidance that Jains may consider themselves even now to be truly Guided (on "the right path ... the most excellent path" [*Uttaradhyayana Sutra* 23.63])[12] without being fundamentally at risk of missing the right Guidance. Note that this solution is possible only because primary authority is *not* placed with a text (although nonorthodox texts can interfere with the transmission and therefore must be rejected).[13]

A scripturalist might also make the general claim that to worry too much about short-circuiting the quest for Truth amounts to perversely avoiding truth and the benefits of relationship with it. "The object of opening the mind, as of opening the mouth, is to shut it again on something solid," wrote G. K. Chesterton, an orthodox Roman Catholic, perhaps pulling too strongly toward authoritarian resolutions of inquiry.[14] In the optimal use of scripture in seeking truth and rightly balanced guidance relations, the horizon of free inquiry and critical correction is never closed; there is a fruitful relation between the confident orientation toward a supreme appellant and humble diligence in continued research and conversation.

Continuing in somewhat the same vein:

(4) Scripturalism is deeply *arbitrary* insofar as it has no noncircular way to distinguish acceptable from unacceptable determinations of scriptural guidance – whether in deciding which texts count or which textual interpretations are correct, or in relating particular offers of guidance to eternal ideals, or in ordering older and newer meanings in the layers of the text, or in ordering older and newer situations in the scriptural community. For example, some current forms of scripturally justified Zionism and jihadism are surely unacceptable, but it is not so clear that there is anything wrong with them specifically as interpretations of scripture.

---

[12] In *Sacred Books of the East*, vol. 45 (trans. Hermann Jacobi, Oxford University Press, 1894).

[13] See Paul Dundas, *History, Scripture and Controversy in a Medieval Jain Sect* (Routledge, 2007), chap. 3 on Jain scripturalism.

[14] *The Autobiography of G. K. Chesterton* (Ignatius, 2006), p. 217. The remark draws a contrast between himself and H. G. Wells, who apparently "thought that the object of opening the mind is simply opening the mind" (ibid.).

The structural problem here is that the text is passive, a *determinandum*. When a scripturalist treats the text as an active *determinans* of directive meaning, there is still no getting around the fact that the reader is *making* the text speak directively; the text acquires the virtual intention of saying what it says, of "meaning" X or Y, from its interpreter, even if the interpreter is working conscientiously with data supplied by the text and historical knowledge about the text's origination. A careful reading of a scriptural text will indeed be constrained very extensively by the text's recorded language, and scholarship will bring in further constraints of related facts. But readers will nonetheless disagree endlessly and momentously about how to read and apply a scriptural text. This is because multiple interpretive frameworks are always available to guide their construal of the text's purport, and divergent approaches are sure to be taken for at least three reasons: (a) interpreters differ in sensibility and in practical preferences; (b) interpreters are competitive, vying with each other for attention and influence; and (c) in the spirit of committed communication, it is the ideal fulfillment of every conversation to explore all possibly meaningful alternative views of the subject matter.[15] Thus guidance comes out of the process of conversing about scripture and other things; ascribing guidance to scripture itself is illusory.

Those who regard scriptures as religious "classics" in the general sense of classic texts may as well accept this description of the situation, for on their view the classic texts merit their high valuation just in being the texts we find we have the best conversations about. But scripturalists intent on receiving the Guidance are not satisfied by this valuation.

There are quite different scripturalist solutions of the problem. The simplest is to affirm that a certain community has historically arrived at agreement on a certain construal of scriptural guidance and finds itself able now and for the foreseeable future to ward off any disagreements that would disrupt its working agreement by honoring all consensually helpful texts and policing the lines of shared belief. On this view, the text designated Scripture is an instrument of communal self-guidance. It may

---

[15] Jorge J. E. Gracia observes rightly that "theological differences cannot be resolved by just looking at revealed texts. They can be resolved only by identifying the sources of theological disagreement and addressing them. To do otherwise is like trying to compare and reconcile Freudian and non-Freudian interpretations of a text. No reconciliation is possible in terms of the texts themselves, because the source of disagreement is to be found in the theoretical framework used to interpret the texts, rather than vice versa." *How Can We Know What God Means?: The Interpretation of Revelation* (Palgrave, 2001), p. 141.

be further affirmed that the scripture-using self-guiding community is inspirationally guided in turn by divine being, as, for example, personal experiences of God or a larger action of the Holy Spirit on the community may be thought to guide the Christian church.[16] But it may be insisted that scripture is an instrument used or projected more directly by divine being – not through the mediation of other human experiences of the divine – to provide Guidance to humans. It may be thought that the scriptural Word contains the very form and energy of primal being. Or it may be argued that the Word can summon and cue humans in a uniquely life-optimizing way – speaking *now*, from *beyond* the horizon of what the hearer already sees and feels, *teaching* in the eminent sense. The human writers and interpreters of scriptural language can be seen as deputies carrying out the divine communication.[17] The divine gift of guidance may thus be "arbitrary" in relation to ordinary procedures of validation but at the same time supremely nonarbitrary – the one remedy for the arbitrariness of the whole human position in the world – in enabling a rectified relationship with transcendent being, as when the stellar person at a party solves your impossible problem of approach by speaking to you first.

(5) Because they are human linguistic formulations treated as divinely meaningful, scriptures typically present *insoluble interpretive issues* that make scripturalism cognitively insecure and socially unstable. The incongruity between the human qualities of scriptural texts and the divine target meaning calls forth problematic theories of allegory and divine accommodation in defense of religious reading.

Allegory is the optimistic idea that a text can say more than it says, putting its audience in touch with a religiously relevant higher meaning. Divine meaning is thought to be accessible in this way due either to its eternal omnipresence or to a specific divine initiative.

In practice, allegorical readings are not ecstatic visitations of unheard-of meaning (which would create a different problem) but rather predictable impositions of contestable theories of being and the communicative situation. For example, allegorical reading in the Abrahamic traditions is dominated by Platonic emanationism and Platonic psychology. Reading the biblical interpretations of Philo or Origen or Ibn 'Arabi, one is

---

[16] Karl Rahner, "Über die Schriftinspiration," *Zeitschrift für katholische Theologie*, 78 (1956), 127–168; David H. Kelsey, *The Uses of Scripture in Recent Theology* (Fortress, 1975), pp. 207–217.

[17] Nicholas Wolterstorff, *Divine Discourse* (Cambridge University Press, 1995), chap. 3.

drawn back repeatedly to basic theses of Platonism. But allegorism is a weak premise of teaching insofar as it involves, on the one hand, a familiar global thesis about the ultimate message of scriptural texts and, on the other hand, a reckless freedom to arrive at that thesis by any interpretive route, no matter how fanciful. In both of these respects, allegorism seems to fail as a strategy for relating responsibly to a text or to the divine.

Allegorical reading also reinforces the social division of classes of scripturalists that Ibn Rushd described. There is a higher allegorical meaning that the philosophically educated can understand and benefit from that others cannot. But this means a breakup in the Guidance that is supposed to unite a universal community – or else an intolerably author-itarian rule of ignorant laypeople by the allegorically enlightened elite.

Divine accommodation is a more humble counterpart to the allegory idea, looking at the situation the other way around. (At any rate, I will discuss the humble version of it; there is also a proud version that takes for granted that enlightened people do understand the spiritually highest meaning of scripture while the common people cannot and so must be accommodated by anthropomorphic depictions of the divine and recipes for bloody rituals.) Divine being, the source of divine meaning, is thought to be abundantly powerful and loving so that communication with humanity is sure to take place. The Guidance is going to be here some-where. But a scripture is obviously a human production. Therefore we must appreciate that divine being has condescended to speak to us as we are capable of understanding – to "lisp to us as nurses are wont to speak to little children," as Calvin put it.[18] In another formulation, the divine has *appropriated* human utterances in such a way as to make points for our ultimate benefit.[19]

Divine accommodation may be affirmed a priori, in confidence that divine being *would* reach us through our own language (given the crucial human importance of language); then the category of scripture may pick out the texts and interpretive traditions in which readers have the best reason to believe that such condescension has actually occurred. There may be a history of successful religious community building with the texts as charters or impressive spiritual fruits produced by reception of the texts. There may be a somewhat haunted experience of communion with

[18] Jean Calvin, *Institutes of the Christian Religion* (trans. Henry Beveridge, Hendrickson, 2008), 1.13.1, p. 66.
[19] Wolterstorff, chap. 12.

the divine by means of what is felt to be the best of available books even in the absence of breakthrough to an extraordinary articulated divine meaning.

The interpretive problem generated by the accommodation premise is the inverse of the allegory problem. Rather than inserting the reader's preconceived theory in the space of divine meaning, accommodation theory voids that space by placing the divine meaning behind an opaque screen. The audience needs to have some basis for believing that scriptural texts point them in the Right direction, but divine guidance is present in the text incognito. Everything in it, after all, is anthropomorphism; even when the text says, "Thus says the Perfect One," no sense of perfection is given beyond a human conception and thus no guidance superior to that of human wisdom. When a later sanctified text offers a different guidance than an earlier sanctified text, there can be no unmistakably divine indication that the one supersedes the other; the human audience makes its own decision about this. As with allegory but more indirectly, scriptural interpretation is turned over to interpreters' theories about divine purpose – theories that will always be eminently contestable. The critic may conclude that it is more honest and productive to settle for discerning the best of human wisdom than to believe in cognitively unsupported hints that scripture serves a greater purpose.

Although allegorical reading is an unsatisfactory basis for interpretation of the Guidance, a world-religion scripturalist community must resort to it in order to patch together the historically, linguistically, intellectually, and ideologically diverse pieces of its canon, as Hindus for example must read the Rig Veda's myths allegorically to orient them to the Upanishadic meditation on Brahman and Atman or to theistic devotion to Vishnu or Shiva, and as Christians must read Jewish scriptures allegorically to orient them to Christ and the Christian life and to explain Christian scripture to the educated. Although accommodation theory is an unsatisfactory basis as well, scripturalists must resort to it in order to acknowledge the plain fact that scriptures are embedded in the history of human communication and so in cultural evolution – so that Mahayana Buddhists must regard unacceptable Theravada teachings as "skillful means" accommodations to the spiritual situation of earlier Buddhists.

A general scripturalist response to these concerns might be called, not with Kant's approval, roughly Kantian: there is an intelligible *ideal* of divine Guidance even though the empirical *actuality* of guidance is humanly structured just as allegorical and accommodationist readings suggest it is – that is, by theoretical framing, insofar as there is construable meaning in religious texts, and by ignorance, insofar as there is a permanent opacity of the divine. (Kant would disallow the metaphysical knowledge on which allegorists often presume but would encourage us to recognize that certain concepts are bound to be applied in making sense of experience.) The ideal is meaningful a priori and relevant to religious life because religious life is, of its essence, maximally optimistic and responsible; it is that side of life where we do not ignore the Other, where we endeavor to bring the ordinary human horizon notionally and emotionally within a farther horizon. As religious communities muddle through the endless debates that the critic correctly predicts they will have, their interpretive frustration is not disabling, after all, since they take their debates to be tracking, never definitively resolving, the ideal Guidance.

Defenders of allegorical and accommodationist interpretation might claim that they transcend the limitations imposed on them in these critical portrayals. In his study of the seminal Christian allegorist Origen, Henri de Lubac argues that the scriptural meanings found by Origen's allegorizing are typically more Christological than Platonic – that is, inspired directly by Christ in his New Testament attestation, in the conjunction of that attestation with Jewish scriptures – and that Christological allegorizing is enabled by the epochal situation-changing divine initiative of Christ's life, death, and resurrection rather than by freely available ideas.[20] Equipped with the newly provided manifestation of Christ, the symbolic resonance of many items in scripture is allowed to strengthen in certain directions. (De Lubac believes that "symbolism" anchors interpretive discoveries in the datum more firmly than "allegory" does.) When Job, for example, says, "I know that my Vindicator lives!" (19:25 – "Redeemer" in Christian Bibles), he is *not* in fact talking about Christ, but once Christ has appeared, any religious reader can judge that Job *may* be talking about as *much as* a vindicator of that kind, and a devotee of Christ can hardly not think that Job's exclamation reaches toward Christ specifically. Further, de Lubac shows that Origen's interpretations are often represented as journeys into surpassing mystery, presuming a growth in "spiritual understanding" but no capture of the truth by a philosophical theory and no definite boundary between one person's understanding and another's.[21] Whatever one

---

[20] Henri de Lubac, *History and Spirit: The Understanding of Scripture according to Origen* (trans. Anne Englund Nash and Juvenal Merriell, Ignatius, 2007).

[21] Ibid., p. 103.

thinks of Origen's own results, this approach seems a religious possibility in any scriptural tradition.

Generally, it seems fair to say that any optimistic or responsible reader – and a fortiori any religious reader – will be sympathetic to the implicit reaching of human expressions, even textually polished expressions, toward meanings beyond what they have clearly formulated. Some silly inferences have been drawn from the small differences of wording between two phrases or lines in a Hebrew poetic couplet, but it is not silly to suppose that a Hebrew couplet's repetition somehow extends the reach of the thought.[22] Nor is it gratuitous to suppose that the characters and situations of compelling narratives are originally charged with the profound significance of the soul or the cosmos. Allegorical reading is an organized way of exploring these possibilities. Accommodation, too, can be defended by a basic epistemological consideration. Humans understand only what they are capable of understanding and more broadly speaking are helped only as they are capable of being helped; moreover, human capacities are culturally, which is to say also historically, determined, and sudden great changes of thought or practice are not humanly possible.[23] Or, to shift emphasis to the infinite greatness of the holy: "If the Torah did not put on the garments of this world the world could not

---

[22] De Lubac states that Origen's "ignorance of Hebrew parallelism makes him seek all sorts of distinctions and gradations when there is only a duplication of more or less synonymous expressions" (350). But Philo before him had modeled the avid scripturalist approach of finding distinct meaning wherever the text gave any hint of the possibility. According to Moshe Idel, a major theme of the Zohar is grounded in biblical parallelism: "One of the most astounding characteristics of the Zoharic exegesis of the Bible is the exploitation of the biblical stylistic phenomena of parallelism between the different parts of a verse, in order to introduce a bipolar reading that is in many cases seen as representing the polarity between male and female. This approach is related to the comprehensive arcanization of the biblical text as it implies that mere repetition of synonymous terms would diminish the semantic cargo of the text. By reading a dual vision into the parallels in the verse, which are synonyms in the biblical style, the Zohar creates a drama, often implying a sexual or erotic mythical event that occurs in the sefirotic realm." "The Zohar as Exegesis," in Katz, p. 94.

[23] "Man, according to his nature, is not capable of abandoning suddenly all to which he was accustomed ... and as [in Moses'] time the way of life generally accepted and customary in the whole world and the universal service upon which we were brought up consisted in offering various species of living beings in the temples in which images were set up, in worshiping the latter, and in burning incense before them ... His wisdom ... and His gracious ruse ... did not require that He give us a Law prescribing the rejection, abandonment, and abolition of all these kinds of worship." Moses Maimonides, *The Guide of the Perplexed* (trans. Shlomo Pines, University of Chicago Press, 1962), p. 292, 3.32.

endure" (Zohar 3:152a).[24] Accommodationist interpretation takes account of these limitations consciously. It opens up the significant topic of divine providence in the history of religious awareness; in a secular offshoot of providential thinking, the theme of "the education of the human race" powers the rise of historical consciousness.[25]

(6) The published text of a scripture is supposed to provide definitive Guidance, which places scripturalism, unlike a living guide, in a *fixed guidance dilemma*: either the followers of a scripture must comply with its demands throughout their generations, with no adjustment of the guidance prompted by the changing shape and need of the world they live in – the validity of their scripture and their frozen or tacitly adjusted understanding of it becoming more and more questionable as the cultural ground moves under their feet – or followers must use extrascriptural means of substantially adjusting the directives of scripture, in which case the authority of the text becomes less than fully scriptural.

There is a related *unsurpassability dilemma*, if unsurpassability is understood as a fixed limit of valid Guidance. Any momentous new learning or insight in a scriptural community would have to be rejected or else disguised as falling within the limit set by scripture. Here too an observer would be bound to think that human understanding is actually screening itself away from the best help rather than seeking and following it. (The objection assumes that *what* is understood to be fixed or unsurpassable in the Guidance is relatively concrete – something formally more like the shape or height of Mount Everest than the direction "up.")

A central objective of axial guidance, according to the conservative thesis on axial "revolution," is to hold a maximally inclusive communicating community together in spiritual harmony through time. The entrenching of normative teachings in scripture is a likely strategy for achieving this. But a fully entrenched guidance would be paradoxically defeated as guidance by its removal from the community's critical thinking and constructive communication. (Vedic mantras that lack appreciable sense provide guidance only by courtesy of other texts and practices

---

[24] *Zohar*, trans. Daniel Chanan Matt (Paulist, 1983), p. 43. Compare Kabir's dictum: "Brahma suits His Language to the understanding of His hearer." *Songs of Kabir* (trans. Rabindranath Tagore, Macmillan, 1915), p. 92.

[25] On the history of accommodationist thinking in Judaism and Christianity and this adaptation of it, see Stephen D. Benin, *The Footprints of God: Divine Accommodation in Jewish and Christian Thought* (SUNY Press, 1993).

they are linked to.)[26] This is why every world-religious scripture has generated a large and endlessly growing commentarial literature, to say nothing of the much larger body of differently structured or less pious responses to scripture that contribute to the ongoing guidance discussion. Pointing to this evidence, scripturalists can argue that their Scripture can play its chartering role while its understood directives evolve.

A foundationalist style of scripturalism does indeed try to minimize changes of scriptural interpretation and generally to constrain thoughts about scripture.[27] But it seems that any existing foundationalist school is doomed to shrink in size and intellectual and spiritual respectability as it shuts out factors contributing to what will widely be seen as spiritual progress – for example, the rise of historical consciousness and critiques of racism, sexism, and speciesism. The axial traditions have all shown a capacity to interact progressively with new cultural factors. But foundationalists will foreseeably continue to arise not only as cultural conservatives but as sober guardians of the scriptural definitions of the supreme ideals of axial religion. Their continuing influence will renew the dilemma of fixed guidance.

(7) Insofar as scripturalism binds responsibility and access to the divine to membership in a particular historical community, it is essentially provincial, partisan, and *fanatical*. Both spiritually and politically, it is a divisive curse. The axial claim of universality is belied by the inescapable anchoring of the scriptural community in a language and a specific historical project, which, joined to the ultimate high-stakes demand to recognize the Guidance, unavoidably produces conflict over doctrine and authority (though not necessarily physical violence), domineering, and interpretive distortion of "heathen" alternatives.

In principle, axial traditions are able to spread and establish themselves independently of an ethnic rationale. In practice, Buddhism is one of the best examples. But even Buddhism is always the religion of a Buddhist community on the ground somewhere, already defensive of its particular heritage and primed to enter polemically into intercourse with other

---

[26] Barbara Holdrege, "Vedas in the Brahmanas," in *Authority, Anxiety, and Canon: Essays in Vedic Interpretation* (ed. Laurie L. Patton, SUNY Press, 1994), pp. 37–39.

[27] A major religion scholar writes: "When we consider a religious text to be divine – whether it be a book of the Bible or a Buddhist sutra – we greatly delimit the thoughts we can think about it." Donald S. Lopez Jr., *The Lotus Sutra: A Biography* (Princeton University Press, 2016), p. 11. One knows what he means; fortunately, this delimiting is not mandatory for all scripturalists, many of whom regard divinely sponsored texts as the most thought-provoking of all.

communities. Very typically, a particular scriptural canon will be an influential and practically indispensable element defining that community's identity and agenda. Even a great Buddhist leader can apparently go off the deep end of fanatical espousal of scripture, as Donald Lopez relates about Nichiren:

> In a place [like Japan] where the *Lotus Sutra* was well known, the other forms of Buddhism, which in Nichiren's view were all provisional teachings, had no purpose. It was now time for all of them to dissolve into the great ocean of the *Lotus Sutra*, so thoroughly that even their names would be forgotten. Thus, all those who failed to abandon other forms of Buddhism – and in some of his writings this seemed to include the entire population of Japan – were guilty of the sin of slandering the dharma and were destined for rebirth in the Avici [that is, the worst] hell ... [Nichiren] wrote that he was the greatest man in Japan because he was the man in Japan most hated and persecuted for his devotion to the *Lotus Sutra*.[28]

Optimists may hope that the scriptures of the various communities will all teach peace and harmony and will share an understanding of human good with each other so substantially, so well complemented by reasonable philosophies and political stances, that any decently developed scriptural interpretation will knock the props out from under fanatical formulations of scriptural religion. Thus, fanaticism will not be able to base itself plausibly on a world-religious scriptural rationale.

But even if there were, in spite of the deeply polemical conditioning of the formation of each world religion, a widely shared scriptural irenicism, scriptural fanaticism would always overwhelm it – because the particular Text, like the particular savior or scheme of which it speaks, claims to mark the Right Path.

Scripturalists may respond that it is not clear that scripturalism plays a negative role in this unwelcome expression of religious psychology. Instead, the premise of textual guidance may provide the best defense against fanaticism, for it is only an illiterate who claims to possess ultimate guidance in nonnegotiable terms, "in black and white," on the basis of a complex text. It is true that there are forms of guidance such as laws and treaties that work properly only when there is an enforceable directive in a text and that such texts have served as models for the guidance of scripture as a whole. But whoever thinks of scriptural

---

[28] Lopez, pp. 84, 86; Nichiren, "Rectification for the Peace of the Nation," in *Sources of Japanese Tradition*, 2nd ed., vol. 1 (ed. William Theodore de Bary et al., Columbia University Press, 2001), p. 298.

guidance on such models exclusively is overlooking other equally important constituents of scripture and models of guidance – philosophical, poetic, devotional – and failing to appreciate how the whole scriptural conversation works.

(8) Scripturalism is unreasonably *inegalitarian* in presupposing and taking advantage of literacy as it does. Because the social elite will always control education, scripturalist thought will generally reflect and reinforce the advantages of the dominant ethnicity, sex, and class, weaving their outlook into scriptural interpretation so that the hierarchical social order cannot be *radically* challenged for religious reasons (despite chronic disputes between leaders about their relative powers and priorities and who is and is not behaving properly). Among Hindus, the boon of ultimate Guidance is tied to the privilege of being able to deal with classical Sanskrit texts – that is, a privilege of males of the Brahmin caste – and male Brahmin equivalents are in charge of scriptural teaching in every world-religious community. The impressive contributions of individual female scripturalists, a Hildegard here and a Mirabai there, have not disturbed this imbalance of power.

The axial ideal of universal literacy is subverted by the social structure of literacy itself, given that literacy is intrinsically a social advantage. Imagine that sexual oppression were eliminated thanks to technological advances affecting work and reproduction, with the result of women and men sharing equally in literate leadership. Still a power difference would open up between the men and women who, thanks to their talent and disposition and good fortune, take advantage of the society's utilities of communication and the men and women who do not. No educational system can prevent some from becoming more literate than others. The well-informed, rhetorically empowered literates would be able to act more intelligently than the relative illiterates in many practical applications, besides enjoying the delights of good discussion. This difference would be perpetuated by a literate class on the basis of superior literacy much as the power of the rich is perpetuated on the basis of wealth – unevenly at the level of families, but irresistibly at the level of class.

Sincerely egalitarian scripturalists ought to be bothered by the historical evidence of structural inequality in scriptural communities and the relative alienation of subjugated classes from the benefits of literate religion. Still, they might say, the problem is not rooted in the premise of literate Guidance. The glass of our moral culture can be seen as half-empty or half-full of effective respect for human equality, and optimistically we should plan to increase its fullness on the basis of such encouraging recent developments as the vastly wider publication of scriptures and scriptural discussions in all traditions and the rise of female leadership in a number of scripturalist communities. We should remember that we are in the middle of a still-developing axial revolution. Only within the last few decades has a majority of the world's population become literate and a majority in the richest countries gotten access to higher education.

(9) A scripturalist community claims to draw from its scripture both the best of teachings, striking powerful *initial* sparks for spiritual exploration, and the best of rulings, providing a needed *finality* in resolving spiritual issues. As the comprehensive Guidance, it must perform both of these functions. But it cannot succeed, for each function undermines the other. A living spiritual guide can skillfully balance and combine promptings for exploration with reminders of unchangeable standards. A scripturalist guide will draw on scripture in doing this. But then the scriptural text will be given incompatible illocutionary characterizations: Is it suggesting how we might think or telling us what we must think? Scripturalist communication will be chronically polarized between liberals embracing the teaching model and conservatives embracing the ruling model; there will be no effective consensus about how to take scripture, greatly reducing the meaningfulness of scriptural unity.

Faced with this challenge, a Christian might say, "Of course: Paul distinguishing between what he received from the Lord and his own reasoning about sexual issues, where he says 'Judge for yourselves!'" (1 Corinthians 7, 11); a Buddhist might say, "Of course: the Noble Truths, but also the parables and legends"; and scripturalists in other traditions can cite similarly differentiated points of reference. The still-expanding axial initiative of bringing literate guidance to the most inclusive community includes a sensitivity to this illocutionary complexity. No scriptural canon reads exclusively like a suggestive philosophical or literary text or exclusively like a slate of edicts either.

(10) A scripture need not be believed to be perfect and so need not generate the *"wax nose" problem* of unreasonably ingenious interpretation to save the supposed perfection of the text.[29] But this and many other disasters of unreasonable interpretation are strongly encouraged by the

---

[29] Wolterstorff's example is an inerrantist conclusion that the ancient psalmist who said that the earth does not move (Psalm 93 1:1) could not have shared the false ancient belief in geocentrism and so must have been speaking figuratively (228–229).

premise of ultimate Guidance. Reasonable scripturalists can fend off unreasonable interpretations of the text, but often the pertinent way to do this is to invoke historical or literary considerations that carry less religious weight than maximized reverence for the Guidance.

*

I do not think that our discussion of substantial worries about scripturalism brings us closer to a general verdict for or against its rationality or reasonableness or intelligence. As long as the basic premise of religiously expansive optimism, responsibility, and prudence is not rejected out of hand, it seems that scripturalists have sufficient resources to withstand criticism on every front. The implication all along the line is that critical assessment must focus on specific implementations of scripturalism that may or may not tally with axial optimism and may or may not fulfill the intrinsic standards and promise of the guidance relationship. The premise of scripturalism should not be judged solely by the felt value or disvalue of a particular scripturalist experience; instead, particular scripturalist experiences should be evaluated in light of the general hopes and hazards of scripturalism.

6.6 PHILOSOPHERS' VIEWS OF SCRIPTURE

Philosophy and scripture are closely related axial enterprises. Scriptural teachings are philosophically empowered, philosophical agendas are scripturally informed, and philosophical discussions are based on quasi-scriptural canons. Various relationships have been realized between the two modes of considering supreme ideals. Some philosophers have used the resources of free reasoning to avoid engaging scriptural religion directly, some to criticize it, some to provide their own reconstruction of it, and some to serve it. Relatively rarely, philosophers have thought carefully about what scripture is in principle – but almost never with a comparative perspective reaching farther than the constitutive polemics of their own religious cultures (Christian vs. Jewish, Hindu vs. Buddhist, and Daoist vs. Confucian).

In the postclassical age, the most influential philosophers were perforce religious philosophers working within the parameters of scriptural religion. Their stance was generally deferential. For Vasubandhu, Shankara, al-Ghazali, Maimonides, and Aquinas, scripturally "revealed" knowledge was unchallengeable and interpretively dominant. Yet these philosophers found considerable room to rationalize the purport of scripture, making axial sense of the whole package of scripture.

Al-Farabi aroused suspicion of philosophy in the Islamic world by relegating prophecy (which in his frame of reference means scripture) to the rank of imagination, inferior to reason, and by viewing the contents of religious belief qua religious as "similitudes" of the truth, acquired by persuasion, distinct from the demonstrated truth of philosophy.[30] His successor Ibn Sina restored prophetic knowledge to the highest rank, in principle, but made it clear that he viewed scripture as a means of conveying to common people a measure of the truth about God and the soul that philosophers know on the basis of Platonic and Aristotelian arguments.

[The prophet's] duty is to teach men to know the Majesty and Might of God by means of symbols and parables drawn from things which they regard as mighty and majestic, imparting to them simply this much, that God has no equal, no like and no partner. Similarly he must establish in them the belief in an afterlife, in a manner that comes within the range of their imagination and will be satisfying to their souls; he will liken the happiness and misery there to be experienced in terms which they can understand and conceive. As for the truth of these matters, he will only adumbrate it to them very briefly, saying that it is something which "eye hath not seen nor ear heard" ... [there is] no harm in his discourse being interspersed with sundry hints and allusions, to attract those naturally qualified for speculation to undertake philosophical research into the nature of religious observances and their utility in terms of this world and the next.[31]

This "skillful means" suggestion seems likely to unsettle confidence in the supreme validity of scriptural Guidance.

The crux of postclassical philosophy of scripture is the capacity of a natural language to express an effective intention with regard to ultimate reality and goodness despite its human sense-making limitations. Origen's theory of allegory, Maimonides's theory of negation (that knowledge of God advances only by insightful negation of creaturely characterizations of God), and Aquinas's theory of analogy (that statements about God can be true analogically though not univocally) are high points in the

---

[30] Abu Nasr al-Farabi, *On the Perfect State* (trans. Richard Walzer, Kazi, 1998), chaps. 14, 17, and "The Attainment of Happiness," in al-Farabi, *The Philosophy of Plato and Aristotle*, rev. ed., (trans. Muhsin Mahdi, Cornell University Press, 1969), §55, p. 44; and see Richard Walzer, "Al-Farabi's Theory of Prophecy and Divination," *Journal of Hellenic Studies*, 77 (1957), 142–148.

[31] Avicenna (Ibn Sina), *Avicenna on Theology* (trans. A. J. Arberry, J. Murray, 1951), pp. 44–45.

Abrahamic discussion. In the South and East Asian traditions, the more negatively oriented thinkers like Nagarjuna and Shankara aim for an enlightening effect in demonstrating precisely that our language never does escape its formal and material limitations, while the more linguistically optimistic thinkers like Zhu Xi use the theoretical discourse of supreme appeal (Principle) and generally prescribed attitude (sincerity, etc.) as a ladder on which to mount to a more-than-notional understanding of the highest good.

We have two themes to follow, then: the categorical *improvement* on scriptural guidance that philosophy can provide for those capable of it – which will either be destabilizing or stabilizing for the larger religious community, depending on whether it can accommodate the philosophical option – and the auxiliary *help* that philosophy can give in recognizing how scripture works and what it accomplishes.

Al-Farabi's and Ibn Sina's patronizing view of prophecy and scripture is a prototype for many Western philosophers to come, most articulately Spinoza and Kant. Philosophy realizes with the higher faculty of reason what scripture suggests persuasively using the lower faculty of imagination. The philosopher's rational religion has the great advantage that it is not circumscribed by the positive historical commitments of the organized religious communities and so can steer clear of harmful and needless disputes. All of the leading Jewish, Christian, and Muslim philosophers of the Middle Ages are on the same page, rationally, thanks to their shared Platonic-Aristotelian intellectual background; they have philosophical disagreements, to be sure, but for purposes of discussing God, the soul, and nature, they are not separated by intractable dogmatic disagreements. (The eminent Asian postclassical thinkers also live in a kind of philosophical *oikumene*, sharing rational appreciation of Buddhist and Hindu arguments in India and of Confucian, Daoist, and Buddhist arguments in China.)

Although al-Farabi and Ibn Sina clearly stake a claim for the epistemically superior position of philosophy, they might also say that they are helping us to form appropriate expectations of scripture. Scripture is not the definitive disclosure of the Truth to the rationally inquiring mind; rather it is the authorized teaching of the Truth to the common people and thus the instrument and guarantor of the inclusive community's unity – the Guidance indeed, in that social-pragmatic respect. This two-sided claim will be made explicitly by Spinoza.

*

In China, one of the founding thinkers of Neo-Confucianism, Zhu Xi, took an approach to scripture that was spectacularly assertive. He successfully argued for a major change in the Confucian canon based on requirements of rational sense making – for him, an organized effort to discern Principle in everything. Traditionally, the primary canon consisted of the five oldest text collections: the *Yijing* (*Classic of Changes*), the *Shijing* (*Classic of Poetry*), the *Shujing* (*Classic of Documents*), the *Liji* (*Book of Rites*), and the *Chunqiu* (*Spring and Autumn Annals*). By Zhu Xi's time, however, four later and more thoroughly rationalized books had assumed commanding importance in the interpretation of the canon: the *Da Xue* (*The Great Learning*), the *Zhongyong* (*The Doctrine of the Mean*), the *Lunyu* (*Analects of Kongzi/Confucius*), and the *Mengzi* (*Mencius*). Zhu gave the Four Books preeminence over the Five Classics, and from then on they received the greatest emphasis in the official curriculum. Zhu Xi's adjustment can be seen as a major step in the axialization of Confucian tradition.

The reader will have perceived that my own vision of Confucian tradition is centered on the *Lunyu*. If I were a more faithful follower of Kongzi, my prime material of discussion would be in the *Shijing* or the history Classics, not the *Lunyu*! Instead, I accept the priority of Kongzi's own remarks in a scheme legitimated by Zhu Xi. (If I were a participant in the "Boston Confucianism" scene described by Robert Neville, I might accept Neville's argument for including the *Xunzi* among the primary scriptures because of its apparent great relevance to our life today.)[32]

Zhu Xi also said: "Once we have grasped principle, there is no need for the Classics."[33] The point is to understand what the textual data indicate: in Zhu Xi's mind, the possibility of philosophically superseding the labor of textual interpretation does not entail dismissal of scripture from the curriculum. But he seems to have taken a step further Kongzi's claim that one principle runs through all sound teachings (*Lunyu* 4:15).

*

[32] Robert C. Neville, *Boston Confucianism* (SUNY Press, 2000), pp. 4–6.
[33] Chu Hsi (Zhu Xi), *Learning to Be a Sage* (trans. Daniel K. Gardner, University of California Press, 1990), 5.52, p. 157 (from the *Zhuzi Yulei*, chap. 104, section 47); cf. 4.3, p. 128: "Book learning itself is of secondary importance. Moral principle is complete in us, not something added from the outside." Compare Zhuangzi: "Words exist because of meaning. Once you've gotten the meaning, you can forget the words. Where can I find a man who has forgotten words so I can have a word with him?" (chap. 26 [HY 26/14], p. 302).

In early modern Europe, once philosophical discussion of religion had been sprung free by the shock of the religious wars and persecutions of the Reformation period, Spinoza radicalized the idea of scripture as vulgar teaching in his *Theological-Political Treatise*.

Moses desired to teach the Hebrews in such a manner and inculcate into them such principles as would attach them more closely to the worship of God on the basis of their childish understanding. (44)[34]

Moses ... introduced religion into the commonwealth, so that the people would do its [civic] duty more from devotion than from fear (74) ... the ceremonies of the Old Testament, and indeed the entire Law of Moses, related to nothing but the Hebrew state and consequently nothing other than material benefits. (76)

Those who are most powerful in imagination are less good at merely understanding things ... Consequently those who look in the books of the prophets for wisdom and a knowledge of natural and spiritual things are completely on the wrong track. (29)

Pioneering a historical-critical approach, Spinoza insists on impartially reading the text of the Bible to see what it says and reveals about itself.

The more vehemently [the religious leaders] express admiration for its mysteries, the more they show they do not really believe Scripture but merely assent to it. This is also clear from the fact that most of them take it as a fundamental principle (for the purpose of understanding Scripture and bringing out its true meaning) that Scripture is true and divine throughout. But of course this is the very thing that should emerge from a critical examination and understanding of Scripture. It would be much better to derive it from Scripture itself ... but they assume it at the beginning as a rule of interpretation. (9)

An attentive reader of the Bible finds that there are many inconsistencies and much evidence of corruption and loss of information in the text as we have it and that there is much in the moral and political circumstances of the ancient Hebrews that is not relevant to readers today. More importantly, though:

That there is a God, one and omnipotent, who alone is to be adored and cares for all men, loving most those who worship Him and love their neighbor as themselves, etc. ... Scripture teaches so plainly and explicitly throughout that no one has ever called its meaning into question in these matters. But Scripture does not teach expressly, as eternal doctrine, what God is, and how he sees all things and provides for them, and so on ... the prophets themselves have no agreed view about these matters, so that on these questions nothing can be regarded as the

---

[34] Benedict de Spinoza, *Theological-Political Treatise* (trans. Michael Silverthorne and Jonathan Israel, Cambridge University Press, 2007), Gebhard ed. pagination.

teaching of the Holy Spirit, even if they can be decided very well by the natural light of reason. (102–103)

Spinoza's boldly stated separate-spheres position could evoke either tolerance or intolerance of philosophy among the religious: "Scripture leaves reason absolutely free and has nothing at all in common with philosophy ... each of them stands on its own separate footing" (9). He is ignoring the shared axial formation of philosophy and scriptural religion. The "nothing in common" thesis obviously goes too far, as does the forced corollary that scriptural prophets never reason with their audience (156–157).[35]

Spinoza writes sweetly that "true knowledge of God is not a command but a divine gift" (172), yet it seems impossible to separate awareness of *this* gift from feeling that we are ordered to align ourselves with it. Conversely, it seems impossible to separate the kind of obedience that is the prime concern of the Law of Moses from insight, even among commoners, into what makes the aim and method of obedience appropriate. The distinction between knowledge and obedience is not so simple.

Seizing on the Bible's self-surpassing idea of a new covenant written in people's hearts by which they will *know* God (Jeremiah 31:31–34), Spinoza claims that the rational idea of God is "God's true original text, which he himself has sealed with his own seal, that is, with the idea of himself as the image of his divinity" (158). We end up with a split, then, between a tattered historical relic-text that happens also to be an estimable religious classic, on the one hand, and on the other a "true original text" that is not a text at all but a rational conception. Spinoza often seems to be saying that for nonrational persons the first text works appropriately as the Guidance, while for rational persons the first text works as the Guidance only as an indicator of the second text (the rational conception). He does show awareness, however, of a reason why rational persons should welcome the first text as the Guidance: the

---

[35] "The [New Testament] Apostles always employ arguments, so that they seem to be engaged in a debate rather than prophesying. By contrast prophecies contain nothing but dogmas and decrees, since in them it is God who is presented as speaking, and God does not engage in discussion but issues edicts on the absolute authority of his nature. Equally, prophetic authority does not permit participation in argument, for whoever seeks to confirm his dogmas by means of reason is thereby submitting them to the judgment of each individual for decision ... This is how all of Moses' arguments in the Pentateuch are to be understood; they are not drawn from the repertory of reason, they are simply turns of phrase by which he expressed God's edicts more effectively and imagined them more vividly" (156–157).

quality of their lives, as of everyone's, is deeply affected by the conduct and salvation prospects of fellow citizens, and Scripture is indispensable in maintaining the moral discipline, good morale, and optimal future of communal life. Thus rational persons should realize not only that the nonrationals need Scripture but also that the rationals need the nonrationals to obey and be consoled by Scripture (186–188). (In his tortuous argumentation of this point, Spinoza also seems to suggest that rational individuals need the guidance of scriptural commandments in conducting *their own* affairs, since the light of reason does not fully illuminate the risks and benefits of concrete actions [187]. It is a point that Dharmakirti or Shankara or al-Ghazali or Maimonides might make.)[36]

Kant, too, patronizes scripture from a rationalist standpoint, but his *Religion* book, published under the eye of the Prussian authorities, contains a relatively thoughtful appreciation of scripture's importance in supporting rational religion. (The great supersessionist Hegel, in contrast, will not be bothered to think about scripture to this extent; scripture has shrunk to nothing in his Enlightenment rearview mirror.) Seeing that the more basely motivated "ecclesiastical" version of religion naturally precedes the purely moral version, Kant reflects, somewhat in a Protestant-vs.-Catholic vein:

We must also concede that the preservation of the pure faith unchanged, its universal and uniform diffusion, and even the respect for the revelation assumed within it, can hardly be adequately provided for through *tradition*, but only through *scripture*; which, again, as a revelation to present and future generations must be the object of the highest respect, for this is what human need requires in order to be certain of the duty to divine service. A holy book commands the greatest respect even among those (indeed among these most of all) who do not read it, or are at least unable to form any coherent concept of religion from it; and no subtle argument can stand up to the knockdown pronouncement, *Thus it is written* ... history proves that never could a faith based on scripture be eradicated by even the most devastating political revolutions, whereas a faith based on tradition and ancient public observances meets its downfall as soon as the state breaks down. How fortunate, when one such book, fallen into human hands, contains complete, besides its statutes legislating faith, also the purest moral doctrine of religion ... In this event, both because of the end to be attained thereby and the difficulty of explaining by natural laws the origin of the enlightenment of

---

[36] Cf. Dharmakirti, *Pramanavarttika* 1.216 (according to Tom Tillemans, "Dharmakirti" [ed. Edward Zaita, *Stanford Encyclopedia of Philosophy* (plato.stanford.edu), 2017]); Shankara, *Brahma Sutra Bhashya* 3.1.25; al-Ghazali's *Deliverance from Error*, in *The Faith and Practice of Al-Ghazali* (trans. W. Montgomery Watt, Oneworld, 1994), pp. 85–87; Maimonides, *Guide* 3.31.

the human race proceeding from it, the book can command an authority equal to that of a revelation.[37]

The pitfall, of course, is that the religious may believe superstitiously in their scripture (as something to obey slavishly in order to please an Almighty Being) or in the authorities of scriptural interpretation. The church must be protected against this degradation by rational leaders.

Since the sacred narrative is only adopted for the sake of ecclesiastical faith, and, by itself alone, it neither could, nor ought to, have any influence whatever on the reception of moral maxims but is rather given to this faith only for the vivid presentation of its true object (virtue striving toward holiness), it should at all times be taught and expounded in the interest of morality, and the point should thereby also be stressed, carefully and (since the ordinary human being has in him a constant propensity to slip into passive faith) repeatedly, that true religion is not to be placed in the knowledge or the profession of what God does or has done for our salvation, but in what we must do to become worthy of it.[38]

Rational leaders have *always* provided morally purifying readings of *all* the world's religious literature, Kant claims.[39] This stands to reason, on Kant's view, because wherever there is rationality, there is consciousness of the ideally prior moral demand.

*

In the nineteenth century, religion scholars like Max Müller began to think seriously about the category of scripture in global perspective, but the leading Western philosophers either held scripture at arm's length or raided particular scriptures for ideas of interest.[40]

There is a thunderous silence about scripture in two of the twentieth-century philosophical initiatives that possibly imply the most about it: the Wittgensteinian turn to investigation of "language-games" and Habermas's neo-Kantian turn to ideals of communicative action. In the neglect of scripture by these thinkers (except belatedly and tentatively by Habermas) one can feel the force of many philosophical prejudices old and new – how the venue of philosophical discussion must be a separate literature dedicated to free thinking with a critical detachment from

---

[37] Immanuel Kant, *Religion within the Boundaries of Mere Reason* (trans. Allen Wood and George di Giovanni, Cambridge University Press, 1998), Ak. 6:106–107, p. 116.

[38] Ibid., Ak. 6:132–133, p. 136.   [39] Ibid., Ak. 6:110–114, pp. 118–122.

[40] Schopenhauer makes an interesting case study. See *Understanding Schopenhauer through the Prism of Indian Culture* (ed. Arati Baruta, Michael Gerard, and Matthias Kossler, de Gruyter, 2013).

cultural tradition; how religious meaning, when it becomes an object of philosophical inquiry, is to be addressed as "myth" or "prophecy," the production of a different type of experience and communication than the philosophical, or as "faith" bound to a nonrational object; and how the modern Enlightenment has broken decisively (again) with mythic thinking and intellectual authoritarianism.

Many have assumed that the formation of a global cultural community could only be hindered by continuing attachment to religious traditions. Karl Jaspers challenges this assumption but also falls back into it. He points out that all the world's literate cultures realize enlightenment, or axialization, in their own culturally distinctive ways; but he elucidates enlightenment in a Western-philosophical idiom of existentialism that resolutely disallows religious obedience to scriptures. His confrontation with scripture is placed strictly in the Western debate about the authority of the Bible.[41] He defends "liberality" and a free philosophical version of religious experience, in which the transcendent field of meaning possibilities that the lucidly existing individual grapples with is never reified into a "revelation" that must be believed in. A scripture can be a great resource for grappling with clues to transcendence, he admits, but only if it is treated as a collection of suggestive texts, not as a more decisive teaching than a mythology – not as the Guidance.

The Bible is as rich as life ... The Bible is full of contradictions, a meeting-ground of irreconcilable spiritual forces, views of life and ways of life ... to share in its truth, one must move in its contradictions. They alone cast light upon the truth....

While searching for a harmonious unity of faith, men would assert it prematurely and design it rationally in theologies ... Neither historically nor conceptually can we fix upon a center of biblical thought and experience. Therein lies part of the Bible's vast, life-giving power.[42]

Philosophy is older than the biblical revelation ... existentially more original, being accessible to all humans as humans, and ... fully capable of hearing and adopting truth in the Bible as well.[43]

Paul Ricoeur follows Jaspers in using philosophical tools to construct a not-specifically-religious conception of revelatory experience supporting a nonauthoritarian interpretation of religious thought.[44] He goes quite a bit

---

[41] See *Philosophical Faith and Revelation* (trans. E. B. Ashton, Harper & Row, 1967) and his book with Rudolf Bultmann, *Myth and Christianity* (Noonday, 1958).

[42] *Philosophical Faith and Revelation*, p. 333.   [43] Ibid., p. 337.

[44] Paul Ricoeur, "Toward a Hermeneutic of the Idea of Revelation," in *Essays on Biblical Interpretation* (ed. Lewis S. Mudge, Fortress, 1980), pp. 73–118.

farther in rendering help in recognizing the character of scripture. Whereas Jaspers conceives the prime clues to the ultimate human situation as "ciphers,"[45] Ricoeur speaks of "symbols" in continuity with religious tradition. The general proposition that anchors his hermeneutics is "The symbol gives rise to thought."[46] Poetically great texts contain symbols from which we receive an "impulsion" to reflect on human existence in deeply illuminating ways. For example, the biblical symbol of an original divine commandment not to eat a certain fruit, lest one die, testifies to our primal dread of what will follow from putting ourselves in the wrong.[47] Thus the interpreter of potent symbols is in a good position to articulate the meaning of human existence both philosophically and religiously. The reader of a sacred text is invited to explore a figured world of spiritual drama with real relevance, such as the Adam-and-Eve world figured by Genesis.

Scripture is distinguished as the great text that is centered on a supreme appeal, where "all ... forms of discourse are referred to that Name which is the point of intersection and the vanishing point of all our discourse about God, the Name of the Unnameable."[48] But the interpreter should let the world figured by a scriptural text unfold before imposing on the text a previous theological decision about its significance.[49] Scriptural hermeneutics should not override general hermeneutics.

Because of the institution of scripture, religious experience is profoundly conditioned by textual interpretation:

"Ultimate concern" would remain mute if it did not receive the power of a word of interpretation ceaselessly renewed by signs and symbols that have, we might say, educated and formed this concern over the centuries. The feeling of absolute dependence would remain a weak and inarticulated sentiment if it were not the response to the proposition of a new being that opens new possibilities of existence for me. Hope, unconditional trust, would be empty if it did not rely on a constantly renewed interpretation of sign-events reported by the writings, such as the exodus in the Old Testament and the resurrection in the New Testament. These are the events of deliverance that open and disclose the utmost possibilities

---

[45] "Ciphers light the roots of things. They are not cognition; what is conceived in them is vision and interpretation. They cannot be experienced and verified as generally valid. Their truth is linked with Existenz. The magnetism of Transcendence for Existenz is voiced in ciphers. They open areas of Being. They illuminate my decisions." Ibid., p. 92.

[46] Ricoeur, *The Symbolism of Evil* (trans. Emerson Buchanan, Beacon, 1967), pp. 347–357.

[47] Ibid., pp. 32–33.

[48] Ricoeur, "Toward a Hermeneutic of the Idea of Revelation," p. 104.

[49] Ricoeur, "Philosophy and Religious Language," in *Figuring the Sacred* (trans. David Pellauer, Fortress, 1995), p. 44.

of my own freedom and thus become for me the word of God. Such is the properly hermeneutical constitution of faith.[50]

In "Manifestation and Proclamation," Ricoeur works over the old idea that biblical faith breaks with the religion of myth, sacrifice, and nature and ancestor worship – an idea that is either recklessly universalized or given its proper global contextualization in Jaspers's idea of the axial. Ricoeur finds in the Bible not simply a break but a typically axial retrieval of archaic religious elements in the newer "kerygmatic" or proclamatory summons of the hearer to reckon with the Unnameable.

Everything indicates therefore that the cosmic symbolism does not die but is instead transformed in passing from the realm of the sacred to that of proclamation. The new Zion prophetically inverts the reminiscence of the sacred city, just as the Messiah who is to come projects into the eschatological future the glorious royal figures of divine unction. And for Christians, Golgotha becomes a new *axis mundi*.[51]

In this way the Guidance can speak to our imagination and heart as well as to our reason and will.[52]

The new "kerygmatic" element directed to our free will is seen in Jesus' teachings, where there is a shift from the archaic interest in the *wholeness* of the cosmos seen in correspondences among things to limit-expressions indicating a *rupture* of sense where pragmatic insight runs out: "He who seeks to save his life must lose it," "Love your enemies," "The Kingdom of God is among you," and the morally "extravagant" though otherwise prosaic parables.[53] Jesus' teachings have religious appeal without relying on any manifestation of the sacred; one finds one's orientation not by marveling or worshipping but by deciding to be sacrificial and forgiving. The *tremendum* and *fascinosum* of the sacred have been transmuted into moral obedience and fervor.[54] But Jesus also uses an older symbolism of death and rebirth – in baptism and in the

---

[50] Ibid., p. 47.

[51] Ricoeur, "Manifestation and Proclamation," in *Figuring the Sacred*, p. 66.

[52] Ibid., p. 67. Ricoeur's point is related to Robert C. Neville's claim about the need for "archeological depth" in theology: "Theologically formulated conceptions of God are archeologically deep because they combine at once many levels of images, symbols, and abstraction conceptions. Without its historical moment [working in the first place with scriptures], theology could not be archeologically deep. It would have to employ one-dimensional notions, and would most likely be unable to handle the partiality of its dominant prisms without the specter of relativism." *Behind the Masks of God: An Essay toward Comparative Theology* (SUNY Press, 1991), p. 39.

[53] Ricoeur, "Manifestation and Proclamation," pp. 59–60.   [54] Ibid., p. 65.

conversation about being "born again" (John 3:1–9) – to characterize the invited arrival at the right orientation.

While Ricoeur's discussion of scripture is thoroughly theistic and biblical, there is nothing in his analysis that prevents applying it to other axial traditions or prevents a religious person from participating in other traditions. A crucial contributing factor is that he shares with Jaspers a very indeterminate philosophical conception of the supreme appeal, quite different from the Perfect Being theology that has ruled philosophical theology in the West.

*

Peter Ochs, an architect of today's Scriptural Reasoning movement, joins Maimonides, Spinoza, and Kant in the tradition of conceiving scripture as an instrument of moral formation. But he is not a rationalist. By developing the Peircean pragmatic turn toward grounding philosophy in the search for solutions to concrete problems of belief, he has created a generalizable model of deferential scripture use.[55] Ochs agrees with Hermann Cohen that Western civilization derives from its "prophetic" biblical heritage its definitive moral orientation toward human equality – an equality most basically of vulnerability to suffering.[56] (Similar moral commitments are carried forward from non-Western scriptures as well.) This moral orientation now requires a pragmatist self-critical consciousness in philosophy, a consciousness that Spinoza may have hinted at but, with his commitment to a priori rationalism, did not adopt:

> From the command to care for those who suffer comes the pragmatic maxim for academics: that you may wield the sword of theoretical reasoning only for the sake of repairing institutions that fail in their work of helping repair suffering by repairing broken practices of everyday life. Were it not for our prior commitment to the commands of scripture, we would have no irresistible warrant for choosing "care for those who suffer" as one of the indubitable purposes of our academic work as well as our interpersonal engagements. Nor would we have sufficient warrant for adopting pragmatism as a primary resource for our critique of the modern academy.[57]

---

[55] Peter Ochs, *Peirce, Pragmatism and the Logic of Scripture* (Cambridge University Press, 1998).

[56] See Hermann Cohen, "The Social Ideal of Plato and the Prophets," in *Reason and Hope: Selections from the Jewish Writings of Hermann Cohen* (trans. Eva Jospe, Norton, 1971), pp. 70–77.

[57] Peter Ochs, "Philosophic Warrants for Scriptural Reasoning," *Modern Theology*, 22 (July 2006), 469.

Thus in quite a different way than Shankara or al-Ghazali or Aquinas, but with as profound a deference to religious tradition, Ochs finds the agenda of philosophy set by scripture. Scripture in turn is properly read with a philosophically sensitized eye for the "vagueness" of its symbolism – productively "vague" in requiring for the completion of its sense relations to actual other persons and their needs and to other human perspectives, including common sense and science.[58]

*

The first philosophical assessment of scripture that is genuinely global in conception is Shlomo Biderman's *Scripture and Knowledge* (1995).[59] Rejecting noncognitivist construals of the meaning of religious language, Biderman asserts that scriptures are distinguished both religiously and philosophically by their unique offer of knowledge. He is dissatisfied with "textual" approaches that treat scripture as one among various interpretable texts and with "contextual" approaches that treat scriptural guidance as one among various normative social practices. "The two approaches diminish the feeling of amazement, even bewilderment, that scripture often arouses and is originally meant to arouse."[60] Biderman finds the special character of scriptural communication in a twofold "entanglement" such that, on the one hand, descriptions of empirical realities are mixed with descriptions of nonempirical realities (so that scripture is the site of "revealed" knowledge), and on the other hand, propositional meaning is mixed with a uniquely urgent nonpropositional affective and motivational meaning (so that scripture reading is a religious act) – an entanglement of "outward" and "inward" meaning.[61] This doubly entangled meaning is justified and authoritative on scripture's own terms, as scripture itself provides the necessary rules and evidence for it. The character of the entanglement differs in different traditions, however – for example, depending on whether scriptural validation depends on the existence of God or only on operations of the mind.[62]

*

[58] Ochs, *Peirce, Pragmatism and the Logic of Scripture*, pp. 288–295.
[59] Shlomo Biderman, *Scripture and Knowledge* (Brill, 1995). Biderman does not attend to Chinese scriptures, but I do not see why his program could not reach that far.
[60] Ibid., p. 74.   [61] Ibid., p. 89.   [62] Ibid., pp. 94–95.

It seems that these four views are strongly represented by philosophers:

(1) A *deferential* philosophy of scripture is normatively bound to a particular scripture and considers others, if it does, strictly in comparison and contrast with that point of reference. The governing philosophical commitment is to a conception of Being or Beyond-Being – or, as in Ochs, to a conception of the proper work of reasoning – that harmonizes the vision projected by scripture with rational analysis. The deferential approach does not feel bound to address the global phenomenon of scripture but does produce ideas worth testing for their generality.

(2) A *patronizing* philosophy of scripture subordinates guidance derived from scriptural interpretation to rationally formulated guidance, possibly assigning to scripture a necessary educational and political role. (Spinoza's friend Lodewijk Meyer, who like Spinoza subordinated scripture epistemically to natural reason, was nevertheless willing to concede that without scripture we could not be sure we were thinking about everything that is most worth thinking about – though the role of scripture "is only to rouse its readers and to impel them to think about the matters set out therein.")[63] The philosophical agenda is to resolve all important questions on a base of rational knowledge or, in Kantianism, rational will and faith. No other form of justification may overrule reason's requirements for justification. The patronizing approach is self-confidently universal, but that makes it overconfident and unfair as a frame for scriptures. It is hard to see how a Kantian could take Hindu scriptures nearly as seriously as Christian scriptures, for example, given the proximity of the Kantian ethical program to Christianity.[64]

(3) A nonauthoritarian, non-patronizing *hermeneutical* philosophy of scripture endeavors to show how scriptural texts, like any powerful texts except with explicit religious interests, illuminate human existence. The philosophical commitment is to a hermeneutical existential ontology inspired by a Kierkegaardian destruction of objectivity in ultimate truth (received by Ricoeur via Jaspers). A theory of religious axialization supports the premise that religion participates along with philosophy in the turn from naïve realism, supernaturalism, and objectifying rationalism. Because the ultimately guiding truth of Being or the Situation cannot

---

[63] Lodewijk Meyer, *Philosophy as the Interpreter of Holy Scripture* (trans. Samuel Shirley, Marquette University Press, 2005), pp. 238–239.

[64] But for a noble attempt to put a global array of religious perspectives fairly in a Kantian order of ethical requirements, see Ronald M. Green, *Religion and Moral Reason* (Oxford University Press, 1988).

be known objectively and must be figured by a free subject, scripture gets the benefit of hermeneutically optimistic philosophical examination just as any evocative text or experience would. The chief limitation of the hermeneutical approach is that it can make nothing positive of scripture's authority.

We should mark Jaspers's oppositional formulation of hermeneutical philosophy as a distinct option. Recognizing the existential meaningfulness of scriptural expressions but also the normative strength of scripture's claim to obedience, Jaspers concludes that free philosophizing and scripture following are irreconcilable. Jaspers's framing of the issue makes evident sense in his historical Christian context. Zhu Xi did not feel constrained as a philosopher by scripture in this way. But then there must have been Confucians who told Zhu Xi that he should feel more constrained than he did – and so the relevance of Jaspers's conception does seem general.

(4) A *neutral normativist* philosophy of scripture acknowledges the special authority and commitment involved in the religious Guidance. Biderman's epistemological approach emphasizes a cognitively amazing world that scripturalists obsessively live in; my own priority is to place scripture in the pragmatics of linguistic guidance, which I think shows better the religiously amplified directivity that for Biderman is strangely "entangled" in religious discourse. Nonetheless I agree with Biderman that the world-figuring epistemic work of scripture is essential. Most importantly, both Biderman and I find basic philosophical motivation in a cross-cultural examination of scripture.

7

The Scripturalist

How amazing is the profundity of your utterances! See, they lie before us with a surface that can charm little children. But their profundity is amazing, my God, their profundity is amazing. One cannot look into them without awe and trembling – awe of greatness, trembling of love. – Augustine[1]

One night, some time after, I took up the *Lotus Sutra*. Suddenly I penetrated to the perfect, true, ultimate meaning of the *Lotus*. The doubts I had held initially were destroyed and I became aware that the understanding I had obtained up to then was greatly in error. Unconsciously I uttered a great cry and burst into tears.
– Hakuin[2]

Scripturalism is a form of religious organization that we observe worldwide, a method of defining and propagating teachings that large-scale, long-running literate communities rely on. It is an indispensable concept for historians of religion and an inescapable principle for leaders in the world religions. To some degree it applies to nearly everyone, because nearly everyone's thought and practice are affected in one way or another by ideas that have been scripturally formed and continue to be scripturally benchmarked. It stands before all readers as a kind of aspirational ideal, if we think of the height of serious reading as the receptive counterpart to the height of serious expression that a communally enshrined Text represents: just as writers worked to get the text right and the community worked to get the choice of text right, with an eye on the

[1] Augustine, *Confessions* 12.14 (trans. Rex Warner, New American Library, 1963), p. 294.
[2] Hakuin, *The Zen Master Hakuin: Selected Writings* (trans. Philip B. Yampolksy, Columbia University Press, 1971), pp. 121–122.

greatest issues and their worthiest address, scripturalist readers work to get from the Text all the benefit that can be gotten, with an eye on the greatest consequences.

But we may conceive scripturalism also as a particular way of being religious that individuals can choose to go in for – or rather a variety of ways:

(1) One can engage scripture as supreme Guidance in the way that is prescribed for all members of one's religious community – for example, by attending to readings of scripture in regular worship, or by obtaining rulings from scripture on specified issues. This is the exoteric end of the spectrum. It is not a matter of outward observance merely, for the religious quality of the community's life and of the authority of its scripture depends on the seriousness of its readers about their relationship with scripture. Depending on the occasion, the emphasis could be on incorporating scriptural information in one's model of life-in-the-world, motivating actions, or renewing a sense of community.

(2) One can spend discretionary time studying a scripture to gain better understanding or to extract additional applications of scriptural guidance. By joining discussions on this topic, one can participate in a more intently scripturalist community within a larger community. One can relish the historical, intellectual, or spiritual clarity in the textual presentation of one's supreme ideals. Practically, one can be keen on living out scriptural guidance in much the way an English-speaking actor is keen on acting Shakespeare – rising to what one takes to be the greatest, most rewarding challenge of self-development. This is a practical requirement for sustaining the leadership and the élan of a scripturalist community.

(3) One can actively promote scriptural guidance of life in one's religious community and in other communities, either professionally (as a bishop or imam, for example) or by private initiative. One can practice the ideal that the Text contains benchmarks for whatever is really worth saying – whatever is more, on the closest examination, than transient sound or willful fury.

(4) One can give maximal attention to the body of scripture – right down to its letters and voicings, even to numerological or other hidden structures – for the sake of acquiring the greatest possible personal intimacy with scriptural meaning. Now we are at the esoteric end of the spectrum.

(5) One can regard scripture as substantially divine and the reader's relationship with scripture as spiritually sufficient. With this extreme attitude to scripture, it becomes a question whether *guidance* is any longer the character of the reader's relationship with the text and whether a *text*, as such, is any longer the venue of the relationship. For if one communes with scripture as with the divine, then one finds in scripture itself the dance, not directions for the dance. (In seeming to undermine basic assumptions about scriptural guidance, ecstatic mystical scripturalism will be in considerable tension with mainstream scripturalism in some communities.)

In this chapter I would like to get clearer on what an individual stands to gain or lose by taking seriously the guidance of a scripture. To this end I will make certain generalizations about "the scripturalist"; of course, such generalities are actually inflected by many ways and degrees of engaging scripture meaningfully – including many ways of combining the pursuit of scriptural guidance with other pursuits.[3]

7.1 THE RELIGIOUS READER

Paul Griffiths has drawn a bold distinction between two main kinds of reading, religious and consumerist.[4] Religious reading is seriously engaged with all that the text is meant to offer and opens the reader to transformation. The religious reader takes the text to heart and is never done with it. Consumerist reading, on the other hand, is free and instrumental. Skimming a text for any useful information it may or may not have is completely in keeping with consumerist reading and completely antithetical to religious reading. One can be *interested* in world religions and pay considerable attention to their scriptures, learning quite a bit from them, within the mode of consumerist reading, but no text is really irreplaceable in building the edifice of learning *about* religion. Consumerist students of religion should bear in mind that devout readers are on another wavelength.

Griffiths's dichotomy is a useful warning shot but greatly oversimplifies. There are not just two primary kinds of reading, and religious reading is not the only seriously engaged reading; scholarly and legal

---

[3] For anthropological widening of this topic, a good introduction is the collection edited by Vincent Wimbush, *Theorizing Scriptures: New Critical Orientations to a Cultural Phenomenon* (Rutgers University Press, 2008).

[4] Paul Griffiths, *Religious Reading* (Oxford University Press, 1999), pp. 40–54.

reading, for example, are very serious modes of reading with high-stakes outcomes in their own frames of reference. "Consumerist" reading varies widely from the random, shallow, and exploitative to the purposeful, intelligent, and respectful. Nor does dutiful religious reading always have the flavor of passionate attachment that scripture lovers like Anselm sometimes manifest, as quoted by Griffiths:

> Taste the goodness of your Redeemer, burn with love for your Savior. Chew the honeycomb of his words, suck their flavor, which is more pleasing than honey, swallow their health-giving sweetness. Chew by thinking, suck by understanding, swallow by loving and rejoicing. Be happy in chewing, be grateful in sucking, delight in swallowing.[5]

Nevertheless, it is good to check back in with classic text lovers, the *hafiz* or *shishta* or *ru* type, to be reminded of our culture's debt to such people for generating and sustaining an atmosphere of seriousness about guiding texts – the atmosphere in which scriptures and other charter texts arose.

As David M. Carr shows, the earliest literate culture in the ancient Near East was geared to taking culturally and spiritually precious texts *to heart*.[6] Written documents, at first not easily legible, were auxiliary to the remembering and contemplating of textual utterance in the minds of scribes. If a library were destroyed, its contents could be recreated because they would have been well and truly received. In receiving that meaning, scribes were enabled to live the best humanly accessible life, optimally informed, a distinctly higher life than that of the nonliterate.[7]

The nonwriting Indian counterparts of ancient Near Eastern scribes likewise found high value in taking texts to heart. According to some scholars, the Brahmins were not primarily interested in the meaning of their memorized texts; they were more like musicians or magicians concerned with correct performance of sounds than scholars concerned with discursive interpretation.[8] Even if that were true, the Brahmins must have been serious receivers and transmitters. But the startling thoughtfulness in

---

[5] Quoted by Griffiths (trans. Griffiths), p. 43.

[6] David M. Carr, *Writing on the Tablet of the Heart* (Oxford University Press, 2005), chaps. 1–2.

[7] In parallel to the transmission of the wisdom and virtue of sage-kings in China, Mesopotamian scribes talked interchangeably about "becoming human" and "being Sumerian," both of those meanings often centering on celebration of the royal exemplar. Carr, pp. 31–32.

[8] "In the oral transmission through recitation sound is all that counts. The words have to be handed down in exactly the same form in which they have been heard. There is no

the content of the Vedic texts shows that the characterization cannot be wholly accurate. We can see that numerous axial or proto-axial authors intended to build on a heritage of precious religious and philosophical wisdom.

Perhaps not every scribe or priest was an earnest seeker of Guidance or a spontaneous devotee of inspiring teaching; many must have simply taken up their parents' occupation. But even those dutiful children found themselves on a spiritually distinctive plane by entering into a demanding collegiality of attending to Guidance. In the axialized religions, this becomes the condition of every scripturalist. The community that actively attends to the texts of Guidance preserves everyone's access to the highest life; everyone in that community shares a momentous responsibility, in principle to everyone, for sustaining the project and participates in a collective realization of its nature and reward.

Most religious readers will start, at least, in a purely compliant position.[9] They belong to a community that directs them to seek and find Guidance in a scripture, perhaps even as a matter of civil law as in Hobbes's England.[10] They will be cued to find the forms of Guidance

---

tradition for the preservation of meaning, a concern regarded as a mere individualistic pastime. The Brahmans' task is more noble: to preserve the sound for posterity, maintain it in its purity, and keep it from the unchecked spread and vulgarization which attaches to the written word." Frits Staal, "The Concept of Scripture in Indian Tradition," in Mark Juergensmeyer and N. Gerald Barrier, eds., *Sikh Studies* (Graduate Theological Union Press, 1979), p. 122. With more practical emphasis, David Carpenter asserts that Vedic speech was classically seen as "more important for what it is and for what it does than for what it 'means.' It is first and foremost a reality of sacred power ... [It] makes manifest the objective structures (known collectively as *dharma*) through which the world of time and space is related back to its ultimate ground ... More than through reading and reflection, one appropriates the Veda through embodiment: one does not 'understand' the Veda, one enacts it and ideally one *becomes* it." "Bhartrihari and the Veda," in *Texts in Context: Traditional Hermeneutics in South Asia* (ed. Jeffrey R. Timm, Sri Satguru, 1992), pp. 20, 28.

[9] Eric Seibert has proposed two ideal types of scripture reader, the compliant and the conversant, in *The Violence of Scripture: Overcoming the Old Testament's Troubling Legacy* (Fortress, 2012), pp. 54–56.

[10] According to Hobbes, the category of scripture rests on political compliance: "The question of the Scripture, is the question of what is Law ... It is true, that God is the Sovereign of all Sovereigns; and therefore, when he speaks to any Subject, he ought to be obeyed, whatsoever any earthly Potentate command to the contrary. But the question is not of obedience to God, but of *when*, and *what* God hath said; which to Subjects that have no supernatural revelation, cannot be known, but by the natural reason, which guided them, for the obtaining of Peace and Justice, to obey the authority of their several Commonwealths; that is to say, of their lawful Sovereigns. According to this obligation, I can acknowledge no other Books of the Old Testament, to be Holy Scripture, but those

that are considered necessary or best in their tradition, and that will variously determine for them what is reasonable in working with Guidance – as, for example, Buddhists, unlike Christians, will not be encouraged to learn from scripture "the will of the Lord for my life," but, on the other hand, both Buddhists and Christians may be encouraged in interpreting scripture to take the measure of the dark age humanity now lives in. They will be advised that scripture provides the most solid and rich resource for spiritual reflection so that they have the option of realizing for themselves that, as the Psalmist says, the sacred directive "is perfect, restoring the soul" (19:8).

Reaching in this direction for a greater self-realization, religious readers may expect to find new and better selves as the subjective correlate of their textually altered world.[11] Or they may want the text to read *them*. "I learned to relinquish initiative to the text ... in Ignatian contemplative prayer I began to learn how to let the text *read me* and to let it bring my needs and the Spirit's movements within me to consciousness" (James Fowler).[12] The idea here is that the communicative stimuli of the text trigger disclosures of the reader's disposition in relation to the offered guidance so that both guidance and following can be dynamically individualized.

In a tradition that supports the option of monastic life, the religious reader can take up with others a daily discipline of scriptural meditation and enactment. For example, the Pachomian model of Christian monasticism demands that monks constantly recite and "breathe" scripture. "'A man shall be filled with the fruit of his mouth, and he will be paid the price of his labors' [Proverbs 12:14]. These are the [words] which lead us to eternal life" (Horsiesius).[13] From a purely psychological point of view, scripture seems tailor-made for people who want to go on permanent retreat together sharing a cognitive focus. It provides them replacement language for the imperfect language they would otherwise speak; it provides *enough* replacement language to carry them through

---

which have been commanded to be acknowledged for such, by the Authority of the Church of *England*." Thomas Hobbes, *Leviathan* (E. P. Dutton, 1950), 3.33, p. 327.

[11] "The text, with its universal power of world-disclosure ... gives a self to the ego." Paul Ricoeur, *Interpretation Theory* (TCU Press, 1976), p. 94.

[12] James W. Fowler, *Stages of Faith* (HarperCollins, 1981), p. 186.

[13] Quoted in William A. Graham, *Beyond the Written Word: Oral Aspects of Scripture in the History of Religion* (Cambridge University Press, 1987), p. 130. On Pachomian scripturalism, see all of chap. 11 in Graham.

each day and through their lifetime.[14] One may object that they have transgressed a limit of wholesome guidance in filling their mouths with words not their own, but they would reply that they are dedicated to making the holy words authentically their own so that their worldly particularity may be sincerely subordinated to the Guidance as required for salvation.

There is a comparable lay version of scripturalist zeal. One can be committed to scripture study and application to the greatest extent allowed by secular life. The premise may be that a divine will for one's life is knowable via scripture. The theological challenge then is to prevent reliance on the Text's guidance from collapsing into a superstitious and inevitably frustrating use of scripture as a tool for resolving any given choice.[15] To safeguard a measure of individual self-possession on the part of the guided, it may be necessary explicitly to limit the force of scriptural direction, by implication limiting the divine being's exercise of power: "Thesis: an *individual will* of God for every detail of a person's life is *not found in Scripture* " (Friesen).[16] The view that God specifies the direction of life in every detail is incompatible with the view that God promotes human wisdom; but the pro-wisdom view, in this monotheist frame of reference, must be reconciled with belief in God's perfection and with confidence that what is necessary for salvation is revealed.

In a highly extroverted manifestation of scripturalist zeal, Nichiren posited that devotion to the Lotus Sutra was necessary for the national well-being of Japan. He did not mean that monks working with the Lotus Sutra were accumulating spiritual merit from which all of Japan benefited (an old idea that had encouraged patronage of a religion by laypeople and the state); he meant that only a prescribed fully national devotion to the Lotus Sutra would protect Japan from such perils as a Mongol invasion.[17] Nichiren was evidently using scripture in a sectarian attempt to vanquish other religious and political options in Japan.[18] But he can also be seen as

---

[14] Graham, p. 139.

[15] A very illuminating book on this issue is Garry Friesen with J. Robin Maxson, *Decision Making and the Will of God*, rev. ed. (Multnomah, 2004).

[16] Friesen, p. 41.

[17] On Nichiren's scripturalism, see Donald S. Lopez Jr., *The Lotus Sutra: A Biography* (Princeton University Press, 2016), chap. 4.

[18] "All those who failed to abandon other forms of Buddhism – and in some of his writings this seemed to include the entire population of Japan – were guilty of the sin of slandering the dharma and were destined for rebirth in the Avici hell. Indeed, Nichiren wrote that anyone who failed to denounce those who slander the dharma would be unable to achieve enlightenment, even if they had copied the *Lotus Sutra* ten thousand times ..." Lopez, p. 84.

drawing one of the ultimate conclusions of the premise of scriptural Guidance: if human well-being really depends on divine Guidance, which is actually obtainable in the true Scripture and only adequately known there, to be grasped in just one or two ultimately compelling thoughts that can be shared with all ... and if the national format of human well-being is, for various practical reasons, the most relevant spiritually ...

According to communicative expectations that are supported in the axializing guidance situation, Nichiren's appeal has glaring flaws. It does not respect individual mental freedom. His interpretation of the sutra – interestingly, a read-between-the-lines doctrine of "three thousand realms in a single moment of thought" – treats the scripture purely as a final resolver of questions.[19] To raise these objections against Nichiren, how-ever, may seem deeply threatening to the basic premise of scripturalism. For how will any scripture be maintained if not by inculcating reverence for it and implementing its guidance in an actual, viable community? An axial response must distinguish scriptural reverence and implementation from forced obedience and must affirm a spiritually actual (though ideal) global community – what Christians call "the true church" – distinct from existing communal administrations.

7.2 SCRIPTURE AND SPIRITUAL FUNCTIONALITY

Sapere aude! Kant quoted from Horace, epitomizing the Enlightenment premise: Dare to be wise, using your own resources of reason! Here, let us say, is a manly individual who actually dares to judge for himself what to believe and how to live. Should he take supreme guidance from scripture? That seems like wrapping him in chains – forcing him to acquire crucial information from a historically untrustworthy source, to follow rules imposed for suspect communal reasons, and to march in step with a company of fellow captives whose choices are under the same restraint. Throw off those chains!

But we might set a more realistic scene. Here is an individual of any gender who is naïve about important matters, imperfectly informed, biased by prejudice and passion, and as a reasoner altogether a work in progress. It is easy to see that our not-yet-epistemically-and-morally-reliable individual has something to gain from *education* both in the

[19] An idea formulated earlier by the Chinese Tiantai master Zhiyi – Lopez, pp. 57–59, 82, 84, 91.

normal sense of following a curriculum and in the broader sense of participating in all of a society's instructing and orienting communications. Might scripturalism contribute positively to the ideal education?

In the patronizing view of philosophers in the tradition of al-Farabi, nonliterate or passionate persons will hit their ceiling of spiritual competence with the imaginative impression made by the stories and exhortations of scripture. To advance further, they would need to philosophize effectively; given philosophical understanding, they could dispense with scripture. Kant's position is superficially like this to the extent that he treats pure practical reason as a complete replacement for historic religious organizations and prescriptions. But Kant also argues that people are aware of the demands of pure practical reason regardless of their degree of intellectual sophistication and that all of us are morally weak in fact, and so, to improve ourselves, we are all obliged to seek support in morally oriented fellowship. Practically, this means we are all obliged to leave the "ethical state of nature" and to join a "visible church" to serve the ultimate aims of the invisible and perfectly universal church of Reason. The head of this church must be God, on the basis of God's knowledge of our hearts. Such a church must teach ideas and statutes of morality, and such content can be maintained reliably over time only with the support of scripture.[20]

Kant gives essentially patronizing reasons for the necessity of scripture: people are naturally in awe of what is written, and we are fortunate that a historical writing happens to teach the highest ideals.[21] He does not directly link the *social* need of every moral agent for supportive fellowship with an *educational* need of every moral agent to get authoritative literate help from a church's charter text. He does not move from the idea that a church embodies a moral "republic" of moral purpose to the idea that scripturalism embodies a "republic" of thoughtful readers of textual Guidance. But he might have. He carries out a reading of the New Testament on this very premise, using famous teachings of Jesus as loci for the examination of moral norms and values.[22] We will probably have to part company with Kant if we want to assert that the scriptural articulation of life's most important ideals is the *best* way to apprehend those ideals; in his view, that would be to elevate what is historically particular and arbitrary above what is universal and rationally necessary.

---

[20] Immanuel Kant, *Religion within the Boundaries of Mere Reason* 6:95–107.
[21] Ibid., 6:107.   [22] See esp. the reading of the Gospel of Matthew in ibid., 6:159–162.

But he does grant that scripture is a normal and obligatory element in our moral-religious life.

How does scripturalism affect the broadly educational intercourse among members of an intellectually diverse community? It seems that a number of attitudes and cognitive sets that are conducive to personal growth and social harmony can be identified uncontroversially, including (to make a short list) thoughtfulness, curiosity, objectivity, coherence, humility, charity, and practicality – all with optimal forms found in between intentional or behavioral extremes.[23] With these reference points, we can make another pass in assessing the promise and risk of scripturalism, this time with our focus on the capacities of the individual. In line with our earlier discussions, the overarching thesis of interest here will be that scripturalism can enhance an individual's most important capabilities, though not without exposure to major hazards for which defenses are needed.

(1) *Thoughtfulness.* Every human being has a knowledge base and a set of guiding ideas for interpreting experience. A person who is abnormally lacking in factual knowledge or who lacks a firm grasp of ideas from which inferences can be drawn is in a poor position to learn or to engage interlocutors in a cognitively rewarding way. But the position of a person who is always ready to bury a discussion under an avalanche of pet facts or whose guiding ideas are too centralized and rigidly invoked is no better. The person in the best position is one who effectively uses a somewhat diverse set of guiding ideas flexibly and who has enough information to evaluate new information intelligently.

The intellectual life of a community can be ruled by scripture in such a way as to limit members' access to significant information or to install a rigidly centralized orthodox system of ideas in their minds. That approach may conduce to a desired uniformity in thought and practice. The individual scripturalist, however, as a mentally independent agent, is not necessarily in tune with that restrictive program. He or she *may* be persuaded that the proper aim of attending to scripture is to march in step with the community. But even if that view is taken, the activity of serious reading will pull against it, for it will summon before the reader's mind diverse questions and diverse possible answers respecting both facts and principles relevant to the Guidance.

---

[23] My list is largely inspired by Peter Levine's recent work on moral networks (private communication). See also the literature on intellectual virtues.

A modestly positive thoughtfulness thesis about scripture would run as follows: *The historical, intellectual, and moral complexity of meaning offered accessibly by a scripture is such that a mentally normal reader is more likely to become more thoughtful as a result of seriously reading scripture.* A stronger version: *Scriptural reading can bolster thoughtfulness at least as much as any other program of serious reading.* It will not be possible to confirm such a thesis, of course, because the key variables cannot be standardized or measured. I cannot answer for you; perhaps George Eliot equips your mind better than any scripture ever will. But scripturalists who wish to embrace the thesis for themselves can encourage thoughtful scripture reading and enjoy that aspect of the writing of the great scriptural commentators.

(2) *Curiosity* is allied with thoughtfulness. A curious person is open to acquiring new awareness of facts and ideas. An incurious person is hard to have any sort of productive discussion with. The same is true of an overly curious person who is always racing off toward novelty. Healthy curiosity is inseparable from being disposed to start and also to cultivate relationships with fellow subjects.

Scripturalism inhibits curiosity if it settles on a complacent understanding of the upshot of the Text. Then the definite bounds of the Text and its acceptable interpretation are walls behind which the scripturalist withdraws from normally curious conversation. But scripturalism excites and productively channels curiosity when scripture's historical, intellectual, and pragmatic complexity is recognized, provided the reader does not thoughtlessly romp among the riches of content. Thus a positive curiosity thesis is warranted: *Scripturalism can support healthy curiosity.*

(3) *Objectivity* is a crucial intellectual quality in referring to things. Logical objectivity is cultivated in the normative disciplines; empirical objectivity is cultivated in the sciences; and communicative objectivity is cultivated in the arts and humanities. One can be "too objective" at the expense of sensitivity in a communicative relationship, and objectivity can interfere with creative flow. But there cannot be a deduction or observation or reading that is "too objective." (An observation of a communicative act or situation can be *too objectifying* if it misses the subjectivity of what is observed – by missing the actuality of guidance, for example.) Scripturalism involves heightened respect for a Text and thus heightened seriousness about communicative objectivity in textual format. Although scriptural guidance can be taught in a way that is far more emotive than objective, the most telling correction of that distortion of guidance comes

from responsible scripturalists pointing out what the Text contains and what those contents probably mean or could mean.

The objective *validity* of the scriptural representation of life-in-the-world – how logically consistent it is or how empirically accurate – is of course another question. The scriptural text collections were created by a process that was neither deductive nor observational, even if some scriptures have strongly deductive and observational components. It is likely, therefore, that a scripturalist can achieve logical consistency or empirical accuracy in a worldview not by drawing that objectivity directly from scripture but only by combining scriptural guidance with other considerations. The fullest objectivity is achieved by the scripturalist, not by scripture.

An optimistic thesis about scripture and objectivity would be this: *Scripturalism demands textual objectivity to the highest degree; partly because of this encouragement of an objective attitude and partly because the Text makes far-reaching criticizable claims about the order of life-in-the-world, it is supportive of logical and empirical objectivity.*

(4) *Coherence.* In ethical and epistemological writing, there is a strong presumption for a unified system, best of all if every choice and belief is grounded in one or a small set of basic principles. Thus a mature agent is expected to have a "plan of life," and a mature knower is expected to have a smoothly functional worldview. But there is an excess of coherence when the subject becomes impervious to learning and conversational exchange. The overcoherent subject is like the incurious subject. At the other extreme, the subject who thinks incoherently is unable to form stable evaluations of kinds of action and situation and so cannot participate in guidance or any meeting of the minds at all, except as led by momentary promptings.

Scripturalism is a school of coherent thinking in three different dimensions: (a) the reader must make sense of relations among diverse textual components, reflecting diverse cultural frames of reference and cognitive modes (myth, morality, metaphysics, poetry); (b) the reader must make sense of relations among his or her own interpretations and many other interpretations, some already inscribed in tradition and some newly proposed by fellow readers; and (c) the reader must effectively relate the various ascertainable meanings of scripture and scripture interpretations to always-looming general religious questions about the structure and goal of life-in-the-world as well as to moral, political, historical, scientific, and other sorts of questions. With so complicated a challenge, scripturalists are strongly tempted to tighten their hold on the Great Ideas of the

Guidance (and indeed are encouraged by the supreme appeals of scripture to do this) and to shirk the labor of interpreting the many subsidiary elements of the Guidance and the many significant relations between the Text and the worlds beyond the text. But the better scripturalists continually refresh the challenge for all.

A modestly positive coherence thesis is suggested: *The models of life-in-the-world and of thinking that a scripture accessibly offers a mentally normal person are such that serious attention to scripture will result in a more-than-ordinarily coherent grasp of and ability to articulate a defensible life direction.*

(5) *Humility and charity.* Nearly everyone is deferential to others to the extent of waiting one's turn to speak and act. Less common is the desirable capacity to defer to others to the extent of allowing them to unfold and lead larger initiatives and considering how their ideas and actions might be justified, which is essential to reasonableness and good citizenship. However, humility and charity can be carried to the timid or evasive extreme of always playing host to others' ideas and asserting no ideas of one's own.

Scripturalism provides a format for arrogance, as the person whose main motive is to prevail in discussion is given the weapon of an epistemic base in the scriptural text that can be mastered and deployed overbearingly in many situations, or for diffidence, as the unassertive person can disappear into scriptural pleasantries. Scripturalism can also be a school of virtuous humility, however, due to the complexity of scripture's content and the demand for both responsibility and self-transcendence in its invitation to relationship with divine being. And it demands charity in linking up with others in the collective realization of scripture's significance.

A positive thesis about scripturalist humility and charity, and indeed about all of the generally desirable mental traits we have so far considered in connection with scripturalism, would be encouraged by Augustine's liberal inference from the plenary meaningfulness of the Text:

My God, you who give height to my humility ... since you tell me to love my neighbor as myself, I cannot believe that you gave less gift to your most faithful servant Moses than I would have wished and desired from you myself ... [If] I had been then what he was and had been given by you the task of writing the Book of Genesis, I should have wished to be granted to me such a power of expression and such stylistic abilities that those who cannot yet understand how God creates would still not reject my words as being beyond their capacity, and that those who have understanding would find in the few words of your servant every true opinion which they had reached themselves in their own thinking, and I should wish too that if another man were to see some other true opinion by the light of truth, that that opinion also should be discoverable in these same words of mine ... In this diversity of true opinions, let Truth herself bring forth concord.[24]

Thus: *Scripturalism can be supportive of an epistemically as well as interpersonally rewarding humility and charity.*

(6) *Empathy.* A person understands the significance of choices and experiences better and can communicate with others better in proportion to his or her empathetic awareness of the intentions and satisfactions and dissatisfactions of other subjects. Rational awareness without empathy is flat; responsibility without empathy is insensitive; intelligent calculation without empathy is one-sided.

One could well argue that the strongest school of empathy is in the arts, most articulately in literature, where the character of people's lives is made vivid. Or one could counterargue that while artistic representations draw us into musing on human possibilities, it is uniquely the law that forces us to face human strivings and vulnerabilities as real.

Scripture often has both of these kinds of value, but its literary and legal human realism is limited by its governing idealization. For example, the humanly relatable stories of the patriarchs in the Hebrew Bible have been tightly fitted into the exposition of covenant history, and most of the biblical statutes are no longer practicable. More alarmingly, many human figures, including whole peoples like the Amalekites, are reductively portrayed in a symbolic role as enemies of God. It must be remembered that the human content in any scripture is a signifier of its supreme message and that even if the message centers on love or compassion, it will register in a relatively abstract way compared to a strong literary or legal focus on human experience.

An appropriately cautious thesis about scripturalism and empathy would be this: *Although scripture by itself is not inherently the best school of empathy, a scripture may give the scripturalist a strong reason to cultivate empathy.* Scripture may at least function as a diagnostic: those who "have not ears to hear" the scriptural appeal may be too self-absorbed.

(7) *Practicality.* A person may have a mind well furnished with information and ideas and yet have no drive or feel for relating those assets to practical challenges in the given world. The grasping of significance is cut

---

[24] Augustine, *Confessions* 12.26, 30, pp. 308, 313.

off at the point of possible applications and so, accordingly, are any effects of being guided. Such a person is hard to have a serious discussion with, in most channels of seriousness. But so is the overpractical person who blocks every extension of a line of thinking by insisting on a direct application, thus preventing any enlargement of our vision for practice.

A scripture will probably contain some materials that lend themselves to impractical contemplation and some that support short-sighted practicality as well. One can take pure reading pleasure in contemplating Indra's feats in the Rig Veda, and one can thoughtlessly insist on specific behavioral rules from the Laws of Manu. But there is sure to be material at the normative core of a scripture that confronts the reader on the level of practical principle: "Those in the wilderness, calm and wise, who live a life of penance and faith, as they beg their food; through the sun's door they go, spotless, to where that immortal Person is, that immutable self" (Mundaka Upanishad 1.2.11).

A positive practicality thesis is implied: *The serious reader of scripture is directed to a spiritually wholesome balance of followable, life-reshaping policies of practice with reflective insight into the significance of that conduct of life and the situation it addresses.* While external critics might protest that the whole scriptural system is off base – that scripturalists would be better guided by other forms of guidance, given the epistemic and moral hazards of the scripturalist premise – at least it can be said that scripturalism draws from its religious base a commitment to specially intent scrutiny of the spiritual quality of human practice and its principle. It would be a rare secularist who has attended to practice as carefully as a monk has.

7.3 COLLECTIVE REALIZING

To be a reader is to be able to understand what is written. This definition of the reader can pass for minimal if we have a minimal expectation of understanding script – say, being able to pronounce written words, words that one could use in sentences of one's own that make sense. Or the definition can prompt larger expectations of understanding. The reader in the *best* case grasps the *significance* of what is written: (1) what the writer probably meant or could conceivably have meant, considering both the passage and the whole text; (2) how the writer's meanings relate to the probable and possible meanings of other writers and texts belonging to a common intellectual network; (3) how the meanings of the writer and relevant others relate to what we know or can guess about their practical situations; (4) how any or all of these elements relate to what is true, good, and beautiful, in one's own judgment; and (5) how one's own interpretation of the text's meaning and evaluation of the text's claim relate to other actual and possible interpretations and evaluations.

Individual scripturalism is a way of trying to be a best reader. In this respect it is like the most serious literary, philosophical, and legal reading. These are all intensively communal practices, for in each realm of ambitious reading there is a unifying commitment to sharing the reading experience with as many fellow readers as possible: sharing the discernment of literary achievement, of philosophical illumination, of the legal and social sense that laws and rulings make, and, in the case of scripture reading, of the sense of the Guidance. Members of the ideally diverse, overlappingly interested community of writers and readers in each realm have an auxiliary role of simply helping each other not to miss gettable meanings; they also have a more substantially collegial role of sharing in the responsibility for judging meaning and living out its implications.

To grasp significance is to realize. I can *notice* an animal before me and *know* that it is a rattlesnake without *realizing* that I need to back away immediately. Once I do realize the danger, the other shoe has dropped – there is a final determination of the meaning of the encounter for me; various things I notice and know come together decisively, "crystallize," in a compelling update of my model of life-in-the-world. We call this "realizing" because the real constitution of life-in-the-world has been unveiled – our situation is *so*, including a specification of our own practical position.

Realization is final in its moment but subject to amendment by later realizations as life goes on.

Realizing is collective whenever my grasp of significance is shared with others – thematically so when I realize the grasp sharing as a current activity. The relevant views and desires of others may differ quite a bit from mine and still factor into the collective realization. For example, in the United States there is a well-established collective political realization that the authorities of church and state must be kept separate, even though secularists and the various churches have very different aims for benefiting from the policy. This is not merely a political equilibrium that has emerged among rival parties – almost everyone *grasps* that the desired American life cannot go forward unless this premise is respected, all of the participating individuals and groups knowing also that their own grasps of the significance of church-state separation are part of a larger, more complicated grasp. Within a church, meanwhile, there are ecclesial real-izations as to which points of doctrine must be affirmed by all – otherwise church life would no longer be the life of that church – and which questions must be left open. These realizations are variously entertained and would be variously explained by individual constituents.

In all the realms of serious reading some, at least, of the most valuable realizations are collective. Grasping that *Middlemarch* is a terrifically smart portrayal of the horror of Edward Casaubon (among other things), I need to know what others see in *Middlemarch* (including even the possibility of defending Casaubon) and how it is placed in the work of Eliot, the history of the novel, and the history of England and Western culture. My realization about *Middlemarch* is a work in progress with many evolving elements so long as I remain in communication with the text itself and with other readers and writers. My happiness in "getting" *Middlemarch* is not undone by openness to revising my understanding. On the contrary, it is intensified. My realizing state seems greater insofar as I directly enjoy the stimulating fellowship of the interpretive commu-nity and continue to reap benefits of additional awareness.

A scripture reader's participation in realizing the meanings of scripture can be similarly expansive. It is true that a scripturalist, like a literary snob, can be geared wholly to finality of judgment, effectively shutting down communication with most other readers and thus deadening col-lective realizing. It may seem that scripturalists are doomed to this fate because of their religious interest in following the correct ultimate life direction, which must be gotten once for all. And indeed a particular scripturalist culture may be constraining in this way. But generally it is possible for a religious reader to grasp a spiritually sufficient significance of a guiding Text while still actively asking about its further reaches of significance. Some of the most robust examples of scripturalist communi-cation bear this out, including discussions of scripture by sage-commentators that have themselves become scriptural.

As the continuity thesis about axial community suggests, the scriptur-alist can seek to fulfill historical responsibility to everyone in a multi-generational community of followers of the Guidance. Besides the spiritual privilege of interpreting for one's own direct benefit the deliver-ances of the scripturally featured seers or sages or prophets, there is the challenge of meaningfully activating one's historical relationship with everyone else involved in the scriptural project – the friends, foes, and reference points of the scriptural protagonists in their own contexts and the writers, editors, implementers, and actual audiences of the Text in other situations along with one's own. Sharing with *everyone* the realization of scripture's significance is an impossibly large assignment, but working in that direction, or merely being oriented toward that comprehensive sharing, qualifies one's understanding with a transcendent horizon, motivating a more widely and deeply interested study of the Text.

7.4 SCRIPTURE AS A (HUMOROUS) FRIEND

The Axial Age teachings arose in times of social disintegration.[25] In China, for example, the Confucian appeal to the ways of the Zhou is almost desperate: those ways have been lost, and the scripturalism of Kongzi and the *ru* is a strategy not merely for articulating best ideals and practices but for riding out the storm of community disarray. Possessing proto-scriptural Texts makes it possible for Kongzi's group to live in a more nearly ideal way in good-enough spirits and for Kongzi to say, "What have I to fear from such a one as Huan T'ui [a threatening official]?" (*Lunyu* 7:22). The situation must have been similar for the Yahwist prophets of Israel, the philosophical communities in the Greek world, and the critics of Brahminism in India.

The problem of maintaining personal morale in a hostile world is a great theme for those whose spiritual disaffection from mainstream culture is confirmed and deepened by their radically new orientation to the divine. They feel painfully the discrepancy between the ideal and the actual community. To be a follower of God is to be persecuted, the Psalmist exclaims:

Willful sinners have heaped false accusations upon me, but I keep your precepts
     wholeheartedly.
Thick like fat is their heart, but I engage in Your Torah.
It is good for me that I was afflicted, in order that I learn Your Statutes ...
Were not your Torah my occupation, then I would have perished in my affliction.
                                                                 (Psalm 119:69–71, 96)

From the scripturalist's own point of view, scripturalist ideology provides the key to sane living in a grossly flawed world. A morally sensitive person must admire anyone who is consistently honest, thoughtful, and considerate and a forceful upholder of good standards of conduct – who, in many actual milieus, must stick out somewhat as a misfit. Our

[25] See *The Origins and Diversity of Axial Age Civilizations* (ed. S. N. Eisenstadt, SUNY Press, 1986).

traditional type for a person who consistently acts virtuously in spite of adversity is a Knight. (I offer a gender caveat at this point: the Knightly image is masculine, but I do not think there have been fewer female Knights than male.) The Knight may live by a partly implicit, minimally articulated code, like the virtuous private detective Marlowe, the knight of the mean streets, or may go about as one of the representatives of a widely known program like the Knights of the Round Table. A scripturalist is the Knight of a maximally articulate, exhaustively vetted program with the most eminent sponsorship possible. Certainly there is a hazard of arrogance and bullheadedness in the Knight position. But it will be a demand of the scriptural code and part of the communally fostered image of a scripturalist Knight, as it was of the Knights of the Round Table, that the Knight be among the most considerate of persons.

The anachronism of the Knight theme in a modern context is quite to the point, for one of the first specimens we will think of is the Knight of the Woeful Countenance, Don Quixote, whose idealistic life was by all realistic measures doomed to disappointment. Anyone stepping into the Knight position today must reckon not only with the likelihood of persecution by the non-virtuous but also with a lack of social credibility in the supporting code and a ridiculous lack of vindication in outcomes. The official solution, of course, is integrity – Job's integrity or Sita's in the Ramayana. The very substance of virtue, in its deep accord with the ultimate grain or power of the universe, will see the Knight through. But there is also a less official help for the Knight, not a standard component of scripture but not absent from scriptural literature, either, and possibly more widespread than we think, given the relentless sobriety in most scripture translations: a higher humor relishing the very incongruity of scripturally informed life.

There is humor in Job's case. It is in how the narrator and God handle Job, subjecting him to grotesque suffering and then to the counsel of pompous friends, and in how the speeches hit back with scriptural parodies, such as Job's inversion of Psalm 8: "What is man that You should give him importance, or that You should pay attention to him? That you should visit him every morning and try him every moment" (7:17–18).[26]

The *Zhuangzi*'s characteristic humor is seen in this passage in chapter 6 in the playful use of the "Creator" idea (without any commitment to

---

[26] On humor in the handling of Job's problem, see J. William Whedbee, *The Bible and the Comic Vision* (Fortress, 1998), chap. 5.

theism) and the antics of the characters acting out the "free and easy" life of nondiscrimination:

> Master Ssu, Master Yü, Master Li, and Master Lai were all four talking together. "Who can look upon nonbeing as his head, on life as his back, and on death as his rump?" they said. "Who knows that life and death, existence and annihilation, are all a single body? I will be his friend!"
>
> The four men looked at each other and smiled. There was no disagreement in their hearts and so the four of them became friends.
>
> All at once Master Yü fell ill. Master Ssu went to ask how he was. "Amazing!" said Master Yü. "The Creator is making me all crookedy like this! My back sticks up like a hunchback and my vital organs are on top of me. My chin is hidden in my navel, my shoulders are up above my head, and my pigtail points at the sky. It must be some dislocation of the yin and yang!"...
>
> "Do you resent it?" asked Master Ssu.
>
> "Why no, what would I resent? If the process continues, perhaps in time he'll transform my left arm into a rooster. In that case I'll keep watch on the night. Or perhaps in time he'll transform my right arm into a crossbow pellet and I'll shoot down an owl for roasting. Or perhaps in time he'll transform my buttocks into cartwheels. Then, with my spirit for a horse, I'll climb up and go for a ride. What need will I ever have for a carriage again?
>
> "I received life because the time had come; I will lose it because the order of things passes on."[27]

The humor is part of the integrity of these exemplary friends; they could not wholeheartedly accept the vicissitudes of worldly life and responsibly treat these troubles as all right for each other as well as for themselves without relishing the incongruity.

The persecuted Psalmist, in contrast, is committed to discrimination between righteousness and wickedness and in this respect seems the right representative for all the prophetic religions. If any consoling or redeeming humor is to be found in the trials of the righteous, the humor must acknowledge a chronic spiritual pain. For a monotheist, there is considerable pain in the thought that it was in God's power to create a harmoniously virtuous universal community, as the Qur'an notes: "Do not those who believe understand that if God had willed, He would have guided mankind all together?" (13:31).

The Qur'an addresses this problem by ridiculing the ungodly. They pass judgment on the Eternal from their pitifully parochial vantage point:

---

[27] *The Complete Works of Chuang Tzu* (trans. Burton Watson, Columbia University Press, 1968), chap. 6 (HY 6/45–54), pp. 83–84.

[A skeptic] who, when passing by a ruined and desolate city, remarked: "How can God give life to this city, now that it is dead?" Thereupon God caused him to die, and after a hundred years brought him back to life.

"How long have you stayed away?" asked God.
"A day," he replied, "or part of a day." (2:259)[28]

Unbelievers are playing a fool's game with the All-Knowing:

If you question [the Meccan unbelievers], they will say: "We were only jesting ..."
    [Or] they swear by God that they said nothing. Yet they uttered the word of unbelief and renounced Islam after embracing it ... Are they not aware that God knows what they conceal and what they talk about in secret?
    Whenever a Chapter [of the Qur'an] is revealed, they glance at each other, asking: "Is anyone watching?" Then they turn away. (9:65, 74, 78, 127)

Some of them indeed listen to you, but no sooner do they leave your presence than they ask those endowed with knowledge: "What did he say just now?" (47:16)

Idolaters invoke idols that "could never create a single fly though they combined their forces. And if a fly carried away a speck of dust from them, they could never retrieve it" (22:73). On Judgment Day they will be asked: "Where are your idols now, those whom you supposed to be your gods?" and they will say: "By God, our Lord, we have never worshipped idols" (6:22). Or else they will claim that they were in good faith because they *were* worshipping idols; but on that scenario, their idols will call them liars, and the idols themselves will offer submission to God (16:86–87).

The Qur'an directs Muhammad and by implication all its readers to "bear with" the unbelievers: "They scheme and scheme: and I [God], too, scheme and scheme. Therefore bear with the unbelievers, and let them be awhile" (86:11–17). Believers will be equal to this challenge because "you are the best of those that show mercy" (23:118). On being apprised or reminded by the Text that we have been granted the mercy of being able to confront a spiritual scandal without being defeated by it, we suddenly overcome the infirmities of our condition – we laugh.[29] By making fun of

---

[28] Fooling the resuscitated about elapsed time is a favored way of showing God's mastery; see also 17:52, 18:9–26 (the story of the Seven Sleepers), 23:112–116, 30:55, 79:46. Throughout this section I use N. J. Dawood's translation in *The Koran* (Penguin, 1990), which is especially good for the drier humor and an important influence on my interpretation.

[29] Hobbes suggests that the typical occasion of laughter is "sudden glorying" in comparison of one's own relative strength with one's own former weakness or the weakness of another. *The Elements of Law, Natural and Politic: Human Nature*, in *Human Nature*

unbelievers who hamper the formation of the good community, the Qur'an offers the reader a lighter attitude than despair toward what we experience as evil and a more humane attitude than fanatical partiality toward what we understand to be good.

A moral hazard of scripturalist community is that it can unreasonably close down awareness of the vexatious incongruities in spiritual existence, maintaining an illusion of perfect order within the righteous or enlightened circle. No laughing: there is supposed to be serene assurance only. But this is cramped guidance.

7.5 RELIGIOUS TYPES OF SCRIPTURALIST

It is not wrong to say that typically different views of the nature and authority of scripture are held in different scripturalist traditions. At least, my remarks in this vein have been consistent with generalizations that are commonly made. But actually we cannot predict from, say, "the" instrumentalist Buddhist view of scripture that literate Buddhists will all relate to scripture in an instrumentally calculating way or from "the" ontologically committed Hindu view that literate Hindus will all be disposed mainly to bask in the divine presence of Vedic language. Nor can we predict from the orthoprax norm in Judaism and Islam that all Jewish and Muslim scripturalists will be concerned primarily with the behavioral regulation of daily life. Other factors are in play, both generally human and individual, and some of these factors can plausibly be construed not merely as natural variations – as some humans happen to be engaged more by statements of principle, others by narratives, others by ritual performance, for instance – but as religious ideals.

It is worth considering the impact of religious attitude ideals on scripture following to develop a more concrete picture of individual scripturalism, even though the implications for the justification of scripturalism are not of a different order than the spiritual functionality issues we discussed above.

Different ultimate priorities of devotion correspond to temporal dimensions of concern.[30] The *pious* person reveres what is already constituted and places emphasis on acknowledgement of the text and the

---

and De Corpore Politico (ed. J. C. A. Gaskin, Oxford University Press, 1994), 9.13, pp. 54–55.

[30] See Section 6.5, note 8.

objects of the text's claims as a great fact that must be seen clearly and dealt with scrupulously. For this attitude, scripture speaks loudest as decree. The person of *faith* looks forward to a future of amazing gain; the excellence of scripture is to promise what the person of faith is then challenged to steadfastly expect while paying any necessary price. The person of religious *love* is oriented to the present actualization of divine possibility, not an already-achieved fullness of being or a promised fulfillment but rather a fulfilling of being, preeminently in encounter with a supreme Thou; a reader with this attitude would like to find in scripture, perhaps especially in poetry and narrative, a masterfully active demonstration of the loving orientation. All three sorts of readers are especially sensitive to the pathos of scriptural texts insofar as their respective attitudes are prompted and reinforced by them.

The religious styles of reading are paralleled by and may be integrally related to intellectual styles. Congenial to piety, there is a disposition to concentrate on what is definitely given for our attention that often takes the form of literalism, as regards the construal of language, and empiricism, as regards the gathering of relevant information. Congenial to faith, there is a disposition to maximize the further discovery made possible by what is given, which is much friendlier to extensions of sense and meaningfulness by analogy, symbol, and metaphor and to apophaticism. Congenial to love, there is a disposition to participate fully in the encounter with what is given, which is most sensitive to process – in the case of textual discourse, how the text works and how minds respond.

The optimal conversation in any thoughtful community involves all these styles, even though inclusive conversation means unending conflict between partisans of divergent interpretations, for each sort of thinker is positioned to illuminate points of enduring interest that thinkers of the other sorts tend to miss. The thesis that inclusive conversation is most rewarding would be hard to prove to those who insist narrowly on their own most congenial standards of worthwhile conversation. One must have experienced a succession of pious, hopeful, and loving interpretations, learning to sympathize with them all, to have a basis for knowingly preferring the inclusive conversation to a more restrictively channeled one.

Scripturalists will, I suggest, go in for preferred styles of interpretation just as they will stick with their styles of devotion; but it is a compelling ideal for them, not an implausible expectation, that they will also want to participate in the inclusive conversation, which will balance and redeem their partiality. We can speak of a collective realization of the larger meaning of scripture in this inclusive conversation – a true sharing, more than a mere equilibrium among coexisting perspectives – with no one participant able to be the perfect cognitive host of that realization. Each will remain most attuned to his or her own priorities while trying not to disrespect differently oriented claims.

We can sketch a profile of each religious style to anticipate its best and worst possibilities in a general evaluative perspective.

(1) Potentially, at least, the pious scripturalist exemplifies a highly rational type of thinker and guide. No one could be more serious about recognizing whatever has presented itself to be dealt with. But one who is passionately pious is liable to be carried away with exaggerated construals of what seems of greatest import and perhaps as a consequence is liable to fail in responsibility to human interlocutors by fanatical partisanship for what seems indisputably Great. Given the extremest pious slant, a divinity or a tradition of awesome fixed decrees cannot be lively or optimistic; it is despotism and doom. Pious interpretation at its best is clarifying of the given situation, to which end it is resolutely backward looking – as in the Targum's insistence on reading the desired kisses in the Song of Songs ("Let him kiss me with the kisses of his mouth" [1:2]) as representing a major episode in the sacred history of Israel:

Solomon the prophet said: "Blessed be the name of [Yahweh] who gave us the Torah by the hand of Moses the great scribe, inscribed on two tablets of stone, and [gave us] six orders of the Mishnah and the Gemara by oral tradition, and conversed with us face to face (as a man who kisses his companion) out of the great love with which He cherished us, more than the seventy nations.[31]

One may feel that some of the power of kissing has been lost in this interpretation, but it does solidly remind its audience of the intimacy that counts the most: their communicative contact with the Eternal. So, analogously, would a point of law be resolved by going back to the relevant precedent or code.

(2) The scripturalist of loving submission is liable to be obsessed by a Beloved but is also in a position to be among the most responsively reasonable of thinkers and guides. In his sermons on the Song of Songs, one sees that Bernard of Clairvaux is well launched on a personal adventure of intimacy with God with the aid of that text; one sees also that he is

---

[31] Aramaic Targum to Song of Songs (trans. Jay C. Treat, ccat.sas.upenn.edu/~jtreat/song/targum/, 2004).

maximally interested in explaining all this to his monastic comrades in the liveliest way, inviting them to test the meaning in their experience.

Today we read the book of experience. Let us turn to ourselves and let each of us search his own conscience about what is said. I want to investigate whether it has been given to any of you to say, "Let him kiss me with the kiss of his mouth" (Song of Songs 1:1) ...

Hear the demand of one who has experienced it: "Restore to me the joy of your salvation" (Psalm 50:14). But a soul like mine, burdened with sins, cannot dare to say that, while it is still crippled by fleshly passions (2 Timothy 3:6), and while it does not feel the sweetness of the Spirit, and is almost wholly unfamiliar with and inexperienced in inner joys.

But I should like to point out to the man who is like this that there is still a place for him on the road to salvation. He may not rashly lift his face to the serene Bridegroom [Christ] [for the holy kiss], but he can throw himself timidly at the feet of the most severe Lord with me, and with the publican (Luke 18:13) tremble on the earth and not look up to heaven.[32]

A holy kiss is coming, but the recipient must work through every stage of preparation for it. Bernard is dealing with difficulties that anyone would find in spirituality somewhat as Darwin deals with difficulties raised by evolutionary theory in the long, immensely reasonable chapters of *The Origin of Species*.

(3) The scripturalist of faith is in a position to take the most comprehensively optimistic perspective on the future and thus to encourage doing the greatest justice to everything's potential for good. The openness to good can be unfortunately narrowed by an object of faith that is world-rejecting, as in harsh forms of transcendentalism and apocalypticism, or unhelpfully weird; therefore there is a religious as well as a philosophical need to discriminate between smarter and less smart faiths. Origen's interpretation of the Song of Songs' kisses opens up to every form of enlightenment that can ever come to the soul – preeminently, of course, scriptural enlightenment:

Let the soul say in her prayer to God: "Let Him kiss me with the kisses of His mouth." For as long as she was incapable of receiving the solid and unadulterated doctrine of the Word of God Himself, of necessity she received "kisses," that is, interpretations, from the mouth of teachers [including teachers of ethics and

---

[32] Sermons on the Song of Songs, in *Bernard of Clairvaux: Selected Works* (trans. Gillian R. Evans, Paulist, 1987), Sermon 3, p. 221; verse numbers are those of the Christian Bible.

natural philosophy].³³ But, when she has begun to discern for herself what was obscure, to unravel what was tangled, to unfold what was involved, to interpret parables and riddles and the sayings of the wise along the lines of her own expert thinking, then let her believe that she has now received the kisses of the Spouse Himself, that is, the Word of God.

Moreover, the plural, "kisses," is used in order that we may understand that the lighting up of every obscure meaning is a kiss of the Word of God bestowed on the perfected soul. And it was perhaps with reference to this that the prophetic and perfected soul declared: *I opened my mouth and drew breath* [Psalm 119:131].

And let us understand that by the "mouth" of the Bridegroom is meant the power by which He enlightens the mind and, as by some word of love addressed to her – if so she deserve to experience the presence of power so great – makes plain whatever is unknown and dark to her. And this is the truer, closer, holier kiss, which is said to be granted by the Bridegroom-Word of God to the Bride – that is to say, to the pure and perfect soul.³⁴

Origen thinks that the key to enlightenment is Christ but also that Christ as the eternal Logos is the basis of everything's intelligibility.³⁵ Thus his confidence in discovery and human perfection is not very different from an optimistic secular rationalist's confidence in the prospects for human reasoning. Origen's loyalty to Christian revelation and to the Church as the platform for the pursuit of truth and the "perfection" of soul does not keep him from discussing with anyone what is true and, most importantly, what does and does not satisfy the soul.

Religious readers are enlisted in an amplified usage of language in aid of an enlargement of human life. They risk going too far so as not to fail to go far enough. Rising to a textual offer of Guidance, understanding themselves and their own situations as needy and as capable of Guidance, they may or may not be good guides to the rest of us; that depends on their good sense in harmonizing their scripturalizing with their other human modes of awareness and communication and on what we can make of the enlargements they figure to us. If the scripturalist asserts the authority of scripture as a cover for imposing his or her own will on others or as a peremptory termination of the search for the best reasons in any area of inquiry, then *that* scripturalism, we have reason to declare in advance, is disqualified.

---

³³ Origen, Commentary on the Song of Songs, in *The Song of Songs: Commentary and Homilies* (trans. R. P. Lawson, Newman, 1956), pp. 76–77.

³⁴ Ibid., pp. 61–62; Psalm verse number that of the Christian Bible.

³⁵ *On First Principles* 1.2.4, 1.3.1.

7.6 A SCRIPTURALIST POST-SCRIPTURALIST: VIVEKANANDA IN THE "PARLIAMENT OF RELIGIONS"

The scriptural text collection works against itself, in a way, in the very moment it becomes considerable for us as scripture by setting forth its sharpened main points. Once the supreme ideals have been announced, what need is there for the rest of the sacred material? Once you have read the Chandogya Upanishad, why spend any more time reading other texts in the Veda? Advaita Vedanta carries the sharpening further by picking out a small number of short "great sayings" (*mahavakyas*) in the Upanishads, all asserting that Brahman-Atman is the supreme and sole reality, all containing the essential scriptural Guidance. So abstractly comprehensive are these great sayings that one can barely see any cultural scaffolding around them. Concentrating on "You are that!" for instance, one seems poised to realize a unitive awareness in which the distinctions between speaker and hearer and the game of linguistic communication will have disappeared.

Like other great philosophical scripturalists, the classic Advaitin Shankara intimates that the ladder of the scriptural text can be kicked away once its import is realized, but he assumes that the meaning of the optimal realization is funded by its scriptural articulation. Thus he consistently asserts that the Vedas are an essential source of knowledge.[36] Without saying so directly, he implies that Vedic *communication*, dealing discursively with a variety of received sacred texts, is essential to optimizing life-in-the-world – not to the liberated state as such but to our enlightened comportment toward the goal of liberation.

The modernizing neo-Advaitin Swami Vivekananda seems to make a turn from Shankara's scripturalism. Although he addresses the 1893 World Parliament of Religions as a representative "Hindu" and predictably relates his remarks to "the teaching of the Vedas," he boldly undercuts the scriptural premise:[37]

The Hindus have received their religion through revelation, the Vedas. They hold that the Vedas are without beginning and without end. It may sound ludicrous to this audience, how a book can be without beginning or end. But by the Vedas no books are meant. They mean the accumulated treasury of spiritual laws

---

[36] See Anantanand Rambachan, *Accomplishing the Accomplished: The* Vedas *as a Source of Valid Knowledge in Shankara* (University of Hawai'i Press, 1991), and his summary discussion in *The Limits of Scripture: Vivekananda's Reinterpretation of the Vedas* (Sri Satguru, 1994), pp. 113–115.

[37] My guide to this material is Rambachan, *The Limits of Scripture*.

discovered by different persons in different times. Just as the law of gravitation existed before its discovery, and would exist if all humanity forgot it, so is it with the laws that govern the spiritual world. The moral, ethical, and spiritual relations between soul and soul and between individual spirits and the Father of all spirits were there before their discovery, and would remain even if we forgot them.

The discoverers of these laws are called Rishis, and we honor them as perfected beings. I am glad to tell this audience that some of the very greatest of them were women.[38]

Vivekananda signals that his primary appeal is in the category of holy experience rather than in sacred guidance. As he makes clear elsewhere, for him an overwhelming argument for the supreme competence of personal experience is the example of the holy man Ramakrishna, who "discarded all learning."[39] He also maintains that holy experience must be accessible to all regardless of social position.[40] Yet he continues to introduce some of his main points with the phrases "the Vedas declare" and "the Vedas proclaim," "Vedas" now making a double reference to the transtextual discovery of spiritual laws and to Hindu texts still regarded as prime textual indicators of religious truth.

The key claims in scripture, most importantly in the Upanishads, are substantiated and even displaced by experience, according to Vivekananda, but the experience we need is marked out for us by scriptural testimony:

The mighty word that came out from the sky of spirituality in India was *anubhuti*, realization, and ours are the only books which declare again and again: "The Lord is to be seen"... Religion is to be realized, not only heard; it is not in learning some doctrine like a parrot. Neither is it mere intellectual assent – that is nothing; but it must come into us. Ay, and therefore the greatest proof that we have of the

---

[38] "Paper on Hinduism" at the World's Parliament of Religions, Chicago, September 19, 1893, in *Complete Works of Swami Vivekananda*, vol. 1 (Advaita Ashrama, 1964–1971), p. 7.

[39] "Hinduism and Shri Ramakrishna," in *Complete Works*, vol. 6, p. 184.

[40] "If there is ever to be a universal religion, it must be one which will have no location in place or time; which will be infinite like the God it will preach, and whose sun will shine upon the followers of Krishna and of Christ, on saints and sinners alike; which will not be Brahminic or Buddhistic, Christian or Mohammedan, but the sum total of all these, and still have infinite space for development; which in its catholicity will embrace in its infinite arms, and find a place for, every human being, from the lowest groveling savage not far removed from the brute, to the highest man towering by the virtues of his head and heart almost above humanity, making society stand in awe of him and doubt his human nature. It will be a religion which will have no place for persecution or intolerance in its polity, which will recognize divinity in every man and woman, and whose whole scope, whose whole force, will be created in aiding humanity to realize its own true, divine nature." "Paper on Hinduism," p. 17.

existence of a God is not because our reason says so but because God has been seen by the ancients as well as by the moderns.[41]

It counts as a proof, then, that the ancients as well as the moderns share the relevant experience. We are in a long conversation about the experience framed by a tradition. The tradition proof consists of recorded communication and its disciplined interpretation. Since we are able to identify ancients who had the benchmark experience, their linguistic presentation cannot be incidental to the understood meaning of the experience.

A fundamental question to be posed to Vivekananda from a scripturalist perspective is this: Even granting the accessibility of a tremendous unitive experience to *you*, to Ramakrishna, or to a classic seer, what is the relevance of such an experience to *us* as we discuss this prospect now? If we are to share a world in which we position ourselves with respect to each other and to items and situations we figure by speaking, what marks out the path, and what describes the end of the path, liberation, such that we could collaborate on moving toward that end? Shankara offers the answer of the Vedic tradition of Brahminism coming to a point in the nondual teachings of the Upanishads. Vivekananda, too, adduces Vedic revelation, especially when speaking in India, as a platform of religious communal unity. Indeed, he sets up the Vedas as the norming primary scripture (in the category of *shruti*) for the rest of the world's scriptures (placed in the dependent category of *smriti*).[42] Thus he recognizes that overcoming the alienation of authoritarian, dogmatic, or blind-faith religion ought not to come at the price of alienation from the literate religious conversation.

*

The idea of putting down our scriptural baggage and making a fresh spiritual start is not foreign to the scriptures; in fact, it is prominent in normative core texts, as in Jeremiah saying that the most important covenant is not written (31:33–34), Laozi saying that the true Way is not stated (1), and the Brihadaranyaka Upanishad saying that in the highest realization the Vedas fall away (4.3.22). Jesus' emphasis comes down squarely on a new start based not on what anyone had read but on what he personally embodied at that moment – like Ramakrishna – for the benefit of anyone who could notice, and on the "kingdom of God" realized in his motley circle. Muslim tradition asserts that Muhammad

---

[41] "The Common Bases of Hinduism," in *Complete Works*, vol. 3, pp. 377–378.
[42] "Hinduism and Shri Ramakrishna," p. 182.

was an illiterate, which assures us that the revelation of the Qur'an is unfiltered. The idea of a universally accessible personal realization is more perfectly axial than a traditional view that restricts the ultimate guidance to members of a class or ethnic community. Thus Vivekananda seems to be on the high ground in his disagreement with Shankara about eligibility for realization.

But the wonderful reward of getting the upshot of communicated guidance and making one's own fresh start with it cannot be separate in reality from the linguistic community's provision of the guidance that maintains the structure of the guidance's meaning – the sharable meaning even of mystical experiences, which are inevitably understood and explained differently by the mystics themselves according to the different resources and constraints in their respective traditions.[43] Though Vivekananda pushes away forcefully from traditional Hindu scripturalism, he does not thereby leave the scripturalist conversation: we cannot understand his position without recognizing that he is making a new-Advaitin, scripture-linked move.

When Vivekananda speaks across tradition lines, as at the Parliament of Religions, he can expect to be understood and taken seriously by non-Hindu audiences because he uses a broadly intelligible language of God, soul, and love. These terms are so widely circulated now that they might seem independent of their traditional sources – all the better for rallying everyone to them without sectarian division. But the ideal relevance of such terms depends on their scriptural benchmarks in the literate traditions. Any serious conversation about their meaning must draw on scriptural traditions.

For this reason, I take it that the most important new development in the religious communicative situation is not post-scripturalism but multiscripturalism.

Vivekananda acknowledged a multiplicity of scripturally supported paths, affirming (with strong support from the Bhagavad-Gita as well as religious modernism) that the "many paths" all lead to "one goal."[44]

---

[43] On the tradition specificity of mystical experiences, see Steven T. Katz, "The 'Conservative' Character of Mystical Experience," in *Mysticism and Religious Traditions* (ed. Steven T. Katz, Oxford University Press, 1983), pp. 3–60.

[44] "Paper on Hinduism," p. 18. The Gita supports all four respected paths of spiritual attainment – the way of worldly action (*karma yoga*), the way of knowledge (*jnana yoga*), the "royal way" of direct realization through the practice of austerities (*raja yoga*), and the highly endorsed way of devotion (*bhakti yoga*) – and has Krishna say that all who worship, worship him (9:23).

The thought of a multiplicity of paths could suggest a labyrinth with many exits or no exit; for Vivekananda it must suggest at least the possibility of a common destination, something like the summit of a many-shouldered mountain. That mountaintop is still shrouded in cloud, its outline necessarily vague; any serious questions about its presumable character and the practicalities of reaching it must turn our attention back to path finding and following, which, in the communicative action of literate religion, means scripturalism – yet not a simply parochial scripturalism, but one that knows about many scripturalist possibilities.

8

Multiscripturalism

8.1 MULTISCRIPTURALIST SITUATIONS

What situation are we in, knowing about multiple scriptures? Do they cancel each other's pretensions, like rival kings of the world? Or does global citizenship demand that we harmonize them in some sort of "global theology"?[1] Short of that, how strong an acknowledgement of the ideal relevance of multiple scriptures is possible?

The question can be approached with the concerns of global citizenship or the concerns of religious thought uppermost.

On the side of global citizenship, there is a way of appealing to scriptural rapprochement that presses toward a kind of post-scripturalism. It is to impose ethical standards of relevant guidance as a filter so that scriptures are allowed to speak only in a manner that is at best indirectly and weakly scriptural. (Imposed cognitive standards, perhaps tied to historical or natural-scientific knowledge, may have the same effect.)

In one representative agenda for interreligious conversation, Paul Knitter asserts that the traditions are required by the current global situation to provide fruitful direction toward these goals:

(1) Liberation from physical suffering, meeting the still-unmet basic physical needs of the majority of the world's population

---

[1] Leading proposals for "world" or "global" theology – even that of Wilfred Cantwell Smith, in *Towards a World Theology* (Westminster, 1981) – are notably silent on scripturalism. An honorable slight exception is Robert C. Neville, *Behind the Masks of God: An Essay toward Comparative Theology* (SUNY Press, 1991), pointing to the need for a scriptural "archeological depth" of the guiding ideas of the world religions (36–39).

(2) Liberation from socioeconomic oppression, ending the vast victimization of people denied basic control of their lives

(3) Liberation from nuclear oppression (the reign of terror we live in, knowing that just one or a few people could trigger nuclear war) and holocaust

(4) Liberation from ecological disaster

These concerns determine a "common core" of relevant religious teaching regardless of what each tradition teaches distinctively.[2] Thus there is a mandatory concern for Buddhists about physical well-being regardless of the Buddhist proclamation of the Noble Truth that all life has the character of dissatisfaction, a mandatory concern for Hindus about social equality regardless of the social discrimination in the Laws of Manu, and a mandatory concern for Christians about nuclear safety and ecological preservation regardless of the apocalyptic hope of the New Testament. All of these goals can be espoused without following scriptures, but scriptures still have value because many people are most likely to be ethically aroused and persuaded in scriptural-religious settings.

Undoubtedly there have always been ethical conditions on scriptural guidance. Our attention is captured by Yahweh's or the Buddha's or Laozi's utterances in the first place because they are promising interventions in our struggle to rectify our lives. But the hallmark of religious communication is to expand decisively our view of what constitutes good and evil and what is possible and impossible in that struggle. An ethically or politically driven interpretation of religious proposals is liable to subtract the religious addition of meaning. Indeed, religious meaning is deliberately bracketed in the pluralistic secular arena; when I make claims for justice, though I may call my God and my ideal of righteousness to witness, I cannot demand that my neighbors be followers of my God and my prophets.

It may be asserted that scriptural interpretations in the various religious communities, even though on a different track from the ethico-political conversation in the public square, will nevertheless be commonly oriented to the needs of global humanity so that what will seem most relevant to readers looking to scriptures for Guidance will be precisely the

---

[2] Paul F. Knitter, "Interreligious Dialogue: What? Why? How?" in Knitter et al., *Death or Dialogue?: From the Age of Monologue to the Age of Dialogue* (Trinity, 1990), pp. 27–30.

common or complementary meanings across traditions that can be found in multiple scriptures. At least we can expect this to be true for the most humanly responsible scripture readers in the various traditions. To the extent that this pattern obtains, these readers will be multiscripturalists in a religiously thin way, hard perhaps to distinguish from the influence of the Zeitgeist; but it is still an important harmony.

More squarely on the side of religious thought, there is a popular way of thinking about religious pluralism that produces an easy and misleading answer to the question of multiscripturalism. It is the idea that the supreme Real and Good must be the sponsor of all religious experience of enduring interest and thus, via all necessary accommodations to human limitations, must be the sponsor of the meanings of all scriptures, which must therefore be unifiable on their best interpretation. One may point to the Sikhs' Guru Granth Sahib as a demonstration of the idea – theologically the manifesto of a Hindu-Muslim unification movement and textually a showcase for diversely sourced sacred texts.

But "Real"-ism is misleading logically when its identification of the divine is merely a category in which claims about the divine are located, not a specification of what or who the divine is (as when Ibn 'Arabi calls God "the Reality"). "The Real" can be an empty placeholder that puts off the determination of whether religious experiences actually are informed in commensurable ways. The abstract ultimacy of the referent – that we are thinking about that which *must be* the basis of everything – guarantees that we cannot know what we are referring to, for we posit that it is in back of whatever we think we know. The religious traditions, for their part, point not to the abstract Real and Good – or to a correlated subjectivity of openness to whatever the transcendent might be – but to a somehow perceived *That* that is ultimately real and good (God, Brahman, Emptiness, the Way) whither all non-delusory paths must lead. And this relatively definite religious ultimate determines the main practicalities of the religious life. Thus the Sikhs attest to the One Creator and enact social-egalitarian implications of that Creator's transcendence.

The notion of a generic Ultimate is misleading substantively because in fact the ultimate religious ideals of religious traditions are divergent. Emptiness is not Brahman, far from it; devotion is not detachment; filial piety is not faith. We can characterize this situation with another thesis on axiality, a thesis of axial diversity: *The similarity of the axial communities in their allowance for the mental independence of individuals and their reliance on ideals that are ultimate trumps in reflective discussion entails not an ultimate commonality of those ideals but, on the contrary, that all the different possible ultimate positions are taken.* We could not be confident that we had plumbed the depths of spiritual possibility had we not discovered very momentous choices to be made. Nor could we adequately respect the disagreements that are constitutive of the traditions, as Buddhism rejects fundamental premises of Hinduism, Daoism maintains a running criticism of Confucianism, and Christianity puts its polemical twist on Judaism.

Existing scriptures are bound to be ideologically and rhetorically diverse due to having been composed and transmitted in the various concrete circumstances of the scripturalizing communities, but that is not the whole explanation of their diversity; we should also expect scriptures to reflect diversity among the ultimate religious ideals that *can* be held. A thicker, more religiously serious multiscripturalism must take up that challenge.

*

Assuming best practices in education, we all have multiscriptural awareness because multiple scriptures are in our curriculums. We sample and curiously discuss the texts as scriptures without necessarily being committed to following any of them. On this cognitive plane, we are indeed *compulsory* multiscripturalists, for an educated person cannot think that any one revered Scripture holds the patent on the category of scripture. As is true of language and religion, one's understanding of one's own scripture is unfortunately limited if one lacks acquaintance with other scriptures as well. But beyond this acquaintance that we all ought to have, one might also find oneself convinced of unavoidable Guidance from a hitherto non-holy scripture. In that event one is on a multiscripturalist path as a matter of personal fact, and objections about logical incompatibility or psychological disunity are already in the course of being overcome.

Multiscripturalism is a religiously compelling ideal for those who are disposed to find the Guidance in the fullest communion with all apparently relevant texts. They may reason that just as the Confucian canon, the Vedas, and the Bible came to be assembled from diverse components and unified as the Guidance for their historical communities, so the totality of spiritually essential-seeming texts should now, if possible, be unified as the Guidance for everyone. They may argue for multiscripturalism in the key of optimism: *The most optimistic seeker of Guidance will not be daunted by the challenge of appropriating material from diverse frames of reference.* Or in the key of responsibility: *One cannot show adequate respect for the transcendent being and goodness of the divine or for the spiritual experience of known and knowable fellow agents by insisting on the sole relevance of one scriptural tradition.* Or in the key of intelligence: *Full religious intelligence does not overlook any of the best offers of guidance, particularly those that have been judged necessary by axial religious communities.*

Multiscripturalism also seems practically impossible, however, because being a scripturalist means being on a path, committed to that path for the optimization of life. Here "path" is a figure for a concrete complex of guidance in which the agent is embedded both by factual circumstances and by choice. One cannot cross a mountain on different paths at the same time; one cannot speak different languages at the same time; one cannot learn different dances at the same time; one cannot be a wholly loyal subject of the House of David and the House of Zhou at the same time.

It may be objected that teleologically meaningful living is path-bound yet not like being on just *one* path. True, I cannot cross a mountain on two paths at once, but I can cross on one path today and another next week, thus getting to know the mountain much better. I cannot speak two languages at once (properly), but I can spend time in two countries or two literatures, thus getting to know language and ideology much better. Certainly I can learn different dances and indeed very different styles of dancing. I cannot be a faithful subject of two political regimes if they are at war – but are they necessarily at war? Does either necessarily forbid me to participate in the life of the other community?

Though the image here is blurry, it is possible to talk of "blending" paths.[3] This notion provides for some fluidity in the handling of the cognitive demands made by new appeals and for an underlying reformation of religious subjectivity. But actually following guidance is different from merely entertaining ideas. While I could listen to two ranger talks

---

[3] "What we are interested in is the unique blending of two or more paths in order to realize their inbuilt creativity." K. P. Aleaz, "Pluralism Calls for Pluralistic Inclusivism," in *The Myth of Religious Superiority: Multifaith Explorations of Religious Pluralism* (ed. Paul F. Knitter, Orbis, 2005), p. 170. Aleaz has articulated a blending of Christianity and Neo-Vedanta in numerous works. Charles Wei-Hsun Fu writes of pursuing a blending project: "In religious search and philosophical inquiry, I always want to be a nonpartisan cosmopolitan, somewhat like ... a fastidious bee trying to make the best possible honey out of various nectars (I mean, various sources such as Christianity, Buddhism, Confucianism, and so on)." "A Universal Theory or a Cosmic Confidence in Reality?" in Leonard Swidler, ed., *Toward a Universal Theology of Religion* (Orbis, 1987), p. 154.

and form a blended idea of the best way to hike across a mountain, I could not follow two paths across the mountain in a blended manner (unless they conveniently cross each other at many points). Or in a more urgent situation, I could have studied fire-escape plans in hotels around the world, thus gaining an advanced understanding of the possibilities of fire escape, yet only one of those plans is the unavoidable guidance for the fire in the hotel where I am.

Many models for the scene of religious pluralism are worth considering. Raimon Panikkar discusses the strengths and weaknesses of four of them – paths on a mountain, colors in a rainbow, topological transformations of a religious invariant, and languages – and points toward a fifth model in the multiple reverberations (so to speak) of mystical silence.[4] The path model seems especially strongly connected to the premise of guidance inasmuch as guidance's second essential task, after identifying or confirming the desirable goal, is identifying the best steps toward the goal.

Living in readiness for guidance is indeed like being on a path to the extent that one sees sequentially constrained choices ahead. The most interesting choices have some aspects that are sequentially constrained but others that are not: for example, if I decide to travel from Jackson to Chicago, I have to choose a road, rail, or flight path connecting the two cities, and I will take various further steps accordingly; but at the point of choosing to go to Chicago, I might have chosen to go to Seattle instead or to stay home, without having been on any definite mental path of evaluating travel options. Where there is no constraint of sequence, there can be no guidance regime. If I suddenly decide to go to Seattle instead of Chicago, we might say that I have been swayed by the *appeal* of Seattle; we are not seeing the guidance regime in which I turn that way.

If I *am* in a regime of guidance, I am not making pathless choices. To be a follower of a scripture is to be in a regime of guidance. Simply switching to a different scriptural regime would be like suddenly deciding for Seattle over Chicago. Unless there is such a thing as a multiscripturalist guidance regime, multiscripturalism as mere regime switching cannot count as the following of a guidance and so cannot be regarded as a mode of scripturalism.

Could there be multiscripturalist guidance?

---

[4] Raimon Panikkar, *The Intrareligious Dialogue*, rev. ed. (Paulist, 1999), pp. 12–22.

The phenomenon of multiple religious belonging is seen now in individual cases worldwide and is long established in East Asia, where persons are accustomed to receive guidance from different scriptural traditions according to the social occasion or the spiritual need. The guidance regime of the religious culture coordinates the guidance offers of the texts. Ideal disagreements between the texts cause disharmony only if the texts themselves are the focus of dogmatic attention.[5] The East Asian "Three Teachings" system depends on selective awareness of and deference to the Teachings. A kind of "blending" is at work. It can be said nevertheless that the religious guidances in play are scripturally normed.

There is a more individually autonomous version of the same pattern. At the eclectic extreme, an individual might have a personal regime of guidance in a diversely inspired philosophy of spiritual fulfillment, drawing on scriptural assets as they seem most helpful – say, reading scripture A for directives in social ethics and scripture B for advice on overcoming attachment. Used in this way, the scriptures have the status of religious classics rather than scripture. None makes a claim to paramount authority; if it did, it would interfere with eclectic freedom. An individual's adherence to scriptures may however be governed not so much by free personal discrimination as by an adapted traditionalism (perhaps as a result of living in multiple communities) or personalized obedience (perhaps as an adjustment called for by familial or professional relationships) so that different scriptures do guide the individual as paramount textual authorities in the situations where they speak most pertinently. In this case the multiscripturalist individual is obviously not in perfect agreement with scripturalists who are committed to deriving all life Guidance from one scripture within one scriptural tradition. But neither are millions of religious East Asians.

On the other side of the Himalayas we find relatively domineering Vedic and Abrahamic views of scriptural authority. On the Vedic view, a certain deployment of Sanskrit is uniquely eternal and divine; other scriptures might very well reflect portions of divine truth, but they must be secondary. One of the most potentially far-reaching concessions to scriptural pluralism in a classical Hindu frame of reference is made by the Kashmiri Shaivite Abhinavagupta, who argues that the meaning of any

---

[5] Judith Berling testifies: "As one who has sojourned extensively along the paths of Chinese religion, it is my observation and experience that relations with other religions are more readily built upon practice and symbols than on doctrine and scripture ... doctrine and scripture [can be] stumbling blocks." *A Pilgrim in Chinese Culture* (Orbis, 1997), p. 36.

scripture is, at bottom, a self-realization of Shiva, the ultimate consciousness that is the ultimate Real, and that any such realization necessarily obtains within the spiritual horizons of a particular person and tradition. Here the idea of divine accommodation to human limitations is interpreted not as "skillful means" in communication but as a range of divine creations of consciousness:

[Every scripture] produces a [sure] judgment as restricted only to those who are eligible, at a particular place and time, with cooperating factors ... A particular person is created by the Lord such that he recognitively apprehends himself in union with that apprehension which is understood to be engendered by this or that god or siddha [perfected one]. Another [person is created who apprehends himself in union with] another [apprehension of some other god or siddha].[6]

Scriptural diversity is to be expected, therefore, and scriptural perspectives will not be harmonized easily:

It is compulsory that texts which teach only aspects of oneself and [consequently] *yield limited fruits be taken up by that one* [who desires such fruits] ... *Inasmuch as one has not attained identity with Shiva, he does not doubt such a conviction as accords with his own nature* [as a limited being]. *He will be doubtful about other convictions and regard* [his own] *as much better.*[7]

Members of each scriptural community will be bound tightly to their scripture by their consciousness.

Confirming this principle in his own case, Abhinava asserts that only his own Shaivite Trika scripture can guide followers to the true goal of identity with Shiva. *His* scripture is the essence of scripture; other scriptures are subordinate to it like other parts of a body are subordinate to the head. Non-Indian "barbarian" scriptures are too contaminated with falsehood to count as scriptures at all.[8]

In Abrahamic scripturalism there is a strong emphasis on God summoning us such that we are responsible to our Creator. The biblical or Qur'anic believer is pinned to a particular scripture not so much by ontic or epistemic limitations (which do have to be taken into account) as by the accountability generated by the communicative event. To look for

---

[6] *Ishvarapratyabhijnavivritivimarshini* 2.3.1–2, trans. David Peter Lawrence in "Aspects of Abhinavagupta's Theory of Scripture," *polylog: Forum for Intercultural Philosophy* 4 (them.polylog.org/4/fld-en.htm#n61, 2003).

[7] *Tantraloka* 35.21–22, in Lawrence.

[8] *Ishvarapratyabhijnavivritivimarshini* 2.3.1–2. Lawrence notes the similarity of the early Christian apologists' argument that the eternal Logos partly informed the thought of Plato et al.

Guidance curiously in other texts is thoughtless rudeness at best, infidelity and idolatry at worst. But even orthodox biblical or Qur'anic guidance is complex and requires checking in with many component texts. Extending this recognition, an Abrahamic scripturalist contemplating multiscripturalism might be open to being divinely addressed and held accountable by *all* texts designated as scripture by historic religious communities, on the theory that the world Creator must have been communicating somehow with all human communities and with literate communities by means of scriptures.

Something like this view informs *Nostra Aetate*, the watershed statement on world religions by the Second Vatican Council of the Roman Catholics, which recognizes God's revelation in multiple traditions.

The Catholic Church rejects nothing that is true and holy in these religions. She regards with sincere reverence those ways of conduct and of life, those precepts and teachings which, though differing in many aspects from the ones she holds and sets forth, nonetheless often reflect a ray of that Truth which enlightens all men.[9]

Yet the "sincere reverence" avowed by *Nostra Aetate* does not constitute an encouragement, let alone a commitment, to *follow* any non-Christian edition of the Guidance. The recognition of holiness in other traditions does not generate accountability to *God*; it generates accountability to fellow human beings whose scriptural religions deserve respect.

Given the basic Abrahamic premise, the master Sufi theorist Ibn 'Arabi offers a remarkably positive view of multiple scriptures, construing the acceptance of multiple scriptures as a requirement of Islamic faith. He builds on the Qur'anic assertions that God has sent messengers to all peoples and that the Peoples of the Book have valid Texts of Guidance:

All the revealed religions are lights. Among these religions, the revealed religion of Muhammad is like the light of the sun among the lights of the stars. When the sun appears, the lights of the stars are hidden, and their lights are included in the light of the sun. Their being hidden is like the abrogation of the other revealed religions that takes place through Muhammad's revealed religion. Nevertheless, they do in fact exist, just as the existence of the light of the stars is actualized. This explains why we have been required in our all-inclusive religion to have faith in the truth of

---

[9] *Nostra Aetate: Declaration on the Relation of the Church to Non-Christian Religions* (www
.vatican.va/archive/hist_councils/ii_vatican_council/documents/vat-ii_decl_19651028_nostra-
aetate_en.html, 1965).

all the messengers and all the revealed religions. They are not rendered null by abrogation – that is the opinion of the ignorant.[10]

As in *Nostra Aetate*, however, the recommended acceptance of other scriptures is not a directive to consult them. Given the fully solar illumination of one's own scripture, why would one, how could one, look elsewhere? And if one did, how could one glean any valid directive other than a repetition of the normative directives one had already received? But Ibn 'Arabi maintains that such gleaning cannot be ruled out:

One who believes [in the ordinary way] believes only in a deity he has created in himself, since a deity in "beliefs" is a [mental] construction ... Beware lest you restrict yourself to a particular tenet [concerning the Reality] and so deny any other tenet [equally reflecting Him], for you would forfeit much good, indeed you would forfeit the true knowledge of what is [the Reality]. Therefore, be completely and utterly receptive to all doctrinal forms, for God, Most High, is too All-embracing and Great to be confined within one creed rather than another, for He has said, *Wheresoever you turn, there is the face of God.*
(Qur'an 2:115)[11]

Ever since the first publications of scriptures there have been religious leaders who gave some attention to other traditions' scriptures and took relatively respectful positions toward them. But global literacy had to be far advanced, along with a questioning of European cultural hegemony in the world, before any *religious guide*, someone like Raimon Panikkar (the Catholic/Hindu author of *The Vedic Experience*), could have a constituency for encouraging multiscripturalism.[12] And Panikkar is still an outlier among theologians, not to say a rogue. In scripturalist religion, exercising religious leadership is still closely tied to representing the paramount authority of the community's already-enshrined Text. Serious moves toward honoring religious authority in other traditions, such as Matteo Ricci and the pro-Confucian Jesuits made in China, have understandably been disallowed by higher church authorities, while religious movements with a modernizing cosmopolitan perspective have undercut seriousness about scriptural guidance altogether by embracing deism and the idea of natural religion. Thus, although an interest in multiscripturalism is

---

[10] Ibn 'Arabi, *The Meccan Revelations* III.153.12, in William Chittick, *Imaginal Worlds* (SUNY Press, 1994), p. 125.
[11] Ibn 'Arabi, *The Bezels of Wisdom*, chap. 10 (trans. R. W. J. Austin, Paulist, 1980), p. 137. Probably the doctrinal forms he has in mind are all within the Abrahamic family, but the reference of his thought cannot be contained within that limit.
[12] Raimundo Panikkar, *The Vedic Experience* (University of California Press, 1977).

unavoidably generated by our awareness of many scriptural traditions that deserve respect, the premise is still in doubt.

8.2 WHY MULTISCRIPTURALISM SHOULD NOT BE POSSIBLE

(1) *The issue of incompatible beliefs.* A commonsensical view of religion holds that as long as the specific guidance offers of religious traditions are taken seriously, the religions will be committed to incompatible *beliefs*. A follower of the Christian Bible must believe that Jesus Christ (not Krishna) is the unique divine incarnation, a follower of the Vedas must believe in an endless cosmic cycle (not a Day of Judgment and single resurrection), a follower of the Confucian Classics must believe in the practical priority of filial piety (not seeking satori), and so forth. Since a lucid mind cannot believe mutually excluding propositions, a lucid multiscripturalism is impossible. Following genuinely diverse guidances is psychologically schizophrenic.[13]

This conception of the religious situation can usefully be challenged along several lines.

First, we are not entitled to assume that propositional beliefs are the controlling standard of religious orientation. Buddhists explicitly warn against attachment to beliefs, and analogous warnings are found in many of the traditions – for example, in the attacks on idolatry in the Hebrew scriptures. Wilfred Cantwell Smith has developed the case for defining religiosity primarily by devotion (he says "faith") rather than by belief.[14] The claim is not that cognitive engagement and commitment are unimportant in the religious life but that they are at the service of relationship with the holy rather than being ends in themselves. Beliefs lose their religious utility when they are treated as fully formed, permanent logical commodities.

Second, even if one wishes to retain the ideal of a fully definite, fully believable belief as a cognitive touchstone in religious life, one is not entitled to assume either at the beginning or in the midst of inquiry that one can fully specify the content of ideal belief. Christians believe in God,

---

[13] On the schizophrenia issue, see David J. Krieger, *The New Universalism: Foundations for a Global Theology* (Orbis, 1991), pp. 35–37. He argues that intercultural encounter occasions two unsatisfactory responses, jumping back from the new option or jumping over to it, but also a third, more satisfactory response, jumping in between to a space of dialogical encounter.

[14] Wilfred Cantwell Smith, *Faith and Belief* (Princeton University Press, 1979).

but the content of their belief is subject to discussion. The same is true of Hindus believing in Brahman or Ishvara or the Devi. Not only do we not *know* that belief in God is irreconcilable with belief in Brahman, it is not easy to say that we *know* that *any* important belief option is excluded by either of these beliefs, except perhaps that being (that is, simply to be) is evil. Moreover, a belief that really is religiously essential, like "God is most great," is not actually a specific cognitive commitment in the same way that, say, "God is impassible" is, so it is not appropriate to think even ideally of fully specifying one's ultimately orienting belief.

These points about belief may be applied also to the claim that a religious person is necessarily invested in an "account" of life-in-the-world that is necessarily "central" and exclusively controlling for that person's understanding. "If you say that you are a Jewish Buddhist, for example, you typically mean that you offer a religious account some elements of which are historically Buddhist and some historically Jewish. You do not mean, because you cannot, that you simultaneously offer two religious accounts" (Paul Griffiths).[15] But this is to require philosophical consistency where the assumed determinacy of ideas does not obtain.

There is indeed a prima facie incompatibility between many prominent claims found in different scriptures. But there is plenty of prima facie inconsistency within scriptures as well. Most scripturalists do not treat their scriptures as philosophical systems; the few who insist on a formulable cognitive consistency tend to place themselves at an esoteric remove from generally reasonable readings of the texts. Meanwhile, the interpretive approaches that many thoughtful scripturalists use to make a usable whole of their home scriptures – namely, distinguishing various kinds of linguistic meaning and various contexts of utterance, responding creatively to the symbolic potentials of the texts, invoking divine accommodation and skillful means – are available to multiscripturalists as well.

The history of polemical relations between the traditions encourages the notion that the incompatibilities in religious claims become too great to negotiate at the tradition level, but nonpolemical inquirers are entitled to test that notion. Now, the very idea of nonpolemical multireligious

---

[15] Paul J. Griffiths, *Religious Reading* (Oxford University Press, 1999), p. 13. Griffiths cites Dan Sperber's parallel claim about symbol systems: "If one could internalize several different symbolic devices, as one can learn several different languages, the task of the anthropologist would thereby become considerably simpler. But the anthropologist, who little by little penetrates the symbolism of his hosts, is never able to pass from one symbolism to another as easily as he passes from one language to another" (quoted on p. 13).

inquiry may be rejected on the grounds that the religious traditions are *intrinsically* polemical: one cannot understand Christianity and Judaism except as pushing away from each other, and so too with Hinduism and Buddhism and with Confucianism and Daoism. But the *specific* polemics that historically helped certain traditions bring some of their main claims into focus do not constitute a *general, permanent* refusal on their part to participate in multireligious discussion, or at least such a refusal should not simply be taken for granted.

(2) *The issue of intelligibility barriers.* Multiple scriptures present us with cultural multiplicity. Except perhaps in the Chinese context where Daoists and Confucians share a language and many conceptual points of reference, it is wise to admit that leaving one scriptural world to visit another raises some of the same issues of intelligibility and translation that visiting another culture does. One cannot assume that one adequately understands what the members of a culture are getting at or that one is able to apply appropriate criteria in resolving the sense and validity of their expressions unless one has become one of them. One must cross over. Translation is always possible but can never be assumed to capture all of the important meaning of any token of the source culture. But multiscripturalism depends on gleaning scriptural directives by translation; therefore, multiscripturalism can never be religiously satisfactory.

The most obvious answer to this objection is that multi*culturalism* is an accepted possibility – one can be both Yoruba and English, for instance, not perhaps to the extent of having two "mother" tongues of equal emotional depth but certainly to the extent of having a perfectly good understanding of what Yoruba and English persons are getting at when they express themselves on a full range of topics. When translations between the two cultures fail, as they admittedly must, the multicultural person understands from both sides how they fail.

It might be thought that the pluralism of scriptural traditions runs deep in a specific way that prevents full understanding of more than one. For a scripture is linked not only to its own language (or languages) and host culture (or cultures) but to its own extraordinary spiritual life in which its followers participate – extraordinary in the ventures of its utterances and in its actual involvement with divinity. There is a profound practical specificity to the life it guides attained through long experience and discipline. A passerby cannot jump into it as into a swimming pool.

Faced with such a warning, the would-be multiscripturalist approaching target scriptures might say: I would like to see how far into these depths I can get. But some gatekeepers for a community will insist on qualifications for following their scripture that effectively keep out anyone whose mind is not completely formed by their tradition. For example, Shankara stated these prerequisites for "inquiry into *Brahman*," assuming they could be met only by a twice-born male Hindu: "The discrimination of what is eternal and what is non-eternal, the renunciation of all desire to enjoy the fruit (of one's actions) both here and hereafter, the acquirement of tranquility, self-restraint, and the other means, and the desire of final release."[16] However, these requirements, insofar as they are stated in a spiritually substantive rather than socially arbitrary way, *could* be met by someone who had not grown up Hindu.

(3) *The issue of incompatible community involvements.* A scripture is a publication that anyone may acquire, but its religious nature as someone's Scripture is a function of the role it plays in the historic life of a community. For this reason it may be argued that there is no genuine access to scriptural guidance except by joining and actively living in the community it serves. One is required to assume responsibility toward fellow scripturalists as well as toward the scripturally indicated divinity. A kind of spiritual intimacy is involved that is exclusive by its very nature.[17] Christians are directed by their scripture to adopt the ideal attitude of *agape* love, for example, which can only be realized in an agapist community (or so many Christians have argued).[18]

There are different ways of construing community, however, and the feasibility of one might not exclude the feasibility of another. Because of

---

[16] Shankara, Introduction to the Vedanta Sutras (trans. George Thibault), in *Sacred Books of the East*, vol. 34 (ed. F. Max Müller, Oxford University Press, 1890), p. 12.

[17] Griffiths argues that religious reading communities are something like marriages. "Many temples in India these days post signs forbidding entry to non-Hindus; Christians do not welcome non-Christians to participate in the celebration of the Eucharist; Tibetan Buddhists often will not let you study a particular work unless you've had the proper initiations. These are all forms of insularity. But they are entirely proper, best likened to the exclusion from the marriage bed of anyone but the spouses, and certainly not a moral reason for rejoicing at or conniving in the continuing extirpation of religious readers.... [Marriage requires] knowing your spouse: knowing a good deal about her, remembering her name, her likes, her dislikes, and her history; and having the skill to behave toward her in a way that both expresses and deepens your love. To be Christian or Jewish or Buddhist is to have an institutional form as your spouse, an institutional form with a history." Griffiths, pp. 186–187.

[18] On arguments for and against this construal of Christian agapism, see Gene Outka, *Agape: An Ethical Analysis* (Yale University Press, 1977).

the historically fraught relationship between Jewish and Christian communities, the "Messianic Jewish" decision to follow Christian together with Jewish scriptures is rejected in principle by mainstream Jews and Christians alike, most strongly by Jews. Yet there are Messianic Jews. In the East Asian world of the Three Teachings, on the other hand, the religious community is ordinarily conceived as benefiting from multiple divine guidances – that is a mainstream attitude – and yet there are Daoist, Buddhist, and Confucian leaders who insist on the sole validity of their own tradition's guidance. In short, one has options in how to place oneself in scriptural community, even if the options are not equally easy to practice or defend.

A scripturalist may protest that the essence of divine guidance is to determine an individual's membership in an ideal community chartered by a scripture; one cannot properly be a scripturalist without being obedient to that determination. Multiscripturalism is therefore ruled out because one cannot be obedient to different supreme determinations of this kind.

But it seems that it is not impossible to be subject to more than one ultimate authority. Children are normally subject to the ultimate authority of multiple parents and quasi-parental figures. That is for their own good, as the different authorities provide needed guidance of complementary kinds and on different occasions.

Obedience to an axial ultimate cannot be like that, it may be replied; the ultimate Director is *absolute,* and its authority cannot be alternated or superseded in successive moments like the mother's or father's authority over a child. This point is made by Jesus' assertion that natural family relationships are replaced by orientation to God's will (Matthew 12:49–50). But Jesus spoke there as an adult among adults and did not deny that children are under the authority of parents; nor did he prove, nor could he have proved, that being subject to the authority of his heavenly Father absolutely excludes the possibility of finding himself subject also to a differently named, somewhat differently conceived divine authority.

A recently created option of multiscriptural community is called Scriptural Reasoning.[19] It is a fellowship of readers from different traditions who share the expectation that scriptural guidance is needed to meet human needs. The members are not committed to being

---

[19] On Scriptural Reasoning, see *The Promise of Scriptural Reasoning* (ed. David F. Ford and C. C. Pecknold, Blackwell, 2006).

multiscripturalists in the sense that each will become a devout follower of multiple scriptures – it is a program of meeting and discussing, not of persuading – but they have accepted a responsibility to fellow readers that is scripturally determined in multiple directions: they believe that reasoning out scriptural meaning in a multiscriptural curriculum and in a nonsectarian forum is a way of being faithful to their own scripture,[20] and for the sake of being collegially faithful to the other readers whom they have accepted as their peers, they are methodically, seriously oriented to what their peers are oriented to. The Scriptural Reasoners say that their interest is strictly in becoming better Jews, Christians, and Muslims respectively, but their practice is a vestibule of multiscripturalism.

8.3 HOW MULTISCRIPTURALISM MIGHT BE POSSIBLE

An inquirer might go canvassing for religious truths, curious to see which claims from which sources satisfy general criteria of credibility.[21] That would produce a kind of philosophical religion. But multiscripturalism is not in the first place a search for truths. It is an adventure in receiving Guidance – an action in relationship. A multiscripturalist has gotten drawn into that position. Following those scriptures has become his or her format for living.

One can read a multiscripturalist author and decide for oneself whether the multiscripturalism is shallow, more academic than devout,

---

[20] Christian theologian Susan Ticciati writes: "The world of the Bible, as a world which can never be possessed, cannot be equated with any particular appropriation of it, but ... its strangeness is, on the contrary, embodied in the Bible's *resistance* to interpretation ... [which] finds indispensable embodiment in the resistance of others to inscription within its universe." "Scriptural Reasoning and the Formation of Identity," in Ford and Pecknold, p. 78. Ibn 'Arabi's ideal of openness to God is supported in Scriptural Reasoning: "I am freed from my own, self-enclosed readings of Scripture and ... Scripture is freed again to be the locus of God's acts" (Ticciati 92).

[21] On criteria for credibility (e.g., substantially appealing religious experiences, compatibility with facts, ethical and psychological fruitfulness), see the papers by Ninian Smart, William J. Wainwright, and Mary Ann Stenger on "Cross-Cultural Truth in Religion," in *Religious Pluralism and Truth* (ed. Thomas Dean, SUNY Press, 1995), pp. 67–107. Let this note serve as a side door into the religious pluralism and interreligious dialogue discussions, which are extensive. Another important collection is Swidler, op. cit., and see also Krieger, op. cit., who helpfully analyzes Panikkar's ideas about multi-religious experience.

or disloyal to one or more of the communities involved. What one sees will be determined partly by what one thinks is possible.

My own sense of what is possible in this area is affected by personal experience. I was raised Christian, and the Christian Bible is still the one scripture I read both methodically and devoutly. In my academic life I am an eager student of all religious traditions, especially as represented by their most authoritative texts; because of my specializations, however, I am better versed in scholarship on the Bible than on other scriptures.

As everyone knows, the Old Testament read by Christians is pervaded by historical and theological preparations for Christ and so is very different from the Jewish Tanakh, in which there is no Christ. The difference lies in the two communities' divergent interpretations of the same textual legacy.

Thus I read the Servant Songs in Isaiah 40–55, and as Christian liturgy reminds me regularly, I always find Christ there, the one who was wounded for our transgressions and bore our infirmities (53:4–5). These passages, especially the fourth song (53), are not just electively assignable to Christ as any prophecy of future redemption might be; they closely concern the very idea of Christ as a universal redeemer who redeems by humble suffering. It is plausible that Jesus himself was guided by the idea of the Servant; it is certain that the New Testament writers were inspired by it (Isaiah 53 is quoted seven times). So the fourth Servant Song is a central and intensely Christian text for me.

At the same time, however, I, like many other Christians, have long studied Judaism for the sake of understanding the Jewish background and counterpoint to Christianity as well as for its own sake. In becoming more aware of Judaism, one becomes more sensitive to the meanings of the Jewish Tanakh. One thus comes to see that the Servant Songs in Isaiah have intensely Jewish application to the Jewish people as a whole, represented at this juncture by the Babylonian exiles and by a prophet embodying their predicament. It is impossible not to perceive and in some way take to heart the Jewish scripture in that text, just as it is impossible not to see it as a core Christian text. For the Jewish people are Jesus' people and mine too insofar as I am a Gentile grafted onto the Jewish root, to use Paul's expression (Romans 11:17–24). Christian interpretation enwraps the Jewish text, as the sufferings of the Jewish people are impressively Christlike, but Jewish interpretation likewise enwraps the Christian text, as the sufferings of Christ form a repetition of the unexpected "light to the nations" (42:6) that Jews claimed was shining in their perseverance six centuries earlier.[22]

If one wants to insist that the Christian meaning of the text excludes the Jewish meaning and vice versa because of the Christian-Jewish disagreement about the Messiah, one would seem to be missing some main points of interest.

I am not a Jew in the sense of being obligated to keep the Jewish commandments. But am I a multiscripturalist with respect to Christian and Jewish scriptures because of the extent to which both canons matter to me? I do not merely notice the Jewish meaning of the text, but rather my spiritual sensitivities are captured by it – I follow it. Nevertheless my Jewish following is always reined in by my Christian following.

More for professional than personal reasons, originally, I began some years ago to pay attention to the Qur'an, realizing in a preliminary way that Islam is extensively connected to the other Abrahamic traditions both historically and theologically. I have now experienced the same sort of partly involuntary spiritual response to certain Qur'anic texts. This is a significantly different case than the Jewish scriptures, which are rhetorically very familiar to a Christian. To a Christian, the Qur'an sounds very different from the Bible, somewhat as (I am told) the New Testament sounds strange to a Jew. The difference is in its quasi-poetic idiom, in its organization, and very often in what it wants to talk about besides its expected witness to God as creator and judge. Partly because of this intriguing difference and partly in spite of it, I find myself not only impressed by the Qur'an but already loyal to certain Qur'anic texts and meanings.

For a non-Muslim like me, Qur'an following can start in at least two ways. One way is simply by reading. For instance, I have been struck by this text about the creation of humanity, among others:

When thy Lord said to the angels, "I am placing a viceregent upon the earth," they said, "Wilt Thou place therein one who will work corruption therein and shed

---

[22] On one line of thinking, the "light to the nations" version of Judaism is the road the Jews did not take. Judaism had the possibility of bringing ethical monotheism to the Gentiles, in effect implementing Christianity in advance of Christianity, but instead concentrated on its distinctive vocation of keeping all the commandments. My interpretation favors this proto-Christian but superseded element in historical Judaism. I suggest that this meaning is not entirely superseded as a Jewish meaning. Do I have standing to make this suggestion? I do not have fully Jewish standing, clearly, but it seems to me that I do not lack standing altogether if I speak in loyalty to the text with respect for its context.

blood, while we hymn Thy praise and call Thee Holy?" He said, "Truly I know what you know not." (2:30)

The verse breaks off without revealing what we most want to know – how things will turn out so that everything we have suffered and done wrong will be part of a good whole. It does not tell us what the result will be; it only implies that it will be affirmable. It teases us by leaving the future and the deeper logic in the dark. Indeed, these things are beyond human knowledge. But it is amazingly encouraging to be told that, even with a full supply of flawless angels, God evidently wants our human contributions too. The tingle of suspense in "I know things you do not" converts by chemical reaction into a spiritually charged "Here we go!" My interpretation becomes more than merely academic as I place myself in the "we" of *that* "Here we go!" – the "we" who are the people of *that* very bold and smart Creator.

At times the Qur'an speaks tellingly in what, for me at least, is a guidance gap left by the Christian scripture. "Then, shall ye be questioned that Day about the joy (ye indulged in!)" (102:8).[23] The idea that all one's pleasures go toward determining the spiritual quality of one's life now seems to me inescapable. As a Christian, I enjoy the sense that divine revelation is circling back around to give me more help by means of this utterance, a sense that presumably most Muslims would not have, as their Guidance baseline is the Qur'an itself. The implied timing is obviously personal, not world historical: for all I know, the gist of the guidance I discover in the Qur'an is already available in the Bible, though I had missed it. Or the content that appeals to me was formulated earlier in Jewish tradition (as is not infrequently true for Qur'anic content, though the Qur'an always puts its own stamp on the material). In such retransmissions, the scriptural deal is not broken; after all, readers of the Jewish Bible are already aware that some biblical material comes from extrabiblical sources, like the Akhenaten Hymn to the Sun in Psalm 104.

The second opening to the Qur'an comes in apologetic argumentation. The Qur'an denies that Jesus is the divine Son of God, challenging my

---

[23] *The Holy Qur'an* (trans. Abdullah Yusuf Ali, revised by the Presidency of Islamic Researches, IFTA, Call and Guidance, King Fahd Holy Qur-ān Printing Complex, 1992). In some translations, including *The Study Qur'an*, the last word, *na'im*, is rendered "blessing," and the interpretation is that we will be questioned on what we have recognized or done with divine blessing in our worldly lives. In others, including the one that struck me and that I have reproduced here, the word is understood as "pleasure," and the idea is that we will be called to account for our pleasures according to their spiritual quality.

Christian understanding of Jesus. To confirm and develop my Christian understanding of this point, I feel obliged to restate it in response to any serious challenge.[24] In this case I am obliged to determine as best I can the real thrust of the Qur'an's objection and the most pertinent Christian response, not ruling out the possibility of adjusting some of my assumptions about Christian guidance – for I must not fall short or make any avoidable mistake in recognizing what is needed for the optimization of life, even if that means I can never entirely finalize my religious metanoia. I do not want to simply repeat the usual Christian assurance that the doctrines of incarnation and trinity do not infringe on the unity and unique realness and goodness of God. I must read the Qur'an, then. I find that its rejection of the "son of God" and "Trinity" notions is connected to its rejection of the Meccan trinity of deities, the "daughters of God" (16:53–57), and to its general rejection of reliance on intercessories in one's dealings with God (19:87–93, 39:43–47, 53:19–26). The Qur'an's negative view of the "son of God" notion is thus substantially related to internal Christian debates about human responsibility and "cheap grace." There is bound to be Christian-Muslim disagreement here, because Christians think that God is in Christ and that Christ does fundamental intercessory work for humanity. But the Christian explanation of Christ's relationship to God and of human accountability to God is somewhat movable in my own mind, which in fact is now moved by the Qur'an; I am now more wary in a Qur'anic way of the hazard of idolatry and miscalculated optimism in the New Testament proclamation "Behold the lamb of God who takes away the sin of the world" (John 1:29).

The Qur'an also seems to deliberately problematize the notion of a divine daughter or son as part of its critique of sexism. "And they assign unto God daughters – glory be to Him! – while they have that which they desire [i.e., sons]. And when one of them receives tidings of a female [child], his face darkens, and he is choked with anguish. He hides from the people on account of the evil of the tidings he has been given" (16:57–59). I find this to be a compelling scriptural prompt for theological feminism.

---

[24] Paul Griffiths makes a principle of the Necessity Of Interreligious Apologetics, stated as follows: "If representative intellectuals belonging to some specific religious community come to judge at a particular time that some or all of their own doctrine-expressing sentences are incompatible with some alien religious claim(s), then they should feel obliged to engage in both positive and negative apologetics vis-à-vis these alien religious claim(s) and their promulgators." Paul Griffiths, *An Apology for Apologetics* (Orbis, 1991), p. 3. I am interpreting the apologetic obligation more broadly, as applying to any thoughtful believer and any sort of scriptural meaning.

It is a prompt that could not be in the Christian Bible because of its investment in the Father-Son format of divine-human relation.

While I am blocked from identifying as a Muslim by considerations such as the Muslim-Christian disagreement about Christ, it does seem to me that I am spoken to by God via the prophetic activity of Muhammad, and I am committed to staying in conversation with Muslims about what I hear and what they hear from the Qur'an. Given that there is no likely prospect of incorporating the Muslim guidance in an expanded canon of Christian scripture, I must conclude that something of the nature of multiscripturalism is afoot in this. I can say this only because the inter-religious reckoning in this example has to do with concerns and cautions about adjustable understandings rather than clashing fixed truth claims.[25]

It is possible of course that my self-interpretation is faulty. In the first case, I may be having an experience of appreciating a *religious classic* that I am pressing to interpret as scripturalism because of my great interest in that category. In the apologetic channel, I may be pressing to create a more friendly discussion between Christianity and Islam than their essential doctrines will permit. But here I stand: I am unwilling not to respect these texts as obligatory references in that strong scriptural sense.

For contrast, I will cite one of many Hindu texts that I am strongly impressed by spiritually yet am unable to follow. It is the great theophany scene in the Bhagavad-Gita where Krishna-Vishnu shows Arjuna his terrifying form as "destroyer of worlds":

[Arjuna:] Gazing upon your mighty form with its myriad mouths, eyes, arms, thighs, feet, bellies, and sharp, gruesome tusks, the worlds [all] shudder [in affright] – how much more I!

Ablaze with many-colored [flames] You touch the sky, your mouths wide open, [gaping,] your eyes distended, blazing: so do I see You and my inmost self is shaken: I cannot bear it, I find no peace, O Vishnu!

I see your mouths with jagged, ghastly tusks reminding [me] of Time's [devouring] fire: I cannot find my bearings. (11.23–25)

I see and accept the point of this passage; I just cannot handle it. For me, the reader, as for Arjuna within the scene, it is too harsh. The more humorous exchange between Yahweh and Job in the Bible (Job 38–42) shows as much as I can face in the cosmic sausage making. This example indicates a constraint on multiscripturalism that figures to be pervasive.

---

[25] "It will often be the case that the most direct and obvious benefits of engagement in the apologetical enterprise will be heuristic, and will accrue to the constructor of the apologetic rather than to its recipient." Griffiths, *Apology*, p. 82.

The more deeply one accepts guidance G1 in scripture S1, the less available one can be for guidance G2 in scripture S2 when there are clashing intellectual, emotional, or practical implications. But of course the same constraint operates within a scripture and often requires to be mitigated by earnest interpretation.

I expect that I will keep circling back around the Gita.

8.4 A MULTISCRIPTURALIST PATH TO GLOBAL SOLIDARITY

If in the future ... faith is going to exist, communicate itself, and link men together, one thing is certain: We can do nothing to plan the future realities of faith. We can only be ready to receive it, and live in such a manner that this readiness increases. – Karl Jaspers[26]

Even if many of us have not yet begun to read them seriously, we have multiple scriptures in hand as a cultural legacy. We are the People of the Books. Leaving aside the enthusiasm that some readers and religious aspirants will feel for delving into an eminently interesting category of literature, our ideally shared attitude toward the scriptural legacy must be determined partly by our ideally shared sense of practical need. Without taking all our cues from the Zeitgeist, we can still say with general certitude that under any circumstances we will need to (1) change conditions of life that are ethically intolerable, (2) improve our techniques to act more successfully in general, (3) be collegial, and (4) sustain spiritual identities. Many religious persons will want to argue that all of these needs call for a renewed commitment to scripturalism because scriptures are still our most powerful devices for realizing the axial ideals of individual dignity, critical discernment, discussion that is maximally serious and maximally accessible at the same time, and solidarity with a historic community. But it can equally be argued that our needs dictate a post-scripturalist stance because the scriptures that have carried us a certain way in optimizing our action are now holding us back. Although scripturalism is not the same as fundamentalism, the recent surge of fundamentalist movements around the world shows that the predominant role of scriptures *now* is to wall people up in communities of resistance to modern cosmopolitanism, to the ethico-political program of equalizing human rights, to the intellectual programs of naturalism and the

---

[26] Karl Jaspers, *The Origin and Goal of History* (trans. Michael Bullock, Yale University Press, 1953), p. 223.

comparative study of cultures, and to the aesthetic program of following artistic and lifestyle innovations wherever they lead. One would perhaps like to think that scriptures are fully coming into their own as vectors of cultural improvement, with an approximation of global literacy being imminent for the first time in human history, but that is not how communicative action seems to be working out. Instead, scriptures are everywhere being deployed to restrain the further development of literacy.

I think the horizon of concern about scripturalism shifts when we ask specifically about multiscripturalism's significance for the future. We may well use a Jaspersian point of departure for this question, since the Axial Age concept opens the door to it.

Jaspers argued that the religious future might break with organized religion as we now know it but could not break with "the fundamental positions and categories of the Axial Period ... [because] the spiritual paramountcy of those centuries of origin is so great."[27] If the classic Axial principles of the literate civilizations are indeed spiritually paramount, then they must be controlling for any global communication about supreme guidance that we can foresee. There may be a distortion, however, in Jaspers's conception of the Axial principles in that he makes heroes of the likes of Heraclitus, Jeremiah, the Buddha, and Kongzi in too individualizing a way, detaching them from the specific cultural processes in which they were embedded, and in too leveling a way, construing their ideas as convergently transcendentalist. His vision of spiritual "world unity" may be unrealistically and unhealthily unifying.

Accepting that caution about "unity," let us think about the "world" side of the proposition. Jaspers was writing in the aftermath of what he took to be the utter destruction in the World Wars of any European claim to cultural supremacy or centrality in the world. European culture appeared to be a smoking ruin, spiritually as well as materially speaking. Yet to give up the very premise of cultural heritage or of touchstone texts would be nihilistic. The way forward was to open up the categories of heritage and classic to everyone capable of contributing so that there could be a maximally discerning, critical, and corrective conversation among the most profoundly meaningful human options. To frame such a global conversation, it would be necessary to appreciate how the axial heroes are comparably profound, but it would also be necessary to appreciate the differences in their situations and ideas. Jaspers used his

[27] Ibid., p. 225.

own philosophical language to indicate the profundity that the axial heroes shared, thus creating a misleading impression that they are all on his own intellectual page. But it is possible to swing the emphasis to the diversity in the profound possibilities that the philosophers, prophets, and sages variously explored – a diversity grounded not only in the sensitivities of the individual thinkers but in the exigencies of competitive ideologizing in different cultural contexts. In Judah, Jeremiah *had* to address Covenant-related beliefs and concerns; in China, Kongzi *had* to talk about the Way. (Yet for us Jeremiah and Kongzi are clearly in conversation about the ideal base and unity of personal motivation.)

Another distinctive Jaspersian emphasis is on communication, idealizing "boundless communication" as axial.[28] Communicative boundary crossing can make us aware of things we were previously unable to see and of our cognitive frame that prevented our seeing them so that our limitations are changed by what Panikkar calls "dis-closure."[29] Dis-closure will come about in fruitful instances of contact with alien thought forms, as in the more adventurous kinds of interreligious dialogue.

Even in everyday speech, communicative and epistemic expansion is assured by the basic linguistic-pragmatic condition that the grasping of meanings is never separate from their sharing and their sharing is never definitely limitable. My relationship with a word is a relationship to all who ever used or may use it, and my relationship with you, as a fellow communicator, is a relationship with all the words we have used or may use and with all the things that have been or might be said to us. Ordinarily most of these relationships are passive and implicit, lacking in conscious significance. It is not automatically a good thing to make them active and explicit. Consciousness normally keeps most of life's meaningful elements in the background, neutralizing the questions or corrections they might motivate so that our lives are manageable. When we do need to confirm or intelligently shift to the best terms of living, however, we want to become conscious of how our lines of communication are functioning, and we want to deliberately communicate along those lines in an exemplary way.

---

[28] Jaspers, *Origin and Goal*, p. 19. For his fullest discussion of communication, which is primarily concerned with delineating the dynamics of intersubjectivity, see Jaspers, *Philosophy*, vol. 2 (trans. E. B. Ashton, University of Chicago Press, 1969), chap. 3, pp. 47–103.

[29] The term is appropriated by Krieger, p. 64.

Scripturalism is a school of broadening communication. The reader of scripture is immediately conscious of relationship with the scripture orig- inators and the Text's words and is somewhere on a path of increasing awareness of relationship with all the hearers and users of scriptural language in a multigenerational community. The *devout* reader will intentionally take on as much as possible in the whole network of relevant relationships, much as a close friend will take on a friend's network. This communicative intention is a strong prosocial force. Any Christian scrip- turalist is unavoidably in solidarity with some set of fellow Christians; given a reasonable religious education, he or she is in solidarity with a huge historic community of Christians, with Jews at a certain remove, and more distantly with many other communities. There are antagonisms within this solidarity, to be sure – the course of passionate life sharing does not run smooth. But throughout the network it becomes impossible to turn away from the sharing.

As large and complexly affiliated as the monoscriptural community may be, however, it still tends to confirm ignorance of many other communities' ideals and arguments, at best, or to promote categorical hostility to other communities, at worst. It seems that scripturalism cannot advance the Axial cause of "boundless communication" past this barrier.

A secularist might wish to argue that boundless communication and global community are far better served by a common-denominator values program such as the human rights movement chartered by the 1948 Universal Declaration of Human Rights. The priority is then placed precisely on concerns and standards virtually all humans actually share, setting aside the divisive implications of religious beliefs. But while the Declaration of Human Rights indeed has a towering significance in global politics, for most citizens the interest of any secular text is sliver-thin compared to the interest of scriptures for scripturalists. For scriptures are vehicles of the Guidance and the most passionate sharing of life that is possible on a large scale of community. Readers of scriptures will study them all their lives; that is not a reasonable expectation for a text like the Declaration that purposely excludes most of what people might seriously disagree about or be puzzled by.

Multiscripturalist respect for all scriptures engages us far more chal- lengingly and therefore profoundly than either monoscripturalism or a common-denominator program can by fostering awareness that ultimate ideals are identified and represented very differently and are not readily reconcilable. The communicative breakthrough in accessing a different

Guidance tradition imposes a new degree of intentional difficulty, first in detecting the religious plausibility of the foreign material and then in trying to see how one could be responsible to it. Only by undertaking this difficulty is the issue of interreligious relationship handled fairly – not by mere avoidance or by a willful imposition of one party's paradigm.[30]

Looking at the scripturalism prospect in this way motivates this last suite of theses on multiscripturalism:

(1) Although full multiscripturalism in the sense of being a devout follower of multiple scriptures is a deeply problematic spiritual goal, *the more modest multiscripturalism of studying and actively appreciating as many scriptures as possible is feasible*, as the current state of academic religious studies shows.

(2) *Multiscripturalism is the most robustly optimistic approach to cultivating global solidarity*, as it positions and affirms members of the global community in their own most optimistic stance as seekers of the highest optimization of human life. In purely humanistic perspective, it is more encouraging that humans share religious optimism than it is discouraging that they disagree on their goals and methods.

(3) *Multiscripturalism is the most appropriately responsible approach to cultivating global solidarity*, as it takes members of the global community with the greatest seriousness in the aspect of their lives that they themselves are most serious about. No disrespect for the nonreligious is implied – one can also endeavor to respect them as they wish to be respected.

(4) *Multiscripturalism is the most intelligent approach to cultivating global solidarity* for two reasons. The first is the same basic reason that church disestablishment has been the most intelligent approach to supporting religious life together with civic harmony in the United States: by granting all parties access to the "public square" of inclusive discussion, the vigor of both intramural and interreligious conversation is increased, among laity as well as among specialists. The second is that scriptures disclose relatively fully the sources and issues attached to a community's ultimate ideals, enabling a thicker understanding of them than if they are merely summarily defined and rationally analyzed.

---

[30] Krieger, pp. 139–140.

(5) A final axiality thesis: *Multiscripturalism is on the main path of axialization* (the most promising development of literacy) because it freshens the requirement for individual discernment in the face of live spiritual options and disrupts the common and oft-condemned religious complacency of living within the bounds of an orthodox codification of the Guidance. More revolutionarily, it brings a nonreductive cosmopolitanism to the original axial premise that ultimate identifications of supreme appeal and right attitude are available to the discerning individual. It brings a more optimistic, responsible, and intelligent embrace of a spiritual problematic of living among many ultimates.

Concluding Thoughts on the Necessity
of Guidance and Ideal Scripturalism

In this study I have foregrounded the pragmatic variable of guidance and paid relatively little attention to semantics or hermeneutics, although successful reference and serious *explicatio* and *applicatio* are necessary conditions of any ideally tenable life guidance; or to epistemology, although mental perspicuity and grounding of belief are also necessary; or to the aesthetic quality of projected images of life-in-the-world, although guidance is powered also by imaginative stimulation. I have wanted to examine the guidance relationship's own force. It is a neglected fact of the highest practical importance that often the main reason we are following a guidance is just that we are going along with a guide in what we take to be an adequate guidance scheme, consenting to allow that guide to define part of our action, and we are in that position not because we have made a radical decision to be guided but because as communicative human beings we are always already being guided by many guides – this is our basic mode of living – and we have allocated a greater portion of our confidence to a particular guide and guidance relation that seem right for a given situation. We are following a crowd toward the presumed exit of the railway station; we are following a uniformed ranger up a mountain trail; or we are following each other down the sidewalk (both corporeally and mentally) while having a conversation. We follow a guidance as long as it is congenial. Full analysis of that congeniality would indeed seek to exhibit the elements of successful reference, credibility, and strong imaginability – as the ideally thoughtful agent will want to catch up to the implications of living in a guidance relationship by clarifying these conditions and testing their quality – but the ground supporting all these qualifications is that we are subject to a specification of our practical dependency and action-in-coordination that seems acceptable for the time being. We are in an action-defining association that seems in itself a basic personal and human success.

To consent to share the defining of one's action, including one's thinking, with a guide is not to give up responsibility for thought. It is refusal to share the defining of action that is irresponsible. Going one's own way is also highly imprudent. I offer a parable:

> There once was a religious thinker who said, "God is most great. I shall conceive God as the sole reality, all-powerful" – and in achieving that thought was instantly squashed out of existence.

We have to start over. Once there were *two* religious thinkers. One said, "I shall conceive God as the sole reality, all-powerful," and was squashed out of existence. The second saw what happened and said, "I see that if one wishes to conceive God as supremely real and powerful, one must be careful not to affirm that God is 'sole reality' or 'all-powerful' without some qualifications to preserve the possibility of creaturely existence. I am not sure what these qualifications would be. I will search out the most relevant testimonies, including any that may count as divine guidance, and on that basis discuss this question with others."

Some mystics would enthusiastically endorse the approach of the first religious thinker, but those of us who are committed to discussion of our supreme ideals would find our role model in the second. The second thinker may have been the Arch-Scripturalist, Moses or Vyasa or the Duke of Zhou, the one who arranged for a transmissible textual platform for carefully considered, humanly adequate offers of guidance that could be reckoned as Guidance.

The second thinker was followed by a multitude. Within that multitude, the truest successors of the second thinker were those who chose to participate actively in an ambitious scriptural project, capitalizing on one of the greatest extraordinary powers of language, rather than simply accepting the terms of life collaboration that their circumstances imposed on them. In committing to scripture, they took on the issue of the mission and ground rules of scripturalist collaboration; they entered the distinct scripturalist problematic as a way of comporting themselves most optimistically, responsibly, and intelligently in the human problematics of guidance, speaking, writing, and religious life.

Scripturalism is sometimes associated with a suspension of individual thought. "The Holy Scriptures are not to be interpreted according to one's own mind" was a principle that the Roman Catholic church asserted against Luther, who had dared to set Catholic tradition aside and say on his own account what the Bible says, and that Luther hurled back at the Catholics, claiming that their tradition substituted sinful human judgment for the saving divine revelation.[1] In the dust raised by this debate, one may lose sight of the absurdity of the proposition insofar as it implies an utter collapse of the guidance relationship. Without the engagement of the mind of the guided, there could not be understanding; without understanding, there could not be guidance following.

Scripturalists have chosen to interpret life and scripture not according to their own minds alone. They have accepted that a major part of sense making and meaningfulness finding will be carried out by divine Guidance, eminently as provided in the Text, and by their fellow scripturalists. In their own religiously ambitious view, they seem to have energized, not suppressed, their own minds in this mode of receiving guidance, much as eager trail walkers feel called upon to be collegially intelligent, perceptive, and surefooted in order to make the most of a good ranger-guided experience, or as eager actors rise to the challenge of partnering with the Bard.

I see that the present elucidation of guidance has a logic in common with Erasmus's defense of free will in his debate with Luther over the role of human action in salvation. "God ... has called us while we turned away from him, has cleansed us through faith ... [but] has also granted that our will can cooperate with his grace."[2] Those who side with Luther on this issue (or, analogously, with Shinran about the sole efficacy of Other-power) will presumably not be moved by appeals to a collaborative norm of guidance. They will think: As spiritually perverted and as needy as humans are, how can it be said that we in any way "cooperate" in our salvation without giving us delusory grounds for self-confidence? They will deny cooperation for the sake of magnifying God's grace and sovereignty and to follow key scriptural texts (Romans 9) – but they will thereby annihilate the guidance relationship and with it all genuine scripturalism, on the conceptions of these things I have identified as main attractors of communicative action. That would be a strange result, seeing

---

[1] Gerhard Ebeling, "Word of God and Hermeneutic," in *The New Hermeneutic* (ed. James M. Robinson and John B. Cobb Jr., Harper & Row, 1964), p. 79n. In the scriptural background is 2 Peter 1:20–21: "First of all you must understand this, that no prophecy of scripture is a matter of one's own interpretation, because no prophecy ever came by human will, but men and women moved by the Holy Spirit spoke from God."

[2] Erasmus, *The Free Will*, in Erasmus and Luther, *Discourse on Free Will* (trans. Ernst F. Winter, Continuum, 1989), p. 62.

that a scripture has brought Christians the message of grace, maintains benchmarks for understanding it, and encourages discussion of it.

Luther seems to show that from a religious point of view the drawing of divine Guidance from a Text can overshoot and destroy the very premise of guidance. And yet there is a rich ongoing Lutheran discussion of free will; thoughtful scripturalism was *not* ended by Luther's argument, which may imply that Lutheran theology (like Pauline theology before it) understands itself to be hyperbolic. I cannot say, therefore, that Luther's scripturalism was untenable. I say only that he posed a concerning risk to scripturalism.

From a religious point of view, the possibility of coming up short religiously in one's scripturalism is no less concerning. If we assume that the religiously flourishing person is optimistic, responsible, and intelligent in as fully enterprising a way as general reasonableness allows, then we must judge any half-heartedness in these channels to be religiously sub-optimal. But suboptimality is hard to pin on any established religious position. It might seem that a Buddhist instrumental view of religious language is suboptimal when measured by the standard of Vedic Hindu-ism's high ontological view. For Buddhists, however, that relative detach-ment from language is an integral part of an extraordinarily promising strategy of escape from attachment and dissatisfaction altogether. Or it might seem that a Confucian naturalist is leaving a lot of possible human fulfillment on the table by abstaining from theist and apocalyptic beliefs that are main sources of spiritual excitement in Christianity and Islam. But from a Confucian perspective, it is the height of wisdom and respon-sibility to be realistic about human embeddedness in society and the natural Way.

Anyone committed to "enlightened" thinking would have to reject forms of scripturalism that are adverse to rational discernment, social responsibility, and pragmatic prudence. But the constraints of enlighten-ment on an ideal scripturalism may not be as tight as one would at first suppose. I do not see why an enlightened scripturalist cannot be a *super-naturalist*, given that various forms of supernaturalism are defensible in philosophical debate. Nor can a scripturalist *fideism* be ruled out, since reliance on faith is an axial option and can be explained in the public square. (Some forms of fideism do constitute a flight from human respon-sibility, but not all.) It is indeed hard to be an enlightened *literalist* in any simple sense of literalism, given that both everyday language use and religious ambition push the horizons of linguistic meaning far beyond the quasi-photographic reproduction of perceptible states of affairs; but some literalists hold sophisticated, supple views of literal meaning. Finally, I do think it is hard for an enlightened person to be a religious *exclusivist*, if by exclusivism we mean categorically denying the religious value of scriptures other than one's own; such an exclusivist would have to keep his or her own religious ideals on a different plane from analogues and challenges in other traditions. But some well-informed exclusivists do that.

I conclude that the force of a conception of ideal scripturalism is not so much to narrow down the principles on which a tenable scripturalism may rest as to put critical pressure on interpretations and applications of principles that may be attractive to scripturalists yet hazardous to their guidance project. The ideal scripturalist's general understanding of language, judgment, religion, and being will be strict enough, on the one hand, to correct or reject insensitive religious positions and capacious enough, on the other hand, to affirm the merits of all great ideals and their serious appropriations.

Bibliography

Aleaz, K. P., "Pluralism Calls for Pluralistic Inclusivism," in *The Myth of Religious Superiority: Multifaith Explorations of Religious Pluralism* (ed. Paul F. Knitter, Orbis, 2005), pp. 162–175.

Alper, Harvey L., *Understanding Mantras* (SUNY Press, 1989).

Anderson, Michael L., and Gregg Rosenberg, "Content and Action: The Guidance Theory of Representation," *Journal of Mind and Behavior*, 29 (2008), 55–86.

Aquinas, Thomas, *Summa Theologica* (trans. Dominican Fathers, Benziger Bros., 1947).

Aramaic Targum to Song of Songs (trans. Jay C. Treat, ccat.sas.upenn.edu/~jtreat/song/targum/, 2004).

Assmann, Jan, *From Akhenaten to Moses: Ancient Egypt and Religious Change* (American University in Cairo Press, 2014).

   "Cultural Memory and the Myth of the Axial Age," in Bellah and Joas, pp. 366–408.

   Of God and Gods (University of Wisconsin Press, 2008).

Assmann, Jan, and Aleda Assmann, et al., "Schrift," in *Historisches Wörterbuch der Philosophie*, vol. 8 (ed. Joachim Ritter and Karlfriend Gründer, Schwabe, 1992), pp. 1417–1429.

Augustine, *Confessions* (trans. Rex Warner, New American Library, 1963).

Austin, J. L., *How to Do Things with Words* (Clarendon Press, 1962).

Avicenna (Ibn Sina), *Avicenna on Theology* (trans. A. J. Arberry, J. Murray, 1951).

Babrius and Phaedrus (trans. Ben Edwin Perry, Harvard University Press, 1965).

Barth, Karl, *Church Dogmatics I/1* (trans. G. W. Bromiley, T&T Clark, 1975).

   The Epistle to the Romans, 2nd ed. [1922] (trans. E. C. Hoskyns [from the 6th ed.], Oxford University Press, 1933).

   The Word of God and the Word of Man [1924] (trans. Douglas Horton, Harper & Row, 1957).

Barthes, Roland, *Image Music Text* (trans. Stephen Heath, FontanaPress, 1977).
Mythologies (trans. Annette Lavers, Hill & Wang, 1972).

Baruta, Arati, et al., eds., *Understanding Schopenhauer through the Prism of Indian Culture* (de Gruyter, 2013).

de Bary, William Theodore, and Irene Bloom, eds., *Source of Chinese Tradition*, 2nd ed. (Columbia University Press, 1999).

Beck, Guy, *Sonic Theology: Hinduism and Sacred Sound* (University of South Carolina Press, 1993).

Bellah, Robert N., "The Heritage of the Axial Age: Resource or Burden?" in *The Axial Age and Its Consequences* (ed. Robert Bellah and Hans Joas, Harvard University Press, 2012).
Religion in Human Evolution (Harvard University Press, 2011).

Bellah, Robert N., and Hans Joas, eds., *The Axial Age and Its Consequences* (Harvard University Press, 2012).

Benin, Stephen D., *The Footprints of God: Divine Accommodation in Jewish and Christian Thought* (SUNY Press, 1993).

Berling, Judith, *A Pilgrim in Chinese Culture* (Orbis, 1997).

Bernard of Clairvaux, *Sermons on the Song of Songs*, in *Bernard of Clairvaux: Selected Works* (trans. Gillian R. Evans, Paulist, 1987).

Bhagavad-Gita (trans. R. C. Zaehner, Oxford University Press, 1966).

Bhagavata Purana, *Original Sanskrit Texts on the Origin and History of the People of India, Their Religion and Institutions*, 2nd ed., vol. 3 (trans. J. Muir, Trübner, 1868).

Bhartrihari, *Vakyapadiya* (trans. K. R. Pillai, Motilal Banarsidass, 1971).

Biderman, Shlomo, *Crossing Horizons: World, Self, and Language in Indian and Western Thought* (trans. Ornan Rotem, Columbia University Press, 2008).
Scripture and Knowledge: An Essay on Religious Epistemology (Brill, 1995).

Bilimoria, Purushotta, *Shabdapramana: Word and Knowledge as Testimony* (Kluwer, 1988).

Blanchot, Maurice, *The Infinite Conversation* (trans. Susan Hanson, University of Minnesota Press, 1993).
The Space of Literature (trans. Ann Smock, University of Nebraska Press, 1982).

Blumenberg, Hans, *Die Lesbarkeit der Welt*, 2nd ed. (Suhrkamp, 1983).

Boy, John D., and John Torpey, "Inventing the Axial Age: The Origins and Uses of a Historical Concept," *Theory and Society*, 42 (2013), 241–259.

Boyce, Mary, *Zoroastrians: Their Religious Beliefs and Practices* (Routledge & Kegan Paul, 1979).

Brown, C. Mackenzie, "Purana as Scripture," *History of Religions*, 26 (August 1986), 68–86.

Cabezón, José Ignacio, *Buddhism and Language: A Study of Indo-Tibetan Scholasticism* (SUNY Press, 1994).

Calvin, Jean, *Institutes of the Christian Religion* (trans. Henry Beveridge, Hendrickson, 2008).

Carlson, Thomas, *Indiscretion* (University of Chicago Press, 1999).

Carlyle, Thomas, *A Carlyle Reader* (ed. G. B. Tennyson, Cambridge University Press, 1984).

Carpenter, David, "Bhartrihari and the Veda," in *Texts in Context: Traditional Hermeneutics in South Asia* (ed. Jeffrey R. Timm, Sri Satgru, 1992), pp. 17–32.

Carr, David M., *Writing on the Tablet of the Heart: Origins of Scripture and Literature* (Oxford University Press, 2005).

Chesterton, G. K., *The Autobiography of G. K. Chesterton* (Ignatius, 2006).

Chittick, William C., "Ibn al-ʿArabi's Hermeneutics of Mercy," in *Mysticism and Sacred Scriptures* (ed. Steven T. Katz, Oxford University Press, 2000), pp. 153–168.

  Imaginal Worlds: Ibn al-ʿArabi and the Problem of Religious Diversity (SUNY Press, 1994).

Chu Hsi (Zhu Xi), *Learning to Be a Sage* (trans. Daniel K. Gardner, University of California Press, 1990).

Chung-Shu, Tung, *Luxuriant Gems of the Spring and Autumn Annals*, in *A Sourcebook in Chinese Philosophy* (ed. Wing-Tsit Chan, Princeton University Press, 1963), pp. 273–288.

Clement of Alexandria, *Stromata* (trans. William Wilson), in *The Ante-Nicene Fathers*, vol. 2 (ed. Alexander Roberts and James Donaldson, Hendrickson, 1994).

Clooney, Francis X., *Seeing through Texts: Doing Theology among the Shrivaish-navas of South India* (SUNY Press, 1996).

  Theology after Vedanta (SUNY Press, 1993).

Coburn, Thomas B., "'Scripture' in India," in *Rethinking Scripture* (ed. Miriam Levering, SUNY Press, 1989), pp. 102–128.

Cohen, Hermann, "The Social Ideal of Plato and the Prophets," in *Reason and Hope: Selections from the Jewish Writings of Hermann Cohen* (trans. Eva Jospe, Norton, 1971), pp. 70–77.

Coward, Harold G., *The Sphota Theory of Language* (Motilal Banarsidass, 1980).

Coward, Harold G., and David J. Goa, *Mantra* (Columbia University Press, 2004).

Cowell, E. B., *Buddhist Mahayana Texts* (Dover, 1969).

Crollius, Ary A. Roest, *Thus Were They Hearing: The Word in the Experience of Revelation in Qur'an and Hindu Scriptures* (Gregorian University Press, 1974).

Dalferth, Ingolf U., "The Idea of Transcendence," in Bellah and Joas, pp. 146–188.

Dante Alighieri, *The Divine Comedy* (trans. John Ciardi, New American Library, 2003).

Daodejing: The Way and Its Power (trans. Arthur Waley, Grove, 1958).

Davidson, Donald, "A Nice Derangement of Epitaphs," in *Truth and Interpretation* (ed. Ernest LePore and Donald Davidson, Blackwell, 1989), pp. 433–446.

Dean, Thomas, ed., *Religious Pluralism and Truth: Essays on Cross-Cultural Philosophy of Religion* (SUNY Press, 1995).

Deleuze, Gilles, with Claire Parnet, *Dialogues* (trans. Hugh Tomlinson and Bar-
    bara Habberjam, Columbia University Press, 1987).
Dhammapada (trans. John Ross Carter, Oxford University Press, 1987).
Divine Incantations Scripture (trans. Nathan Sivin), in *Sources of Chinese
    Tradition*, 2nd ed., vol. 1 (ed. William Theodore de Bary and Irene Bloom,
    Columbia University Press, 1999), pp. 406–410.
Doctrine of the Mean (trans. James Legge, CreateSpace, 2016).
Dogen, *Shobogenzo* (trans. Hubert Nearman, Shasta Abbey, 2007).
Dummett, Michael, "'A Nice Derangement of Epitaphs': Some Comments on
    Davidson and Hacking," in *Truth and Interpretation* (ed. Ernest LePore
    and Donald Davidson, Blackwell, 1989), pp. 459–476.
Dundas, Paul, *History, Scripture and Controversy in a Medieval Jain Sect*
    (Routledge, 2007).
Dupuis, Jacques, S.J., *Toward a Christian Theology of Religious Pluralism* (Orbis,
    1997).
Ebeling, Gerhard, "Word of God and Hermeneutic," in *The New Hermeneutic* (ed.
    James M. Robinson and John B. Cobb Jr., Harper & Row, 1964), pp. 78–110.
Eisenstadt, S. N., ed., *The Origins and Diversity of Axial Age Civilizations* (SUNY
    Press, 1986).
Eliade, Mircea, *Patterns in Comparative Religion* (trans. Rosemary Sheed, Uni-
    versity of Nebraska Press, 1996).
Embree, Ainslie T., ed., *Sources of Indian Tradition*, 2nd ed., vol. 1 (Columbia
    University Press, 1988).
Emerson, Ralph Waldo, "The American Scholar," in *The Complete Essays and
    Other Writings of Ralph Waldo Emerson* (ed. Brooks Atkinson, Modern
    Library, 1950), pp. 45–63.
Engels, David, "Historising Religion between Spiritual Continuity and Friendly
    Takeover: Salvation History and Religious Competition during the First
    Millennium AD," in Engels and Van Nuffelen, pp. 237–284.
Engels, David, and Peter Van Nuffelen, eds., *Religion and Competition in Antiq-
    uity* (Latomus, 2014).
Erasmus, Desiderius, and Martin Luther, *Discourse on Free Will* (trans. Ernst F.
    Winter, Continuum, 1989).
van Ess, Josef, "Islam and the Axial Age," in *Islam in Process* (ed. Johan P.
    Arnasson et al., Transaction, 2006), pp. 220–237.
Evans-Pritchard, E. E., *Nuer Religion* (Oxford University Press, 1956).
    Witchcraft, Oracles and Magic among the Azande (Clarendon Press, 1937).
Faherty, R. L., "Sacrifice," in *Encyclopedia Britannica*, 15th ed., vol. 16 (Ency-
    clopedia Britannica, 1974), pp. 128–135.
al-Farabi, Abu Nasr, "The Attainment of Happiness," in *The Philosophy of Plato
    and Aristotle*, rev. ed. (trans. Muhsin Mahdi, Cornell University Press, 1969),
    pp. 13–50.
    On the Perfect State (trans. Richard Walzer, Kazi, 1998).
Fernhout, Rein, *Canonical Texts: Bearers of Absolute Authority* (trans. Henry
    Jansen and Lucy Jansen-Hofland, Rodopi, 1994).
Folkert, Kendall W., "The 'Canons' of 'Scripture,'" in Levering, pp. 170–179.

Foucault, Michel, *The Order of Things* (Vintage, 1970).

Fowler, James W., *Stages of Faith* (HarperCollins, 1981).

Fraade, Steven D., "Concepts of Scripture in Rabbinic Judaism: Oral Torah and Written Torah," in *Jewish Concepts of Scripture* (ed. Benjamin Sommer, NYU Press, 2012), pp. 31–46.

Frazer, James George, *The Golden Bough*, abridged ed. (Macmillan, 1922).

Friesen, Garry, with J. Robin Maxson, *Decision Making and the Will of God*, rev. ed. (Multnomah, 2004).

Frye, Northrop, *The Great Code: The Bible and Literature* (Harcourt Brace Jovanovich, 1982).

Fu, Charles Wei-Hsun, "A Universal Theory or a Cosmic Confidence in Reality?" in *Toward a Universal Theology of Religion* (ed. Leonard Swidler, Orbis, 1987), pp. 154–161.

Galileo, *Discoveries and Opinions of Galileo* (trans. Stillman Drake, Doubleday, 1957).

al-Ghazali, *Deliverance from Error*, in *The Faith and Practice of Al-Ghazali* (trans. W. Montgomery Watt, Oneworld, 1994).

Gómez, Luis O., "The Whole Universe as a Sutra," in *Buddhism in Practice* (ed. Donald S. Lopez, Princeton University Press, 1995), pp. 107–112.

Goody, Jack, *The Interface between the Written and the Oral* (Cambridge University Press, 1987).

Goody, Jack, and Ian Watt, "The Consequences of Literacy," *Comparative Studies in Society and History*, 5 (April 1963), 304–345.

Gracia, Jorge J. E., *How Can We Know What God Means?: The Interpretation of Revelation* (Palgrave, 2001).

Graham, William A., *Beyond the Written Word: Oral Aspects of Scripture in the History of Religion* (Cambridge University Press, 1987).

"Scripture," in *The Encyclopedia of Religion*, 2nd ed. (ed. Lindsay Jones, Macmillan, 2005), pp. 8194–8205.

"Scripture as a Spoken Word," in *Rethinking Scripture* (ed. Miriam Levering, SUNY Press, 1989).

Green, Ronald M., *Religion and Moral Reason* (Oxford University Press, 1988).

Griffiths, Paul J., *An Apology for Apologetics* (Orbis, 1991).

Religious Reading (Oxford University Press, 1999).

Guru Granth Sahib: Selections from the Sacred Writings of the Sikhs (trans. Trilochan Singh et al., Allen & Unwin, 1960).

Habermas, Jürgen, *Communication and the Evolution of Society* (trans. Thomas McCarthy, Beacon, 1976).

"Discourse Ethics: Notes on a Program of Philosophical Justification," in *Moral Consciousness and Communicative Action* (trans. Christian Lenhardt and Shierry Weber Nicholsen, MIT Press, 1990), pp. 43–115.

The Future of Human Nature (trans. Hella Beister, Max Pensky, and William Rehg, Polity, 2003).

"Remarks on Discourse Ethics," in *Justification and Application: Remarks on Discourse Ethics* (trans. Ciaran P. Cronin, MIT Press, 1993), pp. 19–112.

The Theory of Communicative Action, 2 vols. (trans. Thomas McCarthy, Beacon, 1984, 1987).

et al., *The Power of Religion in the Public Sphere* (Columbia University Press, 2011).

Hakuin, *The Zen Master Hakuin: Selected Writings* (trans. Philip B. Yampolksy, Columbia University Press, 1971).

Hall, David L., and Roger T. Ames, *Anticipating China* (SUNY Press, 1995).

Harris, Sam, *Waking Up: A Guide to Spirituality without Religion* (Simon & Schuster, 2014).

Hauerwas, Stanley, "The Moral Authority of Scripture," in *From Christ to the World* (ed. Wayne G. Boulton, Thomas D. Kenney, and Allen Verhey, Eerdmans, 1994), pp. 33–50.

Havelock, Eric A., *The Muse Learns to Write: Reflections on Orality and Literacy from Antiquity to the Present* (Yale University Press, 1986).

"The Oral-Literate Equation: A Formula for the Modern Mind," in *Literacy and Orality* (ed. David R. Olson and Nancy Torrance, Cambridge University Press, 1991), pp. 11–27.

Hegel, G. W. F., *The Philosophy of History* (trans. J. Sibree, Prometheus, 1991).

Henderson, John B., *Scripture, Canon, and Commentary* (Princeton University Press, 1991).

Hick, John, *An Interpretation of Religion*, 2nd ed. (Yale University Press, 2005).

Hirshman, Marc, *The Stabilization of Rabbinic Culture, 100 CE–350 CE* (Oxford University Press, 2009).

Hobbes, Thomas, *The Elements of Law, Natural and Politic: Human Nature*, in *Human Nature* and *De Corpore Politico* (ed. J. C. A. Gaskin, Oxford University Press, 1994), pp. 21–108.

Leviathan (E. P. Dutton, 1950).

Holdrege, Barbara A., *Veda and Torah* (SUNY Press, 1996).

"Vedas in the Brahmanas," in *Authority, Anxiety, and Canon: Essays in Vedic Interpretation* (ed. Laurie L. Patton, SUNY Press, 1994), pp. 35–66.

The Holy Qur'an (trans. Abdullah Yusuf Ali, revised by the Presidency of Islamic Researches, IFTA, Call and Guidance, King Fahd Holy Qur-ān Printing Complex, 1992).

Horton, Robin, *Patterns of Thought in Africa and the West* (Cambridge University Press, 1993).

Ibn 'Arabi, *The Bezels of Wisdom* (trans. R. W. J. Austin, Paulist, 1980).

Ibn Hanbal, "Creed," in *Judaism, Christianity, and Islam*, vol. 2: *The Word and the Law and the People of God* (ed. F. E. Peters, Princeton University Press, 1990), p. 47.

Ibn Rushd (Averroës), *[The Decisive Treatise] On the Harmony of Religion and Philosophy* (trans. George Hourani, Gibb Trust, 1961).

Idel, Moshe, "The Zohar as Exegesis," in *Mysticism and Sacred Scriptures* (ed. Stephen T. Katz, Oxford University Press, 2000).

Ingalalli, R. I., "Independence of *Shabdapramana* (Testimony as Autonomous Source of Knowledge)," in *Shabdapramana in Indian Philosophy* (ed. Manjulika Ghosh and Bhaswati Bhattacharya Chakrabarti, Northern Book Centre, 2006).

Jaspers, Karl, *The Origin and Goal of History* (trans. Michael Bullock, Yale University Press, 1953).
  Philosophical Faith and Revelation (trans. E. B. Ashton, Harper & Row, 1967).
  Philosophy, 3 vols. (trans. E. B. Ashton, University of Chicago Press, 1969).
Jaspers, Karl, and Rudolf Bultmann, *Myth and Christianity* (Noonday, 1958).
Josephus, *Against Apion*, in *The Works of Josephus* (trans. William Whiston, Hendrickson, 1987), pp. 773–812.
Kabir, *Songs of Kabir* (trans. Rabindranath Tagore, Macmillan, 1915).
Kant, Immanuel, *Groundwork of the Metaphysic of Morals* (trans. H. J. Paton, Harper & Row, 1964).
  Religion within the Boundaries of Mere Reason (trans. Allen Wood and George di Giovanni, Cambridge University Press, 1998).
  "On a Supposed Right to Lie from Altruistic Motives," in *Critique of Practical Reason and Other Writings in Moral Philosophy* (trans. Lewis White Beck, University of Chicago Press, 1949), pp. 346–350.
Karenga, Maulana, *Odu Ifa: The Ethical Teachings* (University of Sankore Press, 1999).
Kasulis, Thomas P., "The Origins of the Question: Four Traditional Japanese Philosophies of Language," in *Culture and Modernity: East-West Philosophic Perspectives* (ed. Eliot Deutsch, University of Hawai'i Press, 1991).
Katz, Steven T., "The 'Conservative' Character of Mystical Experience," in *Mysticism and Religious Traditions* (ed. Steven T. Katz, Oxford University Press, 1983), pp. 3–60.
  "Mysticism and the Interpretation of Sacred Scriptures," in *Mysticism and Sacred Scriptures* (ed. Steven T. Katz, Oxford University Press, 2000), pp. 7–67.
Kelsey, David H., *The Uses of Scripture in Recent Theology* (Fortress, 1975).
Kloppenburg, Bonaventura, "Superstition," in *Encyclopedia of Theology: The Concise Sacramentum Mundi* (ed. Karl Rahner, Seabury, 1975), pp. 1652–1654.
Knitter, Paul F., "Interreligious Dialogue: What? Why? How?" in Knitter et al., *Death or Dialogue?: From the Age of Monologue to the Age of Dialogue* (Trinity, 1990), pp. 19–44.
The Koran (trans. N. J. Dawood, Penguin, 1990).
Kort, Wesley A., *"Take, Read": Scripture, Textuality, and Cultural Practice* (The Pennsylvania State University Press, 1996).
Krieger, David J., *The New Universalism: Foundations for a Global Theology* (Orbis, 1991).
Kumarila, *Shlokavartika* (selections), in *A Sourcebook in Indian Philosophy* (ed. Sarvepalli Radhakrishnan and Charles A. Moore, Princeton University Press, 1957), pp. 498–505.
Lawrence, David Peter, "Aspects of Abhinavagupta's Theory of Scripture," *polylog: Forum for Intercultural Philosophy* 4 (them.polylog.org/4/fld-en.htm#n61, 2003).
Leipoldt, Johannes, and Siegfried Morentz, *Die Heilige Schriften: Betrachtungen zur Religionsgeschichte der antiken Mittelmeerwelt* (Harrassowitz, 1953).

Letter of Aristeas (ed. R. H. Charles, www.ccel.org/c/charles/otpseudepig/aristeas
.htm, 1913).

Levenson, Bernard M., "The Development of the Jewish Bible: Critical Reflections
upon the Concept of a 'Jewish Bible' and on the Idea of Its 'Development,'" in
What Is Bible? (ed. Karin Finsterbusch and Armin Lange, Peeters, 2012),
pp. 377–392.

Levering, Miriam, ed., *Rethinking Scripture: Essays from a Comparative Perspective* (SUNY Press, 1989).

Lévy-Bruhl, Lucien, *How Natives Think* (trans. Lilian A. Clare, Allen & Unwin,
1926).

Lewis, Mark Edward, *Writing and Authority in Early China* (SUNY Press, 1999).

Lopez, Donald S., Jr., *The Lotus Sutra: A Biography* (Princeton University Press,
2016).

Lotus Sutra: Scripture of the Lotus Blossom of the Fine Dharma (trans. Leon
Hurvitz, Columbia University Press, 2009).

de Lubac, Henri, *History and Spirit: The Understanding of Scripture according
to Origen* (trans. Anne Englund Nash and Juvenal Merriell, Ignatius,
2007).

Lucretius, *On the Nature of the Universe* (trans. Ronald Latham, Penguin, 1951).

Lunyu: The Analects of Confucius (trans. Arthur Waley, Vintage, 1938).

Luther, Martin, *Luther's Works*, 55 vols. (ed. Jaroslav Pelikan et al., Fortress and
Concordia, 1955–1986).

Macy, Joanna, *World as Lover, World as Self* (Parallax, 2005).

Madigan, Daniel A., *The Qur'an's Self-Image: Writing and Authority in Islam's
Scripture* (Princeton University Press, 2001).

Maimonides, Moses, *The Guide of the Perplexed* (trans. Shlomo Pines, University
of Chicago Press, 1962).

Malinowski, Bronislaw, *Coral Gardens and Their Magic*, vol. 2: *The Language of
Magic and Gardening* (Indiana University Press, 1965).

Magic, Science and Religion (Doubleday, 1954).

"The Problem of Meaning in Primitive Languages," "Supplement I," in C. K.
Ogden and I. A. Richards, *The Meaning of Meaning*, 7th ed. (Harcourt
Brace, 1945), pp. 296–336.

McFague, Sallie, *Metaphorical Theology: Models of God in Religious Language*
(Fortress, 1982).

McGinn, Bernard, *The Foundations of Mysticism* (Crossroad, 1991).

Mengzi, *Mencius* (trans. D. C. Lau, Penguin, 2003).

Mensching, Gustav, *Das Heilige Wort* (Röhrscheid, 1937).

Meyer, Lodewijk, *Philosophy as the Interpreter of Holy Scripture* (trans. Samuel
Shirley, Marquette University Press, 2005).

Miller, Walter, Jr., *A Canticle for Leibowitz* (Bantam, 1984).

Mimamsa Sutra of Jaimini (selections), in *A Sourcebook in Indian Philosophy* (ed.
Sarvepalli Radhakrishnan and Charles A. Moore, Princeton University Press,
1957), pp. 487–498.

Mosko, Mark S., "Malinowski's Magical Puzzles: Toward a New Theory of
Magic and Procreation in Trobriand Society," *Journal of Ethnographic
Theory*, 4 (2014), 1–47.

Murty, K. Satchidananda, *Vedic Hermeneutics* (Shri Lal Bahadur Shastri Rash-triya Sanskrit Vidyapeetha, 1993).

Nancy, Jean-Luc, *The Inoperative Community* (ed. Peter Connor, University of Minnesota Press, 1991).

Neville, Robert C., *Behind the Masks of God: An Essay toward Comparative Theology* (SUNY Press, 1991).

  Boston Confucianism: Portable Tradition in the Late-Modern World (SUNY Press, 2000).

New Oxford Annotated Bible, 4th ed. (ed. Michael Coogan et al., Oxford University Press, 2010).

Nichiren, "Rectification for the Peace of the Nation," in *Sources of Japanese Tradition*, 2nd ed., vol. 1 (ed. William Theodore de Bary et al., Columbia University Press, 2001), pp. 295–299.

North, John, "The Development of Religious Pluralism," in *The Jews among Pagans and Christians in the Roman Empire* (ed. Judith Lieu et al., Routledge, 1992), pp. 174–193.

Nostra Aetate: Declaration on the Relation of the Church to Non-Christian Religions (www.vatican.va/archive/hist_councils/ii_vatican_council/documents/vat-ii_decl_19651028_nostra-aetate_en.html, 1965).

Nylan, Michael, *The Five "Confucian" Classics* (Yale University Press, 2001).

Ochs, Peter, *Peirce, Pragmatism, and the Logic of Scripture* (Cambridge University Press, 1998).

  "Philosophic Warrants for Scriptural Reasoning," *Modern Theology*, 22 (July 2006), 465–482.

Ogden, C. K., and I. A. Richards, *The Meaning of Meaning*, 7th ed. (Harcourt, Brace, 1945).

Olson, David R., "Footnotes to Goody: On Goody and His Critics" (barthes.ens.fr/articles/Olson08.pdf, 2008).

Ong, Walter J., *Orality and Literacy: The Technologizing of the Word* (Methuen, 1982).

Origen, *On First Principles* (trans. G. W. Butterworth, SPCK, 1936).

  The Song of Songs: Commentary and Homilies (trans. R. P. Lawson, Newman, 1956).

Outka, Gene, *Agape: An Ethical Analysis* (Yale University Press, 1977).

Panikkar, Raimon, *The Intrareligious Dialogue*, rev. ed. (Paulist, 1999).

  The Vedic Experience (University of California Press, 1977).

Phillips, D. Z., *The Concept of Prayer* (Routledge & Kegan Paul, 1965).

Philo of Alexandria, *Allegorical Interpretation*, in *The Works of Philo* (trans. C. D. Yonge, Hendrickson, 1993), pp. 25–79.

Plutarch, "On Superstition," in *Moralia* 2 (trans. Frank Cole Babbitt, Harvard University Press, 1928), pp. 451–495.

Pollock, Sheldon, *The Language of the Gods in the World of Men* (University of California Press, 2006).

Pseudo-Dionysius, *The Complete Works* (trans. Colm Luibheid, Paulist, 1987).

Rahner, Karl, *Hearer of the Word* (trans. Joseph Donceel, Continuum, 1994).

"Über die Schriftinspiration," *Zeitschrift für katholische Theologie*, 78 (1956), 127–168.

Rambachan, Anantanand, *Accomplishing the Accomplished: The* Vedas *as a Source of Valid Knowledge in Shankara* (University of Hawai'i Press, 1991).

The Limits of Scripture: Vivekananda's Reinterpretation of the Vedas (Sri Satguru, 1994).

Rambelli, Fabio, *A Buddhist Theory of Semiotics: Signs, Ontology, and Salvation in Japanese Esoteric Buddhism* (Bloomsbury, 2013).

Ramsey, Ian. T., *Models and Mystery* (Oxford University Press, 1964).

Religious Language (Macmillan, 1957).

"Words about God," in *Words about God* (ed. Ian T. Ramsey, Harper & Row, 1971), pp. 202–223.

Rao, K. L. Seshagiri, *Mahatma Gandhi and Comparative Religion*, 2nd ed. (Motilal Banarsidass, 1990).

Rhees, Rush, *Wittgenstein and the Possibility of Discourse* (Cambridge University Press, 1998).

Ricoeur, Paul, *Essays on Biblical Interpretation* (ed. Lewis S. Mudge, Fortress, 1980).

Figuring the Sacred (trans. David Pellauer, Fortress, 1995).

Hermeneutics and the Human Sciences (ed. John B. Thompson, Cambridge University Press, 1981).

Interpretation Theory: Discourse and the Surplus of Meaning (TCU Press, 1976).

The Symbolism of Evil (trans. Emerson Buchanan, Beacon, 1967).

The Rigveda: The Earliest Religious Poetry of India, 3 vols. (trans. Stephanie W. Jamison and Joel P. Brereton, Oxford University Press, 2014).

Rilke, Rainer Maria, *Ahead of All Parting: The Selected Poetry and Prose of Rainer Maria Rilke* (trans. Stephen Mitchell, Modern Library, 1995).

Rosenstock-Huessy, Eugen, *Practical Knowledge of the Soul* (trans. Mark Huessy and Freya von Moltke, Argo, 1988).

Saadya Gaon, *The Book of Doctrines and Beliefs* (trans. Alexander Altmann, Hackett, 2002).

Sanders, Seth, *The Invention of Hebrew* (University of Illinois Press, 2009).

Sartre, Jean-Paul, *What Is Literature?* (trans. Bernard Frechtmann, Harper & Row, 1965).

Schoeler, Gregor, *The Oral and the Written in Early Islam* (trans. Uwe Vagelpohl, Routledge, 2006).

Scott, Michael, *Religious Language* (Palgrave Macmillan, 2013).

Seibert, Eric, *The Violence of Scripture: Overcoming the Old Testament's Troubling Legacy* (Fortress, 2012).

Seki, Hosen, Commentary in *Buddha Tells of the Infinite: The "Amida Kyo"* (Japan Publications, 1973).

Sen, Prabal Kumar, "Some Alternative Definitions of *Shabdapramana*," in *Shabdapramana in Indian Philosophy* (ed. Manjulika Ghosh and Bhaswati Bhattacharya Chakrabarti, Northern Book Centre, 2006), pp. 53–79.

Shankara, *Brahma-Sutra Bhasya*, in *Brahma-Sutras* (trans. Swami Vireswara-nanda, Advaita Ashrama, 1936).

    Brihadaranyaka Upanishad Bhasya (trans. Swami Madhavananda, Swami Yogeshwarananda, 1950).

    Introduction to the Vedanta Sutras (trans. George Thibault), in *Sacred Books of the East*, vol. 34 (ed. F. Max Müller, Oxford University Press, 1890).

    The Upadeshasahasri *of Shankara* (trans. Sengaku Mayeda, SUNY Press, 1992).

Shapiro, Fred R., "Most Quoted Authors in Yale Book of Quotations" (blog .yupnet.org/2006/12/19/most_quoted_aut/, 2006).

Sherzer, Joel, *Kuna Ways of Speaking* (University of Texas Press, 1983).

Shijing: The Classic of Poetry (Book of Odes), selections (trans. Burton Watson), in *Sources of Chinese Tradition*, 2nd ed., vol. 1 (ed. William Theodore de Bary and Irene Bloom, Columbia University Press, 1999), pp. 37–40.

Silverman, Hugh J., *Textualities* (Routledge, 1994).

Singh, Pashaura, *The Guru Granth Sabib: Canon, Meaning and Authority* (Oxford University Press, 2000).

Smith, Jonathan Z., "Sacred Persistence: Toward a Redescription of Canon," in *Imagining Religion* (University of Chicago Press, 1982), pp. 36–52.

Smith, Steven G., *Appeal and Attitude* (Indiana University Press, 2005).

    "Three Religious Attitudes," *Philosophy and Theology*, 11 (1998), 3–24.

Smith, Wilfred Cantwell, *Faith and Belief* (Princeton University Press, 1979).

    Towards a World Theology (Westminster, 1981).

    What Is Scripture? (Fortress, 1993).

Snell, Bruno, "The Forging of a Language for Science in Ancient Greece," *Classical Journal*, 56 (1960), 50–60.

Some Sayings of the Buddha according to the Pali Canon (trans. F. L. Woodward, Oxford University Press, 1925).

Soskice, Janet, *Metaphor and Religious Language* (Oxford University Press, 1985).

Staal, Frits, "The Concept of Scripture in Indian Tradition," in *Sikh Studies: Comparative Perspectives on a Changing Tradition* (ed. Mark Juergensmeyer and N. Gerald Barrier, Graduate Theological Union Press, 1979), pp. 121–124.

    "Mantras and Bird Songs," *Journal of the American Oriental Society*, 105 (July–Sept. 1985), 549–558.

    Rituals and Mantras: Rules without Meaning (Motilal Banarsidass, 1996).

Steiner, George, *After Babel* (Oxford University Press, 1975).

Stendahl, Krister, "The Bible as a Classic and the Bible as Holy Scripture," *Journal of Biblical Literature*, 103 (1984), 3–10.

Stiver, Dan R., *The Philosophy of Religious Language* (Blackwell, 1996).

Street, Brian V., *Literacy in Theory and Practice* (Cambridge University Press, 1984).

The Study Qur'an (ed. S. H. Nasr et al., HarperOne, 2015).

Stump, Eleonore, *Wandering in Darkness: Narrative and the Problem of Suffering* (Oxford University Press, 2010).

Tambiah, Stanley, *Magic, Science, Religion, and the Scope of Rationality* (Cambridge University Press, 1990).

Tanakh: The Holy Scriptures (Jewish Publication Society, 1985).

Taves, Ann, *Religious Experience Reconsidered: A Building-Block Approach to the Study of Religion and Other Special Things* (Princeton University Press, 2009).

Taylor, Charles, *A Secular Age* (Harvard University Press, 2007).

Thomassen, Bjorn, "Anthropology, Multiple Modernities and the Axial Age Debate," *Anthropological Theory*, 10 (2010), 321–342.

Ticciati, Susannah, "Scriptural Reasoning and the Formation of Identity," in *The Promise of Scriptural Reasoning* (ed. David F. Ford and C. C. Pecknold, Blackwell, 2006), pp. 77–94.

Tillemans, Tom, "Dharmakirti," in *Stanford Encyclopedia of Philosophy* (ed. Edward Zaita, plato.stanford.edu, 2017).

Tillich, Paul, "The Meaning and Justification of Religious Symbols," in *Religious Experience and Truth* (ed. Sidney Hook, NYU Press, 1961).

Tracy, David, *The Analogical Imagination: Christian Theology and the Culture of Pluralism* (Crossroad, 1981).

Tylor, Edward B., *Primitive Culture*, vol. 1 (John Murray, 1871).

Upanishads (trans. Patrick Olivelle, Oxford University Press, 1996).

Uttaradhyayana Sutra, in *Sacred Books of the East*, vol. 45 (trans. Hermann Jacobi, Oxford University Press, 1895).

Vanhoozer, Kevin, *First Theology: God, Scripture and Hermeneutics* (InterVarsity, 2002).

The Vimalakirti Sutra (trans. Burton Watson, Columbia University Press, 1997).

Vivekananda, Swami, *The Complete Works of Swami Vivekananda* (Advaita Ashrama, 1964).

Walzer, Richard, "Al-Farabi's Theory of Prophecy and Divination," *Journal of Hellenic Studies*, 77 (1957), 142–148.

Weber, Max, *The Sociology of Religion* (trans. Ephraim Fischoff, Beacon, 1993).

Whedbee, J. William, *The Bible and the Comic Vision* (Fortress, 1998).

Wilson, Jared C., "The Bible Is Not an Instruction Manual" (www.crossway.org/articles/the-bible-is-not-an-instruction-manual/, 2015).

Wimbush, Vincent, *Theorizing Scriptures: New Critical Orientations to a Cultural Phenomenon* (Rutgers University Press, 2008).

Wittgenstein, Ludwig, *Philosophical Investigations* (trans. G. E. M. Anscombe, Blackwell, 1953).

Wollenberg, Rebecca Scharbach, "The Dangers of Reading as We Know It: Sight Reading as a Source of Heresy in Early Rabbinic Traditions," *Journal of the American Academy of Religion*, 85 (Sept. 2017), 709–745.

Wolterstorff, Nicholas, *Divine Discourse: Reflections on the Claim that God Speaks* (Cambridge University Press, 1995).

The God We Worship: An Exploration of Liturgical Theology (Eerdmans, 2015).

Wyclif, John, *On the Truth of Holy Scripture* (trans. Ian Christopher Levy, Medieval Institute, 2001).

Zagzebski, Linda, *Epistemic Authority* (Oxford University Press, 2012).

Zen Flesh, Zen Bones (ed. Nyogen Senzaki and Paul Reps, Tuttle, 1985).

The Zend-Avesta, in *Sacred Books of the East*, vol. 31 (trans. L. H. Mills, Oxford University Press, 1887).

Zhuangzi: The Complete Works of Chuang-Tzu (trans. Burton Watson, Columbia University Press, 1968).

Zohar: The Book of Enlightenment (trans. Daniel Chanan Matt, Paulist, 1983).

Index